Using Young Adult Literature in the English Classroom

Fourth Edition

John H. Bushman
Professor Emeritus
University of Kansas, Lawrence

Kay Parks Haas
Olathe Public Schools
Olathe, Kansas

PEARSON
Merrill
Prentice Hall

Upper Saddle River, New Jersey
Columbus, Ohio

Library of Congress Cataloging-in-Publication Data
Bushman, John H.
    Using young adult literature in the English classroom/John H. Bushman, Kay Parks Haas.—4th ed.
      p. cm.
    Includes bibliographical references and index.
    ISBN 0-13-171093-1
      1. Literature—Study and teaching (Secondary) 2. Young adult literature, American—History and criticism—Theory, etc. 3. Young adult literature, English—History and criticism—Theory, etc. 4. Youth—Books and reading—English-speaking countries. 5. Language arts (Secondary) 6. Reading (Secondary) I. Haas, Kay Parks. II. Title.
    LB1631.B798 2006
    428'.0071'2—dc22

                                                                                                            2005003473

Vice President and Executive Publisher: Jeffery W. Johnston
Senior Editor: Linda Ashe Montgomery
Development Editor: Kathryn Terzano
Senior Production Editor: Mary M. Irvin
Senior Editorial Assistant: Laura Weaver
Design Coordinator: Diane C. Lorenzo
Production Coordination and Text Design: Thistle Hill Publishing Services, LLC
Cover Designer: Jason Moore
Cover Image: Corbis
Production Manager: Pamela D. Bennett
Director of Marketing: Ann Castel Davis
Marketing Manager: Darcy Betts Prybella
Marketing Coordinator: Brian Mounts

This book was set in Galliard by Carlisle Communications, Inc. It was printed and bound by R. R. Donnelley & Sons Company, Inc. The cover was printed by R. R. Donnelley & Sons Company, Inc.

Pearson Prentice Hall™ is a trademark of Pearson Education, Inc.
Pearson® is a registered trademark of Pearson plc
Prentice Hall® is a registered trademark of Pearson Education, Inc.
Merrill® is a registered trademark of Pearson Education, Inc.

Pearson Education Ltd.   Pearson Education Australia Pty. Limited
Pearson Education Singapore Pte. Ltd.   Pearson Education North Asia Ltd.
Pearson Education Canada, Ltd.   Pearson Educación de Mexico, S.A. de C.V.
Pearson Education—Japan   Pearson Education Malaysia Pte. Ltd.

10 9 8 7 6 5 4 3 2
ISBN: 0-13-171093-1

For all those teachers who strive to meet the needs, interests, and abilities of all students by providing young adults with age-appropriate literature. May these teachers feel the success that is truly due them. May they continue to use young adult literature to help students in their journey to become lifelong readers.

—JHB
—KPH

Educator Learning Center: An Invaluable Online Resource

Merrill Education and the Association for Supervision and Curriculum Development (ASCD) invite you to take advantage of a new online resource, one that provides access to the top research and proven strategies associated with ASCD and Merrill—the Educator Learning Center. At www.educatorlearning center.com, you will find resources that will enhance your students' understanding of course topics and of current educational issues, in addition to being invaluable for further research.

How the Educator Learning Center Will Help Your Students Become Better Teachers

With the combined resources of Merrill Education and ASCD, you and your students will find a wealth of tools and materials to better prepare them for the classroom.

Research

- More than 600 articles from the ASCD journal *Educational Leadership* discuss everyday issues faced by practicing teachers.
- A direct link on the site to Research Navigator™ gives students access to many of the leading education journals, as well as extensive content detailing the research process.
- Excerpts from Merrill Education texts give your students insights on important topics of instructional methods, diverse populations, assessment, classroom management, technology, and refining classroom practice.

Classroom Practice

- Hundreds of lesson plans and teaching strategies are categorized by content area and age range.
- Case studies and classroom video footage provide virtual field experience for student reflection.
- Computer simulations and other electronic tools keep your students abreast of today's classrooms and current technologies.

Look into the Value of Educator Learning Center Yourself

A four-month subscription to Educator Learning Center is $25 but is FREE when packaged with any Merrill Education text. In order for your students to have access to this site, you must use this special value-pack ISBN number WHEN placing your textbook order with the bookstore: 0-13-186208-1. Your students will then receive a copy of the text packaged with a free ASCD pincode. To preview the value of this website to you and your students, please go to www.educatorlearningcenter.com and click on "Demo."

Preface

While there have been changes in the traditional English curriculum in middle and high schools, we believe more must be done. We believe that young adult literature—with its conflicts, themes, protagonists, and language—should be present in the curriculum to provide the necessary transition to the adult literature we hope students will eventually discover and learn to enjoy. This genre deserves the attention that is currently given the classics by those who aspire to teach English and by those who are already teaching English. Therein lies the motive for writing this book. *Using Young Adult Literature in the English Classroom,* Fourth Edition, is written for both prospective and experienced English teachers as they begin and continue the process of selecting the literature curriculum for their students. The book provides guidance both for choosing reading selections and for developing teaching ideas.

New to This Edition

We have made changes in the fourth edition of *Using Young Adult Literature in the English Classroom,* changes we think readers will appreciate. We have updated the literature selections significantly to provide the reader with information about the most current young adult literature. We have significantly changed and updated two chapters: "Diversity in Young Adult Literature" (Chapter 8), and "Media and Young Adult Literature" (Chapter 9). Chapter 9 contains ready-made media activities that can be taken directly into the classroom. In Chapter 6, "Organizing the Literature," we have expanded the section on "Using Young Adult Literature in the Content Classes." We believe that young adult literature has a significant place in the subject areas other than English. What we haven't changed is the conversational tone of previous editions. We believe that both students in preservice programs and experienced teachers who want up-to-date information about young adult literature want to read about it in a short, clearly and concisely written, classroom-oriented work.

Text Organization

The content of the book is very much classroom oriented. In Chapter 1, we discuss the characteristics of young adults and how this literature meets their interests and needs. In Chapter 2, we focus on the literature itself, providing criteria by which teachers may evaluate young adult literature. The research and theory, along with classroom applications, of the reader-response approach to teaching literature is the subject of Chapter 3. In Chapters 4, 5, and 6, we focus on the classroom itself and how teachers can effectively incorporate young adult literature into the curriculum. Chapter 7 encourages teachers to evaluate their use of the classics. Chapter 8 provides literature for a diverse ethnic, cultural, and national population. Chapter 9 emphasizes media and technology and how teachers may use them effectively in conjunction with young adult literature. Chapter 10 focuses on concerns many educators have about censorship. Chapter 11 briefly reviews the history of young adult literature.

To involve readers in this text, we suggest that they keep a "Learning Log" which will allow them to interact with this book. In addition to jotting down ideas as they read, we suggest readers respond to what they have read, guided by the "Learning Log Responses" located at the end of each chapter. Readers are thus able to participate in the reading-writing connection process that we suggest is beneficial for students to use.

In addition, to make this book as useful and accessible as possible, we have supplied three appendices, one providing general teaching information and two supplementing the young adult literature information given in the text. Appendix A provides readers with a variety of resources (books, journals, and organizations) they may use for support when teaching young adult literature. Appendix B lists the works of literature that we have cited in each chapter and indicates which of these titles are more appropriate for the middle school student. Appendix C contains a long list of young adult books in various categories that we feel are appropriate for use in both middle school and high school classrooms. This information supplements the lists of titles and brief annotations that we provide in Chapter 6 as a representative sample of young adult literature.

Acknowledgments

Many individuals contributed in some way to the preparation of this book. Our students, both experienced and prospective classroom teachers, have readily given of their ideas and suggestions about unique and interesting teaching strategies. As we discussed these contributions, they became a part of our thinking of new and interesting ways to look at young adult literature.

Other contributors influenced us in more specific ways. They need to be thanked directly for their contributions to different chapters: Sam Rockford (North Kansas City High School, Missouri), Chapter 3; Rachael Buckley (Baldwin City High School, Kansas), Chapters 6 and 10; Kristina Sestrich (Lathrop, Missouri), Chapter 6; Lisa Hazlett (University of South Dakota) and Judith Hayn (Loyola University), Chapter 8; and Jill Adams (University of Kansas) and Casey Hudson (Columbus, Kansas), Chapter 9. We also thank Lara Squyres, Tiffany Bode, and Erin Foley (University of Kansas). We also wish to thank our production editor at Merrill/Prentice Hall, Mary Irvin, and our copy editor, Karen Carriere, for their valuable contributions to the content and structure of this edition.

In addition, we thank the reviewers of this edition: Sandra Clark, Anderson University; Cyndi Giorgis, University of Nevada Las Vegas; Bette P. Goldstone, Arcadia University; Rodney D. Keller, Brigham Young University, Idaho; and Julie Stepp, Tennessee Technical University.

Finally, we say *thank you* to the creative authors of young adult literature for their devotion to the genre, which has allowed teachers to more easily turn their students on to the world of reading.

Brief Contents

Contents

Note: Every effort has been made to provide accurate and current Internet information in this book. However, the Internet and information posted on it are constantly changing, so it is inevitable that some of the Internet addresses in this textbook will change.

About the Authors

John H. Bushman is Professor Emeritus of Teaching and Leadership (English Education) at the University of Kansas, Lawrence. He is also director of The Writing Conference, Inc., a nonprofit organization established to provide services and materials that support the teaching of writing and literature. Bushman, a frequent contributor to national journals in English education, has written three books in addition to *Using Young Adult Literature in the English Classroom* (with Kay Parks Haas): *Teaching Writing in the Middle and Secondary Schools* (with James Blasingame), *Teaching the English Language,* and *Teaching English Creatively.* He is a frequent workshop leader and consultant on the teaching of English/language arts.

Kay Parks Haas is an Instructional Resource Teacher for the Olathe District Schools (Kansas). She is a former president of the Assembly on Literature for Adolescents, National Council of Teachers of English (ALAN), former associate chair of the Secondary Section of NCTE, and former member of the executive committee of NCTE. She is co-author with John H. Bushman of *Using Young Adult Literature in the English Classroom and Teaching English Creatively* (first edition). She was a finalist for Kansas Teacher of the Year (1993), recipient of the Nancy Landon Kassebaum Excellence in Teaching Award (1993), and a Kansas Master Teacher (2000). In addition, she contributes to national journals in English education and serves as a consultant to publishing companies.

1

Young Adults and the Literature That Meets Their Needs and Interests

I try to write realistically and honestly. I am always aware of being a storyteller. A novel must work as a story; otherwise all the fine writing in the world will not make it successful.
Robert Cormier

Adolescence and preadolescence are interesting, dynamic, and at times unsettling periods. Adolescents are no longer children, but they are not yet adults. It is a time of change: a time for physical growth, sexual awareness, emotional upheaval, and cognitive development. Because we are teachers or librarians who work in some way with young adults, it would seem imperative that we know about the developmental stages through which young people pass. The well-known saying seems appropriate here: We don't teach English; we teach students. Teaching young adults requires familiarity with the characteristics of this age group.

If we agree that the research and theory about young adulthood is accurate and that it gives us important information about what happens to young adults during preadolescence and adolescence, then it is also important that teachers know about young adult literature and how it meets the interests and needs of these young people, who are confronting a range of experiences in their physical, intellectual, moral, and reading development.

Young Adult Literature: A Definition

Young adult literature has been called many names over the years: literature for adolescence, adolescent literature, adolescent fiction, junior teen novels, and juvenile fiction. Because of the pejorative nature of the term *adolescence,* most have moved away from that term and have settled on *young adult literature.* Publishers seem intent on using the term *juvenile fiction,* but most school people do not like the term *juvenile. Young adult literature,* then, seems to be the common term for literature written for or about young adults.

Young adult literature has many common characteristics: Conflicts are often consistent with the young adult's experience, themes are of interest to young people, protagonists and most characters are young adults, and the language parallels that of young people. Most definitions include all of these components (Auten, 1984; Carlsen, 1980; Fuller, 1980). Nilsen and Donelson (2005) offer this definition: "By *young adult literature,* we mean anything that readers between the approximate ages of 12 and 18 choose to read (as opposed to what they may be coerced to read for class assignments)" (p. 1). This description seems very broad, but young readers freely choose specific books because they include the characteristics listed.

Young Adult Literature: The Right Choice

Contemporary adult society is a nonreading society, and some studies suggest that people read less as they grow older (Bushman, 1997; Heather, 1982; McLemee, 2004; National Center for Educational Statistics [NCES], 2003; O'Connor, 1980; Trelease, 1982). Other research indicates that adults read less than one book a year: Angelotti (1981) concludes that the literature programs in schools have produced less than 5% of adults in the United States who read literature. Graves (1990) indicates that "reading, like writing, requires some discipline if you aren't used to it. Most people don't read. A very small part of our population, about 3% buys 95% of the books sold in bookstores" (p. 39).

In a more recent study, the Nation's Report Card indicates that in 2003, 42% of eighth grade children were meeting the *basic* reading level. Thirty-two percent of eighth grade students were reading at the *proficient* level, a 1% decrease in 2003 (NCES, 2003).

In 2004, the National Endowment for the Arts (McLemee) released a study titled "Reading at Risk: A Survey of Literary Reading in America" in which it details the steady drop over two decades in the percentage of Americans who read books of any sort—with a much steeper decline in the consumption of literature (p. A1). Referring to this study, Dana Gioia (2004), chairman of the NEA, writes "the concerned citizen in search of good news about American literary culture will study the pages of this report in vain" (p. A1).

Perhaps Slatoff (1970), while writing some 30 plus years ago, states the problem best even as it relates to literacy today:

It is hard to remember that upon graduation most of them stop reading little more than trivia and go on to live their lives, both inner and outer, as though nothing had happened to them. It is hard to remember that almost everything about a classroom, about the relation of student and teacher, about the structure of the curriculum—in short about the total environment in which we teach literature—helps to produce this unhappy condition and is at best alien and at worst hostile to the fullest comprehension and experiencing of literature. By this I mean mostly that all of this defines a world in which literature is not really relevant except as a subject for study and in which a full literary experience is not likely to take place. (p. 175)

Carlsen and Sherrill (1988) have collected reading autobiographies from teachers and have shared excerpts in *Voices of Readers,* an interesting collection of statements about reading habits. Generally, most respondents stated that their love for reading occurred in spite of what was done in schools. Some developed their appreciation of literature in school, but it usually did not occur until very late in high school or even in college. However, these respondents were English teachers who, we would assume, have a stronger relationship to reading than do other adults.

It seems that schools have accomplished just the opposite of what they intended to do: They have turned students off from reading rather than made them lifelong readers. How has this happened? Teachers have failed to choose literature that enables students to become emotionally and cognitively involved in what they read. If students are asked to read literature that is not consistent with their developmental tasks, they will not be able to interact fully with that literature. As a result, students who do not interact with the literature are left with learning only about literature. For example, most 10th graders know little about *Macbeth* other than a very cursory view of the plot, but they know a great deal about the Elizabethan period, Shakespeare, the Globe Theatre, and the rest of the trappings that accompany the study of this classic play. We know of one school district with a policy that all sophomores read *Julius Caesar.* We also know through our experiences and the experiences of other teachers that many sophomores cannot and will not read that play. As a result, teachers drag students through the play scene by scene over a month-long period. Educators often assume that all students of a particular group can or should be able to do something, in this case read *Julius Caesar.* That is not reality.

Sadly, this is an accurate picture of the literature programs in many middle and secondary schools that still have students move chronologically through the literature anthology and choose the traditional classics as their outside reading. Most students are simply unable to connect the text with their goals, level of development, and experience. Language development affects cognitive development and vice versa: Students at this age read at a much higher level of ability when they are reading something that matches their developmental interests and goals (Anderson, 1983). The attitude found in this classical literature curriculum seems to be that the schools have a body of literature—a canon—to be taught to students, whether they can read it or not. Therein lies the problem. Most students cannot read classical literature well (i.e., they cannot have personal involvement with it). Students think of the literature as something they cannot understand; therefore, they think they are not intelligent individuals. In an interesting study, Bushman (1997) asked students what literature they enjoyed reading, what literature was assigned in the classroom, and what books (if any) they read outside of the classroom. The results clearly showed that students read a great deal in the early grades of middle school but their reading decreases as they proceed into high school. They read what is assigned or do what they have to do to get by in the higher grades, and little outside reading takes place.

This literary elitism encourages students to have an unhealthy, negative attitude toward their ability and, as a result, leads to nonreading when they leave school. If schools and teachers want students to understand what they read, to interact with the literature so that they can make connections to their own lives, to make critical judgments that will enhance their intellectual, emotional, and moral development, and, perhaps most important, to become lifelong readers, schools and teachers must evaluate the literature curriculum and make the necessary changes so that students can indeed achieve success in these areas.

> *There is no advantage suffering through novels that you hate just because somebody else pronounces them "quality." Read the kinds of books you like. It's infinitely more enjoyable, and in the end, you'll be better lifelong readers.*
>
> Gordon Korman

Piaget and Cognitive Development

Piaget and Inhelder (1969) believe that cognitive changes from infancy to adulthood are the result of a developmental process. They suggest that this process occurs in four stages: the sensorimotor period (birth to 2 years), the preoperational period (2 to 7 years), the concrete operational period (7 to 12 years), and the formal operational period (12 years to adulthood). Although these stages give the appearance of a start-and-stop process, the theory suggests a gradual movement from any one period to another. In addition, there are transitional periods between these stages.

Because this book deals primarily with literature read by preadolescents and adolescents, the later periods, concrete and formal operations, are emphasized. During the concrete operational stage, young adults become more independent in their thinking. They can think logically, classify, and show relationships. The real world is extremely important to these young people. Their thinking revolves around immediate and concrete objects rather than concepts and abstractions. The research indicates that at this stage the preadolescent is able to think backward as well as forward in time.

As preadolescents move out of the concrete operational level, they take on more of the formal operations. These operations develop at this time and are retained throughout adult life. During this time, adolescents are able to apply logical operations to all classes of problems. It is during this final stage that abstract thinking prevails. Adolescents are able to reason about abstract propositions, objects, or concepts that they have not directly experienced. At this time, young people are able to hypothesize and use deductive and inductive reasoning.

Middle School: Appropriate Literature, Appropriate Responses

Middle school students have ample opportunity to relate experiences about themselves as they react and respond to what they read. The responses are personal, usually based on real experiences. *Francie* (English, 1999), for example, enables middle schoolers to respond at this appropriate level. The primary emphasis of the novel is prejudice. At the concrete level, students are able to share their personal experiences with this theme. They relate to each other specific examples of how they have faced ethnic, religious, and other kinds of prejudice and what specifically they have done to overcome these prejudicial actions. Other works with this theme—*Daniel's Story* (Matas, 1993), *Walk the Dark Streets* (Baer, 1996), and *Mississippi Trial—1955* (Crow, 2002)—also work well with middle schoolers. Whereas middle school students work with these and other such books at the concrete level, older students may take a different approach, perhaps dealing in a more sophisticated way with the topic of prejudice by exploring its effects on society.

Some students object to the ending of *Whatever Happened to Janie?* (Cooney, 1993). At the middle school level, students explore why the novel ends as it does. Now that Janie has decided to call the Johnsons, her birth parents, will she go back to them? Using this novel as their basis, students can also discuss making decisions and living with the consequences. This approach is especially appropriate for the third book of this series (*The Voice on the Radio*, 1996). Through a variety of ways—writing, discussions, creative drama—middle school students can extend the ending of the novel or work through how Janie feels about hearing her story on the radio.

> *Whatever you write, I hope you decide to make things better in this world, no worse. So tell a really good story that'll make your reader feel wiser and stronger and happier.*
>
> Caroline B. Cooney

Humor plays an important role in *Bel-Air Bambi and the Mall Rats* (R. Peck, 1993). As a response to that novel, students can relate this humor to a concrete experience. For example, mornings around many homes are disastrous. Parents are struggling with each other and with their children. All need to use the bathroom at the same time; all need to eat breakfast and get off to work or school. Items temporarily lost cause further distress. Students may write a humorous response, using an incident that they have experienced while keeping in mind Peck's strategies of writing humorously. In two more current books (*A Long Way from Chicago*, 1998, and *A Year Down Yonder*, 2000), R. Peck portrays a grandmother character that has many humorous attributes. She is a very lovable albeit "crazy" character. Certainly students know of people in their families or friends' families who exhibit similar characteristics.

And who could not find themselves or close friends in the many books about Alice by Phyllis Reynolds Naylor?

Middle school students frequently read *Beardance,* Will Hobbs's 1993 sequel to *Bearstone* (1989). Many readers can relate to Cloyd, the 15-year-old boy who is so determined to make sure that the surviving bear cubs go free. Cloyd's determination is believable. Many young people at this age have strong feelings about social concerns and are willing to act on their beliefs. Although few may be able to travel to the mountain wilderness to save bears from destruction, many can and do take on responsibilities in their own communities. Some of these responsibilities may manifest themselves in working with animal shelters, the focus of Hobbs's 2003 novel *Jackie's Wild Seattle.* These middle school students can share their real experiences and how they overcame obstacles to their goals.

> *Humor is my first love, and I can't resist books like* The Hitchhiker's Guide to the Galaxy *or movies like* Monty Python and the Holy Grail—*anything that's funny.*
>
> Gordon Korman

High School: Appropriate Literature, Appropriate Responses

Research (Piaget & Inhelder, 1969) indicates that most high school adolescents are able to reason at the formal operational level. In general, these students have reached intellectual maturity, and most are able to think in a systematic manner, to reason by implication at the abstract level, and to bring together variables through synthesis. Most students in the upper grades are able to make a statement or pose a problem about a work and defend or solve that particular response, showing the level of reasoning appropriate for students who have moved into the formal operational level.

Using the statement "Sometimes novels leave you with the feeling that there is more to tell," students can develop an idea or thesis that began in the literature but needs to be continued. For example, after reading *Beyond the Chocolate War* (Cormier, 1985), students respond to the condition of Trinity School and what it will be like in 5 years. If there had been a third book in the *Chocolate War* series, what would that novel be like? For example, what would Archie be like as a 30-year-old? Students may also wish to respond to the ending of *The Giver* (Lowry, 1993):

> Downward, downward, faster and faster. Suddenly he [Jonas] was aware with certainty and joy that below, ahead, they were waiting for him; and that they were waiting, too, for the baby. For the first time, he heard something that he knew to be music. He heard people singing. Behind him, across vast distances of space and time, from the place he had left, he thought he heard music too. But perhaps it was only an echo. (p. 180)

Certainly, students have the opportunity to explore the possibilities of what happened to Jonas and the baby. Did they escape? Were memories restored to them? To those left behind?

Weight and young adults' attitudes toward it are probably two of the major issues of adolescents in high school. Although some young adult novels address the issue at the middle school level, few books address the issue for high school students. *Life in the Fat Lane,* by Cherie Bennett (1998), can now fill that void. Bennett discusses the issues of being fat and the related problems that accompany the condition—an image-conscious family, shallow friends, lost love—in stark, frank terms that will demand the attention of overweight young adults. The novel can also be of value to students with friends and acquaintances who have concerns about weight.

Students in high school could certainly explore the theme of heroes. What does being a hero mean to them? Who are the heroes in their lives? What qualities or attributes make up a hero? As a part of this thematic study, students would find Robert Cormier's novel *Heroes* (1998) quite appropriate. Do they see Francis Cassavant and Larry LaSalle as heroes?

Fallen Angels (Myers, 1988) offers readers many opportunities to respond. A character sketch showing the changes that Richie goes through enables students to understand the important incidents of the war and how they affect Richie. Showing growth of a character from the beginning of the novel to the end asks students to bring together important considerations that effect change. Other students may choose to single out the most difficult aspect of fighting a war, based on this novel, and explain why. Still others may conduct a more personal investigation by interviewing Vietnam War veterans about their feelings toward the war, their involvement in specific incidents, and their relationships with other soldiers. Students can then compare this information with that provided in the novel, making some personal comment about how realistic the novel is.

In his novel *Eva,* Peter Dickinson (1988) provides older students with a controversial issue: transplanting the brain of a 13-year-old into the body of a chimpanzee. Readers may dismiss the work as science fiction, but interspecies transplants are getting closer and closer to reality. Human-to-human transplants have existed for many years and now are common. In the late 1980s, the transplanting of a baboon's heart into a human body was quite controversial. Can the reverse, suggested by Dickinson's novel, be far behind? Certainly, the book gives students many issues to investigate, such as the moral and ethical issues of animal and human transplants and the degree to which society will accept the results of medical technology. Higher-level thinking about thought-provoking issues can find its way into student responses, both written and oral.

Responses about freedom, human rights, and the use of language to obfuscate will certainly follow the reading of *Forbidden City* (Bell, 1990). The story of 17-year-old Alex and his father, a cameraman for the Canadian Broadcasting Corporation, tells of the nonviolent-turned-violent demonstration at Tiananmen Square in the spring of 1989. Issues that may surface include the following: How far will people go to secure freedom and human rights? With the use of doublespeak and euphemism, how do we know if the government is telling the truth? What forms of language abuse occur in the U.S. government? Who best serves as agents for change, adults or students? High school students probably have attained the intellectual level to undertake these questions with a higher degree of sophisticated thinking and to respond with more complex, in-depth, and abstract reasoning.

High school students need literature to which they can connect, literature that has moral and ethical issues for them to confront. Williams-Garcia's *Like Sisters on the Homefront* (1995) is such a book. It is the story of Gayle, a 14-year-old mother of one who has just had her second unborn child aborted. The novel addresses the hopelessness felt by teens who are confronted with sex, drugs, poverty, and other social circumstances. The importance of high school students reading this novel is that they can see that hopelessness can be turned around. Gayle transforms her life through her relationship with her extended family.

Janie/Leshaya (*Born Blue*, Nolan, 2001) seems to have this drive as well. Born to a life of hardship, she strives to break away from a very difficult past to something better.

And what happens when a ninth grader just stops talking? Readers can easily relate to the troubled Melinda (*Speak*, Anderson, 1999) as she struggles in the opening weeks of high school. Melinda called the cops—something you just don't do—at an end-of-summer party. Now, she is not spoken to; she is stared at; she simply is an outcast. So she retreats into her head and remains quiet. This irreverent comment on high school is just one part of the powerful novel, which highlights the school culture and the struggle that students often face when trying to cope with that culture.

Developmental Tasks Confronting Adolescents

What are the special needs and expectations of adolescents? What are the major developmental tasks that confront teenagers? Erikson (1963) suggests that the major task of adolescence is the formulation, or reformulation, of personal identity. Middle and high school students are primarily engaged in the task of answering the question "Who am I?" Marcia (1980) describes a series of stages or classifications of identity that teens may adopt as they grow into adulthood. These stages represent products of considerable effort at sorting out concepts of the self in relation to parents, peers, authorities, and society in general.

Havighurst (1972) outlines lifetime developmental tasks for healthy individuals, including a series of tasks that confront adolescents. In his view, the principal needs of adolescence are emotional and social development rather than intellectual growth. Because the adolescent developmental tasks presented are comprehensive and useful to classroom teachers who wish to understand the internal struggles of their maturing students, a closer examination of Havighurst's tasks is warranted. As we discuss each of the tasks, we suggest young adult literature that may reflect the developmental struggle that the young adult is experiencing (Figure 1.1). The literature does not necessarily have the task as its central theme, but the developmental task is part of the character's behavior.

Achieving Mature Relations with Age-Mates

The first task is achieving new and more mature relations with age-mates of both sexes (Havighurst, 1972). Mature relationships are here viewed as adult relationships; girls are looked on as women and boys as men. For younger children, social grouping tends

Achieving New and Mature Relations with Age-Mates

The Chocolate War, Robert Cormier (1974)

Down River, Will Hobbs (1991)

Drowning Anna, Sue Mayfield (2001)

The Long Night of Leo and Bree, Ellen Wittlinger (2002)

River Thunder, Will Hobbs (1997)

Sophie, Guy Burt (2003)

Achieving a Proper Masculine or Feminine Social Role

Jake Riley: Irreparably Damaged, Rebecca Fjelland Davis (2003)

Keeping You a Secret, Julie Anne Peters (2003)

Out of Control, Norma Fox Mazer (1993)

We All Fall Down, Robert Cormier (1991)

Adapting to Physical Changes and Using the Body Effectively

The Cat Ate My Gymsuit, Paula Danziger (1974)

Freak the Mighty, Rodman Philbrick (1993)

Inside Out, Terry Trueman (2003)

Lizard, Dennis Covington (1991)

One Fat Summer, Robert Lipsyte (1977)

The Silent Boy, Lois Lowry (2003)

Achieving Emotional Independence from Parents and Other Adults

Everything Is Not Enough, Sandy Asher (1987)

Hope Was Here, Joan Bauer (2000)

Son of the Mob, Gordon Korman (2002)

Sniper, Theodore Taylor (1989)

Whale Talk, Chris Crutcher (2001)

Preparing for Marriage and Family

Deliver Us from Evie, Kerr (1994)

Dovey Coe, Francis O'Roark Dowell (2000)

The Drowning of Stephan Jones, Bette Greene (1994)

First a Dream, Maureen Daly (1990)

Hanging on to Max, Margaret Bechard (2002)

Preparing for an Economic Career

Born Blue, Han Nolan (2001)

Jesse, Gary Soto (1994)

Make Lemonade, Virginia Euwer Wolff (1993)

True Believer, Virginia Euwer Wolff (2001)

When the Phone Rang, Harry Mazer (1985)

Acquiring a Personal Ideology or Value System

Dark Waters, Catherine MacPhail (2003)

A Distant Enemy, Deb Vanasse (1997)

Razzel, Ellen Wittlinger (2001)

The Second Summer of the Sisterhood, Ann Brashares (2003)

Staying Fat for Sarah Byrnes, Chris Crutcher (1993)

Achieving Social Responsibility

Dogwolf, Alden Carter (1994)

Jackie's Wild Seattle, Will Hobbs (2003)

Meadow Lark, Mary Peace Finley (2003)

Nothing but the Truth, Avi (1991)

Speak, Laurie Halse Anderson (1999)

FIGURE 1.1

Havighurst's lifetime developmental tasks with suggested works that reflect the task.

Tasks adapted from Havighurst, R. (1972). *Developmental tasks and education* (pp. 45–79). New York: David McKay.

to be same sex, characterized by secret gangs and clubs. During adolescence, teens mature sexually and develop strong interests in themselves in relation to the opposite sex. Young people become deeply occupied with social activities and social experimentation.

School is the primary arena where this socialization takes place. Gaining the approval of peers of both sexes becomes a powerful influence on the behavior of adolescents. What may appear to be minor issues of choice develop into shattering dilemmas of conformity or expressions of individuality.

Failing or delaying this developmental task results in poor social adjustment and interferes with progress in other developmental tasks. Havighurst suggests that delay, unlike complete failure, probably means an unhappy adolescence but not a permanent inability to achieve mature adulthood.

Although it is not the primary emphasis in Burt's *Sophie* (1994, England; 2003, United States), this developmental struggle is clearly reflected by Sophie and Mattie as they try to relate to each other and try to gain acceptance by their peers. Certainly, this struggle is also experienced by Jerry, Archie, and Obie in *The Chocolate War* (Cormier, 1974). The struggle that emerges among the young people who travel the Colorado River in the Grand Canyon in *Downriver* (Hobbs, 1991) and its sequel, *River Thunder* (Hobbs, 1997), also shows this concern for peer acceptance, but at what price?

Achieving a Proper Masculine or Feminine Social Role

Achieving a proper masculine or feminine social role is the second developmental task. Again, the point is developing an acceptable adult social role. The task of achieving manhood or womanhood is complicated by the contemporary ferment over social roles, the erosion of traditional models, and the lack of clarity for replacements. Cormier provides for these emerging social roles in *We All Fall Down* (1991). Buddy struggles with who he is, what he has become, and who he wants to be. Jane, the moral model, falls in love with Buddy, as he does with her. The struggle then begins for both young people. Jake in *Jake Riley: Irreparably Damaged* (Davis, 2003) struggles with his manhood and his reputation as he tries to impress his classmate Lainey.

Adapting to Physical Changes

In the third developmental task, the adolescent adapts to physical changes and using the body effectively. During adolescence, young people learn what their adult bodies will be: short, tall, wide, narrow. Not all bodies are shaped or function as their owners desire. The task as defined by Havighurst is pride in or tolerance of one's body and the ability to use and protect the body satisfactorily.

There are at least two components to teenage anxiety regarding physical growth. First is the concern about development of a satisfactory adult body. What if I don't like the way I look, the way I am? Will others accept me as I am? The second and more immediate adolescent crisis regarding physical growth has to do with the timing of physical changes, particularly the development of adult sexual characteristics. Because everyone develops on a different schedule, and girls generally develop more rapidly than boys, adolescents experience keen interest in their own growth in comparison with that of peers. If development is delayed, considerable teenage anxiety and social confusion can result. Teens also struggle at significant depths about physical flaws, real or imagined, that provoke a genuine concern: Am I normal?

Many young adult novels have characters who struggle with their bodies. Paula Danziger's *The Cat Ate My Gymsuit* (1974) and Robert Lipsyte's *One Fat Summer* (1977) seem to be representative of this kind of literature. Lois Lowry tackles the issue in *The Silent Boy* (2003). Dennis Covington's *Lizard* (1991) handles the struggles that come with disfigurement. *Freak the Mighty* (Philbrick, 1993) brings together two unlikely characters: Maxwell, an extremely large boy who has learning disabilities, and Kevin, a very small boy who is a genius. Danny (*Shooting Monarchs*, 2003) puts up with verbal abuse from Chad and other classmates due to his disfigurement. Danny has congenital scoliosis, which gives him a "hump back."

Independence from Parents and Adults

The fourth developmental task is achieving emotional independence from parents and other adults. Again, the goal is an adult relationship with parents rather than the dependence of childhood, a process that is problematic for all parties involved. Young adults are ambivalent about leaving the security of childhood for the strange, complicated, threatening world of adulthood. Parents want them to become mature adults, but they also wish to protect their children, innocent and inexperienced as they are, from the ravages of the adult world. The stage is set for miscommunication, rebellion, authoritarian behaviors, and irresponsibility.

Teachers, as authority figures, are frequently targets of adolescents who are working to establish their personal independence. It's important to understand the conflicts, both internal and external, that drive teenage activity in relation to this task so that teachers can avoid being drawn into misplaced hostility and confrontation.

Sniper (T. Taylor, 1989) involves Ben's struggle in coming to terms with the relationships among adults at the wild animal refuge and simultaneously handling problems associated with a sniper trying to kill the animals. At the same time, Ben's parents are on an adventure of their own. A lot of growing up takes place in a short period. In *Everything Is Not Enough* (Asher, 1987), Michael is perhaps the classic example of someone who is struggling with this developmental task. This 17-year-old has everything a young adult could want: loving parents, summers at the beach, a job waiting for him in his father's business. But Michael wants to make it on his own. He wants to be independent from his parents, but he doesn't want to hurt them. Vince (*Son of the Mob*, Korman, 2002) is adamant that he is not going to follow in his father's footsteps, for his father is head of a powerful crime organization. Vince wants no part of that life.

Preparing for Marriage and Family

The preparation for marriage and family is another concern for the emerging adult. Adolescence is a period in which strong attractions develop between the sexes and the possibility of marriage and family is entertained. Obviously, this fifth task connects with others, especially those of establishing satisfactory peer relationships with the opposite sex and establishing independence from parents. We believe that early young adult literature reflected this struggle more than the current literature does. Perhaps contemporary young people do not feel that the preparation for marriage and family is as important to them at this age as it was 20 years ago; perhaps the shift in attitude toward varying lifestyles has influenced them not to consider marriage and family as immediate concerns. The literature, then, may reflect an alternative attitude, as displayed in the homosexual relationships found in *The Drowning of Stephan Jones* (Greene, 1991) and *Deliver Us from Evie* (Kerr, 1994), rather than an attitude that leads to marriage. This male-male versus male-female relationship is certainly tested in Kerr's novel *"Hello," I Lied* (1997). An earlier work, *Mr. and Mrs. Bo Jo Jones* (Head, 1967), does reflect the marriage and family theme, albeit as a necessary arrangement due to an unplanned pregnancy. Maureen Daly seems to continue this theme from an earlier novel (*Seventeenth Summer*, 1942) in her 1990 novel *First a Dream*. Current literature may lead us to believe that marriage is not necessary for a happy life. Sam Pettigrew in *Hanging on to Max* (Bechard, 2002) is in no hurry to marry, even though he has a very young son named Max.

Preparing for a Career

The sixth developmental task is preparing for an economic career. A significant part of moving from childhood to adulthood is achieving economic independence, the ability to make a living, and choosing a satisfying occupation. During adolescence, the young adult progresses in both these objectives with part-time work, summer jobs, chores, and other means of making money. Readers certainly see the struggles of LaVaughn, a 15-year-old who struggles with her poverty, her family, and her community (*Make Lemonade*, Wolff, 1993; *True Believer*, Wolff, 2001). Certainly at a different level, the three young people in Harry Mazer's *When the Phone Rang* (1985) find themselves in immediate need of financial assistance. Kevin, Lori, and Billy want to remain together as a family after their parents are killed in a plane crash, but it will require sacrifice from each of them. This financial concern is brought about more quickly than usual but nevertheless must be confronted. Jesse and his brother Abel (*Jesse*, Soto, 1994) struggle to make ends meet in junior college because they see education as their only hope of escaping a world of physical labor in the farm fields of California. Janie/Leshaya (*Born Blue*, Nolan, 2001) will do anything and everything to dig her way out of poverty to achieve what she has always wanted to do: sing. She has to overcome many obstacles—many of her own making—to arrive at her self-appointed career.

Acquiring a Personal Ideology

Acquiring a personal ideology or value system to guide the individual in ethical decisions is Havighurst's seventh developmental task. Adolescents tend to be interested in sampling various worldviews, religions, political stances, and philosophical perspectives. Much of life, in both adulthood and adolescence, is made up of choices that reflect the values and ideals of the chooser. Young adults begin to critically evaluate their parents' values and ideas, which they passively accepted as universal truths in childhood.

The British novel *Dark Waters* (MacPhail, 2003) brings together two brothers who at first seem to be alike; however, a near tragedy shows Col just how different he is from his brother Mungo. It takes the tragedy, plus the relationship with the victim's family, for Col to realize what his personal ideology is. Values can also come from the community, as is evidenced in *A Distant Enemy,* a novel by Deb Vanasse (1997). Joseph, a 14-year-old who lives in remote southwestern Alaska, is angry at all the changes that have come to his Yup'ik Eskimo village and is angry at his new kass'aq teacher. He struggles with new ways that, from his point of view, are taking over his traditional community. Why can't he carry on the old Yup'ik ways? Readers experience some of the struggles that Joseph faces and see how he begins to deal with the problems that have been overwhelming him.

Achieving Social Responsibility

The final developmental task Havighurst outlines is satisfactorily achieving social responsibility. Satisfactory interpersonal relationships have already been addressed; this developmental task involves discovering one's role in relation to social groups and participating as a member of the community and a citizen of the state and nation. Adolescents discover that their personal desires, beliefs, and behaviors affect, or potentially affect, groups beyond their own families.

Readers see this struggle in Philip Malloy (*Nothing but the Truth,* Avi, 1991) as he learns quickly how his actions affect many people, some who are closely connected to him and others who are not. His decision to hum along as the national anthem is played during his school's opening exercises sets in motion a series of charges and countercharges regarding respect, freedom, and patriotism. Readers struggle with his motives and those of the others involved. There is a sense, however slight, that Philip Malloy begins to realize the consequences of his actions as the series of events go further than he intended. However, ultimately, as in most good literature, the reader makes the final decision. The 14-year-old Rick Walker (*The Maze,* Hobbs, 1998) can't seem to get along either. He is a foster child who has been sent to a juvenile detention facility. He escapes and believes he can make it on his own. Through his work with Lon Peregrino, a bird biologist who is releasing fledgling California condors back into the wild, Rick begins to develop a sense of his identity and personal growth. He knows now that he has found himself and that he can become a contributing member of society.

Adolescents' Development of Moral Judgment

In Havighurst's (1972) model, the personal value systems or moral ideology that characterizes the tasks is derived primarily from social interaction. Kohlberg (1976) critiques the social learning model of moral development and suggests that the model assumes that the development is the internalization of external cultural rules. He criticizes moral development in the social interaction model by arguing that the basic motivation for morality is rooted in the pursuit of social reward and avoidance of social punishment. "Environmental influences on normal moral development are defined by qualitative variations in strength of reward, punishment, prohibitions, and modeling of conforming behavior by parents and other socializing agents" (p. 48).

As an alternative approach to adolescent development and construction of moral judgment, Kohlberg (1968, 1976, 1987) describes a cognitive developmental approach that builds on ideas and concepts originated by Dewey and Piaget. The primary characteristic of the cognitive developmental understanding of adolescence is the concept of stages. The stages of adolescent development and the establishment of moral ideology are age linked and organized in an orderly sequence.

Dewey (1895/1964) links moral development to cognitive development in a discussion about the objectives of education:

> The aim of education is growth, both intellectual and moral. Only ethical and psychological principles can elevate the school to a vital institution in the greatest of all constructions—the building of a free and powerful character. Only knowledge of the order and connection of the stages in psychological development can insure the maturing of the psychical powers. Education is the work of supplying the conditions which will enable the psychological functions to mature in the freest and fullest manner. (p. 273)

As noted, Piaget's work (1932/1965, 1971) suggests that as a person ages, he or she progresses through sequential stages of intellectual development. These stages are not only age linked but also feature increasing complexity. During adolescence, for example, the teenager moves from a concrete operational stage of intellectual ability to one of formal operational thinking, which is characterized by abstractions and the ability to hypothesize and test for possibility. Formal operational thinking is a significantly higher order of thinking ability than concrete operational thinking.

Kohlberg (1984) develops and refines a hierarchy of moral developmental stages that parallels the intellectual stages of Piaget's theory of human development. The hierarchy consists of three levels: preconventional, conventional, and postconventional (or principled). In turn, each of the three levels consists of two stages, for a total of six stages.

At the preconventional level of moral development that characterizes younger children, the child is self-centered and basically unable to consider the interests and claims of others. Doing right is motivated by the desire to avoid punishment, obey rules, and yield to the superior power of others, usually adults. The conventional level appears in conjunction with the adolescent period. This level is characterized by moral decision making based on interpersonal activity. Motivation for doing right is based more on caring for others, the Golden Rule, and the desire for others to see the individual as a good person. The postconventional, or principled, level is generally attained in adulthood. An individual at this level has distinguished and adopted principles for moral reasoning and action for himself or herself. This person also recognizes that these moral principles occasionally conflict with social rules, posing moral dilemmas that the person resolves with principled ethical judgments. Crucial to Kohlberg's theory of moral development is the idea that higher stages are also better stages of moral reasoning and action—better, not merely different. This concept is important to educators because it implies that students cannot merely change through moral education: They improve or raise their level of moral reasoning and judgments. "Nevertheless, holding development as the central aim of education, we do argue that a higher moral stage is a better stage in solving moral problems as problems of conflicting interests and claims" (Kohlberg, 1984, p. 292).

Kohlberg's theory proposes a close link among age, intellectual development, and moral development. As an individual matures, he or she grows in mental stages (Piaget, 1971) and through the moral stages of Kohlberg's hierarchy (1984), beginning with stage 1 at the bottom and progressing toward stage 6 at the top. Kohlberg further states that intellectual development is linked to moral development, so that an individual could not achieve a higher moral judgment than could be supported by that individual's intellectual development. "Moral stage theory postulates parallelisms between cognitive stages and moral stages, and that attainment of a given cognitive stage is necessary but not sufficient for the attainment of the parallel moral stage" (Kohlberg, 1984, p. 309).

Thus, at age 7, a child may have achieved the concrete operations ability to use logic. Possession of a concrete operations level of intellectual capacity is necessary but not sufficient to rise to the second stage of Kohlberg's hierarchy. At the beginning of adolescence, the individual may begin developing the capacity for formal operations and more complex mental abilities. Formal operations capacity is necessary but not sufficient to rise to the third and fourth stages of moral development.

The key concept here is in the "necessary but not sufficient" relationship between intellectual development and moral development. Kohlberg asserts that individuals may progress in mental capacity through concrete operations, beginning formal operations, basic formal operations, and consolidated operations without progressing past the second stage of moral development. However, an individual with postconventional moral judgment capability must, of necessity, have developed mental capacity well into the formal operations stage. Adequate intellectual development is necessary but not sufficient to cause a rise in moral development.

Other researchers (Gilligan, 1982; Smetana, in press; and Turiel, 1983) have explored this complex field of moral development. Noteworthy is Gilligan, who was a research assistant to Kohlberg at Harvard University and went on to criticize Kohlberg's work by indicating that his work was flawed because he only studied privileged, white men and boys. Gilligan felt that this caused a biased opinion of women. Her detailed study is found in *In a Different Voice: Psychological Theory and Women's*

Development (1982). Gilligan asserts that women have differing moral and psychological tendencies than men. Men think in terms of rules and justice, and women are more inclined to think in terms of caring and relationships. In her view, the morality of caring and responsibility is premised in nonviolence, whereas the morality of justice and rights is based on equality.

Although this book is not a study of social morality, this information may very well be of interest in those reading and studying young adult literature and, thus, we have included it here.

The four young adult novels discussed in the following sections have characters who seem to reflect the developmental theories of Piaget, Havighurst, Kohlberg, and perhaps Gilligan. The characters struggle with their identities, with their relationships with adults and other adolescents, and with their choices, which often suggest their concern with moral questions of right and wrong.

A Distant Enemy

In *A Distant Enemy* (Vanasse, 1997), Joseph enjoys spending time with his grandfather—fishing, hearing stories about the past, and learning about his people, who have made their home in the wet tundra of southwestern Alaska for centuries. Joseph is comfortable in his surroundings. He is not one to encourage or even tolerate change. So when the Fish and Game authorities make changes in the fishing guidelines, Joseph becomes very angry—angry enough to slash the tires of the Fish and Game troopers' airplane in protest. This change in rules for fishing is just one of many changes that have come to his Yup'ik Eskimo village.

Joseph also struggles with people with influence who are not of his lineage. He is angry at his white father for abandoning their family years ago; he is angry at his new white—kass'aq—teacher. To Joseph, any white is his enemy. Joseph not only slashes the airplane tires but also spreads the rumor that the new white teacher had something to do with it. For Joseph, nothing seems to be going his way. He finds a $20 bill on the floor of the shop where he works part time and decides putting the money back into the cash register would be the right thing to do even though he has been told not to open it. Joseph does it, but as he closes the machine, Henry, a coworker with less than positive morals, sees him. Joseph does not know it, but he has set himself up for the charge of stealing because his coworker took $150 and told the owner that he saw Joseph opening the cash register.

Joseph is now in a difficult position. He struggles with what he did with the tires and what others think he did with the money. He contemplates:

> The school, the teacher, the Fish and Game—they were strangers here, just as his father had been. If he were a shaman like those in his grandfather's stories, he would change all the white-skinned men to white-headed eagles that would soar high above the village, and then he would slice their wings from their bodies so they would plummet to the ground. (p. 151)

But for Joseph, there was no shaman's magic, only the routines of the day, the rules, the outside obligations, and the intrusions of the white man's ways. Readers will experience through Joseph this burden that weighs heavily on him. What should he do? His first reaction is to run. Not thinking clearly, Joseph tries to escape. His anger has taken over—no more clear thinking for Joseph. Only a brush with death—falling into the icy lake—forces Joseph to face his mistakes and begin to deal with the problems that have been overwhelming him.

This process, in which Joseph moves from a happy 14-year-old adolescent through difficult troubles—many of his own making—to the realization that he must come to grips with these problems and do something about them, certainly exhibits the moral and developmental stages of which Havighurst and Kohlberg write. Readers sense the struggles that Joseph must confront and move with him as he attempts to resolve them.

Dark Waters

Is family loyalty more important than exposing the truth? This question is troublesome for Col in Catherine MacPhail's Scottish mystery novel *Dark Waters* (2003). Col, a seemingly normal teenager, is growing up in a seemingly abnormal family: his father was killed in a getaway car during a robbery, and his older brother is in and out of trouble. But Col does not see the problem: he loves the memory of his father and he worships his brother. Family loyalty is extremely important to Col; he would never do anything to cause problems for his older brother Mungo. For as his mother explains after a brief altercation: "I will not have you turning on your brother, for any reason. Family's the most important thing in the world. You never turn against your family" (p. 15). But life experiences have a way of changing people. Col becomes a local hero when he saves Dominic, a young boy from a wealthy family, from drowning in the local loch. From this point on, Col's loyalty to his troubled family wavers.

Adding to Col's experience of saving Dominic, he sees something underwater while in the loch, something that is still submerged in his memory. But when that memory resurfaces, Col finds that he must choose between the devastating truth about Mungo and doing what is right. For what Col saw was a face of Klaus, an illegal immigrant, and he knows that Mungo hates these people.

When Col confronts Mungo about Klaus and other atrocities that have happened recently, Col realizes that he must do something. But can he really turn in his brother?

> Mungo's eyes flashed with rage. "Don't you dare talk to me like that. You better show me some respect."
>
> "Respect for you!" Col was every bit as angry. "What respect did you show me? Look at the position you've put me in!"
>
> "What position?" Mungo threw the words at him. "You're my brother. You don't tell on a brother. End of story. You stick to that and you've not got a problem." (p. 147)

Throughout this novel, Col struggles with his identity, his moral fiber, and family loyalty. He decides to compromise. He makes an anonymous phone call to the police indicating that there is a body in the loch. Col believes that he has not been disloyal to his brother, but Klaus will be found and returned to his homeland. The police arrest Mungo anyway, not due to Col's call, but due to Mungo's comrades who have "ratted" on him.

The struggle between family loyalty and doing what is right provides ample discussion material for young people. Readers struggle with Col as he continues looking inward to find out what is the moral decision to make under such dire circumstances. One might argue that Col's mother exhibits much of what Gilligan (1982) believes in terms of the mother's caring effect on human relationships (i.e., her unyielding support for her sons).

> *I'm a poet, a creator, a visionary. I smile often and laugh easily, and I weep at pain and cruelty. I approach the world with the eyes of an artist, the ears of a musician, and the soul of a writer.*
>
> Sharon Draper

Battle of Jericho

The young protagonist in *Battle of Jericho* (Draper, 2003) is Jericho Prescott, a junior at Frederick Douglass High School. He is thrilled with the possibility of being accepted into the Warrior of Distinction Club. While no longer officially sponsored by the school, the Warrior of Distinction Club for all practical purposes is connected to the school. One of the faculty is the sponsor. The Warriors have been around for many years. Jericho's dad and the school's principal are former members. When Jericho is invited to pledge for the Warriors, he believes that he "has arrived." Not only will he be a member of the most prestigious club in the school, but now Arielle, one of the "finest girls around," has started to notice Jericho when the list of pledges is announced. Now Jericho has made the decision to do whatever it takes to become a member.

One major problem exists: "Things are not what they used to be!!!!" When Dad and others of his generation went through the initiation week, the activities were very mild. Jericho soon finds out that what is expected of him and others of this pledge group is far from mild. In fact, as the week progresses and the activities become more and more harrowing, Jericho is forced to make choices that he is not comfortable with.

In addition to the various hoops that the pledges have to jump through, they now are faced with another problem: Dana, a girl who wants to become a pledge in an all-boys' club. Dana believes she has every right to be there if she can, indeed, carry out the rigors of the activities. The problem arises when Eddie, a senior Warrior who is in charge of many of the activities, decides to take it out on Dana and, therefore, she gets the brunt of the hazing. The problem for the pledges is what to do about it when in fact they have agreed to "The Bonding of the Brotherhood, [which] requires not only secrecy and obedience, but also responsibility, loyalty, and honor" (p. 68). So all agree to continue.

What was once thought of as mild, fun, character-building activities now become gross, dangerous hazing: wearing dog collars, paddling, toilet swirlies, scavenger hunts in dumpsters, drinking liquor, and finally jumping out of a two-story building.

Jericho has his doubts as he moves through the hazing. "Everything in Jericho's being screamed inside him—not so much from pain, but from anger. How dare somebody hit him like that. He didn't have to take this" (p. 174). "Jericho looked around desperately; he had no idea what the others were being forced to do. As he lowered his head close to the mud and closer to Rich Sharp's foot, Jericho wondered miserably how he could have sunk so low" (p. 203). "The Warriors did not notice, but Jericho never said a word. He could not bring himself to agree to be marked or branded but he didn't complain or do anything to stop them either" (p. 219). "Jericho felt trapped. He knew he should leave, but there was no way he had the nerve to walk out now. After all, it was almost over. In just a few hours he'd be a Warrior! So he sat where he was" (p. 243).

Although most of the activities are harmless in and of themselves, the impression given to the pledges has been that they are facing a dangerous activity—a red-hot briquette on the back to brand each person, when in fact the Warriors use an ice cube, or blindfolding the pledges and sticking their heads in the toilet as it is being flushed, when in fact the toilet is clean. However, due to Eddie's meanness, Dana receives the real thing. She actually is branded with a red-hot briquette, and Eddie urinates in the toilet before putting her head in the water.

The struggle for Jericho and his friends is where to draw the line, when to quit. Desperately wanting to belong to this prestigious club, not wanting to give up and cause problems for the other pledges, and not really wanting to be quitters, the pledges, although they want to get out, decide to stay—a decision that will haunt them for the rest of their lives because during the last activity, one pledge dies and another gets a broken arm. All do a lot of growing up as they reflect on their experiences and try to determine whether it was all worth it.

> Jericho touched Kofi's cool, slim hand, then turned to leave the room. "I gotta get out of here. Take care of him, Dana."
>
> "Fiercely," she told him. "Jericho?" she called as he reached the door.
>
> "Yeah?" He turned to face her.
>
> "It wasn't worth it."
>
> "I know." (p. 286)

Writing is recycled literature.

Will Hobbs

Downriver

Downriver (Hobbs, 1991) involves some of the issues raised in *The Crazy Horse Electric Game* (Crutcher, 1987) and will also involve students in discussions of moral development. *Downriver* is a tale of adventure as seven young people pirate two boats and equipment and travel through the Grand Canyon. The young people are a part of Discovery Unlimited, an outdoor education program for young people at risk. It is a story about rafting down the Colorado River, but more than that it is a story of how leaders emerge and what they become; it is a story of how young people challenge authority, work through conflicts within the group, and struggle with their own identities.

The novel is written so that students can make connections with the story and the characters. Some will relate to the adventure of rafting down the Colorado River; others will be more concerned with the concept found in Discovery Unlimited. Some readers will wonder why Heather leaves before the Canyon trip. Others certainly will identify with Jessie's problems at home: a father who doesn't understand her and a stepmother who infringes on Jessie's time with her father.

Downriver challenges students with other issues: Is it necessary to have rigid rules in groups such as Discovery Unlimited? How are leaders of unorganized groups selected? Did Troy take on the leadership role, or was it thrust on him? When do young people know that their individual agendas are not as important as that of the group? How does Troy change throughout the novel? What motivates his actions? Do the students know of other students like Troy? What has become of them?

The characters have definite characteristics: Freddy becomes close to Jessie and challenges both Troy's relationship with her and Troy's authority with the group. Star sees dark omens in her tarot cards, and Adam, the practical joker, finds that the group has problems. How does each change throughout the novel, and what do they learn about themselves and each other?

From a moral standpoint, readers can respond to Troy's throwing the map over the falls, Freddy's encounter with the scorpion, and Jessie, Freddy, Adam, Rita, and Star's leaving without Troy and Pug. What is the moral consideration, and how would the students have responded if they had been the characters? How have the characters grown morally? Some would argue that most of the characters move from the first stage to the third stage of Kohlberg's model.

In the end, Jessie and Star are back with Jessie's father. Jessie has reconciled with her stepmother; Freddy is in southwestern Colorado, close to Jessie's home, getting rehabilitated; Rita is back in New York; Troy has been caught by the police in Los Angeles; and Adam is back working with Al, the leader of Discovery Unlimited. Students can discuss their feelings about how each of the characters fared as the novel comes to a close. After what they did, were they treated fairly? Do the students believe that the characters learned from their experiences? Did the students learn from the characters' experiences? One of the reasons for choosing this novel for classroom reading is to help students respond to the moral issues and dilemmas experienced by Jessie and her friends. Through discussion or writing, students try out their ideas, compare and contrast their ideas with those of their peers, and make some moral judgments about the decisions that Jessie and her group made and their consequences. By sharing all of the ideas, moral development is increased. After these activities, students will be ready to read the sequel to *Downriver, River Thunder* (1997).

Young adults experience this moral development of characters as they read other literature as well. They see the growth that takes place with Melinda in *Speak* (Anderson, 1999), with Sarney in *Sarney: A Life Remembered* (Paulsen, 1997), with Billie Jo in *Out of the Dust* (Hesse, 1997), with Destiny in *Destiny* (Grove, 2000), with Isabel, in *Keeper of the Night* (Holt, 2003), and with many, many more characters in young adult literature. Readers also see the ups and down of morality with Mickey, David, Arno, Patch, and Jonathan in *The Insiders* (Minter, 2004).

Many young adult novels offer the quality of literature suggested in these examples. This literature provides the reader with a variety of conflicts and issues, and the student's response depends on the stage of moral development he or she has attained. Young readers may respond effectively to literature in which there are issues of right and wrong. Older readers have more interest in literature that focuses on social expectations. Sometimes the books themselves fit into these categories by emphasizing one level of development.

Other novels have a full range of conflicts and issues—all within the same book. This literature offers settings that are realistic to all young people, characters that include the range of socioeconomic status, and realistic conflicts that help young adults make that transition from the somewhat sheltered life of adolescence to the sometimes stark, cruel life of adulthood. Categories in which we frequently find novels with both positive and negative treatment include family relationships, friends and society, racial and ethnic relationships, identity, and sexual relationships, most of which are mentioned in Havighurst's stages of developmental tasks.

Reading Development of the Young Adult

Students not only develop in stages physically, intellectually, and morally but also in their reading appreciation. Many sources discuss the stages in the development of reading (Brewbaker, 1989; Donelson & Nilsen, 1989; Early, 1960). Carlsen (1980) makes three generalizations about the reading patterns of young adults that are helpful as classroom teachers select reading material for students. First, he suggests that chronological age is more important than mental age in determining what a young adult will enjoy reading. He believes that 13-year-olds of varying cultural backgrounds, development, and school ability will be interested in reading the same kinds of books. For this reason, Carlsen thinks the tendency to push and pull gifted young adults into adult literature and the traditional classics is ill-advised and risks creating resistance and barriers that will carry far into the reader's future. Second, Carlsen suggests that reading preferences are determined culturally as well as by age. For example, there are significant differences between what adolescent boys and girls are willing to read outside of the classroom. Again, lack of awareness and teacher insensitivity to these differences may result in students developing a resistance to reading.

Carlsen's third generalization about adolescent reading habits holds that most young adults make reading selections based on the subject matter of the book rather than the literary merit, language difficulty, or complexity of the story. A young person may choose a difficult book if the subject matter is of significant interest; simple books may be rejected if the subject is boring.

Carlsen (1974) also presents five overlapping satisfactions in reading appreciation. In contrast to some stage hierarchies, a young person moving from a lower to a higher level of reading appreciation does not leave the lower stage for the higher stage. In this construct the higher stages incorporate and expand on the lower stages, much in the way that larger concentric circles incorporate and expand on small circles.

Carlsen labels the first stage of reading appreciation unconscious delight. Here a reader becomes lost in the story, experiencing intensely and personally the events, places, and people. Action and twists of plot are the most attractive parts of the reading experience.

Toward the beginning of adolescence and moving through adolescence, readers are concerned with having vicarious experiences along with seeing themselves in the literature they read, Carlsen's second and third stages of reading development. At this point readers seek situations that parallel their own life situations and issues. Readers also identify with characters in the story; they can test new roles, new feelings, and new responses to challenges through reading experiences.

The fourth concern, philosophical problems, evolves at the point in adolescence when the initial tasks of self-identity are basically resolved and attention shifts to wider society and the happenings of the world in which the teenager lives. Reading interests move beyond the experiences of the characters in the story to the interpretations and meanings of the writing. Issues of relationships, values, and human responsibility characterize the reading interests of adolescents at this level, and they obviously require more complex material.

The last stage Carlsen describes is an adult reading level, or at least a level generally attained in adulthood. This level is aesthetic delight, wherein the literature must be satisfactorily presented and reader concerns focus on the art of the presentation: its style, its thematic treatment, the structure of the story, and the subtlety and harmony of the writer's craft. Obviously, this stage is the most sophisticated and may well be beyond the comfortable ability of most high school students.

The value of Carlsen's hierarchy of reading appreciation for middle and high school teachers lies in the realization that a representative classroom of adolescents generally contains young adults scattered across all five stages. Treating the entire class of students as though they were homogeneous results in problems, potential reading resistance, and frustration for both students and teacher. Not all students find the same books useful, desirable, or even readable. The task for teachers is to know the students, become familiar with the stages of adolescent growth, understand the needs of students, and familiarize themselves with the level of reading the students have achieved. Then teachers can satisfactorily guide and match readers to material that entertains, enlightens, and challenges them to greater maturity.

Meeting the Needs of Special Students

This chapter focuses on meeting the developmental, moral, and reading interests and abilities of students in general. Young adult literature speaks directly to young people in middle and secondary schools. Teachers can meet the range of abilities and interests among young adults by carefully selecting literature appropriate for the developmental levels found in the classroom. Although "regular" students may be easy to describe, teachers may need to pay some attention to two special groups: students who are considered at risk and students who are considered gifted.

> *When I'm working on a new book my purpose is to make the story so compelling that even the most reluctant reader will want to see what happens next.*
>
> Rodman Philbrick

The At-Risk Student

All students are probably at risk to some degree, but some are more at risk than others. Generally, those most at risk are students who are in danger of failure and are less likely to complete school successfully. *At risk* is a new term that describes students who are not specially labeled as special education students. At-risk students may have problems with school success and achievement. In fact, most will probably drop out of school before graduation. Some educators have characterized at-risk students as those who never contribute to class, have little or nothing to say when called on, often daydream, and generally do not respond to classroom activities. These students often see success or failure as beyond their control; they blame others for what happens to them. In the recent past, most at-risk students have been characterized as those with a low socioeconomic status; however, more study has revealed that young people at all socioeconomic levels can be at risk.

For the purposes of this book, we are interested in students who are at risk in reading. These are not necessarily remedial reading students, but students who have not had positive experiences in reading for a variety of reasons. For some, reading and schooling go together. They hate to read and they hate school. As they see it, school has not been good to them. Because the assigned reading has not been appropriate, they have not developed into good readers. They struggle with almost everything given to them in the classroom to read. Other at-risk students have the ability to read the letters and words on the printed page, but they have no desire to read anything that is not required. Even the required literature makes little sense because it has no meaning to these students. In either case, students at risk in reading will not be productive in the academic experience of the classroom and may not become lifelong readers.

What can be done? Some of the risk factors mentioned—socioeconomic status, financial resources, past educational success or failure—may be beyond the direct control of teachers. However, decisions about what literature is used in the classroom and what strategies are used to teach that literature lie right at the feet of the classroom teacher.

As we note throughout this book, young adult literature serves the young adult well. It is written from the perspective of young people and is appropriate for their experiences and levels of reaction. Adult literature (or at least that literature most often found in the middle and high school curricula) is written from different perspectives. Students find it difficult to relate to Brontë's *Wuthering Heights* (1847), Thackeray's *Vanity Fair* (1847), or Austen's *Pride and Prejudice* (1813), but they find delight in reading *The True Meaning of Cleavage* (Fredericks, 2003), *Whale Talk* (Crutcher,

2001), *What Janie Found* (Cooney, 2000), *The Outcasts of 19 Schulyer Place* (Konigs-burg, 2004), *Leaving Protection* (Hobbs, 2004), *Bucking the Sarge* (Curtis, 2004), and the nonfiction piece *King of the Mild Frontier* (Crutcher, 2003).

Why are these novels more attractive to the young adult reader? An adolescent can better relate to the characters and the plot. A youthful protagonist with an adolescent point of view helps at-risk students make connections. The characters are highly inde-pendent. They may not seem realistic to adults, but they are very realistic to the young readers. They offer hope to the young reader, hope that things can change or improve. They give hope to readers that they will be able to cope with all that seems wrong with being a young adult. In these novels, adolescents see their age-mates showing re-sponsibility (e.g., the young adults in the novels have to deal with the consequences of their own decisions).

If we want at-risk students to continue reading in middle and high schools, we must provide them with materials they will read. In discussing reading difficulty, Langer (1984) states:

> While syntax, word length, and vocabulary have been shown to affect text difficulty, more recent views of reading comprehension suggest that ease of comprehension is also a function of the reader's knowledge and experiences . . . the contextual variables that affect and are affected by the purpose for reading and the environment sur-rounding the reading experience. (p. 122)

As noted previously, *The Maze* (Hobbs, 1998) is an action-packed adventure set in the canyons of Utah. It serves the at-risk student well. Rick Walker is a foster child who is sent to a juvenile detention center at an early age. He escapes and heads out on his own. It isn't until he meets Lon Peregrino, a bird biologist who is releasing fledgling condors back into the wild, that Rick begins to understand the importance of working with oth-ers for a common goal. Through the understanding of Lon and the work that needs to be done with the condors, Rick begins to understand who he is and what it will take to get his life back on track. At-risk readers can perhaps see themselves in Rick, a young adult who is down on his luck and does not have much going for him. Although they may never find themselves in the deep sandstone canyons of Utah, they can find themselves work-ing hard to overcome their struggles in life with the help of other people.

Bucking the Sarge (Curtis, 2004) introduces the reader to Luther and Sparky, two young people who live in the projects in Flint, Michigan. Now some might agree that the two boys are at risk primarily due to their living environment, and this may well be true. The reason for choosing this particular book in this section is that *Bucking the Sarge* will certainly meet the needs of at-risk readers. The syntax is clever but not complex; the humor often causes the reader to laugh out loud, and the experiences of Luther and Sparky meet the interest level of at-risk readers. It is true that both boys want out of Flint, Michigan. Flint is not where they want to be for, as Sparky says, "Flint's nothing but the *Titanic*" (p. 127). Luther's mother, Sarge, runs the Happy Neighbor Group Home for Men, also known as slum housing and group homes. She has bilked the system with shady transactions and has developed her "evil financial em-pire." In this oftentimes hilarious story, Christopher Paul Curtis shares experiences of

Luther and Sparky, who often have to do the dirty work with the group homes. Sarge is frequently evicting someone, mainly to make room for another person who has more money and can make more of a "contribution" to her fortune. Luther has a terrible time understanding the evictions, because often there is no reason to remove the individual except to put someone else in who is financially more solvent. Luther cannot accept that. He believes that it may be Sarge's house, but it is someone's home.

Luther's plan of escape is to win the science project competition in school. He has won it 2 years in a row and thinks he can win it again this year. He does. His project is an investigation of the use of lead paint that is still in homes around Flint. What he has not thought through is that his mother—Sarge—is the biggest user of this paint. So when she hears of the winning project, she gives Luther 4 days to leave. So Luther puts his mind to work and while Sarge and her henchmen are off to a 4-day convention, Luther tries to find the many financial resources that Sarge has. He is particularly looking for his $90,000 college fund. Luther finds some money, but it is not in his college fund. He decides that amount is his, and he takes it and heads to Florida. He is to secure travel for Sparky after he gets settled in new living conditions. The revenge is complete: Sarge returns to find little money left, both cars gone—one has been sold, the other is with Luther—and the officials will soon be hot on her tail looking for lead paint in her houses.

The Gifted Student

Some teachers and many more parents believe that young people who are labeled gifted should read only the best literature, and "the best" translates into reading the classics. (Reading the classics is covered in detail in Chapter 7.) If educators accept the developmental processes of young people, the choice of literature becomes paramount in the success of gifted students. It is folly to believe that a gifted student who excels in reading and writing will be able to interact with literature that has been written for adults in a language and style that are quite different from those of contemporary literature. Success in reading relates strongly to the life experiences the reader brings to the literature. If the experience is lacking, if there is no understanding of the moral issues presented, and if the general attitude toward the work is negative for whatever reason, gifted students will have difficulty having the kind of personal response that we want them to have. Educators must present literature with which the student can interact, not just analyze.

> Insofar as we divorce the study of literature from the experience of reading and view literary works as objects to be analyzed rather than human expressions to be reacted to; . . . insofar as we favor form over content, objectivity over subjectivity, detachment over involvement, theoretical over real readers; insofar as we worry more about incorrect responses than insufficient ones; insofar as we emphasize the distinction between literature and life rather than their interpretations, we reduce the power of literature and protect ourselves from it. (Slatoff, 1970, p. 168)

Intellectually gifted students can read the words, phrases, and sentences very well. We are not concerned about the students' ability to mechanically read the works. It is their ability to respond to the literature that is so important. For this reason we believe that teachers should not remove young adult literature from the gifted student reading program. This literature addresses problems in the realm of the moral, emotional, and experiential levels of young adults. The tragedy is that classroom teachers give classic literature to students whose experiences and developmental levels are limited, therefore preventing students the joy and success of reader response at its highest level and, perhaps, encouraging students to function only at the analytical level.

In young adult literature, gifted students can read about themselves, or at least about characters who are gifted in some way. Just as the literature about at-risk students may be helpful for those students, literature with gifted characters may enhance emotional and moral growth for the gifted student. Gifted students may indeed feel some of the same concerns as at-risk students: isolation, emotional instability, and social indecisiveness. Young adult literature may indeed validate their own experiences, attitudes, and uniqueness. Reading literature with characters who have similar concerns and differences may help these students overcome some of their own problems. Painfully aware of how giftedness may lead to isolation and the fear of socializing, gifted students may find some solace in Ursula Le Guin's *Very Far Away from Anywhere Else* (1976). Students may find it easy to relate to the experiences of Owen Thomas Griffiths, the exceptionally bright senior in that novel. Le Guin's novel also lets readers respond to many important issues: the need to conform, the cost of conformity, the "handicap" of being intelligent, boy-girl relationships, and being true to yourself.

Drowning Anna (Mayfield, 2001) also involves a young adult who would be considered gifted but is not labeled as such. Anna Goldsmith is bright but shy and has just transferred from London to a small Yorkshire town. Her dialect differences and her near perfect grades set her apart from the other students. To Anna's credit, she does not flaunt the grades or the dialect, but for some reason Anna is constantly faced with bullying from her classmate and "friend" Hayley. Hayley is gifted in a deviant sort of way: She plays hurtful, cruel games on Anna but always gives the impression that someone else is doing the task or that Anna is simply imagining it. The teasing and cruel jokes continue. They escalate to the extent that Anna can no longer handle them. She gets no help from school officials, other friends, or her parents. They simply do not understand the magnitude of the bullying. Hayley's cunning leaves a deeper impression on Anna than anyone could ever have anticipated. Anna tries to resolve the conflict but fails; however, there seems to be hope as parents and friends find out the severity of the problem. The bullying issue is extremely important for any students, gifted or not.

Especially bright students may find Bruce Brooks's novels enjoyable reads. Protagonists in Brooks's works are exceptionally intelligent adolescents. These bright young adults, however, still have problems. They certainly find their share of adolescent struggles. Students may enjoy *Midnight Hour Encores* (1986), in which Sib, who has great musical talents, still finds herself working through the emotional ups and downs of being an adolescent. Students may also find *Vanishing* (Brooks, 1999) a compelling read. Alice and Res are two highly intriguing characters that help Brooks present important issues to young people—love, death, and controlling one's destiny.

Nonfictional young adult literature meets the needs of gifted students as well as other students. In her study of reading habits of gifted junior high students, Carter (1982) found that many of these students were reading nonfictional works even though most of the assigned reading in the classroom was fiction. We believe students will find *What's Your Story? A Young Person's Guide to Writing Fiction* (Bauer, 1992), *Chapters: My Growth as a Writer* (Duncan, 1982), *How I Came to Be a Writer* (Naylor, 1987), *Blood on the Forehead: What I Know about Writing* (Kerr, 1998), *The Way Things Work* (Macaulay, 1988), *The New Way Things Work* (Macaulay, 1998), *Black Potatoes: The Story of the Great Irish Famine* (Bartoletti, 2002), *Crews* (Hinojosa, 1995), *Speaking Out: Teenagers Talk on Sex, Race, and Identity* (Kuklin, 1993), *Straight Talk about Death for Teenagers: How to Cope with Losing Someone You Love* (Grollman, 1993), *Food Fight* (Bode, 1997), *Girls Speak Out: Finding Your True Self* (Johnston & Steinem, 1997), *Knots in My Yo-Yo String* (Spinelli, 1998), *King of the Mild Frontier* (Crutcher, 2003), *Holes in My Life* (Gantos, 2002), *Guts* (Paulsen, 2001), *With Their Eyes: September 11th, The View from a High School at Ground Zero* (Thoms, 2002), *Escape from Saigon: How a Vietnam War Orphan Became an American Boy* (Warren, 2004), and other such works most interesting and enjoyable. Duncan's *Chapters,* Kerr's *What I Know about Writing,* Naylor's *How I Came to Be a Writer,* and Bauer's *What's Your Story?* would be most appropriate for students who write well and wish to have a career in writing.

In addition to appropriate content and developmental levels, young adult literature provides quality writing, writing that students should read and discuss to help them in their own writing. After reading *The Secret Life of Bees* (Kidd, 2002), *Milkweed* (Spinelli, 2003), *Roll of Thunder, Hear My Cry* (M. Taylor, 1976), *The First Part Last* (Johnson, 2003), *Sang Spell* (Naylor, 1998), *Far North* (Hobbs, 1996), *Out of the Dust* (Hesse, 1997), *Soldier's Heart* (Paulsen, 1998), *Tenderness* (Cormier, 1997), *The Giver* (Lowry, 1993), *Red Midnight* (Mikaelsen, 2002), *Acceleration* (McNamee, 2003), and *The Chocolate War* (Cormier, 1974), for example, readers quickly realize that they have read emotionally powerful, carefully crafted, well-written works of literature. These novels contain all of the components of recognized literary masterpieces. Students can approach these novels in the same way they approach the classics: They can make personal responses, undertake literary analysis, and identify universal themes and specific techniques and strategies characteristic of the author's craft. The issues raised provide students with ample subject matter for creative and critical thinking. Analysis of theme, character development, and plot structure are but a few of the additional literary activities in which students can become engaged.

Using Young Adult Literature as Rites of Passage

As noted in this chapter, young adults evolve through this period called adolescence. Although there are no systematic initiation rites for passage into adulthood in this society as there may be in other societies, young people have some experiences that seem to indicate that they are moving through this period into adulthood. On the concrete, physical level, obvious experiences occur: graduation, getting a driver's license, attending the prom, starting a part-time job, and many others. On the social, emotional level, young people also move through periods of their lives, as Havighurst suggests, by acquiring more mature social skills, achieving a masculine or feminine sex role, accepting the changes that occur in their bodies, achieving independence from parents, preparing for sex and marriage, preparing for an occupation, developing their own moral code, and achieving social responsibility.

As young people move through these experiences or stages, they seem to be so alone in their struggle—albeit oftentimes at their own wishes. Because of the awkwardness of the relationship with their parents and other adults, there seem to be few people other than their peers to help them through this difficult period in their lives. Our society has determined that it is best not to isolate young people during this time, as occurs in some other societies, but rather to let them move through on their own terms.

Books may offer young adults what our society does not. Reading books helps young adults in their journey—their rites of passage—into adulthood. Books provide experiences that may help young adults through their adolescent years. Providing young people with young adult literature, not only in the bookstores but also in the classroom, is imperative if we want adolescents to read about more experiences than they could have on their own. In addition, this literature serves young people in their struggle with identity, with their relationships with adults, and with their choices, which often suggest their concern with moral questions of right and wrong.

Perhaps the greatest gift that our society can give young adults in their journey into adulthood is not a credit card but a library card.

 Learning Log Responses

Write an entry at least a page long that shows your understanding of the periods we call preadolescence and adolescence.

Explain Havighurst's developmental tasks and develop a position statement (two or three paragraphs) on their importance to middle and secondary school classroom teachers.

Write a reflective entry in your journal in which you address the issues of moral development and reading interests as they apply to you as a teacher of literature.

References

Anderson, P. (1983). Practical applications of language learning theory in the middle school and junior high. In D. Bergdahl (Ed.), *Research in the teaching of the English language arts* (pp. 1–7). Athens: Southeastern Ohio Council of Teachers of English.

Angelotti, M. (1981). Uses of the young adult literature in the eighties. *English in Texas, 13,* 32–34.

Auten, A. (1984). All about adolescent literature: Pro and con. *Journal of Reading, 28*(1), 76–78.

Brewbaker, J. (1989). I like happy endings. You don't. *English Journal, 78*(6), 66–68.

Bushman, J. H. (1997). Young adult literature in the classroom—Or is it? *English Journal, 86*(3), 36–40.

Carlsen, R. (1974). Literature IS. *English Journal, 63*(2), 23–27.

Carlsen, R. (1980). *Books and the teen-age reader.* New York: Harper & Row.

Carlsen, R., & Sherrill, A. (1988). *Voices of readers: How we come to love books.* Urbana, IL: National Council of Teachers of English.

Carter, B. (1982). Leisure reading habits of gifted students in a suburban junior high school. *Top of the News, 38*, 312–317.

Cooney, C. B. Poster. Ottawa, KS: The Writing Conference.

Cormier, R. Poster. Ottawa, KS: The Writing Conference.

Dewey, J. (1964). The results of child-study applied to education. In R. D. Archambault (Ed.), *On education: Selected writings* (pp. 271–279). New York: Modern Library. (Original work published 1895)

Draper, S. Poster. Ottawa, KS: The Writing Conference.

Early, M. (1960). Stages of growth in literary appreciation. *English Journal, 49*(3), 161–167.

Erikson, E. H. (Ed.). (1963). *The challenge of youth.* Garden City, NY: Anchor.

Fuller, L. B. (1980). Literature for today's adolescents: A historical perspective. *English Education, 11*(3), 131–141.

Gilligan, C. (1982). *In a different voice: Psychological theory and women's development.* Cambridge, MA: Harvard University Press.

Gioia, D. (2004, July 16). Americans found to read less literature than ever. *Chronicle of Higher Education,* pp. A1, A16.

Graves, D. H. (1990). *Discover your own literacy.* Portsmouth, NH: Heinemann.

Havighurst, R. (1972). *Developmental tasks and education.* New York: David McKay.

Heather, P. (February, 1982). *Young people's reading: A study of the leisure reading of 13–15-year-olds.* Paper presented at the annual meeting of the United Kingdom Reading Association, London.

Hobbs, W. Poster. Ottawa, KS: The Writing Conference.

Kohlberg, L. (1968). Early education: A cognitive-developmental view. *Child Development, 39*(4), 1013–1062.

Kohlberg, L. (1976). Moral stages and moralization. In T. Lickona (Ed.), *Moral development and behavior* (pp. 47–52). New York: Harper & Row.

Kohlberg, L. (1984). *Essays in moral development: Vol. 2. The psychology of moral development.* San Francisco: Harper & Row.

Kohlberg, L. (1987). *Child psychology and childhood education.* New York: Longman.

Korman, G. Poster. Ottawa, KS: The Writing Conference.

Langer, J. (1984). Literary instruction in American schools: Problems and perspectives. *American Journal of Education, 93*, 107–132.

Marcia, J. (1980). Identity in adolescence. In J. Adelson (Ed.), *Handbook of adolescent psychology* (pp. 98–112). New York: Wiley.

McLemee, S. (2004, July 16). Americans found to read less literature than ever. *Chronicle of Higher Education,* pp. A1–A16.

National Center for Educational Statistics (NCES). (2003). *The nation's report card: What does the NAEP reading assessment measure?* Retrieved from www.nces.ed.gov/nationsreportcard/reading.

Nilsen, A., & Donelson, K. (2005). *Literature for today's young adults* (7th ed.). Boston: Pearson Allyn & Bacon.

O'Connor, M. E. (1980). *A study of the reading preferences of high school students.* Arlington, VA: (ERIC Document Reproduction Service No. ED 185 524)

Piaget, J. (1965). *The moral judgment of the child* (M. Gabain, Trans.). New York: Free Press. (Original work published 1932)

Piaget, J. (1971). *Science of education and the psychology of the child.* New York: Viking.

Piaget, J., & Inhelder, B. (1969). *The psychology of the child.* New York: Basic Books.

Philbrick, R. Poster. Ottawa, KS: The Writing Conference.

Slatoff, W. J. (1970). *With respect to readers' dimensions of literary response.* Ithaca, NY: Cornell University Press.

Smetana, J. G. (in press). Parenting and the development of social knowledge reconceptualized: A social domain analysis. To appear in J. E. Grusec & L. Kuczynski (Eds.), *Handbook of parenting and the transmission of values.* New York: Wiley.

Trelease, J. (1982). *The read aloud handbook.* New York: Penguin.

Turiel, E. (1983). *The development of social knowledge: Morality and convention.* New York: Cambridge University Press.

CHAPTER

2

Evaluating Young Adult Literature

*T*he enjoyment of reading must be an integral part of the classroom to foster the positive attitude toward literature that is necessary for lifelong reading. We want our students to enjoy the literature now, but we also want them to continue this enjoyment as they become productive members of society.

The role, then, of the classroom teacher is to walk that fine line between having students read for the pleasurable act that it is and having them read to increase their powers of literary analysis and, thus, become members of an educated, literate society. To this end, teachers will want to make decisions carefully concerning the literature curriculum: its design and how it is delivered to students. In addition, teachers will want to structure lessons that will enable students to independently evaluate the quality of the literature they are reading. To know that we like a work is great; to know why we like it is even better.

Considering Standard Literary Qualities

Authors (writers) are concerned about a number of literary techniques as they bring a piece of literature to publication. Students (readers) are involved with these same literary strategies as they finish their study of the work. Both writers and readers ask questions during the process of writing and reading. What works for young adult readers? What conflict will draw the readers' attention and sustain it throughout the work? How many characters should there be? How involved can they become in the conflict? Will the setting be an integral part of the conflict or a minor consideration? How these literary elements work in the literature determines the degree to which we as readers suggest that the work has quality.

Plot

In interest surveys, young adults usually comment that they like novels that are realistic (i.e., novels that have conflicts in which young adults can find themselves and can realistically decide the solution to that conflict). Authors usually give young adult readers just what they want. They hook them at the beginning and, through a carefully crafted story line, keep the reader to the end.

In the opening lines of *Inside Out* (2003), Terry Trueman grabs the reader and never lets go: "All I want is a maple bar, but I don't think these kids with the guns care about what I want" (p. 3). Kimberly Willis Holt uses the "hook" in the opening lines of *Keeper of the Night* (2003): "My mother died praying on her knees. Her rosary beads were still in her hands when we found her" (p. 3). Certainly, Phyllis Reynolds Naylor, in the opening line of *Sang Spell* (1998), has similar results: "On a night even demons howl for their mothers, Josh stood on the edge of the highway, thumbing a ride" (p. 1). Robert Cormier takes a little different slant in *Heroes* (1998), but he still hooks the reader: "My name is Francis Joseph Cassavant and I have just returned to Frenchtown in Monument and the war is over and I have no face" (p. 1). The relationship to reality is crucial. This holds true for fantasy and science fiction works as well. The reality in this literature may be defined in a different way by the author, but it is defined and attended to. Gordon Korman titillates the reader with his first line in *Son of the Mob* (2002): "The worst night of my life? My first—and last—date with Angela O'Bannon" (p. 1). Again, the first line often is used to hook the reader. Will Weaver in *Memory Boy* (2001) starts his novel this way: "It was the perfect time for leaving. Weather conditions were finally right: a steady breeze blew from the south, plus there was just enough moonlight to see by. July 3, 2008. This would be the date our family would always remember, assuming, of course, that we lived to tell about it" (p. 1).

This reality is found in four plot types:

1. Protagonist against self: *Destiny* (Grove, 2000), *Keeper of the Night* (Holt, 2003), *Driver's Ed* (Cooney, 1994), *Ironman* (Crutcher, 1995), *A Distant Enemy* (Vanasse, 1997), and *Touching Spirit Bear* (Mikaelsen, 2001)

2. Protagonist against society: *I Am the Cheese* (Cormier, 1977), *Beast* (Myers, 2004), *The Giver* (Lowry, 1993), *Miriam's Well* (Ruby, 1993), *Monster* (Myers, 1999), and *Sang Spell* (Naylor, 1998)

3. Protagonist against another person: *Battle of Jericho* (Draper, 2003), *The Insiders* (Minter, 2004), *Whale Talk* (Crutcher, 2001), and *Heroes* (Cormier, 1998)

4. Protagonist against nature: *Fish* (Matthews, 2004), *Blizzard's Wake* (Naylor, 2002), *Dogwolf* (Carter, 1994), *Downriver* (Hobbs, 1991), *River Thunder* (Hobbs, 1997), *The Maze* (Hobbs, 1998), and *Leaving Protection* (Hobbs, 2004)

Nonfiction has similar types. Certainly, Meltzer's works are included in the individual-against-society type, and Bunting's *The Great White Shark* (1982) and Reed's *The Dolphins and Me* (1989) fall into the protagonist-against-nature group.

We have to be careful, too, not to consider one and only one category of plot structure for many of these works because some easily cross over. For example, *Red Midnight* (Mikaelsen, 2003) certainly pits the struggle to escape the village and forest against the individuals, but the sea also plays an important part in the novel. *Nine Man Tree* by Robert Newton Peck (1998) also provides a crossover. Readers might think the struggle to get the killer beast would give the novel plot emphasis, but certainly the development of characters and the setting of 1931 Florida swampland have to be equally important.

How the novel ends also provides criteria for determining quality. Is it predictable from the start how the conflict will be resolved? All quality young adult novels keep the readers guessing. Although most will come to some solution, others may not. Readers may assume that Luther will be free from Sarge (*Bucking the Sarge*, Curtis, 2004) and that he will finally send for Sparky; however, the ending does not absolutely show that. We leave Anna (*Drowning Anna*, Mayfield, 2001) in the hospital recovering from her attempted suicide; however, there are doubts that she will fully recover. Readers are not absolutely sure that Macey (*Burning Up*, Cooney, 1999) will convince her schoolmates to work with her in her drive to elevate the discussion of racism so that all have a better opportunity to confront the issue. Most novels, too, end "the way we want them to." The romance in most of us wants everything to turn out well. However, Cormier jolts us into realizing that life just isn't like that. Most readers want Archie (*The Chocolate War*, 1974) "to get his" and they want Miro (*After the First Death*, 1979) to be caught and Kate to remain alive, but that isn't the way life is.

Other novels that emphasize plot structure:

Avi, *The Man Who Was Poe*, 1989

Robert Cormier, *I Am the Cheese*, 1977

Robert Cormier, *Fade*, 1988

Robert Cormier, *We All Fall Down*, 1991

Robert Cormier, *In the Middle of the Night*, 1995

Lois Duncan, *Don't Look behind You*, 1989

Sherry Garland, *Song of the Buffalo Boy*, 1992

David Klass, *California Blue*, 1994

E. L. Konigsburg, *The Outcasts of 19 Schulyer Place*, 2004.

Walter Dean Myers, *Monster*, 1999.

William Sleator, *The Duplicate*, 1989

Paul Zindel, *Loch*, 1994

> *Good stories are fundamentally about good characters, and for me, writing good characters is all about knowing how to love them. I can't love them if they are too perfect.*
>
> Ann Brashares

Characters

Young adult literature traditionally has characters with whom young adults can identify. Sometimes the plot may not be strong, but well-developed characters allow readers to feel that they are experiencing the conflict. How the characters are presented determines to some extent the quality of the work. If all characters are flat (i.e., they are not fully developed and they do not change), then readers will not relate to the novel.

If, however, they are dynamic, round characters, readers will know fully about the characters and appreciate the many levels of growth that take place. Given the limitations of the young adult novel, most minor characters may be flat, but readers can expect the protagonist to be fully developed. At times, however, perhaps because of the length of the novel, both main characters and minor characters are archetyped (i.e., they play a particular symbolic role). Archie in *The Chocolate War* (Cormier, 1974), Dr. Sterling in *Blizzard's Wake* (Naylor, 2002), and August in *The Secret Life of Bees* (Kidd, 2002) are used this way.

> *Writing for me is the exploration of character; what makes him or her tick and why the reader should care. If someone says of one of my characters, "Hey, that's what I feel," I have succeeded.*
>
> Mel Glenn

Are characters motivated to do what they do? To answer this question, readers look at the interaction between and among characters. Do characters respond realistically to each other and to the events that confront them? Young adult literature has been criticized because the young adults in the literature do not relate positively to adults. This criticism may have been true of earlier young adult fiction, but more recent literature offers a better balance. Of course, adults should not be portrayed in a totally positive way because that is not a realistic view. Many young adults are indeed struggling with their relationships with their parents and other adults, and, to be realistic, their literature should not be presented in any other way. However, positive adult role models can be found: Max the swimming coach in *Stotan!* (Crutcher, 1986), Lainey's mom and dad in *Jake Riley: Irreparably Damaged* (Davis, 2003), Coach Sherman in *Chinese Handcuffs* (Crutcher, 1989), Gran in *Phoenix Rising* (Hesse, 1994), Lon Peregrino in *The Maze* (Hobbs, 1998), and Big Ma, Mamma, and Pa in *Roll of Thunder, Hear My Cry* (M. Taylor, 1976).

Other novels that emphasize character development:

Laurie Halse Anderson, *Speak*, 1999

Sandy Asher, *Out of Here*, 1993

Jane Leslie Conley, *Crazy Lady*, 1993

Dennis Covington, *Lizard*, 1991

Chris Crutcher, *Ironman*, 1995

Christopher Paul Curtis, *Bucking the Sarge*, 2004

Peter Dickinson, *Eva*, 1988

D. Klass, *Home of the Braves*, 2003

Lois Lowry, *The Silent Boy*, 2003

Catherine MacPhail, *Dark Waters*, 2003

Gary Paulsen, *Sisters*, 1993

Gary Paulsen, *Sarney: A Life Remembered*, 1997

Gary Paulsen, *Alida's Song*, 1999

Richard Peck, *A Long Way from Chicago*, 1998

Robert Newton Peck, *Nine Man Tree*, 1998

Ann Rinaldi, *Wolf by the Ears*, 1991

Ann Rinaldi, *Finishing Becca*, 1994

Lois Ruby, *Skin Deep*, 1994

Terry Trueman, *Stuck in Neutral*, 2000

Terry Trueman, *Inside Out*, 2003

Setting

Most readers would argue that *The Chocolate War* (Cormier, 1974), *Beyond the Chocolate War* (Cormier, 1985), *Roll of Thunder, Hear My Cry* (M. Taylor, 1976), *Deathwatch* (R. White, 1972), *The Island* (Paulsen, 1988), and *Wild Man Island* (Hobbs, 2002), to mention a few, would not be successful if it were not for the dull, drab, almost sterile Trinity School, the Mississippi of the early 1930s, the naked desert, an island in northern Wisconsin, and the rough waters of the Northwest. In each of these novels, the setting is crucial to the success of the literature. Even though the setting in each novel is strong, it is not overpowering. It allows for strong characterization and plot development. It adds to the success; it plays a unique role.

In other works, the setting—time and place—enables the readers to move beyond or back from the present. Most fantasy and science fiction would not be possible without mythical worlds or futuristic settings. In *This Place Has No Atmosphere*, Danziger (1986) takes her readers to a new colony on the moon. We move in and out of reality in L'Engle's *A Wrinkle in Time* (1968). Readers find themselves in a city of the future seemingly devoid of human life in Nix's *Shade's Children* (1997) and readers wonder about the possibility of cloning when they read *The House of the Scorpion* (Farmer, 2002). Historical fiction draws on the appropriate time and place for its honest depicting of events. *Across Five Aprils* (Hunt, 1964), *My Brother Sam Is Dead* (Collier & Collier, 1974), *Summer of My German Soldier* (Greene, 1973), *The Bloody Country* (Collier & Collier, 1976), *An Acquaintance with Darkness* (Rinaldi, 1997), *Number the Stars* (Lowry, 1989), and *The River between Us* (Peck, 2003) depend greatly on a particular time in the past. Mildred Taylor's novels and Robert Newton Peck's *A Day No Pigs Would Die* (1972) and *Nine Man Tree* (1998) are in a sense controlled by the 1920s and 1930s of rural Mississippi, rural Vermont, and the Florida swampland, respectively.

The sea kayak is home to Santiago and Angelina (*Red Midnight,* 2002) as they escape their burned homeland and through the forests to reach the ocean and thus head to the United States. There would be no *Fair Weather* (Peck, 2001) if not for the World's Fair.

Other novels that emphasize setting:

Alden Carter, *Up Country,* 1989

Alden Carter, *Dogwolf,* 1994

Caroline Cooney, *The Ransom of Mercy Carter,* 2001

Jean Craighead George, *Julie,* 1994

Karen Hesse, *The Music of Dolphins,* 1996

Karen Hesse, *Out of the Dust,* 1997

Will Hobbs, *Bearstone,* 1989

Will Hobbs, *Downriver,* 1991

Will Hobbs, *Beardance,* 1993

Will Hobbs, *Kokopelli's Flute,* 1995

Will Hobbs, *Far North,* 1996

Will Hobbs, *Jason's Gold,* 1999

Will Hobbs, *Down the Yukon,* 2001

Will Hobbs, *Leaving Protection,* 2004

Hadley Irwin, *The Original Freddie Ackerman,* 1992

Gary Paulsen, *Hatchet,* 1987

Gary Paulsen, *Sarney: A Life Remembered,* 1997

Richard Peck, *Unfinished Portrait of Jessica,* 1991

Robert Newton Peck, *Nine Man Tree,* 1998

Robert Newton Peck, *Cowboy Ghost,* 1999

Ann Rinaldi, *In My Father's House,* 1993

Ann Rinaldi, *Taking Liberty,* 2002

Ann Rinaldi, *Mutiny's Daughter,* 2004

Jerry Spinelli, *Milkweed,* 2003

Paul Zindel, *Reef of Death,* 1998

Theme

Does the work have some redeeming value? Does it speak to readers about universal values and human conditions? Young adults ask these questions when they consider the quality of the literature. Mildred Taylor clearly demonstrates the importance of family, the ownership of land, and the treatment of the human being in her novels. Young adults relate well to the themes found in S. E. Hinton's books because each book has a spirit of hope. Although the protagonists are up against all odds, put there either by themselves or by society, hope remains that the human spirit will overcome the odds. Louis Sachar writes of this human spirit in his book *Holes* (1998), in which Stanley Yelnats is sent to a correctional camp in the Texas desert and finds himself spending most of his time digging seemingly senseless holes.

As in the other literary aspects, there is a balance. In Cormier's *The Chocolate War* (1974), the theme that evil is not limited to any given segment of society is strong, but it does not overpower the plot and characters. And while readers often get caught up with the horrific atrocities of the Holocaust in *Milkweed* (Spinelli, 2003), they soon realize that Misha, Uri, and Janine are more than just victims, they are human beings.

Other novels that emphasize theme:

Avi, *Nothing but the Truth*, 1991

Joan Bauer, *Hope Was Here*, 2000

Cherie Bennett, *Life in the Fat Lane*, 1998

Caroline Cooney, *Driver's Ed*, 1994

Chris Crutcher, *Staying Fat for Sarah Byrnes*, 1993

Chris Crutcher, *Ironman*, 1995

Sarah Dressen, *Dreamland*, 2000

E. R. Frank, *America*, 2002

Mariah Fredericks, *The True Meaning of Cleavage*, 2003

Cynthia Grant, *The White Horse*, 1998

Angela Johnson, *Heaven*, 1998

Steven Layne, *This Side of Paradise*, 2001

Lois Lowry, *The Giver*, 1993

Norma Fox Mazer, *Out of Control*, 1993

Alice Mead, *Junebug and the Reverend*, 1998

Walter Dean Myers, *Somewhere in the Darkness*, 1992

Gary Paulsen, *Nightjohn*, 1993

Richard Peck, *The Last Safe Place on Earth*, 1995

Jon Ripslinger, *Triangle*, 1994

Barbara Wersba, *Whistle Me Home*, 1997

Point of View

Authors have choices to make when they begin to write. What point of view will be most effective to tell the story? Certainly, the omniscient point of view, which establishes the author's presence in all of the characters, is widely used. Readers know the motivations and actions through each character. Robert Cormier chose this point of view in *The Chocolate War* (1974). We get inside the minds of Jerry, Archie, and Goober through the all-knowing storyteller.

The first-person point of view is more limiting. The reader knows events and other characters through the eyes, ears, and mind of one character. The limitation is that the reader cannot get into the minds of the other characters. Some authors get around this problem by moving the point of view from character to character, perhaps making the change from one chapter to another. Ellen Wittlinger uses this technique in *The Long Night of Leo and Bree* (2002) and Todd Strasser uses it, too, in *Give a Boy a Gun* (2000). However, the first-person narrative point of view tends to connect more personally with the young adult reader. A bonding occurs between the young adult character and the reader.

Other novels that emphasize point of view:

Laurie Halse Anderson, *Speak*, 1999

James Bennett, *Dakota Dream*, 1994

Ann Brashares, *The Sisterhood of the Traveling Pants*, 2001

Ann Brashares, *The Second Summer of the Sisterhood*, 2003

Michael Cadnum, *Heat*, 1998

Caroline Cooney, *Whatever Happened to Janie?*, 1993

Carl Friedman, *Nightfather*, 1991

E. L. Konigsburg, *The Outcasts of 19 Schulyer Place*, 2004

Walter Dean Myers, *Monster*, 1999

Gary Paulsen, *Nightjohn*, 1993

Gary Paulsen, *The Beet Fields*, 2000

Nancy Hope Wilson, *Flapjack Waltzes*, 1998

Ellen Wittlinger, *Razzle*, 2001

Paul Zindel, *Loch*, 1994

Style

The storyteller's style affects the decisions the author makes. For example, is the language of the character appropriate? Young adult literature that incorporates profanity is often criticized. On the other hand, the author's style could be criticized if that language was not used by the characters in the novel, especially if the characters would normally use that language. The language found in Cormier's novels fits the characters and events that he chooses. It would be ludicrous if Myers did not use profanity in *Fallen Angels* (1988) when depicting soldiers in the midst of the Vietnam War. The question raised relates to appropriateness. How far does the author go in depicting the reality of the situation?

Another area related to language is the manner in which characters use language appropriate for their ages and educational levels. In telling her story in *Roll of Thunder, Hear My Cry* (M. Taylor, 1976), Cassie does not talk as an adult, and she should not. Appropriate young adult language is found throughout *The Outsiders* (Hinton, 1967), *Down the Yukon* (Hobbs, 1999), *Plunking Reggie Jackson* (Bennett, 2001), *Warrior Angel* (Lipsyte, 2003), *The Insiders* (Minter, 2004), and many other novels, as it should be, because it helps the young narrator tell the story with some credibility.

Style affects more than word choice for dialogue. Most authors will not have their teenage characters involved in events or carrying out actions that most young adults would not normally do. A few authors may come close to crossing over the fine line between the actions of teenagers and adults. For example, Paulsen's *The Voyage of the FROG* (1989) has been criticized because David's thoughts and behavior are very adultlike.

To some extent, the form that the novel takes is related to style. A few authors have chosen to write in verse. Karen Hesse chose to write her Newbery Award–winning novel *Out of the Dust* (1997) using a series of short poems told from the point of view of the main character. Robert Cormier chose to use blank verse for the first time in his 1999 book *Frenchtown Summer.*

Poets are now writing outside the box. While novelists are using verse to write their stories, poets are telling stories with their verse. Mel Glenn uses a series of poems to tell stories (*Foreign Exchange*, 1999; *Split Image*, 2000). Sonja Sones takes a similar approach in her books (*Stop Pretending*, 1999; *What My Mother Doesn't Know*, 2001; and *One of Those Hideous Books Where the Mother Dies*, 2004).

Other novels that emphasize style:

Sandy Asher, *Out of Here*, 1993

Olive Ann Burns, *Cold Sassy Tree*, 1984

Robert Cormier, *The Chocolate War*, 1974

Robert Cormier, *After the First Death*, 1979

Robert Cormier, *In the Middle of the Night*, 1995

Chris Crutcher, *Chinese Handcuffs*, 1989

Chris Crutcher, *Ironman*, 1995

James M. Deem, *3 NB's of Julian Drew*, 1994

E. R. Frank, *America*, 2002

Angela Johnson, *The First Part Last*, 2003

Catherine MacPhail, *Dark Waters*, 2003

L. S. Matthews, *Fish*, 2004

Walter Dean Myers, *Monster*, 1999

Walter Dean Myers, *Beast*, 2004

Gary Paulsen, *Sisters*, 1993

Virginia Euwer Wolff, *Make Lemonade*, 1993

Virginia Euwer Wolff, *True Believer*, 2001

Considering Other Literary Elements

In addition to these standard literary qualities, authors use other literary elements, and young people should explore their use as they read and study this literature.

Metaphor and Simile

Authors traditionally use metaphors and similes to help the reader understand an idea or situation by comparing or contrasting it with another. The important point for young writers is that they should make every effort to use new comparisons rather than trite and overused ones.

Kevin Henkes (*Olive's Ocean*, 2003) uses metaphor to describe the ocean:

> The sky was full—of blue and sun. The ocean reflected it and was flat and glossy like a fancy ballroom floor. To Martha, this was the most beautiful sight, a miracle. (p. 32)

Chris Crutcher (*Whale Talk*, 2000) describes one of the members of the swim team: "Chris Coughlin is so glad to be a part of something he works like one of those potato bugs in my bathtub, and he's as happy stroking away belly down on the bench as he is in the water" (p. 75).

In describing Buddy in *Everything Is Not Enough*, Asher (1987) uses the following metaphor: "He's a human pillow, a 6-foot one-inch, blue eyed pillow with no sharp edges anywhere. Not fat, just fluffed up" (p. 10). Author Alice Childress uses simile to tell the reader about Rainbow's feelings in *Rainbow Jordan* (1981). Rainbow's friend steals a can of sardines for the girls' lunch. When Rainbow finds out, she is so upset she can barely swallow her lunch and thinks it "tasted like sadness, not sardines" (p. 63).

Flashback

A memory or retelling of a past event that has importance to the immediate story line can be used effectively. Both *Dreamland Lake* (R. Peck, 1973) and *The Outsiders* (Hinton, 1967) are told entirely through the use of flashback. In fact, at the end of Hinton's novel, the reader realizes that the story has been Ponyboy's paper for English class. In both novels, the main characters retell events that led to a change in their outlook on life.

Many authors, however, write much smaller sections using flashback. Michael Cadnum uses flashback often in his novel *Heat* (1998). Much of what we learn from Bonnie about her diving accident and about her father's legal problems are through flashback. The author hints of the incident and then writes of it in more detail later, even though it took place in the past.

Robert Cormier had to incorporate some of the story line in *The Chocolate War* (1974) into *Beyond the Chocolate War* (1985) so that the latter could stand alone as a piece of literature without the reader having to have read the first novel. He uses flashback to do most of that. Ray Bannister (and the reader) learns about the chocolate sale that occurs in *The Chocolate War* through Obie in a series of flashbacks. Jacqueline Woodson uses flashback in a similar way in *Lena* (1999), the sequel to *I Hadn't Meant to Tell You This* (1994), because she has to incorporate some of what happened to Lena and Dion in the first book so that the reader will understand why they have run away.

Sue Mayfield (*Drowning Anna*, 2001) uses flashback extensively. For example, at the beginning of Chapter 1, Anna is at home. She has returned from school. As she enters her house, she is very calm and does little things that would seem to indicate that all is well. She hangs her coat on the coat rack, feeds the cat, turns on the radio, and then proceeds to up to the bathroom where she writes a suicide note. Chapter 2 moves back to school, and students and faculty wonder where Anna is. Back home in Chapter 3, Anna's mother returns home from work to find Anna in the bathroom. The story line then moves back and forth from the current time to some time in the past. Over the course of the novel, the past eventually catches up with the present time.

Willo Davis Roberts (*Blood on His Hands*, 2004) also uses flashback extensively. Readers first find Marc on the highway running away from a camp that he has been sent to. He is heading to Washington State to find his father. Then through flashback, readers learn why he was sent to the camp, his family situation, and why he is running away.

Other works that use flashback often are *Sex Education* (J. Davis, 1988), *About David* (Pfeffer, 1980), *Remembering the Good Times* (R. Peck, 1985), *After the First Death* (Cormier, 1979), *The Crazy Horse Electric Game* (Crutcher, 1987), and *Jacob Have I Loved* (Paterson, 1980).

Foreshadowing

Foreshadowing is an author's technique for giving clues or hints to the reader about forthcoming action. In *A Wrinkle in Time*, L'Engle (1968) uses this device to let the reader know that even though Charles Wallace is only 5 years old, he is a very important character. "How did Charles Wallace always know about her? How could he always tell . . . it was his mother's mind, and Meg's, that he probed with frightening accuracy" (p. 11).

Readers are piqued by a statement that Vince (*Son of the Mob*, Korman, 2002) makes early in Chapter 1: "Five o'clock. I'm already nervous by the time Alex drops by to go over the checklist. Alex is always pretty skittish around my family because of what my father does for a living" (p. 1). And then later when Vince opens the trunk for a blanket and finds a body: "To be honest my first thought is that he is dead—which isn't such a stretch. I told you about my family business" (p. 6). And in *High Heat* (Deuker, 2003), a major family problem begins the novel. Shane Hunter, excellent baseball player, learns that his father is being charged with money laundering. Readers get a sense that the Hunter family's lifestyle is going to change. Speaking of the family house, Shane says: "The house was huge—the garage alone was probably bigger than the little duplex we live in now" (p. 8). It isn't until many chapters later that the house is put up for sale.

Readers sense something tragic will happen in the early pages of Cormier's novel *Heroes* (1998). Francis Cassavant has returned to Frenchtown in Monument from the war very disfigured. He has just made arrangements with the landlady to rent an apartment: "After she left, I went to the window and looked at the falling rain outside. I was home again in Frenchtown. I thought of the gun hidden away in my duffel bag, and knew that my mission was about to begin" (p. 7).

Effective Beginnings

Young adults frequently have trouble starting their writing. Although we as teachers have an abundance of prewriting strategies to help these young writers get through this period of "blank paper stare," young adult literature may be an effective source to show how published writers begin. We have on occasion suggested to teachers that when their students are at this stage, they simply bring to class four or five young adult novels and read the opening lines of each novel. After a brief discussion of the strategies and techniques used, students are better prepared to begin their work. These models, coupled with the prewriting ideas that have been generated, make the job of getting started easier. Figure 2.1 gives the opening lines of several well-known young adult novels.

Humor

Making the reader chuckle or even laugh out loud is always a refreshing attribute of literature. Young adult literature is no exception. Whether the author emphasizes humor or simply sprinkles it throughout the work, most readers can find an appreciation for its use. Although Christopher Paul Curtis writes of very serious concerns, he does it with a strong element of humor in *The Watsons Go to Birmingham—1963* (1995); his second book, *Bud, Not Buddy* (1999); and his third novel, *Bucking the Sarge* (2004). They are funny books!

Other writers simply play with the language. Danziger, perhaps, is the most notable. Her works are filled with humor, especially puns. In *This Place Has No Atmosphere* (1986), the reader may react negatively to the abundance of puns, as does one of the characters: "'But Sir Hal . . . how can you rescue me from the dragon when none appears on yon horizon?' He continues to hold my hand and rush me along. 'I'm rescuing you from draggin' along and being late for the meeting.' 'Oh, yeck. That pun

From *Killing Mr Griffin* (Duncan, 1978): "It was a wild, windy, Southwestern spring when the idea of killing Mr. Griffin occurred to them." (hook)

From *What Happened to Lani Garver* (Plum-Ucci, 2002): "I never bought into our island's superstitions about Indian summers being cursed. Not until last year, at any rate." (hook)

From *Keeping You a Secret* (Peters, 2003): "First time I saw her was in the mirror on my locker door. I'd kicked my swim gear onto the bottom shelf and was reaching to the top for my calc book when she opened her locker across the hall. She had streaked blond ponytail dangling out the back of her baseball cap." (informing detail)

From *The Chocolate War* (Cormier, 1974): "They murdered him." (hook, surprise)

From *Shooting Monarchs* (Halliday, 2003): "He was born during the Thanksgiving Day parade. His mother didn't want to miss seeing the big balloons, so she made the nurse haul a TV into the delivery room." (character)

From *Milkweed* (Spinelli, 2003): "I am running. That's the first thing I remember. Running. I carry something, my arm curled around it, hugging it to my chest. Bread, of course. Someone is chasing me. 'Stop! Thief!' I run. People. Shoulders. Shoes. 'Stop! Thief!' " (hook)

From *King of the Mild Frontier* (Crutcher, 2003): "I grew up riding a rocket. If legendary rocket man Wernher von Braun could have harnessed the power of my meteoric temper, we'd have beaten the Russians into space by a good six months." (character)

From *Down the Yukon* (Hobbs, 2001): "The trouble started over a mongrel dog, small, mostly black, shorthaired and shivering." (hook)

From *Hole in My Life* (Gantos, 2002): "The prisoner in the photograph is me. The 10 number is mine. The photo was taken in 1972 at Ashland Medium Security Federal Prison in Ashland, Kentucky. I was twenty years old and had been locked up for a year already—the bleakest year of my life—and I had more time ahead of me." (character)

From *A Wrinkle in Time* (L'Engle, 1968): "It was a dark and stormy night." (setting)

From *Mississippi Trial, 1955* (Crowe, 2002): "My dad hates hate. All my life, if the word ever slipped out of my mouth, he'd snap into me faster than a rattlesnake. 'Hiram,' he'd say, straightening up tall like a preacher, 'the world's got plenty enough hate without you adding to it. I will not tolerate such language—or even such thinking—in my home or in my family!' " (dialogue)

FIGURE 2.1
Opening lines of selected novels.

is perfectly awful'" (p. 108). Danziger also has fun with the characters' names in this novel: Juna, Aurora, Starr, Cosmosa, and Rita Retrograde.

Crutcher tells a funny tale about an overweight youngster named Angus Bethune in the short story "A Brief Moment in the Life of Angus Bethune" (1989). Crutcher treats some serious topics—obesity, homosexuality, bulimia—but with a touch of humor. For example, Angus's dance partner tells him that she is bulimic but under treatment for it. He responds, "'Actually,' I say, 'I even tried it once, but when I stuck my finger down my throat, I was still hungry and I almost ate my arm'" (p. 23). All of Crutcher's novels have a touch of humor sprinkled throughout. For example, in *Whale Talk* (2001), T. J. explains to his kindergarten teacher about his name: The Tao Jones (The Dow Jones). And later T. J. describes Coach Murphy:

> Murphy is sixty-eight years old, having received divine dispensation to teach till two days after he dies, and I have judiciously avoided taking PE or health classes from him for four years. (p. 11)

Sometimes it's just a single line in a novel that promotes a chuckle or an out-and-out laugh. In Vande Velde's *Never Trust a Dead Man* (1999), Selwyn is toying with the idea of asking the witch Elswyth to change him into a woman so that he can safely return to his community to find out who has committed the murder. Selwyn cannot make up his mind about the gender switch. Impatiently Elswyth, wanting Selwyn to decide, grins wickedly: "Last chance to pee standing up" (p. 114).

Other works that emphasize humor include *Bel-Air Bambi and the Mall Rats* (R. Peck, 1988), *Harris and Me* (Paulsen, 1993), *If This Is Love, I'll Take Spaghetti* (Conford, 1983), *Who Put That Hair in My Toothbrush?* (Spinelli, 1988), *Alice in Rapture, Sort Of* (Naylor, 1989), *Outrageously Alice* (Naylor, 1998), *The Crazy Horse Electric Game* (Crutcher, 1987), *Don't Care High* (Korman, 1985), *A Long Way from Chicago* (R. Peck, 1998), and *Way Down Yonder* (Peck, 2000).

Imagery

Novels rely on words to create pictures in readers' minds. These word pictures help readers to know what the characters look like—how they dress, what their features are, and so on. Authors use imagery to help readers see what cannot be shown in pictures. These images also help to set the time and place of an event in the literature. Certainly, authors use imagery to set a mood. Luther and Sparky (*Bucking the Sarge*, Curtis, 2004) have the task of taking the junk and garbage that has been removed from the rooms in the group home to the dump. Curtis describes one such load of junk:

> Along with bent forks and coverless books and ripped-in-half lottery tickets that spilled out was the biggest, baddest, ugliest, nastiest-looking rat that had ever walked the streets of Flint. It tumbled out of the box into the bed of the truck, landing with a smack that sounded like someone had dropped one of those great big Polish sausages on a tile floor. (p. 46)

Will Hobbs (*Jackie's Wild Seattle*, 2003) describes the baby seal that Shannon is trying to rescue:

> The baby looked up at me, its huge liquid eyes running with pus. Some of the whiskers were stuck together. It moaned. Suddenly the smell hit me. It was sickly sweet at first but after a few seconds the odor was distinctly putrid. There were deep bites and gashes all over the seal's back, along its sides, too. I turned and waded back with it to the base of the cliff. (p. 117)

The setting is so important in Hobbs's novels that he must use very effective language to convey the pictures he wants readers to see and the sensations he wants them to experience through his words. Readers begin to see and feel the beauty as well as the danger in the Virginia Falls, the Nahanni, and Deadmen Valley in *Far North* (1996), and they experience the dangers along with Nathan and Lighthouse George in *Ghost Canoe* (1997). Readers also experience the dangers of the Yukon River in *Jason's Gold* (1999) and *Down the Yukon* (2001) and the treacherous ocean waters in *Leaving Protection* (2004).

Personification

Authors often quite effectively give human traits to animals or other nonhuman objects. Sue Ellen Bridgers (*All Together Now*, 1979) uses personification along with sensory experiences to enrich readers' responses: "The metallic thump of the baseball gave the neighborhood a new pulse, a heavy, lonely, throbbing sound. All through the long afternoon it toned, like a knelling bell, their lethargy, their indifference, their unspeakable failure" (p. 151). Readers will remember the wonderful effect of M. Taylor's use of personification in *Roll of Thunder, Hear My Cry* (1976) when she describes the school bus as it approaches the trench in the road:

> The bus rattled up the road, though not as quickly as we had hoped. It rolled cautiously through a wide puddle some twenty feet ahead; then, seeming to grow bolder as it approached our man-made lake, it speeded up, spraying the water in high sheets of backward waterfalls into the forest. . . . The bus emitted a tremendous crack and careened drunkenly into our trap. . . . Then it sputtered a last murmuring protest and died. (p. 40)

Symbolism

In *Dark Waters* (MacPhail, 2003), Klaus serves as a symbol for morality as Col first sees his image when he goes into the water to save Dominic. Klaus's image returns to Col frequently as a reminder of what he must do about his brother Mungo.

As mentioned, Cormier uses symbolism in *The Chocolate War* (1974) to help create the mood: "The shadows of the goal posts definitely resembled a network of crosses, empty crucifixes" (p. 17). In *The Blue Heron* (1992), Avi, to some extent, uses the heron as a symbol for the timidity of the boy who has grown up in a home isolated by wilderness.

Hyperbole

We use hyperbole, or exaggeration, often in our daily conversations, as when we say things such as "I was so shocked at what he said, I almost died." Well, of course, the speaker didn't almost die, he simply wanted to exaggerate his feelings. Authors also use this technique to make points. The title of Cormier's *The Chocolate War* (1974) doesn't suggest a literal war. Chris Crutcher uses hyperbole in a more humorous way, but it is still quite effective. In *Ironman* (1995), Bo is writing to Larry King about the choices he has made (this is a major part of the book, because Bo thinks Larry King is the only adult who will listen to him). Because of his obnoxious behavior, he can either have home tutoring with Ms. Conroy or join the Nak Pack, Mr. Nak's anger management class. Bo says:

> Now Larry, I gotta tell you what kind of choices I was being offered here. I took Geography from Conroy as a freshman, and the woman can flat put you to sleep. And the second your forehead splats onto the desk, she calls your parents; has a phone right there in her room. Next thing you know you're wiping the drool off your chin and she's standing over you with the handset saying your dad wants a word with you. My biggest worry about home tutoring is that she'd then know where I live. On the other hand, there's the Nak Pack. That's what they call it, no kidding, Larry, and if you wanted to put a major crimp in Clark Fork's future crime wave, you'd call an air strike down on their next meeting. (p. 19)

Allusion

An allusion is a reference to something that is generally known or understood. Readers often find biblical and mythological allusions in literature. For example, when someone is under a great deal of stress or is working through a tremendous problem, others may say "that's his cross to bear," making reference to the biblical story of Jesus having to carry his cross to the place of crucifixion. In young adult literature, we find, perhaps, one of the best-known allusions. Robert Cormier's *I Am the Cheese* (1977) is an allusion to the old nursery song and game "The Farmer in the Dell." Cormier connects this allusion even further: the family name is Farmer. Readers may make the connection between the novel and the allusion when they think of the last two lines of the rhyme: "The rat takes the cheese" and "The cheese stands alone!" Cormier calls on a nursery rhyme again in his novel *We All Fall Down* (1991). The allusion is to the singing game ring-around-a-rosy, which refers to the Black Death. When people got a rosy rash, they rubbed themselves with herbs and posies but fell down and died.

Chris Crutcher, a masterful writer, uses allusion in many of his works. Specifically, in *Staying Fat for Sarah Byrnes* (1993), he characterizes one of the orderlies in the hospital as "Schwarzenegger Number One" (p. 121) in reference to the present governor of California and body-building guru Arnold Schwarzenegger.

Main Character as Writer

Like Gary Paulsen's *The Island* (1988) (discussed in Chapter 4), other young adult novels feature a character as writer. A few novels emphasize writing in addition to the central theme. One such novel is Hinton's *Taming the Star Runner* (1988). Travis, a troubled teenager from the city, is sent to stay with his uncle on a ranch in the country. Travis may be the macho, cool city kid, but he is also a writer who has finished his first novel and sent it off to a publisher. The most noteworthy point of Hinton's novel is Travis's attitude toward his writing, the audience for which he thought he had written, and his overall concern with changing any part of this "finished" writing.

In a more current novel (*Olive's Ocean*, Henkes, 2003), Martha Boyle wants to become a writer. She is hesitant as her father has given up his job to emphasize writing. Martha does not want to interfere with that decision. However, Martha's father decides writing is not for him and he plans to return to the law practice. Martha believes she now can write in earnest.

Janet Lee Carey's *Wenny Has Wings* (2001) is a collection of letters that Will North writes to his sister Wenny. Both Will and Wenny were killed in a tragic accident, and Will was brought back to life. Will writes to Wenny hoping that some healing within the family will take place.

> *Keep a journal. This builds within you a writer's eye, a writer's ear, a writer's heart. Listen to the world, feel its heartbeat, record its fascinating detail.*
>
> Vicki Grove

Four novels—some rather old and one rather new—take the form of journals and may help students in the process of writing their own journals. We learn about the troubles and conflicts in Eva by Dickinson (1988), *Z for Zachariah* by O'Brien (1974), and *A Gathering of Days: A New England Girl's Journal, 1830–32* by Blos (1979) through their own journals. *A Gathering of Days* is particularly interesting because Cassie, the 13-year-old narrator, records everyday activities that are important to her as well as personal feelings about events in her life. In the fourth novel, *Breathing Underwater* (Flinn, 2001), Nick has been assigned by the court to an anger management class after he has hit and verbally abused his girlfriend. The judge also assigns Nick to write 500-plus words a day in a journal detailing his relationship with Caitlin and what led to the abuse. Figure 2.2 lists young adult literature that addresses writing in some significant way.

Atkins (1988) suggests that the structure of a novel as a whole can be used to teach the structure of a formal essay. She offers *A Day No Pigs Would Die* (R. N. Peck, 1972)

The Writing Process at Work

Avi, *The Man Who Was Poe,* 1989

Marion Dane Bauer, *What's Your Story: A Young Person's Guide to Writing Fiction,* 1992

C. Bennett and J. A. Gottesfeld, *Heart Divided,* 2004

Betsy Byars, *The Moon and I,* 1991

Chris Crutcher, *King of the Mild Frontier,* 2003

Lois Duncan, *Chapters: My Growth as a Writer,* 1982

Kevin Henkes, *Olive's Ocean,* 2003

S. E. Hinton, *The Outsiders,* 1967

S. E. Hinton, *Taming the Star Runner,* 1988

M. E. Kerr, *Me, Me, Me, Me, Me: Not a Novel,* 1983

M. E. Kerr, *Blood on the Forehead: What I Know about Writing,* 1998

Stephen King, *On Writing: A Memoir of the Craft,* 2000

Walter Dean Myers, *Monster,* 1999

Phyllis Reynolds Naylor, *How I Came to Be a Writer,* 1987

Gary Paulsen, *The Island,* 1988

Susan Terris, *Author! Author!,* 1990

Paul Zindel, *David and Della,* 1993

Therapy or Reflection

Janet Lee Carey, *Wenny Has Wings,* 2002

Chris Crutcher, *Chinese Handcuffs,* 1989

Chris Crutcher, *Ironman,* 1995

Alex Flinn, *Breathing Underwater,* 2001

Linda Glovach, *Beauty Queen,* 1998

Journalism

Sandy Asher, *Summer Begins,* 1980

William Bell, *Forbidden City,* 1990

Dallin Malmgren, *The Ninth Issue,* 1989

Walter Dean Myers, *Darnell Rock Reporting,* 1994

Journals or Diaries

Alicia Appleman-Jurman, *Alicia: My Story,* 1988

Katherine Ayres, *North by Night: A Story of the Underground Railroad,* 1998

Chris Crutcher, *Stotan!,* 1986

James M. Deem, *3 NB's of Julian Drew,* 1994

Farrukh Dhondy, *Black Swan,* 1993

Peter Dickinson, *Eva,* 1988

Robin Jones, *The Beginning of Unbelief,* 1993

Lou Kassem, *A Haunting in Williamsburg,* 1990

Anna M. Martin, *Sunny: Diary Two,* 1998

Sue Mayfield, *Drowning Anna,* 2001

Robyn Miller, *Robyn's Book: A True Diary,* 1986

Joan Lowery Nixon, *A Family Apart,* 1987

Robert O'Brien, *Z for Zachariah,* 1974

Susan Beth Pfeffer, *About David,* 1980

Susan Beth Pfeffer, *The Year without Michael,* 1987

Ouida Sebestyn, *The Girl in the Box,* 1987

Joyce Carol Thomas, *Marked by Fire,* 1982

Sue Townsend, *The Secret Diary of Adrian Mole, Aged 13 3/4,* 1982

Paul Zindel, *The Pigman,* 1968

Paul Zindel, *The Amazing and Death-Defying Diary of Eugene Dingman,* 1987

Paul Zindel, *A Begonia for Miss Applebaum,* 1989

FIGURE 2.2

Writing models in young adult literature.

as an example to follow to teach students how to write a structured three-part essay. She suggests that the first chapter, in which Rob assists the cow in giving birth to twin calves, serves as the novel's introduction. The reader sees Rob's emergence as a man—the central theme or thesis. The body of the book deals with Rob's raising of Pinky through the pig's slaughter. Here, Rob understands what it means to be a man. The conclusion describes the death of Rob's father and Rob's assumption of manhood. Atkins suggests that "With this model before them, the students should understand the basic organizational structure of a piece of writing—be it novel or essay" (p. 202). Atkins then suggests that students write an essay about manhood using all of the components of the writing process.

The connection between reading and writing is clear. Research from a variety of sources is strong: Reading leads to writing and, in turn, writing leads to reading. The author Richard Peck has said many times: "Nobody but a reader ever became a writer." Donald Murray (1982) states it this way: "Writers act as their own first readers, scanning and rescanning their own prose to evaluate the content, form, and language of the material they produce" (p. 146). The two processes are combined: When young people read, they create meaning for themselves; when young people write, they create meaning for themselves and others.

Probst (1986) believes that

> At the basis of the conceptions emerging today of literature and its teaching is the assumption that knowledge is made and that it must be made by each of us. It is an epistemology that ties together language, literature, and composition. The making of meaning is a linguistic process, the formulation and testing of propositions and assertions; literature is the reservoir of meanings made, the visions others have had; composing, both oral and written, is the act of forging our own visions. (p. 67)

In addition, as students make meaning of what they read and what they sense in the world around them, they are more eager to do something with this meaning when they write.

With this attitude in the reading-writing connection, students give more serious attention to both. They feel more comfortable responding and creating. Consequently, they are able to identify and analyze the writer's craft and make some transfer to their own writing. More on the reading-writing connection is found in Chapter 4.

Nobody but a reader ever became a writer.

Richard Peck

Considering Young Adult Audience Appeal

Experience tells us that young adults get turned on to reading when they read literature that meets their interests and fulfills their needs. Experience also tells us that that literature does not, for the most part, come from the literary canon that is part of the curriculum in most middle and high schools. What gets students excited about reading? Why will many young adults not take the time to plow through a Keats poem but stay up half the night reading Paul Janeczko's or Mel Glenn's poetry anthologies? Why is it that juniors won't read Hawthorne's *The Scarlet Letter* (1850) but will read Speare's *The Witch of Blackbird Pond* (1958); won't read Thoreau's *Walden* (1854) but will read Paulsen's *The Island* (1988); won't read much of anything given them from the established curriculum but will read Chris Crutcher's *Running Loose* (1983) and then proceed to read everything that Crutcher has written? The answer is that there are qualities found in young adult literature that simply are frequently not found in the more traditional literature—qualities that draw young adults to read and enjoy.

One of the most significant qualities that draws young adults to reading is the existence of characters with whom they can relate in situations with which they are familiar. For example, students who have had to suffer the threats of peer pressure would be drawn to the conflicts between the main characters in Sue Mayfield's *Drowning Anna* (2001), M. Brooks's *True Confessions of a Heartless Girl* (2003), T. Benduhn's *Gravel Queen* (2003), C. Atkins's *Alt Ed* (2003), Cherie Bennett's *Life in the Fat Lane* (1998), or Vicki Grove's *Reaching Dustin* (1998). Along the same line, students who are experiencing the joys and conflicts of dating would be interested in reading about the teen relationships in Walter Dean Myers's *Beast* (2003), Jon Ripslinger's *How I Fell in Love and Learned to Shoot Free Throws* (2003), or Todd Strasser's *A Very Touchy Subject* (1985). Students having to deal with family conflicts would relate to the situations in Sharon Creech's *Bloomability* (1998), A. Johnson's *The First Part Last* (2003), David Klass's *California Blue* (1994), Gordon Korman's *Son of the Mob* (2002), Michael Cadnum's *Heat* (1998), or C. Mackler's *The Earth, My Butt, and Other Big, Round Things* (2003). Some students might be suffering some personal conflicts or may be dealing with abuse, illness, or death. For outside reading, those students might want to read about the abusive relationship in Brock Cole's *The Facts Speak for Themselves* (1997), Chris Crutcher's *Whale Talk* (2001), Norma Fox Mazer's *After the Rain* (1987), Laurie Halse Anderson's *Speak* (1999), Alex Flinn's *Breathing Underwater* (2001), or David Klass's *You Don't Know Me* (2002). Even given an unfamiliar setting, young adult readers can become interested in the plot because they can relate to the similar feelings, needs, and interests of the teenage characters. As a result, students may connect with the apartheid situation in Sheila Gordon's *Waiting for the Rain* (1987), the persecution of the Jews in Jerry Spinelle's *Milkweed* (2003), the massacre in Tiananmen Square in William Bell's *Forbidden City* (1990), and the fight for civil rights in Chris Crow's *Mississippi Trial, 1955* (2002).

On the other hand, young adults also find themselves interested in unique people and situations—characters, settings, and story lines that are different from them and their lives but with which they can still make some connections. As a result, students enjoy the aliens in William Sleator's *Interstellar Pig* (1984), the facially deformed Lucius Sims in Dennis Covington's *Lizard* (1991), the futuristic attitude toward cloning found in Nancy Farmer's *The House of the Scorpion* (2002), and the adventure of saving the monstrous sea creatures in Paul Zindel's *Loch* (1994) and *Reef of Death* (1998). Readers also may want to explore the culture of the Yup'ik Eskimo village in

Deb Vanasse's *A Distant Enemy* (1997) or read about the culture of the Melungeons in *Sang Spell* (1998) by Phyllis Reynolds Naylor.

Concerning style, many young adults are likely to appreciate a more direct plot than those often found in traditional classics, which include a great deal of description before and within the story line—a story line that often covers a long period. Young adult literature, instead, usually begins effectively and directly with a hook, dialogue, or action and covers a shorter period. Robert Cormier's *We All Fall Down* (1991) exemplifies directness of plot from the very beginning with the intense action-packed description of the trashing of a suburban house. So, too, does *Acceleration* (McNamee, 2003). Seventeen-year-old Duncan finds the diary of a serial killer while working in the lost and found department of the Toronto Transit Authority. The novels of Lois Duncan, Will Hobbs, and Gary Paulsen are also good examples of directness of plot in that, although we have a sense of setting in their books, it comes across through the actions and dialogue of the characters.

A final area of interest to explore in young adult literature is the nature of the ending. Much to many teachers' disappointment, most young adults like a neatly tied-up ending—one with closure that provides all the answers so the student is burdened with no more thinking. However, the characteristic of most young adult literature is to provide a thought-provoking ending—one that frequently leaves some loose ends for the reader to ponder, question, and extend. With the multiple interpretations of Robert Cormier's *After the First Death* (1979), students must decide for themselves not only the interpretation of the title but also whose death or deaths actually occurred. In Lois Lowry's *The Giver* (1993), the reader is left to wonder whether Jonus actually reached Elsewhere and what happened to the society he left. At the end of Myers's *Beast* (2003), the reader is not sure that Spoon and Gabi will be together. There is a hint that Spoon still has positive feelings for Chanelle. And readers are not certain whether Macey in Caroline Cooney's *Burning Up* (1999) will be successful in raising awareness of racism in her New England community. Although these open-ended pieces are conducive to creating activities that will extend the students' thinking and interpretations, it is even more rewarding when the students also grow to appreciate this characteristic of the literature.

Learning Log Responses

How do you determine the quality of a book? Explain what a book has to have or do to be a quality book for use in your classroom.

Choose a specific young adult novel and write a rationale for its use based on the qualities found or not found in the work.

Select a specific young adult novel that has a thought-provoking ending. Explain two different activities you would use to help students extend the story line on the basis of their own interpretation and thus enhance their understanding of the novel.

References

Atkins, J. (1988). *The use of young adult literature to teach writing.* Unpublished doctoral dissertation, University of Kansas, Lawrence.

Brashares, A. Poster. Ottawa, KS: The Writing Conference.

Glenn, M. Poster. Ottawa, KS: The Writing Conference.

Grove, V. Poster. Ottawa, KS: The Writing Conference.

Murray, D. (1982). Teaching the other self: The writer's first reader. *College Composition and Communication, 33,* 140–147.

Peck, R. Poster. Ottawa, KS: The Writing Conference.

Probst, R. (1986). Three relationships in the teaching of literature. *English Journal, 75,* 60–68.

3

Using Reader Response to Begin

*If the writer is open to experience and emotion,
story ideas will come in abundance.*
Alden R. Carter

School boards, parents, administrators, and teachers have often expressed concern about literary study, but middle and high school curriculum planners seldom alter their teaching perspective in response. Perplexing and unresolved issues about teaching and learning persist, despite scholarly attention to literature instruction. Some scholars do provide insight. According to Langer (1990), problems in literature teaching stem from a lack of research:

> There has been little systematic improvement in literature instruction in the past 25 years in spite of the efforts of many individual teachers across the country to bring systematic improvement to the teaching of literature. . . . There has been virtually no research on the teaching of literature, no change in the "objectives" that guide program development, no changes in materials that guide instruction, and no rethinking of what counts as success in literature classes—either for teachers or for students. (p. 812)

Langer's words are alarming to literature teachers, who must confront these curriculum issues and who hope to instill in students a lifelong love of reading. It is distressing that young people—our nation's greatest natural resource—are graduating and leaving school yearly without a desire to read. As was noted in Chapter 1, students are simply not reading in school (Bushman, 1997) or for that matter after they leave school (Graves, 1990; National Center for Educational Statistics [NCES], 2003).

For decades, literature instruction focused on teaching information, analyzing the text, and, in the end, teaching and seeking specific knowledge about the text. Probst (1988a) expresses concern with this informational approach to literature study. According to his analysis, teaching literature as information only evolves from an outdated organizational scheme that directs students to study facts rather than literature:

> Conceived of as a body of information, the literature curriculum tends to become a course in literary history or genre. . . a typical curriculum . . . will focus on American literature in the eleventh grade and British literature in the twelfth. . . . The courses are most often arranged chronologically. As a result, the class is likely to concentrate on historical matters, examining the literature in terms of periods, dates, major authors, major works, and so on. (p. 203)

Historically, literature study developed as an academic discipline centered on information, evolving in the late 19th century from such closely related disciplines as classical studies. Probst (1988a) points out that 19th-century educators viewed literature the same way they viewed the classics, as a subject to study and know; therefore, "knowledge about the literature rather than sensitive reading of the literary works" was the important focus (p. 197). Anderson (1986) adds that literary study was closely aligned with the demands of college entrance exams as early as 1874:

> The study of literature at that time was informed by the arguments of Matthew Arnold on the function and purpose of literature study, and Arnold maintained that the avowed purpose of literature study was initiation into and maintenance of "high culture," representing the best thoughts and words of western civilization. (p. 19)

In the 20th century, attitudes changed about the role education played in the community. The focus shifted from preparing students for college to preparing them for practical pursuits. Reform came to the English curriculum soon thereafter, and an important development in that revision was the Bureau of Education Bulletin Number Two, assembled by James F. Hosic, a founder of the National Council of Teachers of English (Probst, 1988a, p. 197). As the social times changed, and with the help of the Commission on the Reorganization of Secondary Education, more emphasis was placed on individual needs in English rather than focusing attention on college-bound students. The psychological needs of students came to the forefront, and English as a subject was thought of more as "a tool for effective living, so that students would be prepared, not just for the academic life, but for life in whatever role they might have to play" (p. 198). Although some positive things came from this philosophy, such as the change in focus from the discipline to the student, other problems emerged. This period produced the idea that literature was only useful as a pastime: "It was 'English for leisure,' nothing more" (p. 198). There never seemed to be a middle ground wherein both the student and academics were treated with equal consideration.

The academic treatment of English as a discipline attempted to reestablish the course work as a serious and "scholarly" endeavor (Probst, 1988a, p. 200). The late 1960s, however, brought another conference to the fore, and again change was in the offing. The Dartmouth seminar of 1966, "attended by about fifty prominent English educators from the United States, Britain, and Canada" (p. 200), was highlighted with the British philosophy of "making the work personally significant to the students" (p. 201). This was truly a major change in how educators were to view English as a discipline. Finally, many years after Louise Rosenblatt's groundbreaking work on reader-response theory, other scholars were reacting to her philosophy. The change from analyzing to responding to literature was beginning to attract interest, but it was only used experimentally in the United States at this time, and then rarely.

Again, there seemed to be a shift from concern with subject matter back to students' needs. From within the swinging pendulum, between concentrating first on the subject, then on the student, a pervasive influence had emerged—teaching literature as a body of knowledge and focusing on literary heritage. But the main point of this historical influence is that "the vacillation back and forth from student-centered to discipline-centered has not produced a conception of literature adequate to support the curriculum" (Probst, 1988a, pp. 202–203).

In the midst of the pendulum swings, one important perspective has been overlooked—a method that offers hope for revolutionizing an outdated literature curriculum. Murfin and Supriya (1998) write "any school of criticism that sees a literary work as an object . . . misconstrues the very essence of literature and reading. Literature exists and signifies when it is read" (p. 1). Rosenblatt's (1991) reader-response theory, first written about in 1938, provides a theoretical base for students to personally respond to reading material. Her theory embraces a method of teaching literature that has the capacity to change students' view of reading. The following passage outlines her perspective on the reader's potential relationship with literature:

> Our eyes must always be directed toward that dynamic interaction between the work of art and the personality of the reader. The aim will be to increase the student's ability to achieve a full, sound reading of the text, and to broaden the personal context of emotions and ideas into which this response will be incorporated. The development of literary appreciation will depend upon a reciprocal process: An enlargement of the student's understanding of human life leads to increased esthetic sensitivity, and increased esthetic sensitivity makes possible more fruitful human insights from literature. (p. 273)

> *Often a poem or a short story will take me out of my life and into a different enlightened state of being. If I visualize things I did around the farm that day and start to write about them in this state, often the imagery or the remembered experience will take me somewhere (emotionally, philosophically, or spiritually) I didn't expect and couldn't have foreseen.*
>
> Michael Carey

Rosenblatt's perspective on the relationship between the reader and the text opens an opportunity for students to partake in an active process whereby they must accept responsibility for much of their literary experience. Instead of a system in which teachers control and limit anticipated responses with "objective" questions, students now contribute to the knowledge pool by providing personal reactions. Rather than teaching literature as a body of knowledge dispensed by the teacher and digested by the student, Rosenblatt offers a method in which reading literature is merely one segment of a process. Literature is much more than a subject that produces information and knowledge; it is a means that, when fully developed, promotes personal growth and, in the process, aids students in making their own knowledge, knowledge that prepares students to become lifelong readers because they will have gained the confidence to read and discover on their own.

Donelson (1989) both captures the goals most teachers desire their students to reach and provides a sound rationale for changing our traditional curriculum in hopes of developing lifelong readers:

> And that really is what a good literature program is. The authors we read and think about and worry about and doubt become part of us as we become part of them. If literature doesn't become part of our hearts and our guts and the guts and hearts of our students, then what is it good for? And that is our responsibility and our joy, to know so many different books and stories and poems and to present them so that young people will take some of them in and become wiser and nobler people because of the literature—and us. (p. 26)

Writing about the world I see helps me make sense of it.

Chris Crutcher

Theory and Research

We feel strongly that the fundamental purpose of any middle or high school literature curriculum is, through developing the love of reading, to promote lifelong reading, whatever secondary goals a particular curriculum may have. Most scholars applaud this purpose; their research works toward achieving that goal. Rosenblatt (1991) considers it the essential reason for teaching literature: "Few teachers of English today would deny that the individual's ability to read and enjoy literature is the primary aim of literary study" (p. 64). Yet not only have curriculum designs failed to meet this goal, but often literature courses have accomplished the opposite effect. Students are not enjoying high school literature classes, and they aren't reading much, if anything, after school. Research tells us that contemporary adult society is a nonreading society, and some studies suggest that people read less as they grow older (Binz, 1993; Heather, 1982; NCES, 2003; News from the College Board, 1999; O'Connor, 1980; Trelease, 1982); other research indicates that adults read less than one book a year. Angelotti (1981) concludes that the literature programs in schools have produced fewer than 5% of adults in the United States who read literature. From a research perspective, several variables interact to diminish one's desire to read for school or for pleasure. Why this is happening needs closer analysis. Purves (1992) agrees that students "do not read for enjoyment, for enlargement of their understanding, or from a desire to appreciate the classics"; rather, they read with a focus "upon issues of format, spelling, grammar and other surface features rather than on content" (p. 22). Probst (1987) attributes the growing disinterest in reading during and after high school to poor organization of curricula: "it is arranged as if knowledge about literature is the crucial matter, thus the predominance of courses emphasizing literary history, genre, and terminology and of tests demanding the memorizing of information about authors, texts, events" (p. 28).

Applebee (as cited in Probst, 1988a) refers to the established curriculum pattern of teaching literature as a means of teaching literary history, authors, genres, and skills such as analysis of plot or character in order to attain knowledge: "In this arrangement, literature is knowledge—information to acquire, to remember, and be tested on" (p. 28). Reemphasizing the detrimental effects of teaching literature as "information to acquire," Rosenblatt (1991) comments on the long-term impact of an information-driven curriculum:

> It is not at all surprising that so few of even our college graduates have formed the habit of turning to literature for pleasure and insight. The novel or play or poem has been made for them too much something to know "about," something to summarize or analyze or define, something to identify as one might identify the different constellations on a star map. (p. 59)

Developing Lifelong Readers

> A few of our students will write us appreciative letters several years from now telling us of the joys and agonies of their doctoral research in seventeenth-century poetic forms or their pursuit of Melville's white whale, three of them will publish in *PMLA* or *New Literary History*, two will come home to debate feminist readings of Hemingway at the local college, and one lonely but diligent scholar will travel to England, become buried in the library at Oxford, and produce a brilliant and unreadable Freudian analysis of the significance of the three witches. Most of our students, however, are going to be elsewhere. They'll be in some line of work far removed from the literary world. They should, nonetheless, be readers. They should be people who enjoy literature, who read it willingly, even enthusiastically, and who respond to it and think about it in ways that enrich their emotional and intellectual lives. (Probst, 1994, p. 40)

As a result of research, a shift away from an informational approach to literature is beginning to occur, however slightly. With this move, a concern for the role of students is evolving in literature instruction. Probst (1988a) argues "that literature is experience, not information, and that the student must be invited to participate in it, not simply observe it from outside. Thus, the student is very important—not simply a recipient of information, but rather a maker of knowledge out of meetings with literary texts" (p. xii).

Juxtaposed with the problem of teaching literature as knowledge, another misfortune occurs in high school instruction. English teachers often mistakenly think they are teaching literacy when in fact they are teaching and testing students on how well they can determine what the teacher wants. Hynds (1990) explains that teachers often thought they were "measuring performance" (p. 247) when in fact they were actually testing how well students could determine the teachers' expectations and answers. This problem is not unusual in teaching literature. Because the focus is on the text and on testable knowledge, a student's real learning is often overlooked and is rarely tested. "In schools, teachers and curriculum builders often assume that training better readers (i.e., raising scores on competency tests) will result in a more literate populace. As a result, teachers constantly remark, "'I don't have time to let the kids read and write what they like. That won't be on the competency exam!'" (Hynds, 1990, p. 249).

As long as no one challenges our existing literature curriculum, teachers and schools will go on teaching under the same precept—if students can perform on tests, then it naturally follows that they must be gaining knowledge from and loving to read literature. Again, Hynds (1990) illustrates that teachers and administrators continually misinterpret classroom behaviors:

> Thus, through a complex social construal process, students learn what teachers will and will not accept. Because some readers can so easily masquerade reading skills as reading interests, some of them may graduate from formal schooling and then never pick up a book. In this case, no amount of training in literacy skills can make them literate. (p. 254)

She further explains that the social effects of classroom discussion and a student's personal response to the text are the ingredients that produce literacy:

> [R]eaders become literate not simply by learning literacy skills but by participating in an elaborate socially construed system. As they develop notions of themselves as readers through participation in reading communities, they develop both intellectual and social competence for bringing what they know about life into the text. The degree to which they "bring life to literature and literature to life" (Hynds, 1989) is related to the likelihood that they will continue to read beyond their years of formal schooling. (Hynds, 1990, p. 255)

It is essential that teachers and others who help design high school curricula begin reinterpreting student behavior and motivations. Driving home the point that teachers often misinterpret students' motives and learning, Hynds (1990) relates a story about Jay, a student she studied closely to gain a clearer perception of reading behavior. He performed well on his class assignments and essays but actually didn't like English or reading at all. His teacher, however, was under the impression that Jay was an exemplary student and therefore must love reading and English class. According to Hynds's (1990) study, Jay's teacher was wrong: "My studies of adolescents revealed that readers can be competent and can demonstrate that competence in the classroom, yet fail to see themselves as 'readers,' and consequently, seldom read for their own pleasure" (p. 249). Jay doubted that he would read much at all after graduation: "Jay had developed 'literacy skills,' but not 'literate behaviors.' He was capable of comprehending and demonstrating competence to his teacher when a grade was involved.

However, he rarely saw reading as an end in itself, and only occasionally put his competence to use in understanding and identifying with literary characters" (p. 249).

Students, especially middle and high school students, are not likely to pursue literature with a scholarly passion; however, they will read as a form of self-indulgence. When used for the best reasons, self-indulgence can serve as "an attempt to see more clearly who one is and where one stands" (Probst, 1988a, p. 4). This perspective provides students more opportunity to grow with the literature they read and challenges them to create new knowledge. "Exchange with the text can become for the reader a process of self-creation" (p. 21). Curricula that endorse a reader-response base for teaching literature help promote the possible gain for students. As Rosenblatt (1956) explains, it ensures their love of reading:

> Once an organic relationship has been set up between young readers and books, many kinds of growth are possible, and the teacher can proceed to fulfill his function. Above all, students need to be helped to have personally satisfying and personally meaningful transactions with literature. Then they will develop the habit of turning to literature for the pleasure and insights it offers. (p. 67)

Rejection of a curriculum based on studying literature solely for factual knowledge is the first step in aiding students' growth toward an attitude of lifelong reading. Moreover, students who have experienced a classroom wherein reader response is the basis of instruction will discover the transformational process of learning. In his book *You Gotta Be the Book: Teaching Engaged and Reflective Reading with Adolescents* (1997), Jeffrey Wilhelm describes reader response as a process consisting of 10 dimensions, which all fall into one of three categories: *evocative* responses, which includes the activation of prior knowledge; *connective* dimensions, which creates the meaning beyond the text, and *reflective* dimension, in which readers consider the significance of characters and events (pp. 46–47).

Students' Evolving Literary Understanding

Focusing on literature as a means of knowledge is merely one change that must transpire in school curricula. Another problem confronting teachers and administrators in teaching literature to a group of young people is dealing effectively with the students' differing intellectual development. Researchers have identified several stages of, and patterns to, young adults' developing literary understanding. Carlsen (1980) suggests three general developmental stages of literary interest. The first, early adolescence, occurs from about ages 11 to 14. Students at this level are characterized as having interests in animal stories, adventures, mysteries, the supernatural, sports, coming of age in different cultures, stories about the home and family life, and fantasy. Middle adolescence, roughly ages 15 and 16, typically is characterized by interests in nonfictional adventure, longer historical novels, mystical romances, and stories of adolescent life. Carlsen's third stage, late adolescence, approximately ages 17 and 18, is the period of transition to adult reading. This age group searches for personal values, social questions, strange experiences and unusual circumstances, and the transition to adult roles.

Where Carlsen's study suggests a definite trend in interest for students, Hynds's (1990) research challenges the idea that comprehension and literary analysis are enough to promote better reading skills. In her studies, she discovered "that readers operate out of a variety of social perspectives that influence their conceptions of how to read, respond to, and demonstrate understanding of literary texts" (p. 245). Hynds distinguishes between the approaches students take in reading. If, for example, they read for pleasure, students are "story-driven," responding to and "motivated most often by an engaging plot or interesting characters"; however, when they read for school assignments, students read for the teacher's tests and therefore are "largely 'information-driven'" (pp. 245–246). The implication is that students read with a different intent depending on the assigned purpose. But it further suggests that if students are reading for pleasure (in or out of class), they are searching for a story that will entice them to engage and maintain their interest.

Beach and Wendler's (1987) study moves the issue of reading development a step beyond Carlsen's research. They examined differences in ability to respond to literature based on age levels, comparing 8th graders, 11th graders, college freshmen, and college seniors in their ability to draw inferences about characters, acts, and perceptions. The results make evident how significant the developmental differences are both in terms of student performance and in the selection of literature. "The results suggest that from early adolescence to young adulthood, readers shift from a 'describer orientation'—conceiving of characters in terms of immediate surface feelings or physical behaviors—to conceptions of characters in terms of long-range social or psychological beliefs and goals" (p. 286). This important finding reveals that the younger age group does think in terms of analysis beyond the most basic level. Further, Beach and Wendler found evidence that the older, more mature college students had increased developmental abilities to "infer social/psychological meanings for characters' acts" (p. 294). In curriculum planning, this knowledge is salient because part of the problem for students is often that they are developmentally incapable of achieving their teachers' expectations of analysis or interpretation. The maturity factor in older students makes selection of reading material more critical. More difficult works should be geared toward older rather than younger students. This is an important point of contention in the selection of literature.

Probst (1987) provides a challenge to high schools that want to redesign their literature curricula. He suggests that rather than "arranging literature courses in terms of genre or history, we might conceive of the curriculum as an opportunity for students to explore the significant issues in their lives and in the culture, issues about which they must develop convictions" (p. 30). Inherent in his alternative route to teaching literature is the reader-response approach to reading. As noted, Rosenblatt established this theory as early as 1938 and reinforced the idea with instructional information in subsequent publications, but it was only in the late 1960s and early 1970s that some teachers in a few schools actually incorporated the theory into their teaching. Rosenblatt (1991) outlines the significance of the student-reader: "The really important things in the education of youth cannot be taught in the formal didactic manner; they are things which are experienced, absorbed, accepted, incorporated in the personality through emotional and esthetic experiences" (p. 180).

> *I don't know the story before I begin. I only have a vague image in my mind of a character and a place. Then I write in order to find out what the story is.*
>
> Sharon Creech

Teaching literature, then, should be an ongoing process between reader and text, as expressed by Probst (1987) as he expands the concept of literature in the classroom:

> Literature thus invites us to participate in the ongoing dialogue of the culture. It presents to us what others have experienced and how they have made sense of that experience, and it invites us to take those perceptions, combine them with our own, and build out of the mix the conceptions and visions that will govern our lives. Literature provides us not knowledge ready-made but the opportunity to make knowledge. (p. 28)

Probst further explains that predetermined meanings of words, ideas, and issues are nonexistent; rather, it is our interpretation, our response to the words and the writers, and our reflective and critical thoughts that form cultural meaning: "I read Shakespeare, then, and [Richard] Peck, not to submit to them, not to absorb unreflectingly and uncritically their visions and their values but to think with them" (1987, p. 28).

The transaction between reader and text (reader response) is the focus of change in literature curricula. Probst (1988b) identifies this intricate relationship by borrowing a metaphor from Annie Dillard that explains this transaction between reader and text: "'The mind fits the world and shapes it as a river fits and shapes its own banks'" (p. 378). He goes on to explain the metaphor: "The relationship between reader and text is much like that between the river and its banks, each working its effects upon the other, each contributing to the shape the literary text ultimately takes in the reader's mind" (p. 378). This perspective denotes an important distinction between the two types of literature curricula discussed, placing the quest for knowledge at one end of the curriculum continuum and literature as a process focusing on the relationship between the reader and the text at the other.

Response-Centered Curriculum

A response-centered classroom is an important alteration of curriculum, one that meets Hannson's (1992) criteria for a "good" instructional method: "We believe that if students are to see reading as a vehicle for lifelong learning, then, how we teach is just as important as what we teach. In a good reading or literature program, how and what we teach are orchestrated so that no one is in doubt as to why" (p. 260). Inherent in this change of focus from text to reader, and providing another link to middle school– and high school–level interest, is the demand for an alternative selection of literature.

For the transaction between reader and text to succeed, teachers must alter their methods of literature selection for the classroom. Which literature is taught in which classes has been an issue of great importance. According to Kolb (1990), "The question of what books are to be required in our schools is, with the exception of salaries, the chief topic of concern among teachers, administrators, and school boards" (p. 35). Selection is intrinsically connected to the long-standing use of textbooks. According to Applebee (1989), "the literature anthology was the most frequent source of materials (used 'regularly' by 66% of the teachers)" (p. 29). By and large, then, teachers base their literature selection on which textbook the school uses. Hannson (1992) reiterates concern for the near-total reliance on textbooks:

> What we currently see being taught in classrooms—regardless of grade level—is a standard body of texts, primarily narrative, preselected for use by someone other than the teacher or the students. . . . At the secondary and college levels, publishing houses and editors of anthologies do the selecting. As we travel across the country, we see a disappointing sameness to what students are reading. Students and teachers tend to approach these texts in habitual and uninspired ways. (pp. 259–260)

In arguing both sides of an established literary canon, Kolb (1990) suggests that

> Literature can be thought of as the embodiment of the great ideas of human civilization, or as the voice of social protest; as a manifestation of a specific society in a specific time and place, or as the product of an individual artistic consciousness. . . . Literature can be understood as a confirmation of the reader's experience, an explanation of that experience, or an enlargement of experience. (p. 39)

The question remains: Which material best meets these criteria? Rosenblatt (1991) is more concerned that students be provided with literature to which they can relate. She suggests that if students are to truly participate in literature as a process of learning and developing skills and interest, then the selections must provide connections:

> The reader brings to the work personality traits, memories of past events, present needs and preoccupations, a particular mood of the moment, and a particular physical condition. These and many other elements in a never-to-be-duplicated combination determine his response to the peculiar contribution of the text. For the adolescent reader, the experience of the work is further specialized by the fact that he has probably not yet arrived at a consistent view of life or achieved a fully integrated personality. (pp. 30–31)

In other words, no one—not the teacher, the parents, or the critics—can experience literature for us. Rosenblatt (1991) explains:

> The reader of the poem must have the experience himself [as] he is intent on the pattern of sensations, emotions, and concepts it evokes. Because the text is organized and self-contained, it concentrates the reader's attention and regulates what will enter into his consciousness. His business for the moment is to apprehend as fully as possible these images and concepts in relation to one another. Out of this arises a sense of an organized structure of perceptions and feelings which constitutes for him the esthetic experience. (pp. 32–33)

It is essential that teachers adopt Rosenblatt's view of the reader's role in literature if they hope to encourage young people to want to read again and again. But perhaps even more important is her understanding of the importance of connecting student to text in dictating the future for lifelong reading: "If the language, the setting, the theme, the central situation, all are too alien, even a 'great work' will fail. . . . Books must be provided that hold out some link with the young reader's past and present preoccupations, anxieties, emotions" (Rosenblatt, 1991, p. 72).

Rosenblatt (1991) explains the inherent reasons that literature must match students' needs, experience, and maturity levels: "It is not enough merely to think of what the student ought to read. Choices must reflect a sense of the possible links between these materials and the student's past experience and present level of maturity" (p. 42). In particular, the link between a student's emotional maturity and the material selected is crucial in helping students achieve that sense of success that ultimately produces confident readers. Rosenblatt explores how much of the student's whole being is involved in this intricate process of appropriate selection:

> The whole personality tends to become involved in the literary experience. That a literary work may bring into play and be related to profoundly personal needs and preoccupations makes it a powerful potential educational force. For it is out of these basic needs and attitudes that behavior springs. Hence, literature can foster the linkage between intellectual perception and emotional drive that is essential to any vital learning process. (p. 182)

Selection is a crucial dimension of altering our national problem of students' lagging interest in literature classes. One basic problem inherent in the selection process is the insistence on teaching classical literature. We suggest that this insistence is partially due to historical circumstances, which have encumbered literature curricula with selections that don't meet the needs of today's youth. Curricula of the 1980s and 1990s continued this tradition of including the literature of the past—the literature most commonly called the classics. Those who call for school and curriculum reform often make suggestions about the English curriculum, usually demanding literature that will help students understand their literary heritage. (For a more detailed discussion of classroom use of the classics, see Chapter 7.)

We state our concerns about the use of the classics here because this study relates directly to the reader-response theory. A teacher's zest to provide students with the great literature of the world so that they may understand basic cultural issues may have the opposite result—students may very well stop reading altogether. Rosenblatt (1991) provides perspective about overwhelming students with the standard classical selection: "In our zeal to give our students the proper literary training, we constantly set them tasks a step beyond their powers, or plunge them into reading that practically requires the learning of new language" (p. 215). She follows this argument with the notion that classical literature has often been introduced to students when their experience is inadequate to connect in any way to the ideas and issues in those works.

Hynds (1990) suggests many of the merits of including literature of interest to students. It is, after all, a link in helping students "view themselves as literate," which will ultimately lead them to continue a lifetime pattern of reading: "Finally, no matter how sophisticated the curriculum or the classroom library, readers must want to read and must see the value in becoming readers before they view themselves as literate" (p. 251). When reading literature, students must be engaged in some way with the text or novel they read. If they cannot grasp the plot or make meaning from the work, then they really aren't interacting with the text.

More evidence introduced by Hynds (1989) illustrates the effect of teaching young adult literature. Her study provides evidence that students interact with greater success when reading works with which they are capable of connecting: "Readers who brought a greater range of interpersonal constructs to their reading" (p. 31) appeared more internally motivated and not dependent on teachers, parents, and peers. In contrast, readers with little congruence in their peer and character impressions were not consistently motivated to read for its own sake and, as a result, were unable to create connections between literature and life.

Young adult literature adds life to a traditional curriculum that many students find uninteresting. Probst's (1987) compelling argument defines the parameters of gain from young adult literature and dispels the myth that traditional literature is best for students. He also points out the ease with which students may be able to engage in reader response, which may not be the case with the older literature:

> Adolescent literature must have a significant place in the curriculum, then, because it deals with the issues students are likely to be confronting, and so it directly and openly invites the sort of encounter we have been alluding to. It touches their lives, addressing issues that matter, raising questions that are likely to interest them. The transactions they may have with it are likely to be significant, rather than trivial and superficial. We must not judge the literature solely on criteria of worth that deal only with features of the text. We must instead judge it on the likelihood that the students' transactions with it will be of high quality—that is, committed, interested, reasoned, emotional, personal. It is of little significance that students remember twenty years from now the distinction between metaphor and simile—far more significant that they have felt the shaping effect of metaphoric language, and that they have profited by it. (p. 28)

Creating a Climate for Using Reader Response

Like any successful program, a reader-response approach to teaching literature requires careful use of classroom strategies to achieve the desired results. Along with creating a climate conducive to active learning, the teacher must learn and exhibit behaviors that promote trust and consistency for students. The teacher creates classroom atmosphere, and the first step is arranging the room in a manner that promotes an environment for open discussions. Next, the teacher's behaviors must encourage an environment of cooperation and trust. After all, teachers can only hope to achieve the desired results in the classroom if students first feel a sense of security to pursue openly active learning (Bushman, 1994). Classroom climate may predict the success or failure of any diligently planned curriculum. Essential to a response-centered method of teaching is developing trust between the teacher and the students. Preparing the students for a trust relationship begins with room arrangement. The classroom should provide an environment that radiates warmth so that quality communication will result, whether in class discussion or in a one-on-one conversation between teacher and student. The classroom arrangement must enable the students to easily see and hear one another. For example, circular seating often accomplishes the communication goals effectively. It is not necessary, however, to keep this arrangement at all times. Change may keep the atmosphere fresh and alive. Mostly, the teacher's concern should be to promote a feeling to students that he or she cares about their success (Bushman, 2001). In other words, the classroom arrangement should convey to students that this is a place for sharing ideas, discussing freely, and, specifically, feeling safe in that process.

Once the seating arrangement has created an atmosphere of warmth, the most critical ingredient to a successful response-centered program becomes the teacher's behavior. A teacher's attitude is the primary tool that can persuade a student that the lesson, the methods used, and, ultimately, the literature itself are critical to learning. Creating this climate is not easy, and an important balance between inviting students to think and respond freely and maintaining authority and control is just one component that teachers must sustain if success is to prevail. Probst (1988a) addresses one key for success, discussions. Offsetting the teacher's authority role with an attitude of trust in students is one way of establishing student confidence:

> If the discussions are to invite the responses and perceptions of the students, it is necessary that these responses and perceptions be welcomed. The teacher must let the students know that their comments are solicited and will be given consideration. . . .
>
> A delicate balance is required. The teacher must establish an atmosphere in which students feel secure enough to respond openly, but must not deceive them into believing that initial responses are sufficient. Nor, on the other hand, should he make students think their responses are invited to provide the teacher and other students with clay pigeons to shoot. If responses are ridiculed, there will soon be few responses left to ridicule. This is not to say that response-based teaching demands the intimacy of a sensitivity session . . . but it does require reasonable freedom from fear of castigation or mockery, and from obsequious submission to the authority of the teacher or the author. The classroom must be cooperative, not combative, with students and teachers building on one another's ideas, using rather than disputing them. (p. 25)

Teacher behaviors, provided they are appropriate and sincere, can create the potential for an exciting literature experience; excitement is an integral part of connecting students to the literature. Therefore, using a response-centered curriculum requires a special type of teacher, one who teaches rather than instructs. This distinction is basic to ensuring the success of a response-based classroom. The difference in the terms is partially an attitude toward students and is explained in Eisner's (1985) text *The Educational Imagination,* in which he distinguishes between instruction and teaching: "To 'teach' is softer than to 'instruct'" (p. 181). He follows with an integral reason for teaching as opposed to using instructional methods, stating:

> This is why the term instruction is more likely to be used by those whose orientation to curriculum is technological and who want to maximize effective control over the content and form of what children learn in school. Instruction is a term more suited to a manual than is the term teach. Instruction is less apt to be associated with the ad-

ventitious, with what is flexible and emergent, in short, and what is artistic, than is teaching. (p. 181)

Certainly, teachers are called on to be artists in a response-centered classroom. They must be creative in all aspects of classroom management so that students become personally engaged in responding to literature and teachers sustain a fresh approach to students' responses.

One specific behavior that teachers must maintain is discussing student responses. Classrooms that have focused on literary analysis, or on literature for the sake of knowledge, have an especially difficult task because students have learned through experience that teachers have a specific answer in mind. Expected responses and preconceived notions, apart from matters of factual recall, do not enhance response-centered class discussion. Rosenblatt (1991) suggests that students need guidance in evaluating their own reactions to the work, but instead of imposing specific ideas or "patterns, the teacher will help the student develop these understandings in the context of his own emotions and his own curiosity about life and literature" (p. 66). If the teachers display this attitude, they will create an environment wherein students begin to "feel" their responses instead of the anticipated answers that teachers have expected in the past.

The teacher's demeanor determines the success of a response-centered program. Leadership, exhibited through questioning techniques and by facilitating group discussions that reflect the teacher's own insight into what students think about when reading, is the key to the development of trust. When students recognize that the teacher is not guiding them to a specific response and that they can speak without fear of disapproval, they will sense consistent behavior. One way for teachers to prepare for students' responses is through understanding their own reading responses. Buckley (1992) suggests that teachers first explore their own reading habits before leading students through a reading journey. In the context of an imaginary institute for educators, she sets two objectives—the first is to study teachers' reading habits and the second is to have them discover how students read:

> The purpose of the first objective is to develop reflective teachers who seriously think about how they themselves read, discerning as best they can the peculiarities of human comprehension. . . . [The] second objective calls for a new curriculum for teaching literature to elementary and secondary students. This objective . . . is easier only because it follows and benefits from the understandings gained from the first. Generating ideas on how to teach others naturally follows in the wake of discoveries born from self-teaching. To teach literature with poise and confidence, teachers need to experience and internalize the subject. If the institute aspires for a different teaching of literature, then the new ways of literature must first become part of the teacher, not just part of the curriculum. Change the teacher, the institute hypothesizes, and then students will change accordingly. (p. 46)

It is important to remember that teachers cannot be thrust into a response-centered method; they must understand it, believe in it, and, ultimately, want it to work for students.

Critical to response-based literature are teachers who are both sensitive to students and sincerely responsive to the unexpected. Teachers must be able to *hear* what students are responding to, which involves much more than merely listening to answers. Once students learn that the teacher is interested in their insights, trust can evolve. Ultimately, as Rosenblatt (1991) counsels, teachers must establish a classroom climate that will induce students into a "spontaneous response" (p. 108). Achieving this level of facilitation will provide the necessary tools to help students develop a love of reading; however, to obtain the desired results, students must be provided with literature that provokes their interest enough for them to read it.

As noted, reading literature that motivates students and stimulates ideas relevant to them is essential as they enlist response-based skills. Probst (1988a) reminds us,

> If we are to begin our teaching with students' responses, we need literary works that provoke responses, stimulating students to think, feel, and talk. Without such works, awakening interest in discussion and writing can be very difficult. The teacher is forced to trick students into temporary interest in something that doesn't really appeal to them. (p. 113)

Classroom Strategies for Teaching the Literature

As noted, the young adult literature chosen in middle and secondary schools provides young adults with subject matter that relates to areas that are important to them. How we teach that literature is important, too, because what teachers have students do with the literature enables young adults to make the connections necessary between their reading and their world.

Traditionally, teachers have spent considerable time teaching about literature, and students have thus not been truly involved with the literature itself. "We must keep clearly in mind that the literary experience is fundamentally an unmediated, private exchange between a text and a reader, and that literary history and scholarship are supplemental. Studying them may or may not contribute to understanding of the private exchange, but it cannot be substituted for that immediate experience" (Probst, 2004, p. 7). It would seem, then, that teachers must do everything in their power to foster the relationships that students have with the text; therefore, the classroom becomes the nurturing center for that reading experience. Students feel comfortable sharing the meaning of literature and how it relates to their particular world.

Rosenblatt (1938) and Probst (2004) write of the interconnection of teacher, text, and student. Although the literary experience is between the reader and the text, the growth of that experience most often takes place in the classroom, so the teacher and students play an important role in this reading development. To make some sense of the text, readers draw on their thinking about past events, relevant experiences, and general knowledge. Sharing this process with the teacher and classmates fine-tunes their understanding of the text.

Beach and Marshall (1991) suggest that students respond by engaging, describing, conceiving, explaining, connecting, interpreting, and judging. When young adult readers make emotional responses and reactions to the text, this engagement comes in many ways: "I love this book!" "This is great!" "What a dumb story!" Readers can react to the book as a whole, or they may respond to a particular part: "That character was a jerk!" When describing, students reproduce or restate what is in the text. This is a rather low-level response, but the information may be necessary to reach the meaning.

Students move beyond this describing process by making connections between the text and their experience (conceiving). As students explain the text, they are offering reasons for why certain actions occur or why characters do what they do. The process increases the perspectives that students have on their reading. At a higher level of response, students make connections to the text with their knowledge of language, literary conventions, and social conventions to make meaning.

When students interpret what they have read, they say, "What does this text say?" We all understand at one level of reading and generalize to another level. Jerry's decision not to sell chocolates in *The Chocolate War* (Cormier, 1974) is more than just one student's decision not to enter into a school's money-making project. Lastly, students respond by judging the quality of the work. They evaluate the characters, the plot, and the author's craft.

Rockford (2002) builds on questions generated by Berger (1996) by creating a list of questions that he uses for helping students build responses. Rockford suggests six questions:

1. What did you notice?
2. What did you question?
3. What do you feel?
4. What do you relate to?
5. What do you predict?
6. What did you observe about the writing? (p. 23)

Teachers have an important role in fostering this reader response. They also share in the responsibility of helping students with their developmental tasks, growing moral judgment, and reading appreciation. The classroom pedagogy that teachers choose can make or break a student's development in these areas. We believe that creative oral and written activities with young adult literature have a positive effect on young people.

Group Discussions

The interaction that occurs among young people within a large or small group enables students to check their responses to literature against the responses of other students. This interactive process helps students adjust their thinking or reinforce their positions as they hear other responses. Students can ask for clarification if ideas and positions are not presented clearly; they can ask for elaboration if they need more information for a better understanding of the issues under consideration. If students feel that a statement has little supporting evidence, they can ask that the student justify the position.

For example, a student responding to Gordon Korman's *Son of the Mob* (2002) suggests that the treatment of two sets of parents at the end of the novel is inappropriate. Another student quickly agrees. Hearing no further evidence from either student, others may ask for a justification of that position. In their responses, the students show their understanding of the novel in relation to their perceptions of the world in which they live. At this point there is a heightened moral awareness (Yeazell & Cole, 1986) of the incident in the novel as it relates to the world of these two students. Certainly, the additional discussion that follows would enhance further moral reasoning skills.

> *My ideas tend to follow the "what if" model.*
>
> Gordon Korman

Other processes also enhance thinking skills. Students may find that by comparing and contrasting incidents and characters in two or more young adult novels, they have a better understanding of the issues under discussion. Group discussion also fosters evaluation. Students make evaluative statements about what they read. When students make statements with the words *good, great,* and *super* in them, they need to offer sound reasoning why and on what basis they feel that the quality of the work should be described with those or similar words.

One way to help students respond to their reading is by using response questions similar to those listed on page 67 or those listed in Figure 3.1. Questions such as these help students to move through their emotional responses to the work at first. There may be many more questions and areas to discuss, but these questions would get to the

---

What is your first reaction after reading this novel?

What feelings or emotions does this novel evoke in you?

What character(s) do you particularly like? Why?

What character(s) do you particularly dislike? Why?

Do any characters in this novel remind you of people you know?

Are you like any character in the novel?

What fears or concerns do you have for the characters?

What decisions do you believe were particularly good or bad?

What memory does the novel help you to recall?

Would you change any part of the novel? The beginning? The ending?

What questions do you have about his novel?

What do you think is the major point of the novel?

Does this novel remind you of any other literary work?

Comment on the author's writing style.

FIGURE 3.1

Response-based questions.

meat of any novel. Of course, these questions could be used when the discussion slows down. Perhaps the first and foremost question to ask in the response-based discussion is, "What do you want to say about what you read?" These questions may be inserted periodically after the discussion has begun. After students develop a strong sense about their relationship with the literature, they then move to the more analytic questions that cause the reader to think about the genre itself and about the author's craft.

Reading Aloud

Although there is still much controversy over how students best learn to read, every side of this argument agrees that hearing the written word is necessary to literacy development. Advocates for best practice include reading aloud as an integral strategy for lifelong literacy. In their book *Straight Talk about Reading* (1999), Hall and Moats list five benefits for reading aloud. The child

1. develops background about a variety of topics
2. builds his or her vocabulary
3. becomes familiar with rich language patterns
4. becomes familiar with story structure and the reading process
5. identifies reading as a pleasurable activity (p. 53)

Amanda Witty, a teacher at Blue Valley North High School in Kansas, goes one step further. In addition to reading aloud to her students, she uses the shared reading strategy. Shared reading allows students to listen to a fluent reader while having the written word in front of them to use and follow along. Witty believes that teachers should choose high-interest literature and set aside time to read aloud to their students every day, regardless of the age of students or the content area.

Creative Drama

Role-playing and improvisation expand the boundaries of experiences for students so that they develop a more complete understanding of themselves and of the literature they are reading. Through role-playing and improvisation, students are able to think as characters would think and act as characters would act. Students take on a persona different from their own and work at making that character come alive as they perceive what that character would be like if he or she were real. The process is much like Kohlberg's (1987) "role-taking." Although Kohlberg's role-taking may not be solely related to literature study, it certainly seems to be an appropriate model for understanding character motivations and actions. Students get inside the characters and play out their emotions, making choices and decisions based on the readers' understanding of those characters.

Creative drama works well as students respond to and interact with *Blood on His Hands* (Roberts, 2004). Marc Solie confronts a number of issues in this book: the death of his sister, a dysfunctional mother after the death, a dysfunctional family with the addition of the mother's new boyfriend, being sent to a detention camp and then running away. Certainly these issues facing the young adolescent can provide challenging role-playing or improvisational situations in which students can participate. Creative drama works with historical fiction as well. In *A Killing in Plymouth Colony* (Hurst & Otis, 2003), John Bradford struggles throughout the novel with his feelings for his father Governor William Bradford. Students could take on the two roles and try to explore the feelings of each character.

Most young adult novels provide for interesting role-playing situations. The moral dilemma is most often at the heart of the novel's conflict. Students can use creative drama to explore the concerns of Nick Hodges and his father (*The Empty Mirror*, Collier, 2004), Jerry, Archie, and Obie (*The Chocolate War*, Cormier, 1974), Buck and Tunes (*Dangerous Skies*, Staples, 1996), Dinnie, Guthrie, and Lila (*Bloomability*, Creech, 1998), Katy and Jacob (*The Silent Boy*, Lowry, 2003), Kate and Teri (*Catalyst*, Anderson, 2002), Isabel and family members (*Keeper of the Night*, Holt, 2003), Spoon and Gaabi (*The Beast*, Scholastic, 2003), Margaret Rose and her great uncles Morris and Alexander (*The Outcasts of 19 Schuyler Place*, Konigsburg, 2004), Santiago and Angelina (*Red Midnight*, Mikaelsen, 2002), and Col and Mungo (*Dark Waters*, Bloomsburg, 2003).

Socratic Seminars

Sherrill Hayes (2004), a teacher at Olathe East High School in Kansas, suggests that the Socratic seminar connects the reader-response approach and the active engagement of students and their peers. She goes on to suggest that the "truth does not come solely from one person, rather it is the interaction of a group of people from which the real truth comes" (p. 42).

In the Socratic seminar, teachers give students a passage; the students read in preparation for a conversation; the students are divided into two concentric circles; the inside group discusses while the outside group observes; the groups switch; and the whole class reflects (Metzger, 1998, p. 241).

Rockford (2002), who has used the Socratic seminar (see Rockford's model at the end of this chapter) in his teaching at North Kansas City High School in Missouri, indicates "the entire method is based on teachers coaching students to the point where they are conducting their own unassisted discussion" (p. 68). He goes on to say that because "Socratic Seminars are student-centered and because they involve literature and students making their own meaning, they are the perfect complement to a Reader-Response Classroom" (p. 68).

Literature Circles

Literature circles are composed of small groups of students who have read the same novel, poem, or article. Each member has, prior to reading the text, prepared to take specific responsibilities in the upcoming discussion. Each is ready for discussion with notes needed to help with that role (Daniels, 1994). Daniels makes the connection that literature circles "inherently welcome, celebrate, and build upon students' responses to what they read" (pp. 34–35).

The specific responsibilities or roles that students have include discussion leader, literary luminator, experience connector, and illustrator (Daniels, 1994; Hayn & Boatman, 2001). Other roles have been developed to fit particular needs: the vocabulary enricher, a summarizer, or a history master (Allen, 2001).

Daniels states 12 key factors for "authentic and mature literature circles":

1. Students choose their own reading materials.
2. Small temporary groups are formed, based on book choice.
3. Different groups read different books.
4. Groups meet on a regular, predictable schedule to discuss their reading.
5. Kids use written or drawn notes to guide both their reading and discussion.
6. Discussion topics come from the students.
7. Group meetings aim to be open, mature conversations about books, and so personal connections, digressions, and open-ended questions are welcome.
8. In newly forming groups, students play a rotating assortment of task roles.
9. The teacher serves as a facilitator, not a group member or instructor.
10. Evaluation is by teacher observation and student self-evaluation.
11. A spirit of playfulness and fun pervades the room.
12. When books are finished, readers share with their classmates and new groups are formed around new reading choices. (p. 19)

Rockford (2002) believes that literature circles are a part of the reader-response theory that makes up the foundation of the entire instructional method. "Students are choosing the literature they are reading, transacting with the work, making their own meaning on an individual level, bringing that meaning to a small group, and finally making an additional meaning with small group discourse" (p. 40). Judith Hayn and Wendy Boatman of Loyola University in Chicago suggest that "Literature Circles offer readers the opportunity to participate as literate beings. Our goal is students who not only love reading but also think actively and critically about what they read" (p. 3). Elizabeth Dickinson, a teacher at Heartland Elementary in Overland Park, Kansas, uses literature circles often. She says: "Literature circles encourage students to become risk takers, and encourage them to share: interpretations, thoughts, and personal feelings about the books they are reading. Not only does the opportunity for all students to share have a positive effect on the classroom climate, it leads to students gaining confidence in their ability to be readers" (Dickinson, 2004, p. 29).

Writing

A number of activities use writing as the principal mode of responding. Responding reports, journals, the narrative, and the personal essay help students make a personal response that draws on their ability to create meaning of what they have read. We include a brief comment on each of these strategies in this chapter; a more detailed account about the use of writing and its relationship to the literature appears in Chapter 4.

Responding Reports.   Students can write responding reports in place of the traditional book report. Book reports have been the nemesis of students and teachers for years. Responding reports emphasize reading the work and responding to it primarily by writing. They do not emphasize looking up specific information to find "right answers." When all students have read the novel as a class, teachers can use these reports to assess students' understanding of the work.

Responding reports help students to become personally involved with the literature. They begin by having students make personal responses (i.e., they become engaged with the reading). How does the student relate to this novel? What emotions and feelings does the student experience? After students have read and written about the novel on a *personal* level, they are ready to move to a more *intellectual* level. They now think about the author's craft: What strategies and techniques did the author use to generate the responses students have?

Responding reports also integrate reading and writing. Students can thus enjoy the totality of the novel by responding to the ideas presented and by understanding the techniques the author uses. We believe that students feel more at ease when responding to a work in this way because they are in control of how they respond: how they structure their responses, what they include, and what they omit. As a result, they grow in their understanding of their novel in particular and of literature in general. For example, in *Chinese Handcuffs* (1989), students could respond to Crutcher's use of detail and description, the major themes of suicide and sexual abuse, and how they view the novel in terms of what it means to a young adult in today's society. There could also be an open response: Choose any passage in the novel that you find meaningful. Quote it and comment on its importance. (See Figure 3.2.)

The Journal.   We view the journal as a source for making deposits and withdrawals, much like a checking or savings account in a bank. To carry the analogy one step further, the bank account grows as interest is added periodically. Growth also takes place in the journal entries because students have thought about those ideas since their inception. The journal can be the place where students record their reactions to the text as they are reading. This response is not formal and is certainly not evaluated by the teacher. Students may wish to list the characters and a one- or two-sentence description of each; it is a place to record facts and important information about plot, setting, and theme that may be useful in later discussions or written responses. Students may wish to record quotes that they want to remember, connections to their experiences, and interpretations that they make as they are reading. Journals serve students well for continued use throughout the study of a particular novel.

The journal acts as a testing site for students' thinking. Coming to some understanding of a literary text is a process much like the process of writing: Readers do not come quickly to a complete understanding of the meaning of a piece of literature. It often takes time, and it takes a testing of ideas about meaning. Students can write informal drafts in their journals to get at that meaning. We have learned much about the "writing to learn" movement and how writing helps readers and writers in all content areas to increase critical and creative thinking and, therefore, to arrive at understanding. Many readers say that they really don't know what they mean until they can speak

Dillon, the main character in *Chinese Handcuffs,* writes unsent letters to his dead brother as a way of coping with problems that seem unsolvable. In the space below, tell how you feel about that process. Could you use an unsent letter to work through problems that you may have from time to time? Tell how you deal with difficult problems. What outlet do you use to achieve release from the tensions that problems cause?

Respond briefly to each of the following:

- What is your first reaction after reading *Chinese Handcuffs?*
- What feelings or emotions does the work evoke in you?
- Do any of the characters remind you of people you know? Do not name the individuals, but describe how these people whom you know are like the characters in the novel.
- What is the major point of the novel as you understand it?

As has been noted, Dillon uses the unsent letter. Indicate in which situations (about what concerns) did Dillon write the unsent letters and indicate what effect they had on him.

Choose one of Dillon's letters to Preston, take on the point of view of Preston, and respond to the letter. Become Preston for a short time and respond to Dillon's concerns.

Chris Crutcher uses similes frequently in his novel. The following are but a few:

> "I was drawn to her like a masochist to hot tongs." (p. 15)

> "The whistle blew. . . . Coach Sherman motioned to Jennifer, who approached like a racehorse following a tough workout, shoulder-length blond hair clinging to her neck like a wet mane, her long sinewy legs glistening with sweat." (p. 18)

> "My emotions churn inside me like a hurricane, and when it's at its worst, I can only lay back and let them take me away." (p. 59)

- Look through the novel and find at least five more similes and list them below.
- Now, comment on the effectiveness of using such a device. Why would an author use the simile?
- Write two or three paragraphs in which you use similes.

FIGURE 3.2

A responding report on Crutcher's *Chinese Handcuffs* (1989).

or write about it. The meaning often changes as they spend time working through their understanding by writing.

Rockford (2002) suggests, "Different types of Response Journals provide students a structure in which to express their responses. Simply walking into the classroom every day and having students write a 'one-page response' would become tiresome" (p. 30). He suggests four different types of journal use: the *quote journal,* in which students simply respond to a quote from the text that they are reading; the *partner journal,* in which students set up dialogue journals to share with each other; the *character journal,* in which students assume the role of one of the characters in the book that they are reading and write in their journal from that character's point of view; and the *note card journal,* in which students keep their responses on note cards rather than on plain sheets of paper. With this journal, students are making brief entries rather than longer entries (pp. 31–37).

The Narrative and the Personal Essay.   The journal has its uses, but it is not meant for evaluation. At times, however, teachers want students to write a more formal piece of writing, whether it is developing characters and plot in a story or taking a position about what they have read and supporting that position in an organized way. We support this practice, although we believe that for most students in grades 6 through 10, a less formal piece of writing is more beneficial. According to Wadsworth (1978), many students have trouble writing formal essays because of the nature of the writing and their lack of formal operational characteristics. Formal writing can come later.

For example, after reading Minter's *The Insiders,* students who have had experience with groups could respond in a narrative showing the troubling aspects of school cliques, school gangs, or community gangs. Students may choose the personal essay over a narrative to explore the problems of gangs and their effects on the school or social communities. After reading Avi's *Nothing but the Truth* (1991), middle school students may respond by relating a personal experience in which they told the truth as they knew it but others saw it in a different way; older students may write a more formal essay in which they explore the use of half-truths and obfuscated language to achieve a particular result.

Responding to <u>*Touching Spirit Bear*</u>*: An Example*

In this section, we describe a sample reader-response classroom exercise, using Ben Mikaelsen's 2001 novel *Touching Spirit Bear* as our text. An important part of the literature selection for any English or language arts classroom is choosing material that is age appropriate. We have given much attention to this topic in this chapter; it seems appropriate to offer a minimal reminder as we select a novel for study as an example of what can be done in a response-centered classroom. If we expect students to have sufficient experience for a response, they must be able to relate in some manner to the assigned literature. Karolides (1992) states the significance of using appropriate literature:

> The language of a text, the situation, characters, or the expressed issues can dissuade a reader from comprehension of the text and thus inhibit involvement with it. In effect, if the reader has insufficient linguistic or experiential background to allow participation, the reader cannot relate to the text, and the reading act will be short-circuited. (p. 23)

With the wide range of young adult literature available today, it is not difficult to find adequate reading material that meets the needs and interests of all students. *Touching Spirit Bear* is a quality young adult novel that excels in its literary merits as well as in its ability to maintain reader interest. Fifteen- to seventeen-year-old students identify and are involved in reading this novel because of its themes, language, tension, and interesting characters. A brief summary of the novel follows:

Cole Matthews is a very angry adolescent. His behavior goes beyond simple anger, though; it has become filled with rage and hate. Cole, frequently in trouble, has now gone too far. He finds Peter Driscal in the parking lot and smacks his head against the sidewalk. Peter may be permanently brain damaged.

Cole is sentenced to Circle Justice, a system, based on Native American traditions, that attempts to provide healing for the criminal, the victim, and the community.

As part of the sentence, Cole is banished to a remote Alaskan island. There he is mauled by a mysterious white bear of Native American legend. He believes he will die, but he begins to take control of his life. His thoughts miraculously shift from anger to humility. The attack of the Spirit Bear may have saved his soul.

Preparing Students to Read

The first stage of successfully preparing students for a reading assignment is to seize their attention and to focus it, often through writing. (You can choose a variety of methods for focusing students' attention, but writing works very well. Discussion about a relevant topic works well, too; however, for this prereading lesson, we have chosen writing.) Purves, Rogers, and Soter (1990) attest to the strengths of writing and learning, stating that "Extended writing draws out of the mind of the reader more information, more reflection, more wrestling than, for example, either group discussion or brief responses to questions will do" (p. 137). Through writing, students are able to explore topics and at the same time connect these topics to their feelings, fears, and other emotions.

In choosing a topic for the prereading writing assignments, you want to provoke students to think about a central issue in the novel, preparing students for and focusing them toward an issue that is important in what they are about to read. Stirring students' interest is essential to the process of response because if they are not motivated, the chances are slim that they will respond with much effort. Another purpose for prereading writing is to help students make a connection to the novel. Experience teaches us that our connections to people, ideas, or objects are a driving force. The writing will internalize for students that their ideas are important, further empowering them.

Touching Spirit Bear abounds with themes and issues that will evoke student responses. Prereading activities might include, but should certainly not be limited to, having students write about the following:

Revenge: Have students ever felt so put upon, so angry, that they wished to seek revenge from someone? What were their feelings toward that person or persons? Were they really thinking clearly about what they were doing?

Disobedience: Cole has been in and out of trouble over the course of his young life. Why do you suppose that Cole has such a disdain for the law?

Guilt: Have students think about a time when they caused something to happen, but it was an accident. Although they did not act purposefully, others may have believed it was their fault. How did the students feel? How did they overcome any guilt they had?

As you begin, discuss the responses that students wrote in the prereading sessions. Generally, this is a time for students to discuss what they wrote and to share with each other their various topics. At this time, you assign students the novel. After your students have read it, engage them in the following activities. Spread this response-centered work over a few days as students develop their understanding of the novel.

Large-Group Discussion

First and foremost, ask students for an open response to the novel. What did they think about it? What are their reactions to the work? Did they like it? Why? At first it seems important to let students take the lead in the response. Your listening skills are crucial in this initial phase. As students react, you may need to offer follow-up statements, questions, or acknowledgments to help them clarify, justify, or elaborate on their ideas. If the discussion drags, use generic questions early in the discussion and more content-specific questions later in the process. Try to keep these questions at a minimum and emphasize your spontaneous reactions to students' responses because spontaneous reactions are more meaningful to students, and they help move the discussion by using students' ideas rather than yours. However, sometimes you will need to ask questions such as the following:

What is your first reaction after reading this novel?

What feelings or emotions does this work evoke in you?

What character(s) do you particularly like? Dislike? Why?

Do any of the characters in this novel remind you of people you know?

Are you like any character in the novel?

What memory does the novel help you to recall?

Content-specific questions that you may incorporate into the discussion include the following:

To what extent is the cake symbolic of Cole's life?

To what extent do Cole's parents influence Cole's bad behavior?

Is there any justification for Peter getting hurt?

Why didn't Cole strike back at Peter when Peter was attacking him?

Discuss the Circle Justice system. Is it fair? Would it be appropriate for today?

Small-Group Discussion

Small-group discussions may give students an opportunity to discuss some of their most important responses before sharing them in the large group. The small group may also be used to allow students to further explore the general responses that they shared in the large group. Students often feel less threatened in small groups and are more willing to explore ideas in that setting. Like large groups, smaller groups must have rules of behavior that enable students to function effectively in the interaction. Students must feel secure with their responses, and they must respect the responses of others. They will recognize similarities among all of the responses. You should actively participate in each group by circulating and facilitating where and when needed. It is best, however, to allow students to lead the discussion of the novel. This approach teaches students that they can function with self-sufficiency and without teachers influencing their responses. As Rosenblatt (1991) reminds us, "The reader . . . must have the experience himself. . . . The teacher's task is to foster fruitful interactions—or, more precisely, transactions—between individual readers and individual literary works" (pp. 26–27).

Creative Drama

As noted earlier, creative drama—pantomime, improvisation, role-playing—can be effective in helping students to respond to what they have read. Creative drama helps students to expand on their responses and the meanings that they have discovered or defined in the large or small groups. For example, an improvised discussion between Cole and his father concerning the family relationships would help students to understand how Cole feels. A role-playing activity involving Cole and his parents in which Cole asks for another chance instead of going through the Circle Justice system would also be helpful.

Writing

You also may choose to engage students with all of the questions and statements mentioned so far in this section of the chapter through either free writing, journal writing, or personal essay writing. Again, whether you address these issues through writing or discussion is your decision, and it should be based on what is most effective for your students. When you wish to use longer writing assignments, the following ideas may be helpful:

Monologue: Ask students to take on the persona of Cole and have each student tell of his experiences with the Spirit Bear.

Dialogue: In a similar way, ask students to write a dialogue between Cole and Peter when Peter visits Cole on the island.

Character sketch: Use the biopoem (discussed in Chapter 4 and shown in Figure 4.1). After collecting ideas about a character—Cole, Peter, Cole's parents, Edwin—have students take that prewriting exercise and use it in a poetic character sketch.

Personal essay: Have students respond to the statement, "The Circle Justice system is a demanding but fair system." Students can explore that statement in terms of this novel and also in terms of how they find its meaning in people whom they know.

Expository essay: Have students explore the author's craft. How has Ben Mikaelsen crafted this novel to heighten the suspense, tension, and emotional intensity?

In a response-centered classroom, the writing assignments should challenge the students to further develop their thoughts about the novel and to explore a specific area of interest. Your suggestions are precisely that—suggestions. Students should remain free to choose other topics and other kinds of writing that will better suit their needs. Whatever the form of writing, students should be able to focus their writing toward resolving a disturbing issue or a problem that they see in this novel, something that connects with them and makes it a worthwhile experience.

All of these classroom strategies—large- and small-group discussion, creative drama, and writing—enable students to come to some understanding, some meaning, of what the novel is about and how it relates to them. In doing this, students begin to establish criteria that they can use to make generalizations about meaning. The intent is to help students become more independent in establishing meaning. One of the major pedagogical problems with using the classics is that many students never become independent. They are always dependent on the teacher to determine the meaning of the literature; therefore, many become nonreaders because they feel that they cannot make judgments for themselves (Bushman, 1994).

On the other hand, as Rosenblatt (1991) points out, although students' reactions and impressions are valid, sometimes students make incorrect assumptions about a novel, especially when they begin discussing beyond their personal impressions. At this point, you must begin exploring in a way that will help students recognize a mistake without destroying or confusing their personal responses. This problem requires delicate attention, especially while students are in the early stages of learning the response-centered process. You will need to help broaden their base of experience with literature. As students come to recognize that personal responses are only one segment of a response-centered classroom, the hope is they will grow with that experience and continue developing their skills because, as Rosenblatt again suggests, students need to develop "mental habits that will lead to literary insight, critical judgment, and ethical and social understanding" (1991, p. 75).

Classroom Response to <u>Touching Spirit Bear</u>: A Transcription

We reproduce here as illustration a classroom Socratic seminar by a group of students to *Touching Spirit Bear* by Ben Mikaelsen. The portion quoted is only one activity that was done in the ninth-grade Communication Arts class at North Kansas City High School in Missouri. The class is team-taught by Sam Rockford and Toni Hansen.

At this point in the lesson, the class has finished reading the entire novel. Over three weeks prior to this discussion, the students practiced reader-response-directed topics in both writing and discussion.

This is the class's first Socratic seminar. Rockford and Hansen split the room into two groups: an inner circle and an outer circle. The inner circle participates in the first discussion while the outer circle observes, then they switch. (The description of a Socratic seminar can be found on page 70.)

This class's topic is "What is your *response* to the entire novel, *Touching Spirit Bear?*" Rockford and Hansen gave students 15 minutes to prepare the topic prior to the discussion.

Group 1: The Inner Circle

Lisa:	My response to the book kind of changed throughout the book, because at the beginning, I thought that Cole was not a good person at all. But as I read this book, I noticed some things that were happening in his life. In the end he changed a whole lot and became a whole new person.
Pam:	I agree. How do you think he changed?
Lisa:	At the beginning of the book, he was like beating people up, and he wasn't listening to anyone. In the middle of the book, he was getting a little better. Then toward the end, when Peter was trying to beat him up, he wasn't fighting back. That was a sign that he had really changed, otherwise he would have fought him back if it was at the beginning of the book.
Gary:	On pages 235 and 236, what would you have done if Peter would have hit you?
Lisa:	If Peter would have hit me? I would have hit him back, because I wouldn't let nobody hit me and get away with it.
Adam:	I would have hit him back.
Ashley:	For me, it would have been really hard to hold back.
PJ:	I would have just tied him to a tree. [Laugh.] Wouldn't be that hard. Got those poisonous tree branches the dude was talking about and just wrapped him to one of those. And I thought his parents were kind of like ignorant, cause you know you got the father who was like beating on him and he doesn't know he was having an effect to his own child. Then you got the mother who was just sitting back and drinking and just letting the father do it instead of saying something about it. Then, once toward where he is in the court and Garvey says to the mother, "You can protect your son by doing this and doing that. Why don't you do it instead of just being scared?" Once she finally does it, it seems like she could have did that before anything.
Lisa:	I do agree with you, but I also think that she was kind of afraid of the father because of the way he was treating Cole.
PJ:	Yeah, but what she have to be afraid for? She could have just settled it all right then and there.
Amanda:	Yeah, but he could have hit her.
PJ:	So, put a restraining order on him or something.

Glenn: That wouldn't stop him.

Lisa: That's just a piece of paper that says "Stay away 90 feet." . . . Okay, I have another question, you know that cake thing . . . do you guys think that that's kind of like Cole's life was? The different ingredients they were not as good alone, but once you have them all together they made something good at the end of the book?

Glenn: Not really, but I don't know.

Teacher: Better yet, how does the cake represent Cole's life?

Tony: Didn't it say that it had two eggs with it? Well, I think that the two eggs might be his parents. That just kind of popped up in my head.

Pause.

Lisa: It had some good things, like the sugar, that tastes kind of sweet. That could have represented how he felt after he beat Peter up. Then the bad stuff that was alone, like the flour, the baking soda, the eggs, and stuff, that represents all the bad things that happens. But when you put it together, it was a good cake, kind of like his life. All that bad stuff happened, and some good stuff, like when he went to the island and saw the Spirit Bear, kind of tied into the cake.

Tony: That is true.

Gary: On page 239, what would you have carved instead of a circle for anger on the totem pole?

Ashley: I would have carved a face, an angry face.

Lisa: I think I would have carved the bear.

Glenn: He already carved that.

Lisa: Well, I think I would have carved a better picture of the bear. Maybe he could show the claw more, or the angry part of the claw.

Tony: Maybe he could carve his dad's name into it or something.

PJ: I would have put, uh, like two little stick people in a big explosion to represent like fighting and anger and stuff like that.

Tony: What did you guys think of the book at the beginning when we read the first chapter?

PJ: I though Cole was just another kid with problems, basically.

Mike: I didn't think the book was going to be that good.

Amanda: I thought it was going to be boring.

Lisa: I kind of got into it after they was talking about after he beat Peter up, then I got interested. I like to see or hear action. That kind of triggered something to keep on reading the book.

Teacher: Let's focus on that question and get more people involved.

Jennifer: The first impressions of the book I had was that it would be boring, just about some kid going to jail. But then, it got better and better because it got more exciting and caught your attention and stuff.

Ashley: I felt really sorry for Peter after hearing about the fight and everything.

Amanda: Yeah, like how he was having trouble talking and couldn't walk and stuff like that.

Lisa: I agree with them. . . . Oh, you go ahead.

Derrick: I believe Peter deserves some of that, but not that bad. He deserved a little, but . . .

Amanda: That's mean.

Tony: He deserved to get smacked around a little bit just because he told on him?

Amanda: That's wrong.

Teacher: Go ahead, Amanda. Stand up for yourself.

Amanda: He shouldn't get beat up just because he told on something that was right.

Adam: I forgot what Cole did? What did he do?

Amanda: He robbed a hardware store or something like that.

Teacher: Let's focus on that question some more. A lot of people haven't talked yet. What do you think of this book, your first impression? [Pause.] Okay, what were some of your favorite parts of the book and why?

Lisa: One of my favorite parts of the book was when Cole suggested that Peter come to the island, because it might help. I thought that that was a good idea. And I like that part because [Cole] wasn't just thinking of himself, he was going to help Peter so that he wouldn't commit suicide.

Gary: My favorite part of the book was when he was almost dead and all the things he did to survive.

Tony: My favorite part was when Peter was beating up Cole, because at first I had a feeling Peter might try to hit him or something, but then again I thought he was a wimp. But that was my favorite part seeing how Cole didn't do anything.

PJ: My favorite part was like when Peter suggested that Cole go to the lake with him by himself without having Garvey with them. By the time he got there, and they started stripping down to get into the lake, how Peter just got Cole back for every punch and every swing and just inflicted damage on him like he did to him. But it wasn't in the same way, where like Peter was unconscious or anything like that. Just enough to let his anger go away.

Mike: My favorite part was when Cole was getting beat up by Peter and he was thinking about fighting back but he didn't because he wanted to prove to everyone that he really had changed and wanted to prove that he could tell the truth instead of lying like he had been his whole life.

Josh: I really didn't like the book.

PJ: Why?

Josh: Don't know.

Courtney: My favorite part was when Cole heard the boat and he realized that it had come true that Peter would come to the island.

Allie: I like when the bear attacked Cole, cause Cole kind of deserved it, because Cole shouldn't have tried to kill it.

Amanda: I really didn't have a favorite part.

Glenn: At the beginning of the book, I felt sorry for Cole, cause anger will take over your body and he might not admit what he did to Peter.

Teacher: Okay, we have time for one more question. Whoever has a really important one, let's go with it.

PJ: All right, uh, you know how Cole first got to the island, how he burnt the shed down and everything? You know at the end how he got back to the island at the end and rebuilt the shed and everything? What would you have done? Would you have started off like Cole or would you have started off like Cole ended?

Lisa: If I was as angry as Cole was, and those kind of things would have happened to me, I don't think I would have gone as far as burning down the shed. But I think I would have tried to get off the island. And if I wasn't as mad as Cole was, I think I would have started off like he ended up.

Tony: I would have not burned it down. I would have thought more about the escape and just swimming back to another island. I figure if I am in Alaska, it's going to be kind of cold.

PJ: I would have started off like Cole ended, doing everything right instead of burning everything up and fighting with the Spirit Bear. It just probably wouldn't be that worth it to me. It would just be like, okay I carve the totem pole, start pulling the rock up the hill, start swimming in some cold water, live day by day through this and I will get off the island. Then I wouldn't have to see no one else's face again but my mother's. See what I am saying?

Lisa: I agree with that, but Cole wasn't thinking like that. He was just thinking angry at the beginning.

Ashley: It would have been a big chance arriving at the island, and I wouldn't have had that much time to think about it.

Group 2: The Former Outer Circle, Now the Inner Circle

Amanda: Can I go first? What I relate to in *Touching Spirit Bear* is that when Cole's parents yell at him, he goes out and does something that is not responsible. And I relate to when he gets out of control, because when I get mad, I am out of control, and I don't care what people say. I just do whatever I want.

Linda: I agree with Amanda. That's kind of what I do. I go out and do something. I usually regret it later, but I go out and I don't listen to anybody.

Chris: Same here. I do the same thing all of the time.

Pam: I do too. But I think you should think before you do something.

Ronald: Just like everyone else. . . . If you know me, I don't think before I say a lot of things.

Adam: Neither do I.

Kelly: I can't really relate to a lot of the things that happen. They haven't happened to me, so it was hard to relate. Like when his parents beat him, I don't know how he feels, because . . .

Ronald: I have a question. What else would you use to symbolize your feelings besides carving the totem pole?

Linda: Writing.

Lucas: Wood. I would actually write on all the wood.

Pam: I would sing. I would make a song.

Lucas: To describe my feelings even more, I would do something every day, kind of like how he would go to the pond, or when he broke the stick. I would find a routine of how I felt or whatever that day.

Sandy: I would dress the way I feel. I do that anyway every day now.

Lacey: I would cry. Just put all the bad feelings I have into my tears and just cry until all the bad feelings are gone.

Jessie: With me, most time when I am angry, since I am a football player, I like to take it and use it on the field. Use the anger out there, because that is the only place where I can hit somebody and not get in trouble for it. So just hit somebody as hard as I can.

Linda: Cole has paper and stuff for his homework. Maybe he could just write down more of his feelings and stuff and reflect.

Lucas: Just like keeping a notebook or a journal.

Ronald: Going back to what Jessie said, I can relate to hitting people in football.

Jessie: Oh yeah, he's hit me pretty good before when he was mad.

Pam: Do you guys think Cole should have gone to the authorities about his dad?

Mike: I think he should have. All this stuff probably would not have happened.

Ronald: I disagree with that, I don't think he should have, because in that case . . . he could like get his dad put away, have his mom sent away for alcoholism because the dad would have said something. Then he would have ended up in a foster home, which is really twice as bad.

Lucas:	I agree. I have had emotional abuse before, and I know how it feels when you can't go to anyone for help. I don't think he could have done it, because it would have just led to more abuse. What if his dad goes just as out of control as Cole does when someone tells on him? Like when Peter told on Cole and Cole beat him up, same thing would happen with his dad. He would go mad and beat him up.
Sandy:	Didn't he try to do that?
Linda:	His dad has a bunch of money, and the same thing would have happened. He would have gotten out before he was even in jail.
Sandy:	I disagree with Ronald about not going to the authorities. If Cole did go to the authorities, he wouldn't have hurt Peter, he wouldn't have hurt all those people.
Adam:	But if he would have gone to the authorities, he would be hurt, because it is a process that takes a long time. He would still be at home, and you know what. . . . Say if he went to his counselor at school and says, "My dad is an alcoholic and he is beating me at home," it would take a while for the cops to get there. His dad is going to be beating him in the meantime, whether it's three days or three minutes.
Shelley:	And Cole didn't have a very good reputation, so the people really wouldn't believe him. Or his dad would just make an excuse and get out of it like he does at the end of the book.
Sandy:	I still disagree though. It wouldn't have happened. He could have called the authorities and Peter wouldn't be even hurt.
Pam:	I have a different question. What do you guys think about when Peter's family gives Cole the cold shoulder and was like "We don't trust you" and like don't believe that Cole changed?
Kelly:	I can kind of like see why they would do that, but it is not making the situation any better.
Pam:	They didn't even give him a chance to prove his point that he has changed.
Sandy:	Yeah, but Peter's parents did have a right to say that. Think about it, Cole made Peter mentally challenged. How can you trust somebody that has done that to your son?
Linda:	They should have done it in a more mature manner, instead of yelling at him and stuff.
Kim:	It never hurts to give somebody a second chance.
Kelly:	Yeah, they could have told him nicely instead of threatening him and stuff.
Dwayne:	I wouldn't have given him any chances.
Ronald:	I don't understand how you all could try to represent all the parents like Peter's and Cole's parents. For me, it all goes back to the lawyers. The lawyers seem to talk more than they do.
Lucas:	I think that the parents, even though Cole did all that bad stuff, that the parents should have given him a second chance, or more than a second

chance. They are his parents, and if they care about him or love him at all, then they would give him a chance.

Ronald: Then maybe then he should give them a chance.

Linda: Well, maybe his mom wouldn't have tried to stop drinking to take care of him when he comes back from the island.

Sandy: I've got a question. What do you think Cole should have done instead of beating Peter up?

Jessie: I think he should have taken it out on something else. I don't know, like going out and running, instead of hitting someone else.

Lucas: I think he should have gone to his counselor or somebody. Or like Sandy said earlier, he could have gone to the authorities and told them, "I want to beat him up for what he said about me, because I am getting beat up at home."

Ronald: I think he should have beat him up. There is a cause and effect for everything. You know if you tell on somebody, then somebody is going to come looking for you. Obviously, if he really thought about it, he would have knew that Cole was coming for him.

Dwayne: If you say something, then somebody is going to come looking for you.

Kelly: But he didn't have to bang his head into the sidewalk.

[Chatter.]

Ronald: You all are making it sound like Cole came up from behind him and started beating him. Peter could have fought back, but he didn't.

Kelly: Yeah, but Cole had so much anger that he shouldn't have made Peter have a concussion. He could have just fought a little, but not as far as where Peter couldn't fight back.

Trey: All this stuff wouldn't have happened if Cole didn't break into the hardware store.

[Chatter.]

Teacher: Wait a minute. Listening is a huge part of this activity, and I am afraid some of you didn't hear Trey's point. Can you repeat what you just said?

Trey: All of this stuff wouldn't have happened if he didn't rob the hardware store.

Lucas: Yeah, and he wouldn't have broke into the hardware store if his dad wasn't treating him that way.

Pam: Cole's action doesn't reflect on what his dad does to him. What Cole does is what Cole does. It's not because of his dad.

Lucas: But Cole has some emotions about what his dad does to him. Sometimes you can't help what your emotions demand.

Pam:	Yeah, but you can't be like, it's just his dad's fault. He could have thought about it and not did it. But he did it.
Lucas:	But his emotions got carried away, and you can't help that sometimes.
Sandy	Going back to when Ronald and Dwayne said that they would have beat Peter up. Well, there is something wrong with you if you beat somebody up just for telling, because it is just wrong. I got told on a million times and I don't go up and tell them, "Hey, you're going to get beat up." I don't hit people; I just go up to them and say, "Why did you do it?"
Ronald:	Wait, wait, wait. Peter did not have to tell. He was bragging about it.
Trey:	Yeah, but Cole didn't have to rob the store to begin with.
Ronald:	But you guys are acting like his dad was always there giving him stuff. The only thing he gave him was a beating. You know what I am saying?
Pam:	Did Cole ever ask his dad for anything?
Lucas:	Maybe Cole was too scared of his dad to ask for anything because of the beatings that were going on. You can't help your emotions.
Amanda:	I think he knew that somebody would tell on him. . . . He just wanted a reason to beat someone up, because he knew someone would tell. Peter was just the one.
Jessie:	Think about what he said, though. I don't know if it was in the middle of the book or the end of the book, but he said that back in the beginning that was all that he knew. His dad was beat by his father, and that is all his father knew was to beat his son. And so that is all Cole knew was to beat people who did him wrong. Like if you tell on somebody, you beat the living crud out of him.
Teacher:	Okay, I think we only have time for one more question. Adam, go ahead.
Adam:	Do you think that the end of the book should have been different? It should have actually showed his sentencing.
Teacher:	That's a great question, so let's hear from some people that haven't talked yet.
Corey:	I think that it should have showed what happened afterwards. Like, if he still had the same sentence or did he just get off?
Laura:	I like how the book ended.
Ronald:	I think it would have been better if Cole would have been sentenced to a whole bunch of years in prison. In life, once you do something, you can't go back and change it.
Trey:	I think that would have changed his attitude, and made him really mad.
Kelly:	And then he would have been back to his old self again.
Ronald:	Not if he really changed.
Lucas:	If he would have had another sentence, then the people in prison would have made him more angry and made him go back to his old ways. So maybe he could have just had the island sentence. Then, after he became friends with Peter, then that's it.

Learning Log Responses

What advantages do you see when you have your students use the reader-response approach to literature?

How would you build a classroom climate conducive to using reader response? Why is a positive climate important when using the reader-response method?

Choose a piece of literature and design two different reader-response activities for that work.

References

Allen, R. (2001, Summer). English teachers fight back. *Curriculum Update 2–3,* 6–8.

Anderson, P. M. (1986). The past is now: Approaches to the secondary school literature curriculum. *English Journal, 75*(8), 19–22.

Angelotti, M. (1981). Uses of the young adult literature in the eighties. *English in Texas, 13,* 32–34.

Applebee, A. N. (1989). The background for reform. In J. A. Langer (Ed.), *Literature instruction: A focus on student response* (pp. 1–18). Urbana, IL: National Council of Teachers of English.

Beach, R., & Marshall, J. (1991). *Teaching literature in the secondary school.* Orlando, FL: Harcourt Brace Jovanovich.

Beach, R., & Wendler, L. (1987). Developmental differences in response to a story. *Research in the teaching of English, 21*(3), 286–296.

Berger, L. R. (1996). Reader response journal: You make the meaning . . . and how. *Journal of Adolescent and Adult Literacy, 39*(5), 380–385.

Binz, W. P. (1993). Resistant readers in secondary education: Some insights and implications. *Journal of Reading, 36,* 604–615.

Buckley, M. H. (1992). Falling into the white between the black lines. In N. J. Karolides (Ed.), *Reader response in the classroom* (pp. 45–58). White Plains, NY: Longman.

Bushman, J. H. (1994). *Creating a positive classroom climate.* Overland Park, KS: Writing Conference.

Bushman, J. H. (1997). Young adult literature in the classroom—or is it? *English Journal, 86*(3), 35–40.

Bushman, J. H. (2001). *Teaching English creatively* (3rd ed.). Springfield, IL: Charles C. Thomas.

Carey, M. Poster. Ottawa, KS: The Writing Conference.

Carlsen, G. R. (1980). *Books and the teen-age reader.* New York: Harper & Row.

Carter, A. R. Poster. Ottawa, KS: The Writing Conference.

Creech, S. Poster. Ottawa, KS: The Writing Conference.

Crutcher, C. Poster. Ottawa, KS: The Writing Conference.

Daniels, H. (1994). *Literature circles: Voices and choice in the student-centered classroom.* York, MN: Stenhouse.

Dickinson, E. (2004). *Literature circles in the elementary classroom.* Unpublished master's project, University of Kansas.

Donelson, K. (1989). If kids like it, it can't be literature. *English Journal, 78*(5), 23–26.

Eisner, E. W. (1985). *The educational imagination.* Englewood Cliffs, NJ: Merrill/Prentice-Hall.

Graves, D. H. (1990). *Discover your own literacy.* Portsmouth, NH: Heinemann.

Hall, S., & Moats, L. C. (1999). *Straight talk about reading.* Chicago: Illinois Contemporary Publishing Co.

Hannson, G. (1992). Readers responding—and then? *Research in the Teaching of English, 26* (2), 135–147.

Hayes, S. (2004). *The Socratic seminar in a - response-centered curriculum*. Unpublished master's project, University of Kansas.

Hayn, J., & Boatman, W. (2001). *Implementing literature circles in the middle and high schools*. Ottawa, KS: The Writing Conference.

Heather, P. (1982, February). *Young people's reading: A study of the leisure reading of 13–15-year-olds*. Paper presented at the annual meeting of the United Kingdom Reading Association, London.

Hynds, S. (1989). Bringing life to literature and literature to life: Social constructs and contexts of four adolescent readers. *Research in the Teaching of English, 23*(1), 30–61.

Hynds, S. (1990). Reading as a social event: Comprehension and response in the text, classroom, and world. In D. Bogdan & S. B. Straw (Eds.), *Beyond communication: Reading comprehension and criticism* (pp. 237–256). Portsmouth, NH: Boynton/Cook.

Karolides, N. J. (1992). The transactional theory of literature. In N. J. Karolides (Ed.), *Reader response in the classroom* (pp. 21–32). White Plains, NY: Longman.

Kohlberg, L. (1987). *Child psychology and childhood education*. New York: Longman.

Kolb, H. H., Jr. (1990). Defining the canon. In A. L. Brown Ruoff & J. W. Ward, Jr. (Eds.), *Redefining American literary history* (pp. 35–48). New York: Modern Language Association of America.

Korman, G. Poster. Ottawa, KS: The Writing Conference.

Langer, J. A. (1990). Understanding literature. *Language Arts, 67*, 812–816.

Metzger, M. (1998). Teaching reading: Beyond the plot. *Phi Delta Kappan, 80*(3), 240–246.

Murfin, R., & Supriya, M. R. (1998). Critical approaches: Definition of Reader-Response Criticism. *The Bedford glossary of critical and literary terms*. Bedford, MA: Bedford.

National Center for Educational Statistics (NCES). (2003). *The nation's report card: What does the NAEP reading assessment measure?* Retrieved from www.nces.ed.gov/nationsreportcard/reading.

News from the College Board. (1999, August 31). College Board Online, www.collegeboard.org/press/senior99/html/sattl.html.

O'Connor, M. E. (1980). *A study of the reading preferences of high school students*. Arlington, VA: ERIC Document Reproduction Service No. ED 185 524.

Probst, R. E. (1987). Adolescent literature and the English curriculum. *English Journal, 76*(3), 26–30.

Probst, R. E. (1988a). *Response and analysis: Teaching literature in junior and senior high school*. Portsmouth, NH: Boynton/Cook.

Probst, R. E. (1988b). Transactional theory in the teaching of literature. *Journal of Reading, 31*(4), 378–381.

Probst, R. E. (1994, March). Reader-response theory and the English curriculum. *English Journal, 83*(3), 37–44.

Probst, R. E. (2004). *Response and analysis* (2nd ed.). Portsmouth, NH: Heinemann.

Purves, A. C. (1992). Testing literature. In J. A. Langer (Ed.), *Literature instruction: A focus on student response* (pp. 19–33). Urbana, IL: National Council of Teachers of English.

Purves, A. C., Rogers, T., & Soter, A. O. (1990). *How porcupines make love II*. White Plains, NY: Longman.

Rockford, S. (2002). *Reader-response: The "I" in literature*. Ottawa, KS: The Writing Conference.

Rosenblatt, L. M. (1938). *Literature as exploration*. New York: Noble & Noble.

Rosenblatt, L. M. (1956). The acid test for literature. *English Journal, 45*(2), 65–76.

Rosenblatt, L. M. (1991). *Literature as exploration* (4th ed.). New York: Modern Language Association of America.

Trelease, J. (1982). *The read aloud handbook*. New York: Penguin.

Wadsworth, B. (1978). *Piaget for the classroom*. New York: Longman.

Wilhelm, J. (1997). *You gotta be the book: Teaching engaged and reflective reading with adolescents*. New York: Teachers College Press.

Yeazell, M., & Cole, R. (1986). The adolescent novel and moral development. *Journal of Reading, 29*(4), 292–298.

CHAPTER

4

The Reading-Writing Connection

Nobody but a reader ever became a writer.
Richard Peck

Children learn to read from writing and learn to write from reading. The theory that supports this premise is extremely strong, as discussed in this chapter. However, putting the theory into practice in schools has been long in coming. Although in the past each discipline was taught in isolation, today the integration of reading and writing is much more accepted. "Any teacher of composition or of literature over the past decade recognizes that we have experienced a radical shift in our approaches to both subjects" (Burkland & Peterson, 1986, p. 190).

Burkland and Peterson go on to say that reading and writing were formerly considered solitary activities, but new studies indicate that readers and writers develop knowledge through shared and discussed information. In addition, teachers do not need to feel that they are shortchanging either area; rather, they are forging a lasting bond among the student, the literature, and the writing that develops from the literature.

A Rationale

Reasons abound for teaching reading and writing in combination. Although writing and literature can be taught within a thematic process, many times they are not. As a result, students feel a lack of personal involvement, especially with isolated writing assignments. Literature, then, along with the theme approach (if it is used), provides the needed context in which to write and learn about writing. Students may find the literature connection helpful as they make connections to ideas and themes expressed in what they read. Writers must find that commitment toward what they are writing. This commitment is difficult to achieve when working through a sterile writing assignment that has not come out of the writer's own desire to write or is a response to something heard in a class discussion or something read in a literature study.

> *Keep on reading and writing! You will probably find you write best the kinds of stories you most enjoy reading.*
> Sandy Asher

Elbow (1981) suggests that the only valid justification for a writing program is the creation of more capable writers who produce better writing. Practicing writing in isolation may lead to improvement, but at some point student writers need the visual model. For example, they must interact with the published writing of real authors. By interacting with that writing, students come to a consensus about what authors do. When students realize that authors deliberately choose certain words and that they begin sentences and paragraphs differently depending on the effect they wish to produce, students begin to emulate and experiment, trying to find the best strategies for them and thus becoming more capable writers.

It helps students to know that authors first concentrate on the development of ideas and that the emphasis on mechanics comes at the end of the process; that they move through the writing process, rejecting the idea that a polished product can be written in one setting; that they understand that the writing process is recursive and not linear (i.e., they write, think, rewrite, and so on, frequently throughout the process); and that they may use a list of ideas that they want to include—but a list to which they are not restricted. They know that the act of writing produces more thinking, which, in turn, produces more writing.

> *The most important way to be a writer is to be a reader.*
> Ann Brashares

When making the connection between reading and writing, students do not need the grammar book to learn the language conventions used in writing. Through literature, students will see the use of metaphor, simile, dialogue, imagery, and the many other conventions that authors use effectively. By using literature, students see for themselves how these conventions affect readers. Students can carefully examine the choices that the authors have made and transfer them to their own writing.

The study of literature has not gone through the turmoil that the teaching of writing has experienced. Some educators may argue that teaching isolated skills (such as grammar) still benefits young people, and many still believe that answering questions after reading a work is the way to learn the one and only meaning of the piece. However, very few now believe that literature terms and conventions should be taught without experiencing them in the reading process, and most teachers follow, in their own particular way, the reader-response theory.

> *Writers need readers to complete the work of the book.*
>
> Sandy Asher

Most literature and composition anthologies printed before 2000 and used in many classrooms today contain chronologically divided American and British literature with composition suggestions for students that result in what Tchudi (1986) calls "pseudo-academic expository essays" (p. 252) . Tchudi denounces this practice: "For too long, English teachers and professors have ignored the developmental needs and interests of their students while promoting curricula distant from those students" (p. 254). These texts are primarily concerned with a knowledge-level understanding of what was read. Writing is used to respond to questions that check comprehension, rather than using the reading to inspire original, thought-provoking essays. The traditional use of writing does not encourage response with the literature because the intent of most anthologies seems to be to emphasize the "right" interpretation. As a result, students are asked to interact with questions raised by editors of the books rather than with the authors of particular selections.

Teachers who practice the reader-response theory believe that literature provides young people with universal themes that interact with their own goals, desires, visions, values, and morals. Students are able to experience vicariously the actions and emotions of others and compare and contrast these experiences with their own. Literature, and certainly young adult literature, allows students to see that others face similar decisions and share their problems and concerns. Rather than promoting "distant curricula," writing that ties the literature and the student's world together helps students formulate answers to their personal dilemmas.

Theory and Research

The theory and research show a strong relationship between reading and writing, but this relationship has not always been recognized. Even since the early 1990s, many educators were still arguing that reading was simply a decoding task and that writing was the encoding task—two unrelated processes. A move to reconsider the connection between reading and writing began in earnest in the early to mid 1980s. Educational theory and empirical research now provide evidence for this new thinking about the reading-writing connection.

For many years, most classroom teachers have known that skills were not successfully transferred from one area to another. This transfer did not occur because the skills were usually taught in isolation. For example, most educators, from the elementary classroom to the university level, know that a grammatical knowledge base does not transfer to writing ability, although many classroom teachers continue the practice. No research supports it. This grammar issue most clearly represents how research and practice collide, with research losing out to ineffective practice; however, research does not lose out in the reading-writing question. Here, research has led the way.

Noyce and Christie (1989) use schema theory, which explains how the mind assimilates information, to explain the missing link between skills and both reading and writing. "Comprehension occurs when text information is assimilated into an already existing schema or when the schema itself is changed so that it can accommodate new information from the text" (p. 7). Therefore, the authors suggest, if comprehension does not occur, it is due to a lack of assimilation into existing schemata. Given this information, teachers can include additional instruction to help students revise their schemata to lead to better comprehension.

Schema theory not only explains reading comprehension but also enhances the connection between reading and writing. Because the two areas are related, activities aimed at increasing reading comprehension will enhance the writer's skills. "The same schemata that are used for reading comprehension are also utilized during the writing process" (Noyce & Christie, 1989, p. 8). Burkland and Peterson (1986) also found evidence to support schema theory. They examined the work of David Bleich, Louise Rosenblatt, Linda Flower, James Britton, and Lev Vygotsky and learned that these authors believe that our minds make connections between symbols and experience and "out of already developed and developing cognitive schemata" (p. 191). Through experience, readers and writers continually revise their schemata while they read, write, and interpret.

The transactional approach is also used to describe the reading-writing connection (Sternglass, 1986). In this view, as readers read, they are creating new meaning for themselves, "meanings that did not exist independently before either in the mind of the author or of the reader" (p. 151).

Uttero (1989) connects the use of reading, writing, and cooperative learning. Working together, students find meaning in their reading through their writing. Uttero's research indicates that readers and writers complete several steps while reading and writing. Both processes mobilize prior knowledge, create a model of meaning, and ask readers to monitor their thinking and reading strategies. Through cooperative learning, students express their ideas both orally and in writing and receive feedback on their progress. Peer groups and teacher support enhance students' reading and writing development. Blanchard (1988) states that the Report of the Commission of Reading in 1985 "strongly emphasizes the need to view all language processes—listening, speaking, reading, and writing—as interrelated and mutually supportive" (p. 60). He indicates that writing activities enhance reading comprehension. Blanchard and others mentioned in this section are convinced that more learning occurs when students write in response to and about literature.

Ronald (1986) discusses expressive writing (writing for oneself and reflecting on that writing). She states that "expressive writing assignments can begin to accomplish that reintegration of reading, writing, speaking, and listening" (p. 238). By constantly rereading their own writing, students become more aware of their meanings and the connections they are attempting to make.

> *Writing is a joy, as reading is a joy . . . as words themselves are a joy; as playing with them, arranging and rearranging them in rows and patterns and letting them dance and sing is a joy.*
>
> Harry Mazer

Theory into Practice: The Classroom Connection

Bromley (1989) states that "both research and theory support the notion that combining instruction in reading and writing in the classroom enhances children's literacy learning" (p. 122). She presents three major reasons for making connections between reading and writing: Both skills develop at the same time; each reinforces the other; and, through reading and writing, language is used for communication.

To make these connections, Bromley uses buddy journals, a written dialogue between partners about the books they are reading. Buddy journals provide a real audience for writing, promote cooperation between students, and build interest and confidence in writing. Bromley (1989) states that buddy journals "make the connection between reading and writing obvious for children" (p. 129). Gilles (1989) advocates the use of literature study groups. While reading the books they have chosen, students write comments, questions, or concerns in literature logs, and then they meet in groups to discuss what they have read. The literature logs serve as a focus for the discussion and as a reminder to students about concerns they wanted to address. Students involved in literature study groups discuss a book by linking it with their own experiences. Each member of the group, including the teacher, is responsible for critiquing and analyzing the book. Gilles believes that when teachers respond as an equal member of the group, they model more sophisticated interpretation strategies. In addition, this process puts into practice the theory that meaning is made as people discuss and interpret what they read.

Harste (1990) discusses the development of literacy and details suggestions for a successful literacy program:

1. Language is learned through use rather than through practice exercises.
2. Children need to be given opportunities to make language their own by making connections with their lives and background information.
3. Children learn best in low-risk environments where exploration is accepted.
4. A well-designed reading-writing program should provide ample opportunities for daily reading and various types of writing.

Harste emphasizes the need for daily, open-ended discussions and activities based on literature and writing. Open-ended activities allow students to become involved based on their own interests because "reading . . . is sharing meaning about texts, [and] writing is not simply a process of recording on paper already-perfected ideas but also a vehicle for organizing thought" (p. 318).

Improvement of reading and writing skills was Raphael and Englert's (1990) goal. To attain their goal, they administered a set of curriculum materials that guide students through planning, organizing, writing, editing, and revising. Their research indicates that both reading comprehension and writing skills improve as students use language, engage in peer-editing and peer-shaping groups, and internalize the strategies they have learned. The authors conclude that learning modes show students that reading and writing are active, ongoing processes.

> *No tears in the writer, no tears in the reader. No surprise for the writer, no surprise for the reader.*
>
> Robert Frost

McMahan and Day (1983) argue against the sole use of essays as springboards for writing in the composition class. Instead, they assert, imaginative literature, short stories, and poems have several advantages over essays. Literature provides an emotional response often not expressed in essays. "Imaginative literature deals with individual human experience and . . . it can provide an incentive to students to write out of their own experiences" (pp. 111–112). After students read, discuss, and write about the literary work on a personal level, they are ready to analyze the piece itself. The literature provides the writer with specific details and examples for analyzing aspects of the literature, such as character and plot development.

Tierney and Leys (1986) examined studies that show that stories children read influence what they write. For example, a group of first graders who read the traditional first-grade readers full of choppy sentences and little detail wrote in that same style. They conclude that writers are influenced by what they read and mimic the writing style of poorly written as well as well-written works.

Sheley (1983) found that literature could be a model of written language as well as a global view of human experience. "Literature enlarges the student's knowledge and understanding of human behavior for it exhibits thoughts and feelings which are often concealed in real life" (p. 123). When writing from literature, students become aware of the author's intent and discover that writing is not a mysterious event that just happens. As students become more accomplished writers, they begin to see the choices that authors make.

Wilson (1983) found that literature had a positive effect on the writing style of students who speak nonstandard English. Neither weeks of red correction marks on writing assignments nor extensive grammar exercises had motivated students to analyze their writing habits. However, after prolonged exposure to interesting literature, the students' writing skills improved because "students need to read before they write . . . in order to hear mentally and internalize the rhythms and patterns of written standard English" (pp. 116–117).

Wilson also discovered that the quality of writing increased when students first discussed the literary work and then wrote about it. Their compositions showed mature insights often not present in writing without a literature base, and their language patterns improved. Any continuing difficulties in standard English usage or content problems were addressed using student writing during the revision stage.

Fitzgerald (1989) argues that revision in writing and critical reading use similar thought processes because relationships exist among authors, readers, and texts. For example, authors know that readers expect the text to have continuity and to follow a line of reasoning. Because they keep their readers in mind, writers continually compare the actual with the desired text. "Through the comparisons, writers judge the degree of consonance (match) or dissonance (mismatch) between authors' and readers' goals and what's in the text" (p. 44). When dissonance occurs in writing, the revision process begins. Dissonance develops in critical reading when the reader experiences confusion or skepticism over an author's words.

Fitzgerald suggests group conferences to aid the thinking processes involved in revision of writing and critical reading. Students focus on consonance and dissonance among authors, readers, and texts. The teacher sets a positive tone and models comments and suggestions.

Atwell (1998) believes students should choose what they read and write in the English classroom. A workshop atmosphere permits students of all abilities to think and to learn through literature and writing because the classroom workshop "accommodates adolescents' needs, invites their independence, [and] challenges them to grow" (1998, p. 26). According to Atwell, writers must constantly read and be exposed to a variety of written material, including prose, poetry, fiction, and nonfiction. Children who are given the freedom of choice over their own reading and writing material will show the teacher that reading and writing are important to them.

Romano (1987) asks students to be active learners by challenging them to "use written language to uncover their mental processes of reading, their changes in thinking, their developing awareness, and their emerging understanding" (p. 143). Romano often finds that students' literary insights differ from those given in teacher's manuals. Therefore, rather than use the manual and risk stifling his students' mental maturity, he allows students to find their own meaning in the literature they read. Romano gives his students the independence necessary to interact with and write about literature in their own way. Students "need not listen to a teacher tell them what to think. They think" (p. 145).

Burke (2000) emphasizes the importance of incorporating writing activities throughout the reading experience—before, during, and after the reading of the piece—because to do so engages students in the following practices:

- Elaboration strategies, as students respond to questions and prompts the teacher provides and internalize the habits of inquiry
- Thinking skills, as the act of writing about a text requires readers to make meaning
- Verbal articulation, as students use their writing as a script to help them discuss their ideas more confidently
- Textual intelligence, as students use writing to examine and respond to different aspects of the texts they read—this might take the form of imitating, recasting, or reflecting on the texts
- Imaginative capacity, as students occupy the role of writer/creator, one which invites them to see the inherent creativity in all types of writing (p. 238)

Along the same lines, Beers has promoted the use of several different before-, during-, and after-reading strategies that engage students in writing about the literature they read (2003). For example, in writing "probable passages," students examine a list of 10 to 15 key words from the text, preselected by the teacher, and predict the literary categories in which the words will be used: Will they relate to the characters? The setting? The problem/conflict? Or the outcome/resolution? Students also have an opportunity to place any challenging or unfamiliar words into an "unknown" category. After the initial placement, students then write a "gist statement," predicting the plot—the "probable passage"—of the story. Through cooperative learning groups, students share their "probable passages" before reading. After reading the literature, students then discuss, or write, comparison statements between their own predictions and how the author played out the story using the preselected words. As a result, through word analysis, predictions, and reflection, not only are students connecting reading and writing, but they are also connecting them to the entire reading comprehension process (pp. 87–88).

These researchers all acknowledge that learning advances occur when writing and literature are treated as interrelated subjects. As noted in the research, the concept is not relegated only to theorists but has practical application in the classroom. By nurturing the reading-writing connection, teachers encourage students to take more responsibility for their own learning while they become more competent and discriminating readers and writers.

Teaching the Literature

The rest of this chapter suggests how teachers can benefit from the theory and research just mentioned. In the following pages, we show how we would teach, using selected pieces of young adult literature, the reader-response theory, the writing process, literary elements, and writing and reading skills.

Our approach is holistic: We would teach the reading and writing components frequently found in the English classroom through the study of literature. These skills and processes are not taught in isolation but as a comprehensive study of a piece of literature. We are not suggesting tearing apart a piece of literature bit by bit through a minute analysis of these selected skills; rather, we suggest that readers enjoy the totality of a work by responding to the ideas presented and by understanding the techniques the author uses so that readers learn to make that response. We are concerned that readers do not see themselves as writers and writers do not see themselves as readers. Through the rest of the chapter, we hope that teachers of readers of young adult literature will be able to note specific reading and writing strategies that they, in turn, can use when they are helping young adults with their writing.

Although we have chosen to organize the strategies by literature, we want to be clear that it is not our intent to promote the teaching of these skills in isolation. The work is treated as a whole, and the skills are there to be taught as students respond to the work.

Readers will note that we emphasize students' responses to reading and writing. We believe that students need to start with their emotions and feelings and then move forward to more sophisticated responses. Our strategies are to help students make their responses, know why they respond as they do, trust their responses, and respect the responses of others. In earlier writing (Bushman, 2000), that process was described as moving from the emotional level to the intellectual level. Others have used terms such as *engaging, describing, conceiving, explaining, connecting, interpreting,* and *judging.*

Throughout this book we emphasize the importance of young adult literature in the classroom. We use young adult novels because adolescents relate well to them. The ideas presented are often consistent with their experiences, the books have young adults as protagonists, the language of the literature parallels the language of adolescents, and the quality of the literature demands its presence in the English classroom. We strongly believe that the classics are no longer the only quality literature and the only works that teachers can use to teach composition and literature skills. Therefore, we strongly believe that young adult literature must take its rightful place in schools. The bottom line is that all the successful strategies in the world are of no use if students are assigned books they cannot read in the first place.

The eight works selected for this study are *The Chocolate War* (Cormier, 1974), *Roll of Thunder, Hear My Cry* (M. Taylor, 1976), *Chinese Handcuffs* (Crutcher, 1989), *Breathing Underwater* (Flinn, 2001), *Far North* (Hobbs, 1996), *Buried Onions* (Soto, 1997), *The Giver* (Lowry, 1993), and *The Island* (Paulsen, 1988). We have selected these works because they have the qualities that characterize them as "good literature" and because they are often read by students. Most, if not all, can be used in a classroom study. Although any one piece of literature could be censored at some time, these pieces are often taught by English teachers in middle or secondary schools.

The Chocolate War

Jerry Renault, a ninth-grade student at Trinity High, an all-boys Catholic school, refuses to participate in the school's annual chocolate sale. At first Jerry refuses because of an order not to participate given by Archie, an upperclassman who leads the Vigils, a secret organization bent on intimidating non-Vigils and antagonizing the school's administration. The pranks and strong-arm tactics clearly show the power and control that this underground organization has over the student body as well as over the school officials. No one dares to challenge the Vigils.

But Jerry does. After 10 days of not selling chocolates, Jerry is supposed to join in the effort to sell. He doesn't. The challenge has begun. This act is a definite affront to the Vigils, especially to Archie's control, and to the administration, which has engaged the Vigils to make sure the chocolate sale is successful. For a while, Jerry becomes a hero because he made a decision that no one had ever had the courage to make. But the full powers of Archie and Brother Leon, the chief administrator whose reputation is at stake, and the loss of his closest friends cause Jerry to stand alone in his struggle to fight the establishment. The novel ends with Jerry receiving a savage beating before the moblike student body while Brother Leon looks on from a distance. Jerry is defeated physically and emotionally. He had "dared to disturb the universe" and realized that he shouldn't have. The novel ends with the depressing feeling that the bad guys had won and there is no hope. But perhaps this novel reflects, at least to some degree, a realistic society.

Reading and Writing Activities.   You can stimulate interest in reading the novel by involving students in a prereading discussion on fund-raising events in their school. Do clubs and organizations or the school as a whole ask students to sell candy, candles, jewelry, or magazine subscriptions? What do students think of that process? Have parents or members of the community commented about this practice? Have students make a journal entry about how they feel about this practice of selling items for school-sponsored programs.

A second area to investigate involves particular students. Has anyone refused to participate in the fund-raising? Through discussion or a journal entry, have students explore why they chose not to participate. At this time, introduce the novel and briefly describe the story so that students are aware of the relationship between the practice found in their school and one of the many themes found in the novel.

As a third prereading activity, ask students to place a response on a continuum about the statement "Life Is Fair." At the extreme left is the statement "Life Is Never Fair"; at the extreme right is the statement "Life Is Always Fair." Students place their mark somewhere between these two extremes. This activity should be completed before reading in case some students react to the novel as not being realistic. We believe it is important for them to connect to what they and others have said about the fairness of life.

You may choose to assign the novel to be read completely before the discussion over it, or you may choose to assign sections, with discussion following each reading. Certain advantages and disadvantages accompany each procedure. We believe that it is beneficial to discuss the novel as a whole and not in parts; however, assigning chapters or sections helps students who may not be motivated to stay on task. Students, however, usually do not have trouble finishing *The Chocolate War.*

As students begin working with the novel, they will want to respond in writing to what they have read. What is their first reaction to the book? What is their gut reaction to what happens to Jerry? Do they know other students who are like Jerry? Archie? Have they ever had a Brother Leon as a teacher? Specific names are not shared in the class discussion, but students will want to share information about people they know who have these same character traits. Although you may want to return later for further exploration of the ending, have students initially respond in their journals about the ending: The bad guys seem to win, and the innocent character lies there broken, physically and emotionally. Soon after this writing, have students meet in groups to discuss their ideas with each other.

Characters in *The Chocolate War* provide complexities to which high schools students can relate. One way to begin the character study is through a biopoem (Figure 4.1). This structured response helps students understand a variety of character elements. Using the biopoem structure, students choose characters from the novel—Archie, Jerry, Brother Leon, Goober, and others—and write a poem as a tool for understanding. Discuss these biopoems with students. You may want to use the biopoem as a prewriting activity for the suggested character sketch or some other writing assignment.

A number of other writing assignments emerge from a study of this novel. Students may explore the theme of the nature of humanity and respond to Caroni's thoughts after being detained by Brother Leon: "And he did see—that life was rotten, that there were no heroes, really, and that you couldn't trust anybody, not even yourself" (p. 87). Along the same theme, they might write in response to Archie's thoughts on people: "You see, Carter, people are two things: greedy and cruel" (p. 175). Students could very well explore the following questions: Do I dare disturb the universe?

FIGURE 4.1

Biopoem.
From A. Gere (Ed.). (1985).
Roots in the sawdust (p. 222).
Urbana, IL: National Council of
Teachers of English.

Line 1: First name
Line 2: Four traits that describe character
Line 3: Relative (brother, sister, friend, etc.) of _____
Line 4: Lover of _____ (three things or people)
Line 5: Who feels _____ (three items)
Line 6: Who needs _____ (three items)
Line 7: Who fears _____ (three items)
Line 8: Who gives _____ (three items)
Line 9: Who would like to see _____ (three items)
Line 10: Resident of _____
Line 11: Last name _____

Why did Jerry have that poster in his locker? Did he indeed disturb the universe? To what extent was he successful? Do you think Cormier believes that one should indeed distrub the universe? What parts of your universe do you think ought to be disturbed?

In addition, students may choose to do an "I-search" paper, in which they investigate someone who they believe has dared to disturb the universe and was successful. More serious students may study the original source for the "dare to disturb the universe" theme by reading T. S. Eliot's "The Love Song of J. Alfred Prufrock." Through discussion or writing, you also will want to explore other areas: peer acceptance, human motivation, evil manipulation, hypocrisy, and isolation.

You must allow time to analyze the writer's craft. Cormier makes choices that have a direct influence on the reader. We react and respond to the literature because of his decisions about word choice, setting, use of symbols, and other literary techniques. For example, students explore how the mood of the novel is established right from the beginning. Cormier uses three words to begin: "They murdered him" (p. 7). Immediately we wonder who? How? As the book continues, the reader might think that the struggle on the football field answers our questions about the hyperbole. But as we read on, we realize that there is more to it than just trying out for football. Cormier ties the idea of murder together in the next-to-last chapter when Jerry says: "Just remember what I told you. It's important. Otherwise, they murder you" (p. 187).

The setting and its description help to establish the feeling that we carry throughout the novel. "The wind rose, kicking puffs of dust from the football field. The field needed seeding. The bleachers also needed attention—they sagged, peeling paint like leprosy on the benches. The shadows of the goal posts sprawled on the field like grotesque crosses" (p. 14). Cormier continues the description with additional symbolism: "The shadows of the goal posts definitely resembled a network of crosses, empty crucifixes" (p. 17). The plot would not be as disturbing without the contrast with this religious imagery.

The description of the Vigils's meeting place reinforces the dark, drab picture:

> The small room behind the gym was windowless with only one door leading to the gymnasium itself: a perfect spot for Vigil meetings—private, the solitary entrance easily guarded, and dim, lit by a single bulb dangling from the ceiling, a 40-watt bulb that bestowed only a feeble light on the proceedings. (p. 29)

Imagery—the pictures that the writer paints with words—jumps out from the printed page. Imagery is used again and again to help establish tone:

- Scarlet splotches glistened on his cheeks as if he had been made up for some grotesque stage show. (p. 58)
- Leon looked up, smiling, a smile like the kind an undertaker fixes on the face of a corpse. (p. 67)
- Sweat moved like small bugs on his forehead. (p. 10)
- The moist eyes that reminded Coroni of boiled onions (p. 83)
- a toy boat caught in a whirlpool (p. 7)
- through crazy cornflake leaves (p. 9)
- the two pieces of broken chalk abandoned on the desk, like white bones, dead men's bones (p. 84)
- He tossed in his bed, the sheet twisted around him like a shroud, suffocatingly. (p. 90)
- October leaves which fluttered to the ground like doomed and crippled birds (p. 91)

In addition to studying the imagery, you will want to help students see the use of metaphor and simile as they help achieve this picture painting. Cormier also uses flashback, alliteration, allusion, personification, and foreshadowing but not to the same degree.

You may also want to involve students in a study of names so they can see the degree to which Cormier chose names to strengthen the mood. It was not an accident that the gang was called the Vigils. The name is a shortened form of vigilante. Students can investigate the meaning of the term and show why Cormier would make that choice. Students can also investigate the meanings of Archie. Why might Cormier choose that name over some other one? What about Goober? Obie?

Roll of Thunder, Hear My Cry

This novel, winner of the 1977 Newbery Medal, is one of the many books by M. Taylor that focus on the Logan family (others include *Song of the Trees*, 1975; *Let the Circle Be Unbroken*, 1981; and *The Road to Memphis*, 1990). In this novel, the reader experiences the physical survival of the Logans as well as the survival of the human spirit. This tightly constructed novel with strong characterization and universal themes of prejudice, self-respect, and family love tells of the struggle between races in

Mississippi during the Depression. In addition, the central theme of owning one's own land runs through this powerful conflict. Cassie, a 9-year-old Black girl, learns how owning land and having a place of their own put the Logans in a position that their sharecropper neighbors will never achieve. Papa acknowledges this importance in his comments to Cassie: "If you remember nothing else in your whole life, Cassie girl, remember this: We ain't never gonna lose this land. You believe that?" (p. 115). Papa also explains this to Stacey: "You were born blessed, boy, with land of your own. If you hadn't been, you'd cry out for it while you try to survive" (p. 155).

Over a period of a year (1933), we share with Cassie the deterioration of racial innocence. We struggle to understand as Cassie struggles to understand why she and her brothers must attend a Black school, which is below standard; why they must use hand-me-down books; why they must walk to school while the Whites ride buses; and why the Blacks had to put up with the night riders, the burnings, and other discriminating acts of the Whites with seemingly no recourse. Cassie learns through these and many more difficult experiences what it means to be Black.

Reading and Writing Activities.   To motivate students to read this novel, you may wish to have them write what it was like when they were younger and were ready to start a new year of school. When they were 9 or 10, did they ride a bus to school, did their parents take them, or did they walk? Students then discuss their writing in groups. At this point, lead a whole class discussion on the point of choice in the decisions about how students were to travel to school. How would they feel if they were forced to travel in a certain way because of the color of their skin? Once you have discussed this issue, have students read aloud the first chapter of the novel.

A number of incidents in this first chapter can lead to many writing experiences. One of particular interest is the comparison of the two schools that the children of the area attend—Blacks go to Great Faith Elementary and Secondary School and Whites go to Jefferson Davis County School. Taylor describes these two schools well. We learn who goes to each school, how the students travel to the schools, the names of the schools, the conditions of the books and the schools themselves, and many other details that are necessary for the reader to distinguish between the two schools. A writing assignment that could easily follow this reading involves the use of comparison and contrast. Through their reading, students gather details (prewriting), make some order out of the details they have generated and begin the writing process (drafting), and then share their writing with partners and groups for final revision (revising).

Students can study and perhaps use the various techniques that authors use to strengthen their writing. They may use a lot of detail to strengthen characterization, for example. It would seem that Taylor has chosen to use symbols to strengthen the elements of the theme—danger, prejudice, and destruction. To a lesser extent, Taylor uses the school bus as a symbol for oppression and prejudice. The two schools also may be considered symbols representing the conditions under which each race is educated.

To a greater degree, however, Taylor uses thunder as a symbol for impending danger. She uses this strategy throughout the novel to increase the sense of danger, suspense, and power. Early in the novel, when Mr. Morrison comes home with Papa, the reader learns that he has been fired from his job because he got into a fight. As this is revealed, Taylor describes him as having a "deep, quiet voice like the roll of low thunder"

(p. 27). Again, while Mr. Avery is telling about the night riders, there is "a clap of deafening thunder" (p. 46). Thunder is heard again just before Papa, Morrison, and Stacey are to return from Vicksburg with a wagonload of supplies (p. 158). We learn that they were ambushed by night riders. As they are telling what happened on the road, the reader learns that they didn't hear the truck carrying the bullies because "of the rain and the thunder and all" (p. 162).

Thunder strengthens the theme in Chapters 11 and 12. It is used to introduce Chapter 11 and then again as the children return T. J. to his home. We hear it often throughout this section of the novel, and it becomes stronger as the plot moves to its end. When Papa and Morrison go to save T. J. from the lynch mob and Papa sets the cotton on fire to distract attention from the lynching, Taylor builds the suspense: "Then we sat, very quiet, as the heat crept sticky and wet through our clothing and the thunder banged menacingly overhead" (p. 198).

After taking students through this discovery of thunder as a unifying element in the novel, you may wish to have them create an essay in which they examine another object that Taylor has used repeatedly throughout the novel. For example, a particular pattern is developed with trees. In the essay, students could trace the unifying element and identify its effect on the theme. During this activity, students discuss each theme that occurs in the novel and how the theme holds the work together and helps to make the work whole. Therefore, in this writing activity you can help students to pull together the details that support their thesis just as the author did with the theme in *Roll of Thunder, Hear My Cry*.

At the end of the novel, T. J. is taken to jail. We leave him there as the novel closes. This open ending provides an excellent opportunity for students to write about what they believe will happen to T. J. This writing can take many forms. A simple essay can provide a summary of what has happened and what has led to the arrest. It can also include the position of the writer on what should take place. Because a trial takes place in the sequel, *Let the Circle Be Unbroken*, students can divide into groups and write a trial sequence in which the various characters provide the content for judgment. Students will have to predict what will occur in the future. The activity would certainly encourage reading the next Taylor novel because most students would want to know if what they predicted is what Taylor has happen in the sequel.

> *Read all you can to know more about the world and write to know more about yourself.*
>
> Debra Seely

Chinese Handcuffs

Dillon Hemingway has had to deal with his older brother Preston's bout with drugs as well as Preston's crippling injury from a motorcycle joyride. However, when forced to witness Preston's suicide, Dillon is left with guilt, wondering if he could have prevented the tragedy. He fights in his brother's memory by seeking revenge on Preston's gang, which Dillon blames for driving Preston over the edge. Then Dillon struggles to renew a relationship with Preston's girlfriend—to whom Dillon has always been attracted himself—only to learn that she is the mother of Preston's child, a gift left behind. To cope with his brother's death, Dillon writes Preston unsent letters to try to communicate his unspoken emotions. Dillon also seeks refuge in training for the grueling triathlon, which is frowned on by the school's coaches; they wish Dillon would concentrate on using his athletic abilities to better their own high school teams.

When he pursues a relationship with Jennifer Lawless, Dillon learns that her seemingly perfect role as star basketball player is also an escape from her difficult life at home. As their relationship develops and Dillon earns her trust, Jennifer reveals her history of sexual abuse by her stepfather. As much as Dillon wants to help Jennifer, she convinces him that there's no way for her to win because her stepfather is a prominent lawyer who knows how to play the system to his advantage. However, when Jennifer learns that her mother is pregnant, thus creating another child to suffer in a world of sexual abuse, Jennifer's escape through sports is no longer enough. It is Dillon who not only saves her from a desperate suicide attempt but also secretly sets a trap to finally put an end to her misery.

Reading and Writing Activities.   As a prereading activity, students can respond in writing about how they cope with difficult problems. Everyone has an outlet to release tension. Some students go for long walks; others get belligerent and take it out on family and friends. We know one student who was a fairly good piano player, and he would simply stay at the piano until he had worked through his problem or at least found some temporary solutions. Dillon, the main character in this novel, writes unsent letters to his dead brother. How do we cope? One activity asks students to write about something they have had to deal with that they wouldn't wish on anyone else. How did they deal with it? What strategies did they use? Students may wish not to share their particular problems, but they probably will share the techniques that they used to cope with these problems. Following the writing and discussion, introduce *Chinese Handcuffs.*

Once again, it is important for students to make their personal responses to this book. To help them do so, you may wish to have students respond to some of the following questions:

What is your first reaction to the novel?

What feelings or emotions does the work evoke in you?

What character (s) do you particularly like? Dislike?

Do any of the characters remind you of people you know?

What memory does the novel help you recall? Have you been in a similar situation?

Of course, at some point in the activity, you will want to move students to perception, interpretation, and evaluation of what they have read:

Would you change the ending of the novel? If so, how?

What do you consider to be the most important word, phrase, or quote in the novel?

What is your reaction to or explanation of the title?

What fears or concerns do you have for the characters?

What is the major point of the novel?

Does this novel remind you of any other literary work?

What is your final reaction to the work?

Certainly, these are but a few of the questions and areas that you and your students should explore. In most cases, when students begin responding to literature such as *Chinese Handcuffs,* no list of questions is necessary, but it is good to have a few questions in reserve if there is a lull in the discussion.

Dillon Hemingway uses writing in an interesting way. On many occasions, he writes unsent letters to his dead brother, Preston. Early in the novel, Dillon witnesses Preston's suicide, the last resort for Preston after losing his battle with drugs. Dillon is devastated by this act and throughout the novel takes his various concerns to Preston via the unsent letter technique. He writes about his feelings about the suicide; the daily taunting of his principal at school; his experiences in triathlon training and in being the trainer for the girls' state championship-bound basketball team; his interest in Stacy Ryder, Preston's old girlfriend; his interest in Jennifer Lawless, the star basketball player; and the concern he has for Jennifer's history of sexual abuse by her stepfather. Discuss with students how these unsent letters helped Dillon. What effect did they have? How was Dillon able to use them? Dillon uses them to sort through his feelings and concerns. Although the letters are not sent and there really is no audience to respond, Dillon feels that writing will allow him to work things out.

After this discussion, you may choose to have students write an unsent letter. Students may wish to consider questions or responses to the characters' actions, or they may wish to write about a problem that concerns the author. In a more private way, students may wish to write an unsent letter in which they each share private thoughts concerning a problem with which they have had to cope. At the conclusion of this activity, you may want to suggest to students that the unsent letter technique might be helpful as they sort through problems throughout their adolescent and adult lives.

After reading the novel, students know a great deal about Dillon, but not as much about his brother Preston. There is enough information, however, for students to take on the point of view of Preston and respond in writing to one or more of the unsent letters that Dillon writes. If Preston could respond, how would he address Dillon's concerns?

Crutcher uses many techniques well. He uses hyperbole to make a point, metaphor and simile for comparisons, and allusions to Shakespeare. He uses flashback very effectively, and students could learn from its use. The reader learns a lot about Dillon and Preston in Dillon's unsent letters, in which Crutcher uses the flashback technique. We also learn of Jennifer's trauma, her feelings, and her agony through her flashbacks to her sexual abuse. After a thorough discussion of this literary technique, students can practice using this element in their writing. In a narrative, students can relate particular information about characters or the plot through flashback.

Breathing Underwater

When Nick Andreas spots Caitlin McCourt after her return from fat camp, all Nick can focus on is being close to her. He has known her since kindergarten, but now she is beautiful. Not knowing just how good looking she's become, Caitlin is quite taken by Nick's advances, as well as quite vulnerable when Nick's controlling attitude takes over, easily manipulating her to behave "his way."

Keeping her in line with taunts and jabs that she looks as if she is putting on some extra pounds or criticizing her by saying that certain clothes and behaviors make her look like a tramp, Nick dictates how Caitlin dresses, who else she hangs around with, and what activities she participates in. Nick particularly warns her about making a fool of herself by wanting to sing in the school's talent show; however, Caitlin, influenced by the encouraging words of her other friends who claim she has a beautiful voice, defies Nick's wishes. As a result, following the show, Nick becomes enraged and hits Caitlin in the face, resulting in a court appearance where the judge issues a restraining order, assigns Nick to attend anger management classes, and assigns him to write in a journal 500 words a day detailing the events that led to the physical abuse.

Nick enters his therapy in denial, stating that it was a mistake to think he needs anger management. After all, all he'd done was slap Caitlin. As he reluctantly begins his journal, however, and has the opportunity to witness the denial of the others assigned to his class, he becomes more reflective, realizing that he had taken on the characteristics of his own abusive father. Determined to win Caitlin back, Nick sets out to change himself, practice his anger management skills with Caitlin's protective friends, and regain his own dignity in his relationship with his father.

Reading and Writing Activities.   As a prereading activity, students could explore possible interpretations of the title *Breathing Underwater*. How is this concept possible? What does it mean? What could it represent? Then look at the passage in the novel where Mario, the facilitator of the anger management group, mentions the title:

> Anyone feel like that? . . . Like your life's a big act. Like you're trying to be a man when you're just a scared kid, trying to keep under control when you really want to scream, cry, maybe hit someone. Ever feel like you're breathing underwater, and you have to stop because you're gulping in too much fluid? (p. 20)

After students discuss the title and its connection to the passage, have them explore the concept of anger in a stream-of-consciousness writing. Possible prompts could be the following:

> What makes you angry?
>
> What do you do to control your anger?
>
> Have you ever lost control while angry? What happened?
>
> How do you deal with other people's anger?
>
> What suggestions do you have for others who are angry?
>
> When, if ever, is expressing anger appropriate?

Volunteers could share their writings aloud, stimulating a discussion on anger. Throughout the reading of the novel, students could be encouraged to respond in writing to the anger expressed by Nick, his father, and the others in the anger management class. The concept of anger should be revisited through class discussion throughout the reading.

As Nick is assigned to reflect on the events leading to his physical abuse, he begins the process reluctantly and with a flippant attitude. However, he eventually connects to the process, feeling a need to get the story down for his own well-being. In turn, students could be encouraged to target an action they've made that they are not particularly proud of or focus on a concern or conflict that they have not yet resolved. Like Nick, they could write about the events leading to the action, reflecting on what led up to it and what they think about the behavior now. Because the content of these writings could be quite personal, rather than asking students to share them, they could, instead, write a reflection of the process—did going through this writing process lead them to any new realizations about the action and why they did what they did? Emphasize at this point the power of writing in reflecting on life events.

Flinn's writing style includes the use of figurative language, particularly similes, metaphors, and hyperboles:

- Caitlin clutches the tissue like a white flag. (p. 5)
- The planets were orbiting in a different order. (p. 27)
- The wind pushes at me like a defensive lineman. (p. 33)
- I walk, seconds multiplying like amoebas, to my desk. (p. 42)
- Caitlin was my dealer and my drug of choice. (p. 61)
- My brain is an abyss. (p. 180)

Even the title *Breathing Underwater* presents a paradoxical situation. Have students discuss the effectiveness of this language use. Are there alternatives they would suggest? Are there places in the novel where they would suggest the addition of further figurative choices? Then have them examine one of their journal entries, revising it to include effective figurative language.

With the characters from both this novel and *Chinese Handcuffs* coping with abuse, have students role-play Nick, Nick's father, Caitlin, Dillon, Jennifer, and Jennifer's stepfather together in an anger management group. Several groups could occur at the same time or students assigned the same role could tag into the group being observed by the whole class. In Socratic seminar fashion, have the observing class members reflect on the comments made by the role-playing students. What was realistic/unrealistic? Did they offer any new insights into their characterizations? What issues were left out of the role-playing? Students could follow up with a journal entry on the process.

As a concluding project, students could create an informational brochure on anger management for students. In the prewriting process, students could interview school and community counselors as well as investigate the topic and resources online. In a cooperative learning jigsaw design, students could brainstorm the various categories that would go into the brochure, with small groups being responsible for the various sections. Mini-lessons in technical writing should occur throughout the project time to lead students to an end product that could serve as a school resource in the counselors' office.

Far North

Gabe Rogers, a 15-year-old Texan, attends boarding school in Yellowknife. He, his roommate, and Johnny Raven are traveling to the remote village of Dene by floatplane. Gabe has heard many tales of the mysterious Deadmen Valley and of a river called the Nahanni, fabled for its thundering plunge over Virginia Falls. The plane is forced to land on the river; soon after, the three find themselves stranded in the frozen wilderness because the plane and its pilot have tragically fallen over the falls. The story is about true survival. After the death of Johnny Raven, the boys are forced to go it alone in a world of ice, snow, and wild animals.

Reading and Writing Activities.   Again, as with the other novels, students should respond to *Far North* either in a journal entry or in a simple reader-response discussion. Did they like the novel? Why or why not? Was the plot believable? Do they think that they could survive if they found themselves in a similar situation? What character traits would they need to survive? Did Gabe and Raymond have these traits? How would they compare themselves with Gabe and Raymond?

One way to connect the literature with authentic writing is in the creation of a survival guide based on what students learned from *Far North*. Ask students to brainstorm elements and situations in which Gabe had to survive. Match each situation with techniques or strategies that Gabe used to survive that particular situation. Students can then plan a booklet that could be used as a survival guide for people who find themselves in a situation similar to Gabe's. The booklet could include instructions on how to make snowshoes, build a fire, build a lean-to shelter, and trap a beaver. It could also include tips for how to keep warm, store food, keep food away from animals, and so forth. Students could also draw diagrams, pictures, or maps that would be helpful for survival.

One message in the novel is the importance of the environment. Johnny Raven says, "Take care of the land, take care of yourself, take care of each other" (p. 223). Students can respond to Johnny Raven's statement by indicating what that message means to them. Students can then connect that message to their personal lives by writing about how they take care of their environment, how they take care of themselves, and how they take care of each other.

Another important element to the story is Johnny's letter. Students can use the technique of letter writing to tie writing in with the study of the novel. Students can write a letter from Raymond to Johnny after the potlatch, telling him of his plans for the future. Students can write Gabe's letter as well, indicating what Johnny taught him.

In a more formal piece of writing, students can compare and contrast the novel *Far North* with other novels with similar themes. What similarities can students find in a novel such as *Between a Rock and a Hard Place* by Alden Carter (1995)? Are there comparisons between the novel and other works, such as *Hatchet* (Paulsen, 1987), *The Winter Room* (Paulsen, 1991), *Brian's Winter* (Paulsen, 1996), *The Giver* (Lowry, 1993), *Dogwolf* (Carter, 1994), or *Sweet Friday Island* (T. Taylor, 1994)? Students may choose one or perhaps two or three to include in this expository writing in which they explore the theme of nature.

Buried Onions

Living in Fresno, California, 19-year-old Eddie is trying to make a life for himself, but all he can do is face the tears brought on by the "buried onions," the obstacles that his barrio life has dealt him: living in poverty, surviving gang conflict, dealing with the death of friends and family. On his own, he seeks out odd jobs gardening and painting address numbers on curbs to try to pay rent for his cockroach-infested apartment, as well as tuition to learn air-conditioning skills at the local vocational school. He's also torn between his revengeful nature to track down his cousin's murderer and his desire to "rise above" his past and simply do what is right.

Eddie's situation appears hopeful when he is able to earn the trust of Mr. Stiles, an older man who hires Eddie to landscape his yard. However, when Mr. Stiles's truck is stolen on Eddie's first trip to the junkyard, a frightened Eddie irresponsibly does not report the theft and, therefore, loses Mr. Stiles's trust, hides from the police, and still must find a way to pay his bills.

Deepening his unfortunate circumstances, when Eddie's old friend Jose returns from the navy, the two are involved in a scuffle when they find Mr. Stiles's truck on the streets of Fresno, ending with Jose being stabbed and sent to the hospital. Out of desperation and determination to make something of himself, Eddie enlists in the navy to escape his hopeless condition.

Reading and Writing Activities.   Although Soto takes credit in painting a realistic picture of life in the barrio, this is, indeed, a bleak novel, with Eddie finding the only way to escape his supposed entrapment in barrio life is to join the navy. What will students have to say about this? Using their problem-solving skills, what words of advice do they have for Eddie and for other young adults trying to overcome the cards they have been dealt? Have students write letters of advice suggesting how best to tackle the future under these circumstances.

On the other hand, many students may interpret Eddie's choice to join the navy as a viable decision. Guide students to make personal connections to themselves or others in their lives who have overcome the odds. Students could write a personal narrative essay relaying their own accounts of rising above any struggles they have faced, or they could write an expository essay, making a connection between Eddie's experience to someone else they know: a character in another text (perhaps someone like Dillon in *Athletic Shorts* or Jerry in *The Chocolate War*) or a historical figure.

One of Eddie's goals is to achieve independence—emotionally, philosophically, and economically. Lead a class discussion of what it means to be independent, along with both positive and negative ramifications of achieving and maintaining it. The thoughts generated could be synthesized into a concept map focusing on independence. Choosing from a variety of genres—poetry, essay, or narrative—have students write what independence means to them.

At the beginning of Chapter 3, Eddie describes how he envisions "the good life":

> Where you go to work, do an eight-hour shift, and return home to your family where your kids are wild for you. . . . Mountains rise from your shoulders, coins jingle in your pocket, and the food on the table is your doing. A good life is a long, busy evening of watching TV, where every third or fourth joke is actually funny . . . (p. 35).

Have students reread this passage, coding its components—one color for those they agree with and another color for those that don't make up "the good life" they envision for themselves. After a discussion of how their opinions compare, have students write a description of "the good life," according to their own goals and visions.

The symbolism of the "buried onions," along with its extended metaphor for the sorrows and pains we experience in our lives, permeates this novel. Have students search the novel for all its references to the "buried onions," exploring their interpretations and making connections to the "buried onions" they have had to deal with in their own lives. Then, have them create a new extended metaphor for the challenges they have faced and the effects those challenges have had on their lives, synthesizing their thoughts into a poem to share with their peers.

Similarly, Soto's novel is rich in imagery and figurative language. Again, have students search through the work, identifying as many examples as they can find. Possibilities might include the following:

- Noon glared like a handful of dimes. (p. 8)
- I had money in my pocket, and the joyful music of coins clapping like tambourines as I pedaled. (p. 17)
- That was me, a train with empty boxcars but a caboose of problems. (p. 21)
- Each time the door closed with a clean pucker like a kiss. (p. 28)
- The east was one large bruise that was slowly becoming the night. (p. 34)

After a list has been made, have students select the images they find most effective and least effective, providing a rationale for their choices. They could then rewrite the latter to be more appealing.

The Giver

In this futuristic "utopian" society, families are created by selected couples, who may request one son and one daughter. At age 1, children are named and given to their chosen families; at age 9, they receive bicycles; and at age 12, a ceremony is performed to announce lifetime assignments after the children have been carefully observed for their abilities and interests. They may be assigned to be birth mothers, fish hatchery workers, directors of recreation, laborers, caretakers of the old, nurturers of the newborns, or other roles.

As 12-year-old Jonas anxiously awaits the announcement of his assignment, however, he is surprisingly skipped in the traditional alphabetical sequence. After all of the other assignments have been made, he is shocked and confused to be named the new Receiver of Memories, the most respected assignment of all. His training must begin immediately under the current aging Receiver—now to become The Giver—to ensure a smooth transition. Jonas works with The Giver to receive all of the memories that the society had decided generations ago to do away with to make their lives less complicated and more consistent—memories of war, pain, conflict, and divorce, as well as of color, music, snow, hills, and love. Eliminating these feelings and experiences has produced a society of "Sameness."

As Jonas first receives the memories, he is delighted with new sensations of sledding down a snowy hillside. However, as his training continues, he is overcome with grief and depression, not only for the new sensations of sunburn and war-related tragedy but also for the realization that others no longer experience many beautiful feelings and situations.

Jonas is also devastated as he learns the truth behind some of the horrendous acts in his community that, until now, he had been sheltered from. For example, he was aware that as a Nurturer, his father sometimes had to "release" a baby who was not "thriving," allowing the baby to be sent to Elsewhere—an unknown place that everyone views positively. When Jonas learns, however, that to "release" babies is to inject them with a lethal solution, Jonas is moved to persuade The Giver that it may be time to return the memories to the society. The risk for both is great at this point because they know that stopping the transition of memories now may not allow enough time for a new Receiver to be named and trained; as a result, the memories would automatically return to the citizens.

In an ending subject to many interpretations, Jonas attempts to carry out his plan by kidnapping Gabe, a baby soon to be "released," and riding off in search of Elsewhere to save himself, the baby, and the rest of his society.

Reading and Writing Activities.   As a prereading activity, students could describe what they would consider to be a perfect world. Encourage them to consider as many aspects of society as possible, including education, experiences, family life, career opportunity, and relationships. They also could include in their description a list of rules or laws they would like to live by. After students share their writings aloud, make a record of the reactions of the other class members for future comparison with the world in *The Giver.*

On pages 80 to 81 students can experience Lowry's use of vivid word choice and imagery to fully describe Jonas's first experience transferred from The Giver, sledding down a snowy hill. As students read, they will surely want to comment on such vivid words and phrases as "pinpricks," featherlike," "peppered," "whirling torrent of crystals," "propelled," and "glee." Students then choose another event that Jonas might experience for the first time. Writing from Jonas's point of view and using vivid words and phrases, they fully describe the situation.

As a good exercise to promote keen critical thinking skills, select quotations from the novel for students to write reactions to. Students can write the degree to which they believe them to be true, how they relate to the world they live in today, or how they relate to another piece of literature they have read. We suggest the following quotations as possibilities:

- "Honor," [The Giver] said firmly. "I have great honor. So will you. But you will find that that is not the same as power." (p. 84)
- "The worst part of holding the memories is not the pain. It's the loneliness of it. Memories need to be shared." (p. 154)
- "It's the choosing that's important, isn't it?" The Giver asked him.

  Jonas nodded. . . . "But now that I can see colors, at least sometimes, I was just thinking: what if we could hold up things that were bright red, or bright yellow, and [Gabe] could choose. Instead of the Sameness."

  "He might make wrong choices."

  "Oh." Jonas was silent for a minute. "Oh, I see what you mean. It wouldn't matter for a new child's toy. But later it does matter, doesn't it? We don't dare to let people make choices of their own."

  "Not safe?" The Giver suggested.

  "Definitely not safe," Jonas said with certainty. (p. 98)

Throughout their reading of the novel, students should remind themselves of the perfect world they created and described earlier. Having considered the consequences in *The Giver,* students may then reconsider how they would define and describe a perfect world, perhaps discussing and reconsidering as a class. Then, the class can brainstorm the elements of the society in the novel that they would question. Ideas might include the condition of Sameness; the age-level ceremonies, requirements, and behaviors; or the individual elements removed from memory. Students can put themselves into the world of *The Giver,* choose a situation in the society that they believe should be changed, and write a persuasive letter to the editor explaining specifically why this change should occur.

Finally, explore the ambiguous ending of the novel. When Jonas leaves on the bicycle with Gabe, he does so to save Gabe's life as well as to return the memories to the citizens. Readers are left with many questions, however: What really happens to Jonas and Gabe? Do they reach Elsewhere? Do they survive at all? Does the ending have any religious significance? And what about the people left behind? Are the memories transferred to them? If so, what are the consequences? How is Jonas's family affected by his departure? What do they and the other citizens now think about Jonas? What tone is left for the reader—hope or despair? Rather than simply discuss these questions, have students write an imagined next chapter to the novel in which they consider these questions and provide their own interpretations.

The Island

The Neuton family moves yet again. This time the move takes Wil, a 15-year-old, and his mother and dad from Madison, Wisconsin, to a community farther north in the state. Wil soon finds his special place: the island, a place where he can go to be alone and learn to know nature—and himself. It is also a place for Wil to put aside the outside world—the tension between his mother and father and the local bully whom he will have to confront sooner or later. On the island, Wil studies the loons and the fish in the lake. He wants to know all there is to know.

To help him make some sense of the nature that he experiences as well as his own feelings and emotions, Wil writes and paints. He feels the need to create to express himself, and the desire to become a writer or artist is born within him. The people of the community—Wil's father and mother, Ray Brunner, the television crew, the counselor—really don't understand what Wil is doing. A few—his new friend Susan, her parents, and a local newspaper reporter—are moved by his efforts. Their support reinforces Wil's sense of purpose and strengthens his resolution to continue his activities. There seems to be some resolution at the end of the novel when Wil and his father, who has been observing his son from the distant shore, decide to spend time together on the island. Wil realizes that he really doesn't know his father and that he needs to be with him, perhaps on this island, to be able to write about him.

Reading and Writing Activities.   This novel, perhaps better than any other, models the writing concepts that are taught in schools: writing to learn and the writing process. Wil says it best as he reflects on his writing and painting activity on the island: "To paint. To write. To know. To be" (p. 99). You can use this book to help students understand how writing affects thinking and understanding. The power of writing is used as discovery: What do I know and what do I need to find out? In addition, you may show the process that Wil goes through as he collects ideas, reflects on them, writes them down, and then returns to the writing later for additional work.

The novel is truly a remarkable piece of literature, not only as it shows a young man in his struggle with growing up but also as it reflects what we as writing teachers believe to be important in the process of composing. For example, soon after Wil arrives on the island, he sees loons on the water. The reader soon realizes

> There was more here that he did not understand, but he wanted to know. He wanted to know—he wanted to know the loons. Right now he wanted to know the loons and to know all that he could find out about the loons; he wanted to sit and watch them and learn what they were and know them. And if perfection came from that, if harmony came from that, if knowledge came from that, from his being on the island, that was fine. But he wanted to know the loons. This day, his first day on the island, his first full, real day, he would try to learn the loons, learn what made them part of the island as he wanted to be part of the island. (p. 34)

So Wil spends the rest of that day and the following day watching and studying the loons, and he reflects on what he learns. Wil then "kneeled carefully in the grass and willows and took the notebook and pencil out of his pack. At the top of the first page he wrote HERON all in capital letters" (p. 48) and began to write. Throughout the day, "Wil saw many other things, sometimes one thing would lead to two others, and he made side notes about them and would come back to them; but the whole morning he worked on the heron, wrote about the heron" (p. 48). Readers find Wil's finished project in the novel on page 51. Wil writes about his experiences and his search for understanding of his world and how he relates to it. He writes of his encounter with Ray Brunner at the cafe; he writes about his grandmother. " 'So strange,' he whispered. 'So strange to find her here . . . ' 'So strange' " (p. 82). "Then he turned and went to the boat to get his notebook and write about his grandmother while it was still fresh" (p. 82). There is a strong sense that Wil spends a great deal of time writing and rewriting. "He worked all the rest of the day on the piece about his grandmother, and when he had said some of the things he wanted to say and it seemed to be right, he put the notebook aside and ate a cold can of beef stew" (pp. 92–93). We learn about honesty in writing, too.

> The images that came to him were so clear, but when he tried to describe them—no, explain them . . . and there it was, there was the trouble with it. He wasn't writing about his grandmother. He was explaining her. And that, he thought, was not a way to learn about her, about what she had been to him. He took up the notebook again and started to write, and this time he didn't explain or describe; he simply wrote what she meant to him, what she was as he saw her, and it thundered out of him. (p. 108)

It is so important to Wil to write about his experiences. Even when he is fighting with Ray Brunner, he ponders writing about the fight and learning from it. Later Wil writes of his relationship with Ray and how that relationship seems similar to the relationship he sees between a turtle and the lake's fish. So he writes a piece titled "The Turtle."

This book has so much to offer students and teachers. In addition to the process model of Wil, the writer, the book also offers examples of free writing at the start of each chapter. Students could respond to those pieces. In addition, students could write about how Wil leaves the island, or they could write a newspaper article about his experiences. Certainly they could emulate Wil by trying his observation activities and meditation techniques and write about observations and meditations.

 *Learning Log Responses*

Choose a young adult novel not discussed in this chapter and describe how you would use it to teach reading and writing skills.

Discuss the relationship between the reading and writing processes. What benefits do you see for your students?

References

Atwell, N. (1998). *In the middle: Writing, reading, and learning with adolescents.* Portsmouth, NH: Boynton/Cook.

Asher, S. (1992). Ride the horse in the direction it's going. In D. Gallo (Ed.), *Authors' insights: Turning teenagers into readers and writers* (pp. 11–18). Portsmoth, NH: Boynton/Cook.

Asher, S. Poster. Ottawa, KS: The Writing Conference.

Beers, K. (2003). *When kids can't read, what teachers can do: A guide for teachers.* Portsmouth, NH: Heineman.

Blanchard, J. (1988). Plausible stories: A creative writing and story prediction activity. *Reading Research and Instruction, 28,* 60–65.

Brashares, A. Poster. Ottawa, KS: The Writing Conference.

Bromley, K. D. (1989). Buddy journals make the reading-writing connection. *Reading Teacher, 43,* 122–129.

Burke, J. (2000). *Reading reminders: Tools, tips, and techniques.* Portsmouth, NH: Boynton/Cook.

Burkland, J. N., & Peterson, B. T. (1986). An integrative approach to research: Theory and practice. In B. T. Peterson (Ed.), *Convergences: Transactions in reading and writing* (pp. 189–203). Urbana, IL: National Council of Teachers of English.

Bushman, J. H., (2000). *Teaching English creatively* (3rd ed.). Springfield, IL: Charles C. Thomas.

Elbow, P. (1981). *Writing with power.* New York: Oxford University Press.

Fitzgerald, J. (1989). Enhancing two related thought processes: Revision in writing and critical reading. *Reading Teacher, 43,* 42–48.

Frost, R. (1980). Quote in *The writer's quotation book.* Stamford, CT: Ray Frieman & Company.

Gilles, C. (1989). Reading, writing, and talking: Using literature study groups. *English Journal, 78,* 38–41.

Harste, J. (1990). Jerry Harste speaks on reading and writing. *Reading Teacher, 43,* 316–318.

Mazer, H. Poster. Ottawa, KS: The Writing Conference.

McMahan, E., & Day, S. (1983). Integrating literature into the composition classroom. *Writing Instructor, 2,* 115–121.

Noyce, R. M., & Christie, J. (1989). *Integrating reading and writing instruction in grades K–8.* Boston: Allyn & Bacon.

Peck, R. (1992). Nobody but a reader ever became a writer. In D. Gallo (Ed.), *Authors' insights: Turning teenagers into readers and writers* (pp. 77–89). Portsmouth, NH: Boynton/Cook.

Raphael, T. E., & Englert, C. S. (1990). Writing and reading: Partners in constructing meaning. *Reading Teacher, 43,* 388–400.

Romano, T. (1987). *Clearing the way: Working with teenage writers.* Portsmouth, NH: Heinemann.

Ronald, K. (1986). The self and the other in the process of composing: Implications for integrating the acts of reading. In B. T. Peterson (Ed.), *Convergences: Transactions in reading and writing* (pp. 231–245). Urbana, IL: National Council of Teachers of English.

Seely, D. Poster. Ottawa, KS: The Writing Conference.

Sheley, C. (1983). Active learning: Writing from literature. *Writing Instructor, 2,* 123–128.

Sternglass, M. S. (1986). Writing based on reading. In B. T. Peterson (Ed.), *Convergences: Transactions in reading and writing* (pp. 151–162). Urbana, IL: National Council of Teachers of English.

Tchudi, S. (1986). Reading and writing as liberal arts. In B. T. Peterson (Ed.), *Convergences: Transactions in reading and writing* (pp. 246–259). Urbana, IL: National Council of Teachers of English.

Tierney, R. J., & Leys, M. (1986). What is the value of connecting reading and writing? In B. T. Peterson (Ed.), *Convergences: Transactions in reading and writing* (pp. 15–29). Urbana, IL: National Council of Teachers of English.

Uttero, D. (1989). Reading, writing, and cooperation: A dynamic interaction. *New England Reading Association, 25,* 2–7.

Wilson, A. (1983). The study of literature and the development of standard English proficiency. *Writing Instructor, 2,* 115–121.

CHAPTER

5

The Language Connection

*T*he previous chapter noted the extreme importance of the reading-writing connection. We maintain that the language connection is important as well. As teachers strive for an integrated curriculum, using young adult literature to note and study the particular language choices made by young adult authors moves this educational theory closer to an educational reality. Often, little is done with the study of the English language, partly because teachers do not have confidence in the subject matter and partly because of a traditional view that English language teaching means the teaching of formal English grammar. As a result, students often do not enjoy the excitement that can come from a study of various linguistic topics. The beauty of connecting this linguistic study to young adult literature is that students experience how their language works—not through dull, boring worksheets, but through the excitement that can only be found in reading.

It is important that this connection does not turn into a practice similar to dull worksheets that kill both the enthusiasm that can come from language study and the excitement about the literature that the students are finally able to enjoy. As suggested in Chapter 3, teachers must have students work with the material they read with all of the strategies and techniques that we have come to use when asking readers to respond to a piece of literature. It is after the response—after the joy and excitement of reading and reacting to what is read—that teachers and students take note of the writer's craft. Just as students investigated the use of the simile, the metaphor, or the strategy used in the beginning of a piece when looking at particular tools of writing, they will do the same with language study.

The topics are quite broad. We hope that students and teachers will explore the nature of the English language itself. How have young adult authors used words effectively? To what extent do they use slang? Colloquial expressions? Is there a variety of sentence patterns? Students and teachers should also explore the effective use of dialects. How have authors creatively and honestly used social and geographic dialects to help achieve their effect in writing a particular work?

An investigation into the use of language manipulation would interest students. An exploration of how characters relate to each other—how they converse with each other to manipulate each other's thoughts and actions—might offer the right source for study before investigating how this process occurs in their own world.

Young adult literature also provides a source for a historical perspective. How is English used in novels with characters from different cultures? To what extent has English borrowed terms and expressions from other languages?

The last area for consideration is nonverbal communication. How do the characters communicate without using words? What effects can be achieved through nonverbal communication? A study of these areas provides students with realistic settings in which to observe others using language devices or strategies. Because language is observed in this way, it becomes alive and has much more meaning for students than in the traditional approaches to language study. If done appropriately, it takes nothing away from the enjoyment of reading young adult literature, but, in fact, adds to the pleasure by placing some importance on the author's craft.

The Nature of English

Authors use colorful language to make their writing interesting. They use just the right word to convey just the right image. Like painters, they color and shade their writing so that the reader can imagine the scene. For example, in *The Devil's Arithmetic,* Yolen (1990) writes the following:

> She and Shifre were set to work with Rivka in the kitchen hauling water in large buckets from the pump, spooning out the meager meals, washing the giant cauldrons in which the soup cooked, scrubbing the walls and floors. It was hard work, harder than Hannah could ever remember doing. Her hands and knees held no memory of such work. It was endless. And repetitive. But it was not without its rewards. Occasionally they were able to scrape out an extra bit of food for themselves and the little ones while cleaning the pots, burned pieces of potatoes that had stuck to the bottom. Even burned pieces tasted wonderful, better even than beef. She thought she remembered beef. (p. 125)

> *Learn to use language. It doesn't matter how good a story you have to tell is, if you don't have the tools to tell it, you'll be the only one reading it.*
>
> Chris Crutcher

Changing Times (Kennemore, 1984), a British work, tells a unique story about the growth of a 15-year-old girl named Victoria Hadley. Kennemore plays a bit with time travel. Victoria is able to move throughout time by setting the hands of her clock. The novel offers, in both dialogue and narration, a descriptive and vibrant use of language. In describing Mr. Priestly, Victoria states: "He's a revolting disgusting decomposing tail end of a toad's turd. He stinks" (p. 11). Kennemore uses the same vivid language when narrating the story:

> The sound of the alarm was like a pneumatic drill boring into Victoria's brain. She shouted three words at it, all of them obscene in varying degrees, and tried, as usual, to go back to sleep. But there was a noise, an insistent repetitive noise that just shouldn't have been there; try though she might, she couldn't ignore it. Reluctantly she unburied herself, and hazily, through lingering layers of sleep, the truth clicked into place. Her clock was ticking. (p. 24)

Dark Waters (2003), set in the Scottish lochs, provides language that often is different from what students are reading in American schools. Words such as *daft, bruv, Mam, slaggin, keeker, chippie, loch,* and *rucksack* are found throughout.

In *Chinese Handcuffs*, Crutcher (1989) uses language effectively. He describes Mrs. Crummet's cat as

> a three-legged alley Tom with a face like a dried-up creek bed and the temperament of a freeway sniper. Mean cats call Charlie mean. He chewed that other leg off extracting himself from a muskrat trap, and he's utterly willing to let anyone, man or beast, know that experience left him feelin' right poorly toward the world and every living thing in it. (p. 9)

Instead of Dillon saying "this may be long" in reference to a letter he is writing, he says, "This may be a P.S. worthy of perusal by Guinness, and it's late" (p. 17). And instead of saying "spending money," Dillon says, "He knew he'd probably drop a couple of Abe Lincolns or maybe even an Andrew Jackson on bets" (p. 52).

Crutcher shows his flair for language when he describes Dillon's removal from school: "The Nobel Prize for that little theory was a three-day vacation, do not pass Go, do not collect your lunch ticket" (p. 75). The word choice is also interesting in the following passage:

> shoving a plastic bowl under running water in a semivaliant attempt to wash out the SuperBond-like remains of yesterday's granola. He chiseled small bits loose with the handle of a spoon, semiseriously rinsed the bowl again, and filled it to the edges . . . carrying it carefully to the table so as not to break the scientific seal restraining the milk from overflow. (p. 140)

In *The Outcasts of 19 Schuyler Place* (2004), E. L. Konigsburg, too, uses vivid language:

> "I want a refund from Camp Talequa."
> He laughed. "I think your uncle and my mother already settled that between them. Tillie Kaplan does not give refunds."

"I need a refund. Really, really need it."

Putting his pencil behind his ear, he crossed his arms over his chest and said, "Margaret Rose, I really, really hate to tell you this, but the last two people to get a refund from Camp Talequa were the parents of the girl who came down with Lyme disease the second day of camp. They blamed the deer ticks in the woods near the camp even though no one had been near the woods and even though the girl's symptoms could not possibly have shown up that fast. But these were not ordinary parents. They were lawyers. Both of them. They sent Tillie a letter on cream-colored, heavy-bond stationery that was just one step short of parchment. They politely requested a refund of their full deposit. They didn't even threaten to sue—they didn't need to—their letterhead said enough. They got a check by return mail."

"You mean that lawyers can scare even Mrs. Kaplan?"

"Tillie Kaplan would rather risk bungee jumping off the Verrazano Bridge than risk a lawsuit from a husband-and-wife team of lawyers with killer stationery." (pp. 199–200)

In *Taming the Star Runner,* Hinton (1988) uses repetition: "Christopher was the roundest person Travis had ever seen. His chubby face was round. His big eyes were round. His blond haircut was round. His chunky little legs and arms were round" (p. 52). Hinton also incorporates a few slang terms or phrases. Travis says, "What'd Casey do?" Jennifer answers, "Came out and gave me a leg up" (pp. 42–43). Also, when Ken is talking to Travis, he says, "Your mom was a real sweet girl. Pretty, too. She thought Tim hung the moon" (p. 57). And again, when referring to drinking: "Well, yeah, but I can usually hold it pretty good. I can usually put everybody under the table" (p. 99).

Hinton also creates new words, or at least uses words in a slightly different way. Travis's friends are "all those hoody friends" (p. 13). Hinton characterizes sound: "After a while, Travis went to spit in the bug zapper to hear it zit" (p. 39), and "He [Travis] watched the gray horse thunder down the pasture road, clear the gate, and disappear over the ridge" (p. 64). Travis describes his perceptions of what the girls whom he was drinking with thought of him, since he had to go to the bathroom often: "They probably thought he was tooting up or had the world's weakest bladder" (p. 75). When Travis takes a break from the revisions he has been working on, he looks out the window and observes, "There was the Realtor, in her navy suit and plasticized hair, showing someone around the property" (p. 179).

Teachers may want to use *Memory Boy* (Weaver, 2001) to investigate the use of powerful action words used in the narrative:

"You listen to me. I want you all to step off that crazy vehicle," the leader said. The others nodded.

"So much for traveling in broad daylight," I muttered.

The hijackers dismounted and pulled narrow wooden clubs from their rifle scabbards. At least there weren't real guns.

"Step aside," the leader said.

We obeyed.

Just as the gang was about to ransack the *Princess*—like in an old cowboy movie—the sheriff arrived. Not really the sheriff, but a single green humvee with its headlights on.

"Shit!" the leader said. The gang whirled around to look at the humvee. In one motion they leaped onto their little iron horses and cranked the engines. Within seconds they lurched forward and roared up the bank and into the trees. Their dust hung in the air. (pp. 104–105)

After discussing the use of this passage and many others in that book, teachers can have students write a short piece using active, specific verbs rather than overused verbs.

> *There's a magic in words and language and once you discover that, just like Aladdin's magic carpet, you can fly anywhere—the past, the future, or to worlds unknown.*
>
> Sharon Draper

Throughout *Dicey's Song*, Voigt (1982) creates beautiful imagery. Dicey's classroom is very hot, and she looks out the window to see "their leaves drooped down, dis-spirited by the heat. Like dogs' tongues, Dicey thought, and pictured the tree panting with many tiny tongues, maybe even dripping saliva the way a dog's would" (p. 21). Dicey "unrolled the adventures of the summer out, like ribbons. The ribbons unrolled back until Dicey saw her momma's face" (p. 16). Voigt uses language to describe the land, water, and all of nature—particularly the sky and the sun: "The growing darkness turned the sky to the color of blueberries, and long clouds floated gray. Just a band of burning orange was left from the sunset, but the water caught that and transformed it, lying before Dicey like a field of gold. Like a cloth of gold" (p. 16).

Questions often arise in class discussions about characters found in literature and how they are portrayed by the authors. What techniques do the authors use to convey just how they want those characters to be seen? The language they use is often the telling element, and the reader uses this language to help form some type of mental image of each character. Chris Crutcher, the master of word choice, gives the reader an insight about Rick Marshall in *Whale Talk* (2001):

"I say I'm pretty familiar with the way Rich Marshall operates."

"You think you are, but this is completely different from him shooting that deer. That was just mean. When he's in this spot, he's desperate, which means he imagines things, like you sleeping with Alicia. When he talks like that, he isn't telling you what he thinks, he's telling you what he fears. One thing you want to know about Rich Marshall is this: In his mind, what he fears is his worst enemy. Anything that makes Rich Marshall feel weak will bring him at you like a devil. At that point, it isn't about whether you can whip him, it's about whether you see him coming." (p. 127)

Walter Dean Myers, in his book *Slam* (1996), grabs the reader's attention immediately in the opening paragraph. Choosing the right word or words is very important to convey what the author has in mind for the character. Slam's voice—his thumbprint, his identity—comes through loud and clear. The reader has a clear understanding of who he thinks he is:

Basketball is my thing. I can hoop. Case closed. I'm six four and I got the moves, the eye and the heart. You can take my game to the bank and wait around for the interest. With me it's not like playing a game, it's like the only time I'm being for real. Bringing the ball down the court makes me feel like a bird that just learned to fly. I see my guys moving down in front of me and everything feels and looks right. . . . If somebody starts messing with my game it's like they're getting into my head. But if I've got the ball it's okay, because I can take care of the situation. That's the word and I know it the same way. I know my tag, Slam. Yeah, that's it. Slam. (p. 1)

The Dialect Question

In a society like the United States, language patterns are varied. An assortment of dialects are spoken and written daily. Geographic dialects form when the people of a certain region of the country speak and write in a particular way. In general, the United States has three dialect regions: northern, southern, and midland. Within each of these general regions, there are many dialect pockets (Bushman, 2000). In addition to the geographic dialects, many people speak a social dialect. Taylor (1985) cites eight American social, variant dialects: Appalachian English, Athabascan English (Alaska), Black English vernacular, general American nonstandard English, Keaukaha English (Hawaii), New York City nonstandard English, southern American nonstandard English, and Spanish-influenced English. We believe that students and teachers should be informed about dialects, whether they are regional dialects or social, variant dialects. For example, knowing about African American Variant English (AAVE) and the various regional dialects will give both teachers and students a better understanding and appreciation of the English language. One effective way to meet that objective is through the literature that young people read. Authors often use vocabulary, idioms, syntax, and a general style in their writing to reflect the culture and society about which they are writing.

The following excerpt is from *To Kill a Mockingbird* (Lee, 1960/1988), a novel widely read in secondary schools, although not frequently classified as young adult. Teachers can use this section to show the AAVE in general and also an attitude toward language in particular—an attitude that should be discussed in every classroom.

"That's why you don't talk like the rest of 'em," said Jem.

"The rest of who?"

"Rest of the colored folks," Cal. "But you talked like they did in church."

That Calpurnia led a modest double life never dawned on me. The idea that she had a separate existence outside our household was a novel one, to say nothing of her having command of two languages.

"Cal," I asked, "why do you talk nigger-talk to the—to your folks when you know it's not right?"

"Well, in the first place I'm black—"

"That doesn't mean you hafta talk that way when you know better," said Jem.

Calpurnia tilted her hat and scratched her head, then pressed her hat down carefully over her ears.

"It's right hard to say," she said. "Supposed you and Scout talked colored-folks' talk at home—it'd be out of place, wouldn't it? Now what if I talked white-folks' talk at church, and with my neighbors? They'd think I was puttin' on airs to beat Moses."

"But Cal, you know better," I said.

"It's not necessary to tell all you know. It's not lady-like—in the second place, folks don't like to have somebody around knowin' more than they do. It aggravates 'em. You're not gonna change any of them by talkin' right, they've got to want to learn themselves, and when they don't want to learn there's nothing you can do but keep your mouth shut or talk their language." (p. 128)

Another sequence of dialogue, between Huck and Jim in *The Adventures of Huck-leberry Finn* (Twain, 1885/1999), centers on a similar discussion about language and its use. Parts of the novel are not consistent with what we call a young adult novel, but it is read by many young adults and is certainly taught in many English classrooms. This passage, along with the one from *To Kill a Mockingbird,* can lead to an interest-ing class discussion.

"Why, Huck, doan' de French people talk de same way we does?"

"No, Jim, you couldn't understand a word they said—not a single word."

"Well, now, I be ding-busted! How do dat come?"

"I don't know, but it's so. I got some of their jabber out of a book. S'pose a man was to come to you and say Polly-voo-franzy—what would you think?"

"I wouldn't think nuffin, I'd take en bust him over de head. I wouldn't 'low no-body to call me dat."

"Shucks, it ain't calling you anything. It's only saying, do you know how to talk French?"

"Well, den, why couldn't he say it?"

"Why, he is a-saying it. That's a Frenchman's way of saying it."

"Well, it's a blame' ridicklous way, en I doan' want to hear no mo' 'bout it. Dey ain' no sense in it."

"Looky here, Jim, does a cat talk like we do?"

"No, a cat don't."

"Well, does a cow?"

"No, a cow don't nuther."

"Does a cat talk like a cow, or a cow talk like a cat?"

"No, dey don't."

"It's natural and right for 'em to talk different from each other, ain't it?"

"Course."

"And ain't it natural and right for a cat and a cow to talk different from us?"

"Why, mos' sholy it is."

"Well, then, why ain't it natural and right for a Frenchman to talk different from us? You answer me that."

"Is a cat a man, Huck?"

"No."

"Well, den, dey ain't no sense in a cat talkin' like a man. Is a cow a man?—er is a cow a cat?"

"No, she ain't either of them."

"Well, den she ain't got no business to talk like either one er yuther of 'em. Is a Frenchman a man?"

"Yes."

"Well, den! Dad blame it, why doan' he talk like a man? You answer me dat!" (pp. 135–137)

Another piece of literature that is appropriate to use to study language and dialects is the short story "Who Said We All Have to Talk Alike?" (McDaniel, 1985). Even though it was not specifically written for young adults, it will contribute much to the study of tolerance and understanding of someone's dialect and idiolect.

Neffie Pike, the main character, is 51 and a widow. She has spent her entire life in the Ozark Mountains. She decides to take a job in California as a nanny, but she soon returns and tells her story about the discrimination based on her dialect. She added an *r* to many words that did not contain that letter, and she has a rather colorful vocabulary. Her word for toilet was *torelet,* and *worman* for women. The family for whom she worked could not accept Neffie because of her language. A discussion of Neffie, her language and background, and the family's attitude toward her would help students in their understanding of society and its attitude toward diversity in language and people.

African American Variant English (AAVE)

AAVE is a broad topic for discussion in classrooms. A description of the dialect, its characteristics, its history, and its use in America is necessary to meet the needs and interests of our diverse society. After some study of the dialect, teachers and students can investigate how authors have used the dialect in their writing. When it is used, it is often found in the dialogue of the characters. Students will find it interesting that authors are not consistent in their use of dialect. Teachers will want to have students investigate this dialect use in the novels they read.

Teachers may want to secure more background and develop a knowledge base that will help students as they investigate this dialect. Briefly, AAVE, like all dialects, has regular rule-governed obligatory features. Recent linguistic research in this area indicates five systematic differences between AAVE and standard English: optional copula deletion, negative concord, invariant be, dummy it, and negative inversion (DeStefano, 1973). The first three are most prevalent in the literature.

Several young adult books include the use of the optional copula deletion: In their dialogue, characters omit the be form of the verb. For example, in *The Secret of Gumbo Grove* (Tate, 1987), Raisin talks with Bunny Walterboro. Bunny says, "She say she tired of your mouth! I told her she better quit talking about my friend 'cause you don't take no mess. That's when she said she was gonna beat—" (p. 27). Later, when Bunny is trying to get Raisin to go to the disco, she says, "Girl, we missin' everything. They jammin' at the school yard. Can't you hear that music?" (p. 28). Again, at the dance, Cracker's voice rolls out over the speaker: "You messin' up my dance, Big Boy. Leave them little sisters alone" (p. 30).

In *Scorpions,* Myers (1988) also uses the copula deletion. In a dialogue between Jamal and Mama, Jamal makes reference to a pigeon that has just landed on the window ledge: "He don't even know we here" (p. 11). A moment later, Mama asks Jamal, "So what you going to do?" (p. 12). This structure is found throughout the novel: "Then why Randy want Mack to tell you who to look out for?" (p. 12). "Jamal Hicks, you lying" (p. 12). "'He my ace,' Randy used to say" (p. 13). "'You going to eat the corn flakes?' Jamal said" (p. 118). "'He lyin'.' 'You in the Scorpions?' Darness asked. 'Who you, the F.B.I.?' 'No, man, I'm Harlem Vice, I'm Harlem Vice, and we so bad we got to say it twice!'" (p. 119).

In *Won't Know Till I Get There* (Myers, 1988), Earl says, "'You a vandal'" (p. 19).

In *Rainbow Jordan* (Childress, 1981), Rainbow says, "'Truth is, what else is it but abandon when she walk out with a boyfriend, promise to come home soon, then don't show?'" (p. 7).

I Be Somebody (Irwin, 1984) is full of the copula deletion: "The thing is, Nimrod," Spicy said, "you talking cigars before tobacco's planted." "I talking sense, Spicy," he insisted. "We got to move. We ain't stay here. It never going to get better" (p. 1).

The negative concord, or double negative, is found throughout most literature that uses AAVE. In M. Taylor's *Let the Circle Be Unbroken* (1981), a short dialogue between Papa and Uncle Hammer illustrates:

> "Mary still upset with me 'bout Bud?" asked Uncle Hammer, adjusting his mirror.
>
> Papa slid the straight razor down the right side of his face, stripping away the soap lather. "She got a right to be, don't you think?" Uncle Hammer shrugged and began to lather. "Didn't say nothin' but the truth."
>
> "Thought you wasn't gonna say nothin' at all." (p. 156)

Myers uses the structure in *Scorpions*:

> "I know it ain't real."
>
> "The Scorpions don't have no fake guns," Jamal said.
>
> "You ain't no Scorpions." (p. 106)

This feature is also found in the novel *I Be Somebody.*

The invariant be is a third feature commonly found in the AAVE. Without the be, the speaker or writer is expressing a momentary condition. With the be, the speaker or writer is expressing a recurrent action or state. In *Scorpions,* Mama indicates that Jamal will survive over a period of time: "'Mr. Gonzalez don't need nobody [negative concord] every day,' Mama said. 'Jamal be doing okay if he just help us out some'" (p. 123). And again,

> "That's a dollar seventy," Jamal said.
>
> "I got to tell Indian you working here," Blood said, putting two dollars on the counter. "He been looking for you."
>
> "What he looking for me for?"
>
> "You find out when he find your narrow butt." (p. 127)

Rainbow Jordan and *I Be Somebody* also include the invariant be construction. The latter novel even includes this structure in its title.

In *Born Blue* (2001), Leshaya is reflecting on her earlier years:

> My first memory of myself I be drowning. I can close my eyes and feel myself getting pushed back under all that heavy water, my legs kicking and straining for the sandy

bottom. Alls I find be more water rushing at me and over me, big walls of water hitting me whole and tossing me upside down, and I got no breath left, so I open my mouth and I swallow a gallon of salt water and choke, and more water get up my nose and burn in my head, and I go for a breath again, and the whole time I thinking, Mama's gonna be mad at me, Mama's gonna be mad. Then I ain't thinking nothin' and all the struggling stops, and I wake up in a dark room I know ain't mine. I think I be dead, but I scream, anyways, and a lady I never seen come in and holds me till daylight. (p. 1)

In *Slam,* Myers (1996) puts Slam in a confrontation with Mr. Parrish, his English teacher. In the dialogue, Slam uses the invariant construction and Mr. Parrish makes fun of it:

"So, Mr. Harris [Slam], just why are you taking up classroom space?" he was standing over me. "Why don't you just go out to your neighborhood and find a corner to stand on? That's what you want from life, isn't it?"
   "Don't be standing over me, man," I said.
   "Don't be standing over me?" he raised his voice. "Is that directly from your African background? Maybe from the We-Be tribe?" (p. 216)

Other characteristics of the AAVE include lack of the possessive marker, lack of the plural suffix, endings of words lost, the -ed suffix added to strong verbs, and the third-person singular inflection of the verb form deleted (Baratz & Baratz, 1969). Many examples of these characteristics may be found in all of the works of literature mentioned in this section, as well as in *Do Lord, Remember Me* (Lester, 1984), *A Gathering of Old Men* (Gaines, 1983), *Mote* (Reaver, 1990), *A Hero Ain't Nothin' but a Sandwich* (Childress, 1973), and *Cast Two Shadows* (Rinaldi, 1998). Interestingly, in *Mote,* AAVE is discussed quite openly between Billy and the detective, Stienert.

In addition to discussing the dialect that they find in their reading, students should also discuss why they think authors would choose not to use the dialect. For example, there seems to be very little, if any, AAVE used in *Teacup Full of Roses* (Mathis, 1972), *Durango Street* (Bonham, 1965), *Words by Heart* (Sebestyen, 1981), *Hoops* (Myers, 1981), *A Little Love* (Hamilton, 1984), or *M. C. Higgins, The Great* (Hamilton, 1974), although the characters are Black, and there seems to be no indication that the characters have adopted the standard American dialect.

Geographic Dialects

Regional dialects may be a little more difficult to find in literature. Generally, dialects are more obvious in the oral tradition; however, we do find some examples through vocabulary and syntax. Sometimes authors show the readers what the words or word combinations would sound like through clipping of words and variant spellings. On rare occasions, the main character tells the reader just how the language is used in the setting of the novel. A case in point is when Wil tells how people use English in Cold Sassy (*Cold Sassy Tree,* Burns, 1984):

> You need to understand that in Cold Sassy when the word *aunt* is followed by a name, it's pronounced *aint,* as in Aint Loma or Aint Carrie. We also say *dubya* for the letter *w, sump'n* for *something, idn'* for *isn't, dudn'* for *doesn't, raig'n* for *reckon, chim'ly* for *chimney, wrench* for *rinse, sut* for *soot,* as in train or chim'ly sut, and *like* for *lack,* as in "Do you like much of bein' th'ew?" Well, I know that how we speak is part of what we are. I sure don't want Cold Sassy folks to sound like a bunch of Yankees. But I don't want us to sound ignorant, either, and pronunciations like *sump'n* and *idn'* sound ignorant. So I'm trying to remember not to use such—except right now to tell how Loma became Aint Loma. (p. 104)

Carol Otis Hurst and Rebecca Otis (2003) set their historical novel, *A Killing in Plymouth Colony,* in Massachusetts in 1630. As a result readers experience many language choices of the times: *aye, thine, thou, porridge, thy, thee.* A brief passage illustrates:

> "Aye, on the *Anne,*" she agreed.
> "Was the voyage rough?"
> "It was rough. Like thine, I suppose."
> "Were thou sick?" John asked, remembering his own miserable days at sea.
> "Oh, my! I was sick for days."
> "And when thou landed here, did Father come to greet thee?" He kept his eyes directly on his stepmother's, trying to gauge whether or not she told the truth.
> She nodded. "He did."
> "And was he glad to see thee? Did he take thy hand? Did he hug thee? Kiss thee?" (p. 75)

A study of S. E. Bridgers's young adult literature helps readers to come to some generalizations concerning southern literature. Carroll (1990), who thoroughly studied Bridgers's novels, believes "language becomes an important means by which southern distinctions are illuminated" (p. 11). Carroll goes on to state that "particularly effective in *Sara Will* (1985) is Bridgers's use of three elements of southern language: (1) names and phrases that ring true to the southern ear, (2) the tradition of story telling, and (3) reliance on concrete details drawn from the natural world" (p. 11).

Permanent Connections (Bridgers, 1987) is ripe with southern dialect, which is quite evident in the speech of Fairlee, Coralee, and Grandpa. Fairlee reminisces about his sister when he explains to Rob: "She's always had a hankering for rings and bracelets and earbobs and the like" (p. 86). Carroll goes on to show how Grandpa fits into the oratorical tradition, moral absolutes, and the southern Appalachian dialect, all characteristic of southern literature.

Robert Cormier's books take place around the north central section of Massachusetts, specifically the town of Leominster, Cormier's birthplace. Cormier captures the flavor of the small community in Monument, the setting for *The Chocolate War* (1974), *Beyond the Chocolate War* (1985), and other Cormier literature: "It's a thinly disguised Leominster, I suppose—the spirit of the city rather than the actual place. I've changed the name and everything and I've moved the streets around but it's the same. Yes, I'm lucky that I've got that place—that I can take a ride down to Frenchtown anytime and there it is" (Sutton, 1991, p. 31).

Both Monument and Frenchtown are important settings in *Fade* (1988), *Other Bells for Us to Ring* (1990), *Heroes* (1998), and *The Rag and Bone Shop* (2001). Cormier writes in *Fade*: "The family had settled down in Frenchtown on the east side of Monument in Massachusetts along with hundreds of other French Canadians, living in the three-decker tenements and two-story houses" (p. 4). On each of those three-decker tenements is a piazza—a term for porch used in this region of the country. The term *piazza* is used throughout the novel. In *Heroes*, Cormier writes: "Three days later, Marie and Nicole again passed time together on the piazza above mine" (p. 17).

This New England flavor is also felt in the rural areas of Vermont in the superbly rich and moving novel *A Day No Pigs Would Die* (R. N. Peck, 1972). The novel portrays the adventures of Peck's childhood. The setting is rural Vermont, and the language reflects that setting:

> Whatever old Apron decided that I was doing to her back yonder, she didn't take kindly to it. So she started off again with me in the rear, hanging on to wait Christmas, and my own bare butt and privates catching a thorn with every step. (p. 9)

> Somebody told me once that a cow won't bite. That somebody is as wrong as sin on Sunday. (p. 11)

> "We're beholding to you, Benjamin Tanner," said Papa, "for fetching him home. Whatever he done, I'll make it right." (p. 14)

> "Best I be going," I said. "Thank you for the ginger snaps and the buttermilk." "You're more than welcome, Rob," said Mrs. Bascom. "Anytime you come this way, be sure to stop for a how do." (p. 82)

Regional dialects play an important part in the author's craft. Certainly, if the reader could hear the words spoken, the dialect would be even more profound. As it is, the author relies on word choice and expression to convey that added dimension to the work. Students, as they read young adult literature, can note the dialect that authors use.

> *Rewriting is a blessing for a writer. The brain surgeon must do it right the first time—a writer can do it over and over, until he or she gets it right.*
>
> Robert Cormier

Language Manipulation

The use of language to move people to action or to think in a particular way pervades the American culture and quite often targets young people. Adolescents are asked almost daily to buy this product, to act in this particular way, or to accept this point of view. Certainly, activities in the curriculum will share the dangers of blindly accepting

these manipulative devices. Teachers may also find ways of presenting the use of manipulative language—euphemisms, doublespeak—through young adult literature.
What language devices do characters use on each other to get others to act and think
in a particular way? Young people can study this use of language as they read.

Certainly, Cormier's works come to mind as one thinks of this study. In *The
Chocolate War* (1974), how does Archie control his Vigils? What language techniques
does he use to make them believe in particular ways? The strategies of Brother Leon
alone would fill a classroom discussion. Other Cormier novels provoke similar discussions: *After the First Death* (1979), *I Am the Cheese* (1977), *The Bumblebee Flies Anyway* (1983), and *Fade* (1988).

Rescue: The Story of How Gentiles Saved Jews in the Holocaust (Meltzer, 1988), a
nonfictional account of the many self-sacrificing people who risked their lives to hide
the Jews from the Nazi forces in Europe, effectively shows how powerful, emotional
language can be used for propaganda. Students can discuss the following statements
that illustrate this emotional, propagandized language:

> Good Jews? Bad Jews? What difference does it make? All Jews are considered the same.
> Even the baptized and assimilated Jew is worthless to the anti-Semite. It is no longer
> a question of religion. The Jews' race, their blood condemns them. (p. 5)

> A Gentile Polish teenaged girl is quoted as saying, "Oh, I hate them! The Jews are
> horrible! They are dirty thieves. They cheat everybody. Jews are a real menace. For
> Passover they catch Christian children, murder them, and use their blood for matzo."
> (p. 34)

Meltzer's nonfictional book is a source of euphemistic language. Students can find examples similar to those cited in the following (emphasis added). They can also explain
the real meaning of those words.

> Oskar's subcamp would be closed, too, and the prisoners would go back to Plaszow,
> to await *relocation*. (p. 63)

> The Germans declared martial law and took direct control of the government. Hitler's
> *experts* on the *final solution* arrived to plan the deportation to the death camps. (p. 90)

> No letters of safe conduct or foreign passports for Hungarian Jews from whatever
> source would permit Jews to escape the *solution to the Jewish problem*. (p. 110)

Additional language manipulation can be found in *Milkweed* (2003), a historical fiction story set in the Nazi-occupied city of Warsaw. Readers experience firsthand
through the eyes of a young boy who lives in the streets of Warsaw the life of the in-
habitants of this Nazi-controlled city. But he has very little sense of what is going on.
He actually wants to be a Nazi someday, so that he can wear the tall, shiny jackboots
and a gleaming eagle hat of his own. Readers will want to examine the language of the
oppressed, the language of cruelty, the language of heartbreak, hope, and survival.

After (Prose, 2003), certainly a very traumatic novel, is a ripe source for manipulative language. Students should talk about the language the characters use. There is

clear evidence that the characters manipulate each other, persuading each other to do something they may not want to do by using certain words or phrases or by saying words in certain ways. It is clear that Dr. Willner, through his choice of words, makes every attempt to get the students and teachers at Central to do what he wants them to do. For example, when addressing students about appropriate dress, he says: "I trust the faculty is making notes on those students who apparently feel compelled to express their opinions on a subject about which no opinions are needed" (p. 37). And again, when Silas and his mom and dad are brought to Dr. Willner because authorities found a Mexican hash pipe:

> "All too well, my man," said Avery. "We know that pipe all too well."
>
> "Well, the hard thing was convincing them I didn't know it was a pipe. I kept saying I thought it was some kind of Aztec ritual object. I said I bought it on the eighth grade class trip to the science museum in Boston. Nobody went for it, really. Dr. Willner sniffed the pipe and made a face and said he doubted it smelled that way when—and if—I bought it at the science museum."
>
> "My dad said, 'Are you accusing my son of lying?'
>
> "And Dr. Willner said, 'Not exactly,' in this icy Dracula voice that was so . . . so threatening that even my dad shut up. Which was totally demoralizing. I mean, I'd always assumed that when it came right down to it, my parents would stick up for me, no matter what." (p. 117)

Most of the young adult novels that students are reading lend themselves to the study of euphemisms and manipulative language: literature such as *Double Dutch* (Draper, 2002), *The Battle of Jericho* (Draper, 2003), *Friction* (Frank, 2003), *The True Meaning of Cleavage* (Fredericks, 2003), *The Insiders* (Minter, 2004), *Drowning Anna* (Mayfield, 2001), *Keeping You a Secret* (Peters, 2003), *America* (Frank, 2002), and *You Don't Know Me* (Klass, 2001).

> *Read a lot, and notice when a writer manipulates you.*
> Bruce Brooks

A Historical Perspective

American English has often been called the "cosmopolitan language" because it has borrowed so much from so many languages that it includes a little of almost every language. As students read, they may be aware of words that have been borrowed from other languages. Recognizing such words is easier if students have studied the history of the English language, even in its most elementary form. This investigation may just happen as students who have some knowledge of language history read the words on the printed page. In fact, students may want to read novels with characters who use English that is influenced by another language.

Park's Quest (Paterson, 1988) offers students language study in at least two different ways: the English spoken by a nonnative speaker and the English spoken by native speakers long ago. Thanh, a Vietnamese woman, uses what we have come to call "broken English." She leaves parts of the discourse out, which is consistent with her native language but not with English speaking. Thanh says to Park: "'Come out where I see you,' she ordered, stepping aside, confident that he would obey. He did, blinking in the bright sunshine. 'I never see you,' she said. 'What you name?'" (p. 57).

Also in *Park's Quest*, Paterson alludes to the Arthurian legend. Park is on a quest in search of knowledge about his father, as King Arthur and his knights went on quests. As Park dreams of these long-ago quests, he slips into the language of the day. "'Faugh! You are no knight!' the lady cried in disgust. 'You are naught but a kitchen scullion, smelling of garlic and grease. How dare you to presume to be my champion? Dismount fool, and stand aside, lest the Black Knight skewer you on his spear and roast you in the everlasting flames!'" (p. 5).

Students can easily find words with which they are not familiar. They could also discuss the structure of the discourse, giving particular attention to the flair apparent in the language. Some students may want to pursue the investigation further by identifying other characteristics of Middle English.

Kennemore's *Changing Times* (1984) also can be used to study language because it has a British flavor. The American reader may not entirely understand a comment such as "The day you faint'll be the day I win Crufts" (p. 47), but with a little investigation, one can assume that Crufts is some kind of race. Readers may want to study English vocabulary further to find out exactly what Crufts is. The slang used in *Changing Times* is also British in its origin; *blimey* and *bloody* are used frequently. As noted previously, *Dark Waters* (2003), a novel set in Scotland, may be useful to show students the variety of word choices.

As we think about how language changes over the years, we are aware of how words come into the language and how they sometimes disappear. Many of the personal pronouns used in the Puritan days have long since disappeared. Readers may contrast the language of *The Killing in Plymouth Colony* (2003) to language use today. The slang of today may become the standard language of tomorrow. It is interesting to note that words used in earlier times by various groups of people may not now be in use. The disappearance of certain words can be evidenced in the novel *The Sign of the Beaver* (Speare, 1983), the story of Matt, a 13-year-old Caucasian boy, and his relationship with Attean, an Indian boy. As students read this novel, they will invariably find words that are no longer in use: *puncheon tale* (p. 3), *oiled paper* for windows (p. 3), *blunderbuss* (p. 4), *matchlock* (p. 4), *hemlock boughs* for a bed (p. 10), and *boardcloth* (p. 125). Students may then want to ask their parents, grandparents, and much older friends to give examples of common words and phrases that they used when they were young that are not used today.

Teachers could also use *When the Legends Die* (Borland, 1963) to teach students about borrowing words from other languages. Many words that are now a part of the English language were borrowed from Native Americans. Examples include *moccasin, tomahawk, chipmunk,* and *squaw.* In addition to the Native American influence in the novel, the Spanish language is well represented. Words of Spanish origin include *canyon, cinch, rodeo, corral,* and *bronco.* Three additional books are appropriate for reading as students investigate the influence on the English language from other sources. Mary Peace Finly's Sante Fe Trail trilogy (*Soaring Eagle,* 1998; *White Grizzley,* 2000; and

Meadow Lark, 2003) tells of experiences along the Sante Fe Trail from Independence, Missouri, to Sante Fe, New Mexico, of Teresita Montoya and her brother Julio. The books are ripe with examples of the language used by the American settlers, the Mexican residents, and the indigenous Native American peoples.

Julie in *Julie of the Wolves* (George, 1972) expresses her feelings and values by first accepting and then rejecting the English language and then accepting it again at the end of the novel. Students can pinpoint these transitions and speculate on the values Julie believes to be "American" and the values she identifies as "Eskimo." Students with bilingual backgrounds could share how they feel about their first language and their adopted language. Additional language discussion occurs in other George books: *Julie* (1994), *Julie's Wolf Pack* (1997), *My Side of the Mountain* (1988), and *Frightful's Mountain* (1999).

Nonverbal Communication

> Since language is, phylogenetically, one of man's most distinctive characteristics, we sometimes slip into the error of thinking that all communication must be verbal communication . . . but the language of words is only a fragment of the language we use in communicating with each other. We talk with eyes and hands, with gestures, with our posture, with various motions of our body. (Halpin, 1970, p. 107)

Students are aware of how they communicate nonverbally with each other. They know the meaning of the smirk on the face or the raised eyebrow. They recognize the negative meaning that comes through tone of voice, even though the message may be positive. What better way to extend that understanding than to investigate how authors have their characters communicate nonverbally? Readers can note the subtle nonverbal communication that occurs between and among characters.

Here again, young adult literature serves us well. In Lowry's *Number the Stars* (1989), we can see how nonverbal language is used effectively. A few examples are in order: "Kristi clapped her hands in delight" (p. 34); "Ellen stood on tiptoe again, and made an imperious gesture with her arm" (p. 39); and "He made one hand into a fist, and he kept pounding it into the other hand. I remember the noise of it: slam, slam, slam" (p. 41). Students can use these passages and many others to talk about the feelings expressed. Students can explore the novel further to note the facial expressions on the soldiers, how the soldiers move, how they stand, and what messages are sent by these nonverbal communicators. Also in Will Hobbs's *Leaving Protection* (2004), readers can see the nonverbal communication that takes place. "I didn't look over my shoulder to see the scowl" (p. 120); "Torsen's eyes were wild and trained right on me" (p. 124); and "My heart was still thundering when I reached the open air. I took some deep breaths, feeling like I'd been stunned by a gaff club" (p. 125).

A discussion of the greater impact of nonverbal communication over spoken words is bound to occur. The issue of adaptations a writer must make to convey a meaning on paper instead of using oral or spoken delivery with gestures and facial expressions should bring up the importance of the descriptive language that Asher has used. Again, all of this language study must occur after students have made their personal response to what they have read. After this initial emotional response, students are more at ease with the in-depth investigation of these language topics.

Learning Log Responses

Why is it important for you to connect language study with literature in your classes?

Comment on the interaction between Jem and Calpurnia found on pages 120–121. What generalizations can you make about the language concept discussed, and how do they apply to your teaching?

References

Baratz, S., & Baratz, J. C. (1969). Negro ghetto children and urban education: A cultural solution. *Florida FL Reporter, 7*(1), 1–16.

Brooks, B. Poster. Ottawa, KS: The Writing Conference.

Bushman, J. H. (2000). *Teaching the English language* (2nd ed.). Springfield, IL: Charles C. Thomas.

Carroll, P. S. (1990). Southern literature for young adults: The novels of Sue Ellen Bridgers. *Alan Review, 18*(1), 10–13.

Cormier, R. Poster. Ottawa, KS: The Writing Conference.

Crutcher, C. Poster. Ottawa, KS: The Writing Conference.

DeStefano, J. (1973). *Language, society, and education: A profile of black English.* Worthington, OH: Charles A. Jones.

Draper, S. Poster. Ottawa, KS: The Writing Conference.

Halpin, A. W. (1970). Theory and research in administration. In J. W. Ketner (Ed.), *Interpersonal speech-communication* (pp. 177–190). Belmont, CA: Wadsworth.

Lee, H. (1960/1988). *To kill a mockingbird.* New York: Warner Books.

Sutton, R. (1991). "Kind of a funny dichotomy": A conversation with Robert Cormier. *School Library Journal, 37*(6), 28–33.

Taylor, O. (April, 1985). Standard English as a second dialect? *English Today* (ET2), pp. 9–12.

Twain, M. (1999). *The adventures of Huckleberry Finn.* New York: Aladdin Classics. (Original work published 1885)

6

Organizing the Literature

How to use young adult literature effectively confronts teachers as they plan their school year. For middle school teachers, one book for an entire class may be most effective; high school teachers, however, may find that they can place their students in groups of four or five, with each group working with a different book. Some will use a combination of these approaches (Figure 6.1). For reading outside of the class, students normally choose a book from an approved list. Discussion of each of these arrangements follows.

One Book, One Class

Traditionally, all students read the same work in class. Certainly, on the surface there seem to be many advantages to this arrangement. It is easier for teachers to plan for classroom activities because all students are supposed to start and stop at the same time. Teachers and students can discuss the issues presented in the pages read for the day's lesson. All students, then, are involved with the same issues and can learn from each other the differing points of view held.

In addition, after students finish their personal responses, they can more easily move to the analysis of the qualities of the literature. The entire class can examine

Approach	Instructional Purpose	Classroom Management
One book, one class	Attention given to issues presented in one work	Emphasis on large group
Novels arranged thematically	Attention given to issues from a variety of works; able to meet a variety of interests and ability levels	Emphasis on small groups with some large-group work
Thematic units	Attention given to a variety of literacy genres and skills	Emphasis on small and large groups
One book, one student	Attention given to the reading interest and ability of the individual student	Emphasis on the individual

FIGURE 6.1

Organizational approaches for using young adult literature in the classroom.

plots, analyze characters, and evaluate other literary aspects of the work. When teachers feel that the class has thoroughly examined the novel, they have students complete the process with a project, a piece of writing, or a test that evaluates the students' understanding of the book.

Some argue that this arrangement does not meet the needs of every student in the class. Experience tells us that not all students in any given class have the same reading interests and abilities. In fact, we've heard it said that the only similarity about a class of eighth graders is that they are called eighth graders. Some may be reading at the 5th-grade level; others may be at the 11th-grade reading level. All students are moving through the developmental stages—physical, emotional, moral, cognitive—at different speeds.

Consequently, teachers usually teach to the middle: They choose pieces of literature that will satisfy the majority, if not all, of the students. Often, however, those at the top of the class become bored, and those at the bottom can't keep up. These problems can be overcome somewhat by using groups within the class even though each group is working with the same novel. The activities can be changed to meet the needs of the specific groups. Teachers are having some success with this approach.

The books listed in Figure 6.2 can be used for the one book, one class approach. We have annotated a few of the books here and have included a longer, more comprehensive list in Appendix C. We hesitate to say that all these books will work for all students in every class. However, all of the books listed are quality literature and may be used for some classes.

Armageddon Summer, Jane Yolen and Bruce Coville (1998)
   Fourteen-year-old Marina and sixteen-year-old Jed accompany their parents'
   religious cult, the Believers, to await the end of the world atop a remote mountain.
   During this time, they try to decide what they themselves believe.

Burning Up, Caroline Cooney (1999)
   When a girl she had met at an inner-city church is murdered, 15-year-old Macey
   channels her grief into school project that leads her to uncover prejudice she had
   not imagined in her grandparents and their wealthy Connecticut community.

Catalyst, Laurie Halse Anderson (2002)
   Eighteen-year-old Kate, who sometimes chafes at being a preacher's daughter,
   finds herself losing control in senior year as she faces difficult neighbors and the
   possibility that she may not be accepted by the college of her choice.

The Chocolate War, Robert Cormier (1974)
   The struggle among Jerry, a Trinity High student who wants to take a stand;
   Archie, the leader of the Vigils, who wants to control; and Brother Leon, the
   headmaster of Trinity High, who wants his school to succeed at any cost causes
   conflict among the student body.

Dark Waters, Catherine MacPhail (2003)
   Col McCann becomes a local hero when he saves a boy from drowning; but when
   his older brother is suspected of a serious crime, Col must decide if he should be
   loyal to his family or tell the truth about what he saw while under water.

A Distant Enemy, Deb Vanasse (1997)
   Fourteen-year-old Joseph, part Yup'ik Eskimo and part White, struggles to
   maintain his people's ancient culture as the Western world encroaches on his
   Alaska village.

Down the Yukon, Will Hobbs (2001)
   In the wake of Dawson City's great fire of 1899, 16-year-old Jason and his
   girlfriend Jamie canoe the Yukon river across Alaska in an epic race from
   Canada's Klondike to the new gold fields at Cape Nome.

Driver's Ed, Caroline Cooney (1994)
   Three teenagers' lives are changed forever when they thoughtlessly steal a stop
   sign from a dangerous intersection and a young mother is killed in an automobile
   accident there.

Far North, Will Hobbs (1994)
   After the destruction of their floatplane, 16-year-old Gabe and his Dene friend,
   Raymond, struggle to survive a winter in the wilderness of the Northwest
   Territories.

The Giver, Lois Lowry (1993)
   Given his lifetime assignment at the Ceremony of Twelve, Jonas becomes the
   Receiver of Memories shared by only one other in his community and discovers
   the truth about the society in which he lives.

FIGURE 6.2
Representative literature for one book, one class reading.

Holes, Louis Sachar (1998)

As further evidence of his family's bad fortune, which they attribute to a curse on a distant relative, Stanley Yelnats is sent to a hellish correctional camp in the Texas desert where he finds his first real friend, a treasure, and a new sense of himself.

I Am the Cheese, Robert Cormier (1977)

Adam discovers that his family was placed in the Federal Witness Protection Program years ago, and now he is a victim of his father's enemies.

Jake Riley: Irreparably Damaged, R. F. Davis (2003)

The friendship between a boy recently released from reform school and the farm girl who lives next door angers the faculty at their school and leads to a dangerous confrontation.

Jason's Gold, Will Hobbs (1999)

When news of the discovery of gold in Canada's Yukon Territory in 1897 reaches 15-year-old Jason, he embarks on a 5,000-mile journey to strike it rich.

A Long Way from Chicago, Richard Peck (1998)

A boy recounts his annual summer trips to rural Illinois with his sister during the Great Depression to visit their larger-than-life grandmother.

The Maze, Will Hobbs (1998)

Rick, a 14-year-old foster child, escapes from a juvenile detention facility near Las Vegas and travels to Canyonlands National Park in Utah where he meets a bird biologist working on a project to reintroduce condors to the wild.

Memory Boy, Will Weaver (2001)

Sixteen-year-old Miles and his family must flee their Minneapolis home and begin a new life in the wilderness after a chain of cataclysmic volcanic explosions creates dangerous conditions in the city.

Milkweed, Jerry Spinelli (2003)

Readers are taken to one of the most devastating settings imaginable—Nazi-occupied Warsaw—and learn a tale of heartbreak, hope, and survival through the bright eyes of a young orphan.

Olive's Ocean, K. Henkes (2003)

On a summer visit to her grandmother's cottage by the ocean, 12-year-old Martha gains perspective on the death of a classmate, her relationship with her grandmother, her feelings for an older boy, and her plans to be a writer.

The Outcasts of 19 Schuyler Place, E. L. Konigsburg (2004)

Upon leaving an oppressive summer camp, 12-year-old Margaret Rose Kane spearheads a campaign to preserve three unique towers her great-uncles have been building in their backyard for more than 40 years.

Out of the Dust, Karen Hesse (1997)

Billi Jo tells her story in free verse as she survives tragedy and the loss of loved ones during the Great Depression and Dust Bowl in 1930s Oklahoma.

The River Between Us, Richard Peck (2003)

During the early days of the Civil War, the Pruitt family takes in two mysterious young women who have fled New Orleans to come north to Illinois.

FIGURE 6.2

Continued.

Reaching Dustin, Vicki Grove (1998)
   Fifth-grader Carly's assignment to interview a reclusive, brooding classmate leads her to discover some of the events that have caused his antisocial and abusive family's negative impact on their Missouri farming community and on Carly's family in particular.

Sang Spell, Phyllis Reynolds Naylor (1998)
   When his mother is killed in an automobile accident, high schooler Josh decides to hitchhike across the country and finds himself trapped in a mysterious village somewhere in the Appalachian Mountains, among a group of people who call themselves Melungeons.

Son of the Mob, Gordon Korman (2002)
   Vice Luca is just like any other high school guy except for one thing: His father happens to be the head of a powerful crime organization. And the conflict continues: Vince meets the girl he wants to date. The problem is that she is the daughter of an FBI agent.

Son of the Mob: Hollywood Hustle, Gordon Korman (2004)
   Vince Luca heads to California and leaves his shady family and their illegal antics. But soon, the family (at least some members) find Vince, and trouble starts all over again.

Steal Away Home, Lois Ruby (1994)
   In two parallel stories, a Quaker family from Kansas in the late 1850s operated a station on the Underground Railroad, while almost 150 years later, 12-year-old Dana moves into the same house and finds the skeleton of a black woman who helped the Quakers.

Under a Different Sky, Deborah Savage (1997)
   A boy with Olympic dreams and an extraordinary horse struggles to transcend his impoverished family background as he falls in love with the emotionally troubled daughter of a wealthy family.

A Year Down Yonder, Richard Peck (2000)
   During the recession of 1937, 15-year-old Mary Alice is sent to live with her feisty larger-than-life grandmother in rural Illinois and comes to a better understanding of this fearsome woman.

FIGURE 6.2
Continued.

Arranging Books Thematically

For teachers who believe that their class should not read one book, an alternative arrangement using themes can be very effective. If we believe in the diversity that comes with most classes, more than one book may be needed to meet the interests and abilities of the students. For example, some middle school teachers may want their students to read Cormier's *In the Middle of the Night* (1995) but feel that some students would not respond well to that book. These teachers could also choose Cooney's *The*

Terrorist (1997) or Duncan's *Gallows Hill* (1997) for the middle range of students and Hobbs's *Ghost Canoe* (1997) for those in the lower range. All books center on the mystery theme. Groups of eight or so students can read one of the three or four books, and then, because they are bound together with this central theme, students can discuss each book separately and in relationship to each other. Each group may spend time working separately with its book and then join the other groups for a general discussion. Each group may also do projects around its book and then present them to the entire class.

The important concern here is the attempt to meet the needs and abilities of all students and still keep an organization that the entire class can follow. One important benefit from such an approach is that all students read one book and hear about two or three others. Students may then choose to read these on their own at a later time. Figure 6.3 presents books that can be grouped around themes. We have also suggested the range of difficulty for each book: higher range, middle range, and lower range.

Thematic Units

A thematic arrangement of literature may be expanded into an effective curriculum design called thematic units. This design is more than just arranging three or four novels that are thematically related. The unit involves teaching all of the language arts: literature, oral and written English, and language. The emphasis is on integration of the skills and subject matter that are taught in the English classroom. It is much like the whole language approach found in many elementary classrooms. The theme—linguistic or social—is the glue that holds the unit together. The literature, the written and oral processes, and the language activities are centered in some way on the theme. Most thematic units are 6- to 18-week segments of the curriculum. It is important to note that the theme is the means and not the end. It is a vehicle for teaching the language arts.

The thematic unit is designed to emphasize the process of discovery, much like the reader-response approach in literature and the writing process. Students are able to spend their time more wisely, discovering what is important to them as they explore the investigatory topics that comprise the thematic units. With this approach, students are studying in a curriculum that is based on experience, involvement, and response—all of which are related in some way to the study of young adult literature. The literature for each thematic unit is not limited to novels. Although novels may provide the backbone for the unit, other literature, such as short stories, poems, and nonfiction, is included. Whatever literature is chosen, the emphasis is on the response that the student makes (i.e., the literature itself and its relationship to the reader). So often in other curriculum designs—chronology and genre—the emphasis is on historical and formal literary characteristics. With thematic units, students' primary goal is not to find out how a particular work fits into an overall historical survey nor to spend the majority of their time trying to delineate the formal characteristics of the work. (Is it a novel, short story, or poem?) It is important to note these characteristics in literature study, but they do not command primary attention. The attention is given to the

	Middle School	
High Range	**Middle Range**	**Lower Range**
Teen Pressure		
Drowning Anna (Mayfield, 2001)	Stargirl (Spinelli, 2000)	Double Dutch (Draper, 2002)
Friendships		
Wenny Has Wings (Carey, 2002)	Dangerous Skies (Staples, 1996)	Being Youngest (Heynen, 1997)
Prejudice		
Witness (Hesse, 2001)	North by Night: A Story of the Underground Railroad (Ayres, 1998)	Francie (English, 1999)
Strange and Eerie		
This Side of Paradise (Layne, 2001)	A Haunting in Williamsburg (Kassem, 1990)	Reef of Death (Zindel, 1998)
Survival		
Battle of Jericho (Draper, 2003)	Leaving Protection (Hobbs, 2004)	Blizzard's Wake (Naylor, 2002)
War		
Soldier's Heart (Paulsen, 1998)	Soldier Boys (Hughes, 2001)	Escape from Saigon (Warren, 2004)
	High School	
Victims		
America (Frank, 2002)	Blood on His Hands (Roberts, 2004)	Lena (Woodson, 1999)
Illness		
What Happened to Lani Garver? (Plum-Ucci, 2002)	Life in the Fat Lane (C. Bennett, 1998)	The Silent Boy (Lowry, 2003)
Love and Sexuality		
Dreamland (Dessen, 2000)	Speak (Anderson, 1999)	The True Meaning of Cleavage (Frederich, 2003)
Echoes from the Past		
Milkweed (Spinelli, 2003)	Surviving Hitler (Warren, 2001)	Mississippi Trial, 1955 (Crow, 2002)
Government Control		
After (Prose, 2003)	I Am the Cheese (Cormier, 1977)	The Giver (Lowry, 1993)
Unusual Circumstances		
Son of the Mob (Korman, 2002)	The Music of Dolphins (Hesse, 1996)	Bucking the Sarge (Curtis, 2004)

FIGURE 6.3

Literature arranged thematically for middle and high school.

work itself—what authors have to say and how they say it. In the thematic unit, the chronology may be there in the upper grades in high school, but the genre is there at all levels. By reading these various works, students can consider not only differing viewpoints but also how each author uses different genres to express thoughts on similar topics.

The writing that occurs in the thematic unit is much like the writing that occurs in any other curriculum design. Students use the process to arrive at some understanding of the chosen topic. The unit approach may offer one additional component: ideas about which to write. If the theme is relevant to the students' interests, it will provide many opportunities for students to engage in the writing experience. Students may respond to the literature in writing; they may also simply respond to the theme.

Because the thematic unit is designed to include all of the language arts, the language component is easily incorporated into the total unit. It matters little whether the theme is socially or linguistically oriented; a wealth of material exists for study in middle and high schools. Authors' use of dialect, particular word choice, sentence construction, use of euphemisms and doublespeak, and use of manipulative language provide students with ample material for study.

Oral communication is also an integral part of thematic unit planning. Teachers have long recognized the necessity and value of classroom discussion, but its quality has slipped until it is often nothing more than a dull recital of names, dates, and other facts. Even well-intentioned teachers may find that the open discussion session they have envisioned instead becomes the familiar tug of war as they try to pull answers out of unresponsive students. In most cases, these experiences lead to "teacher-talk," which requires students to function as sponges—soaking up information, which is then wrung out at exam time.

It doesn't have to be this way. The thematic unit approach uses speech and creative drama activities to show students the relationships among all the language arts. Group discussions, impromptu speeches, and interviewing are rewarding activities when linked to particular social or linguistic themes. Speech activities should evolve in response to reading, writing, and viewing. Creative drama helps to expand the boundaries of experience so that students may develop a more complete understanding of themselves, their work, and their relationships with other people. Drama is as effective with composition and language as it is with literature. It adds an exciting dimension to learning, and it helps to bring about the effective communication that we described earlier.

Improvisation and role-playing complement thematic units. Students can interpret themes and conflicts in literature by improvising parallel circumstances, or they can take characters from the work and place them in other situations through role-playing. Oral communication is a natural thread that runs not only through thematic units in teaching English but also through the entire educational experience. To teach speech and drama in a way that implies separation from other educational experiences is unfair and certainly unrealistic.

The "Thematic Units" boxes present two skeleton thematic units: one for middle school, created by Kristina Sestrich (Lathrop, Missouri), and one for high school, created by Rachel Buckley (Baldwin City High School, Kansas). They include objectives, materials, and a few representative activities.

Thematic Units

THEMATIC UNIT ON FRIENDSHIP FOR MIDDLE SCHOOL STUDENTS

Thematic Objectives

The student will
- Define the concept of friendship.
- Generate a list of qualities found in a friend.
- Investigate the importance of friendship in society.

Language Arts Objectives

The student will
- Develop confidence in his or her written and oral composition.
- Revise, edit, and proofread his or her own writing to make it clear and effective for the reader.
- Examine qualities of writing in others' work as well as his or her own.
- Identify language items or elements from selected literature that will demonstrate language change and variety.
- Participate in discussion leading toward a goal or solution.
- Describe the power of language found in various forms of communication.
- Identify figures of speech in literature and use those elements in their own writing.
- Come to a general understanding of the meaning of something read.
- Identify major traits of important fictional and nonfictional characters and analyze their influence on each other.

Materials

Novels
 Phoenix Rising, Karen Hesse (1994) (selected students: high level ability)
 Treasures in the Dust, Tracey Porter (1997) (selected students: middle level ability)
 Bridge to Terabithia, Katherine Paterson (1977) (selected students: low level ability)

Short Stories and Poetry
 "The Beginning of Something," Sue Ellen Bridgers (1987)
 "The Dreamer," William Childress (1990)
 "The Cave," Glein Dresbach (1990)
 "Pastures of Plenty," Woody Guthrie (1990)
 "Gone Away," Denise Levertov (1990)
 Very Best (Almost) Friends: Poems of Friendship, Paul Janeczko (1999)

Nonfiction
 Puppies, Dogs, and Blue Northers: Reflections on Being Raised by a Pack of Sled Dogs, Gary Paulsen (1996)
 My Life in Dog Years, Gary Paulsen (1998)
 Love Ya Like a Sister: A Story of Friendship, Julie Johnston (ed.) (1999)

Drama
 Little Old Ladies in Tennis Shoes, Sandra Fenichel Asher (1989)
 Large Fears, Little Demons, Dallin Malmgren (1990)

Activities (a representative selection; teachers will want to create others)

1. Have students brainstorm the term *friendship* by using the process of webbing. Then ask students to choose three qualities they admire most in a friend. Students will then find three examples from their respective novels that emphasize the qualities they have chosen. Afterward, have students begin a piece of writing in which they show how friendship is exemplified in their novel.

2. After reading each of their novels, have students create a biopoem (for example, see Figure 4.1) on one of the characters or the theme. Have them follow the biopoem with a character sketch. Students should take this sketch through the writing process, getting feedback from peer groups and finally finishing the writing into a polished product. Following is an example from *Phoenix Rising:*

   Nuclear
   Radiating, deadly, poisonous, infiltrating
   Son of power-hungry people
   Lover of escape, air, and unassuming people
   Who feels free, light, and crazy
   Who needs air to breathe, people to create, and a place to roam
   Who gives death, cancer, and illness
   Who fears entrapment, lack of war, and no more use for me
   Who would like to be endlessly free
   Resident of anywhere
   Explosion

3. To study effective use of language, have students bring in samples of friendship reported in newspapers. Have students examine the language used to describe the friend. Compare and contrast this use of language with that found in the literature. How does the point of view of the writer influence the message?

4. Have students identify imagery within their novels and use what they find in the literature to enhance their own writing. Following are examples from the novels:
   Bridge to Terabithia: "Entering the gallery was like stepping inside the pine grove." (p. 99) "but she gave him a look with those blue eyes of hers that made him zing like one of the strings she was strumming." (p. 30)
   Treasures in the Dust: "It drifts through our house like a ghost." (p. 2)
   "Where I see abandoned farms and half-buried tractors ruined by dust, she sees camel trains and oasis after oasis circled by palm trees." (p. 22)
   Phoenix Rising: "A stream of condensed moisture rained from the heavy lid, hitting the stove top and hissing." (p. 13)
   "I'd had too many bad dreams about that back bedroom. It had grown too black and hungry." (p. 12)

5. In addition to their novel, have students choose either a short story or a poem to compare and contrast with their novel. Students will utilize a graphic organizer (e.g., a Venn diagram) to do this activity. To help students understand the concept, have them compare cats and dogs using the Venn diagram. They should see that some characteristics are unique to cats and some unique to dogs, but some apply to both. After reading the short stories or poems, students should make their comparisons and contrasts with their novels. Following are examples: *Treasures in the Dust,* "Pastures of Plenty" by Woody Guthrie; *Phoenix Rising,* "The Beginning of Something," by Sue Ellen Bridgers, or "Going Away," by Denise Levertov; *Bridge to Terabithia,* "The Dreamer," by William Childress, or "The Cave," by Glien W. Dresbach.

6. Have students choose one of the Paulsen pieces. The objective of this activity is to show that friendship may involve animals as well as humans. Discuss with students how Paulsen describes his dogs and to what extent they become his friends.

7. Local color is an important concept in literature and in language use. This concept helps to determine character, setting, and so forth. Have students look through their reading to find examples of language that help to determine local color.

8. Have students create a dramatic interpretation of their books. They may use the book as a whole or they may choose one scene they feel was especially important to the novel as a whole. Following are examples:

    Bridge to Terabithia: Students could act out the creation of Terabithia, the museum scene between Jessa and Ms. Edmunds, or Leslie's death (or reaction to Leslie's death).

    Treasures in the Dust: Students could interpret Violet's wild stories, preparing for a dust storm, or the scene in which Violet's family is preparing to leave for California.

    Phoenix Rising: Students could interpret scenes between Muncie and Nyle, scenes with Ezra and Nyle, or the final part of the book when Ezra is dying.

Thematic Units

THEMATIC UNIT ON CRIMES AGAINST HUMANITY FOR HIGH SCHOOL STUDENTS

Thematic Objectives

The student will

*   Demonstrate an understanding of the thematic concept.
*   Define *hatred, intolerance, oppression, and persecution* as evidenced within the literature.
*   Identify the impact of hatred, intolerance, oppression, and persecution on individuals and society.
*   Demonstrate cooperative goal setting and problem solving in heterogeneous groups through activities relating to the theme and the literature.

Language Arts Objectives

The student will

*   Participate in the composing process, demonstrating an increased proficiency in oral and written composition while focusing on a specific form of structured written expression.
*   Demonstrate an understanding of literature that is varied in form but related in content and an understanding of the different effects each has on the reader.
*   Be able to describe the power of language found in various forms of communication, specifically the language that shapes behavior.
*   Participate freely and honestly in small- and large-group discussions.
*   Demonstrate appropriate behavior when presenting an informational report.
*   Identify figures of speech in literature, specifically examining simile, metaphor, irony, point of view, foreshadowing, and flashback.

Materials

Novels

Briar Rose, Jane Yolen (1992) (selected students: high level ability)
A Break with Charity, Ann Rinaldi (1992) (selected students: middle level ability)
Nightjohn, Gary Paulsen (1993) (selected students: low level ability)

Supplemental Materials

Tituba, Reluctant Witch of Salem, Elaine G. Breslaw (1996)
The Crucible, Arthur Miller (1952)
Rescue: The Story of How Gentiles Saved Jews in the Holocaust, Milton Meltzer (1988)
The Diary of a Young Girl, Anne Frank (1956)
Life in the Warsaw Ghetto, Gail B. Stewart (1995)
Caged, Ruth Minsky Sender (1988)
I Have Lived a Thousand Years, Livia Britton-Jackson (1997)
Maus, Art Spiegelman (1986, 1991)
A Women Called Truth, Sander Asher (1989)
Black Out Loud: An Anthology of Modern Poems by Black Americans, Arnold Adoff (ed.) (1970)

Activities (a representative selection; teachers will want to create others)

1. To help students synthesize their feelings and ideas after reading about crimes against humanity, have them list statements indicating what this theme means to them. Use the following format:

   I used to be _____.

   But now I am _____.

   Have students create a listing of 15 to 20 pairs of these statements. When students have finished, discuss the ideas generated. Have students put their list in their journal, because they will be adding to it as they read the various works in the unit.
2. Have students who are reading *Nightjohn* create a collection of thoughts and reactions organized into *Oppression* is _____ or *Persecution* is _____ statements. Suggest that students find examples within *Nightjohn* rather than drawing on outside knowledge.
3. Have students create a found poem based on their reading of *Briar Rose.* The found poem should come from the book as a whole or from a particular section. Following is an example:

Found Poem
Fantasy reality
Briar Rose

But not the bad fairy,
Not the one with big black boots and silver eagles on
her hat.
The angel of death.

Hitler
the SS, the Gestapo

A great mist came over all in the castle
everyone will die

relocation
mass extermination

> curse
> your father, mother, uncles, cousins, aunts,
> all the people who bear your name
>
> solution to the jew problem
>
> a briary hedge grew around the castle
> with the thorns as sharp as barbs
>
> concentration camps.
> Auschwitz, Dachau, Bergen-Belsen
>
> the prince
> the mist, hovering like a last breath on the lips of
> the sleepers
> he marveled at how many lay asleep
>
> an open gravesite
> for those gassed in vans
> at Chelmno
>
> on that bed lay the most beautiful young woman
> that he put his mouth on hers
>
> and she lived.

4. Have small groups of students studying *A Break with Charity* look for sections containing dialogue or descriptions of the girls in Tituba's circle. Suggest that students begin at the beginning of the novel and look for degrees of language manipulation: the use of language to move people to action or to think in a particular way. Suggest that students pay close attention to the words of Ann Putnam and Susannah's reaction to her language. Students should also examine the language of Abigail Hobbs, John Dorich, and Tituba.

5. Have students choose one of the following quotes and develop a well-structured piece of writing. Students should develop their positions on the thesis they choose and support them with ideas offered by authors' works read in the unit.
    Anyone who has begun to think places some portion of the world in jeopardy. —John Dewey
    If there is no struggle there can be no progress. —Frederick Douglass
    The important thing is not to stop questioning. —Albert Einstein
    And the trouble is, if you don't risk anything you risk even more. —Erica Jong
    Discuss these quotes with students and help them get started through prewriting sessions in class. As students write, they should participate fully in all aspects of the writing process.

6. Have students choose a dramatic piece for study, memorization, and performance. They may work with a partner or small group. Students may choose to write and present a dialogue, soliloquy, or monologue from the novel they are studying: *Briar Rose*, *Break with Charity*, or *Nightjohn*.

7. This activity could be used as the final project. Group students and assign each group one of the fictional or nonfictional works listed in the supplemental materials section. After each group has read its work, have students make a presentation about the work to the class. The project should include the following:
    - A brief personal response to the work: how they felt about it, what it made them think about, whether they liked it and why, and other information normally found in a personal response.

- A brief overview of the plot, setting, description of characters, and so forth.
- How specifically this work fits into the theme of this unit.
- How this work parallels themes found in the other literature read in this unit.
- Characters' attitudes toward crimes against humanity.
- Specific devices used by authors to help convey their message.

After the groups have presented their projects, students may give individual oral and written presentations as well.

Poetry, Short Stories, Drama, and Nonfictional Young Adult Literature

Most of the young adult literature mentioned in this book has been of the most common genre: the young adult novel. The reason seems obvious: When one thinks of young adult literature, the novel comes to mind. It has been the mainstay of young adult reading for more than 30 years. However, thematic unit examples include poetry, short stories, drama, and nonfiction.

Writing poetry specifically for the young adult audience is relatively new. Only a small number of collections existed a few years ago. Now, more poetry is written by and for young adults, and writers and editors are creating collections for young people. The same can be said of short stories and drama. Nonfiction has been available longer, but it is just now beginning to become popular in the schools. Young people have been reading it for some time, but it has taken a long time for nonfiction to find its way into the classroom.

> *Writing is a path of self-discovery and survival. To the true poet, it is the way to keep the soul breathing. No criticism or failure can discourage the true poet if he or she is to stay alive.*
>
> Michael Carey

Poetry

One of the earliest collections of poetry used for casual reading as well as for the classroom was *Reflections on a Gift of Watermelon Pickle and Other Modern Verse,* edited by Steve Dunning, Edward Lueders, and Hugh L. Smith (1966/1995). A collection read by children, young adults, and adults, *Reflections* was composed of poetry from hundreds of poetry magazines that got favorable responses from young adults. Two other collections followed: *Some Haystacks Don't Even Have Any Needles and Other Complete Modern Poems* (Dunning, Lueders, & Smith, 1969) and *Zero Makes Me Hungry: A Collection of Poems for Today* (Leuders & St. John, 1976).

Mel Glenn and Paul Janeczko are two contemporary poets who have a primary audience of young adults. Glenn's publications, *Class Dismissed! High School Poems*

(1982) and *Class Dismissed II: More High School Poems* (1986), became very popular with young adults, probably because the poems have the same characteristics as many young adult novels: Adolescents relate well to the topics of the poems; the language is direct, spoken as a young adult would speak; and the protagonists are from a variety of racial and socioeconomic backgrounds. The collections are packaged attractively; each poem carries the name of an individual with an accompanying photo, which gives the impression that the poem is written by the young adult pictured. It isn't; all are written by Glenn. More recent collections are much like the novel in that they tell stories. Recent titles include *The Taking of Room 114: A Hostage Drama in Poems* (1997), *Who Killed Mr. Chippendale? A Mystery in Poems* (1996), *Jump Ball: A Basketball Season in Poems* (1997), *Foreign Exchange: A Mystery in Poems* (1999), and *Spilt Image* (2000).

Janeczko, a high school teacher, has achieved success with many collections of poems for young adults. His first was *Postcard Poems: A Collection of Poetry for Sharing* (1979), a collection of poems short enough to send to someone on a postcard. Other Janeczko collections followed: *Don't Forget to Fly* (1981), *Strings: A Gathering of Family Poems* (1984), *Pocket Poems: Selected for a Journey* (1985), *Going Over to Your Place: Poems for Each Other* (1987), *The Place My Words Are Looking For* (1990), *Preposterous: Poems of Youth* (1991), *Poetry from A to Z* (1994), and *Worlds Afire, The Hartford Circus Fire of 1944* (2004). One additional collection, *Poetspeak: In Their Work, about Their Work* (1983), will eventually be found in most classrooms because it contains not only the poems of many authors but also notes from the authors telling how they came to write the particular poems. Figure 6.4 presents a selection of poetry collections suitable for classroom study.

The poetry of Sara Holbrook is also much loved by middle and high school students. *Chicks Up Front* (1996), *The Dog Ate My Homework* (1990), *I Never Said I Wasn't Difficult* (1996), *Walking on the Boundaries of Change* (1995), and *Wham! It's a Poetry Jam* (2002) all speak directly to young adults.

> *Writing poetry strengthens two of the most important components of good writing: precise and concise language.*
>
> Sara Holbrook

Short Stories

Like poetry, the short story is not new to the secondary school classroom. In most anthologies, the short story is the predominant genre. Most, however, are not written for young adults. The themes are adult in nature; however, a few students relate positively to them.

Today, the reading in this genre for young adults has broadened greatly. Now the works of young adult authors such as Robert Cormier, Joan Aiken, Robert Lipsyte, Susan Beth Pfeffer, Richard Peck, and Jerry Spinelli, to mention only a few, are included in collections of short stories designed specifically for young adults. Three early collections should be noted: *Sixteen* (1984), *Visions* (1987), and *Connections* (1989).

And Still I Rise, Maya Angelou (1978)

Back to Class, Mel Glenn (1987)

Chicks Up Front, Sara Holbrook (1996)

Collected Poems, Robert Hayden (1985)

Cool Salsa: Bilingual Poems on Growing Up Latino in the United States, Lori M. Carlson (ed.) (1994)

A Dime a Dozen, Nikki Grimes (1998)

Dirty Laundry Pile: Poems in Different Voices, Paul Janeczko (2001)

The Dog Ate My Homework, Sara Holbrook (1990)

Feelings Make Me Real, Sara Holbrook (1990)

A Fire in My Hands, Gary Soto (1990)

Foreign Exchange: A Mystery in Poems, Mel Glenn (1999)

Harlem: A Poem, Walter Dean Myers (1997)

Hoofprints: Horse Poems, Jessie Haas (2004)

How to Write Poetry, Paul Janeczko (2001)

I Am the Darker Brother: An Anthology of Modern Poems by African Americans, A. Adoff (ed.) (1997)

If Only I Could Tell You: Poems for Young Lovers and Dreamers, Eve Merriam (1983)

Imaginary Animals: Poetry and Art for Young People, C. Sullivan (1986)

I Never Said I Wasn't Difficult, Sara Holbrook (1992)

In the Trail of the Wind: American Indian Poems and Ritual Orations, John Beirhorst (1987)

Johnny's Song: Poetry of a Vietnam Veteran, Steve Mason (1986)

Jump Ball: A Basketball Season in Poems, Mel Glenn (1997)

Just People and Paper/Pen/Poems: A Young Writer's Way to Begin, K. Appelt (1996)

Keesha's House, H. Frost (2003)

Lifelines, Leonard S. Moor (1994)

Life through Poetry: Original Poems by Young Adults, J. H. Bushman (ed.) (2000)

Locomotion, J. Woodson (2003)

My Friend's Got This Problem, Mr. Candler, Mel Glenn (1991)

Nothing's the End of the World, Sara Holbrook (1995)

One of Those Hideous Books Where the Mother Dies, Sonya Sones (2004)

Opening a Door: Reading Poetry in the Middle School Classroom, Paul Janeczko (2003)

The Other Side: Shorter Poems, Angela Johnson (1998)

Paint Me Like I Am, Bill Aguado (ed.) (2003)

Poems from Homeroom, Kathi Appelt (2002)

Poetry after Lunch: Poems to Read Aloud, J. A. Carol and E. E. Wilson (1997)

FIGURE 6.4

Poetry collections for young adults.

Poetry from A to Z, Paul Janeczko (ed.) (1994)

Quilting the Black-eyed Pea: Poems and Not Quite Poems, N. Giovanni (2002)

Reflections on a Gift of Watermelon Pickle and Other Modern Verse (2nd ed.), Stephen Dunning, Edward Lueders, and Hugh L. Smith (1995)

Seeing the Blue Between: Advice and Inspirations for Young Poets, Paul Janeczko (2002)

Selected Poems, Gwendolyn Brooks (1982)

Selected Poems, Langston Hughes (1959/1990)

Shakespeare Bats Cleanup, R. Koertge (2003)

Sister Slam and the Poetic Motormouth Road Trip, Linda Oatman High (2004)

Some Families, Sara Holbrook (1990)

Sports Pages, Arnold Adoff (1986)

Stardust Hotel, Paul Janeczko (1993)

Stop Pretending: What Happened When My Big Sister Went Crazy, Sonya Sones (1999)

Spinning through the Universe, Heather Frost (2004)

The Taking of Room 114: A Hostage Drama in Poems, Mel Glenn (1997)

Very Best (Almost) Friends: Poems of Friendship, Paul Janeczko (ed.) (1999)

Walking on the Boundaries of Change, Sara Holbrook (1995)

Wham! It's a Poetry Jam, Sara Holbrook (2002)

What My Mother Doesn't Know, Sonya Sones (2001)

Which Way to the Dragon? Poems for the Coming on Strong, Sara Holbrook (1997)

Who Killed Mr. Chippendale? A Mystery in Poems, Mel Glenn (1996)

Words with Wrinkled Knees, B. J. Esbensen and J. Stadler (1987)

Worlds Afire: The Hartford Circus Fire of 1944, Paul Janeczko (2004)

You Remind Me of You, Eireann Corrigan (2002)

FIGURE 6.4
Continued.

Don Gallo, editor of the three collections, indicates in the introduction the importance of *Sixteen*, the first book: "This book you now hold is unique—in two ways. First, there has never before been a collection of short stories written specifically for teenagers by authors who specialize in writing books for young people. Second, none of these stories has appeared in print before" (Gallo, 1984, p. ix).

Although there is much variety in these collections, there is also some similarity. Many of the stories fit into general themes: cultures, death and dying, and coming of age, to mention only a few. The advantage is that these short stories can be used effectively in thematic units. Seeing how different authors treat a particular theme or topic can be beneficial to students. For example, in *Connections*, stories are grouped in four general themes: Encounters, Clashes, Surprises, and Insights. However, each story has a more specific theme such as boy-girl relationships, self-image, and parental and peer relations. It is interesting to note that in *Visions,* more than half of the stories have death or dying as the predominant theme. Gallo has edited many short story anthologies since these three. They can be found in Figure 6.5.

Writers of young adult literature have published collections of their own short stories. Robert Cormier, a prolific writer of short stories, has published *8 Plus 1* (1980), an anthology of his stories that were judged exceptional by readers of his novels. Norma Fox Mazer also published collections of her short stories: *Dear Bill, Remember Me? and Other Stories* (1976) and *Summer Girls, Love Boys* (1982). Chris Crutcher, whose short stories are found in other collections, has published a collection of his own titled *Athletic Shorts* (1991). Avi's *What Do Fish Have to Do with Anything and Other Stories* (1997) is a collection featuring a teen undergoing a personal transformation. Harry Mazer edits a collection of short stories about guns: *Twelve Shots: Outstanding Short Stories about Guns* (1998). Other appropriate collections are listed in Figure 6.5.

> *I write because I have a story to tell. That story might want to tell itself as a poem or as a nonfiction book or as a novel. The important thing to me is to find the best words to tell that story.*
>
> Paul Janeczko

Drama

Perhaps *Center Stage: One-Act Plays for Teenage Readers and Actors* (Gallo, 1990) broke the drought that students have faced in trying to find dramas written specifically for them. As in his short story collections, Don Gallo has called on writers of young adult literature to create plays solely for and about teenagers. *Center Stage* is a collection of 10 one-act plays by Alden Carter, Susan Beth Pfeffer, Lensey Namioka, Cin Forshay-Lunsford, Dallin Malmgren, Jean Davies Okimoto, Ouida Sebestyen, Sandy Asher, Walter Dean Myers, and Robin Brancato. As the book jacket blurb indicates, "Some of the plays are comic, some serious; all offer special insights into the concerns and triumphs of teenagers."

Before *Center Stage,* the field was very limited. Students found Aiken's *Street* (1978), Zindel's *The Effect of Gamma Rays on Man-in-the-Moon Marigolds* (1970), and *Let Me Hear You Whisper* (1974), and Rose's three-act television play *Twelve Angry Men* (1969) to their liking. In 1989, Sandy Asher published a powerful one-act play titled *A Woman Called Truth.* The play tells of the life of Sojourner Truth from the day she is sold away from her family, through her struggle to free herself and her son, to her emergence as a respected advocate of abolition and women's rights. The play is appropriate for young adults as well as adults. Asher has since published *The Wise Men of Chelm* (1992), *Dancing with Strangers* (1994), *Little Old Ladies in Tennis Shoes* (1989), and *Emma* (1997), which are all appropriate for young adults.

Absolute Magnitude, W. Lapine and S. Pagel (eds.) (1997)

America Street: A Multicultural Anthology of Stories, Ann Mazer (ed.) (1993)

American Dragons: Twenty-Five Asian American Voices, Laurence Yet (1993)

Am I Blue? Coming Out from the Silence, Marion Dane Bauer (ed.) (1994)

As Long as the Rivers Flow: The Stories of Nine Native Americans, P. Gunn and P. C. Smith (1996)

Back of Beyond: Stories of the Supernatural, S. Ellis (1998)

Bad Behavior, Mary Higgins Clark (1995)

Baseball in April and Other Stories, Gary Soto (1990)

Big City Cool: Short Stories about Urban Youth, Jerry Weiss and Helen Weiss (2002)

Blue Skin of the Sea, Graham Salisbury (1992)

The Book of Changes, Tim Wynne-Jones (1995)

But That's Another Story, Sandy Asher (1996)

The Canine Connection: Stories about Dogs and People, Betsy Hearne (2003)

Chills in the Night: Tales That Will Haunt You, J. Viveto (1997)

The Color of Absence: 12 Stories about Loss and Hope, James Howe (ed.) (2001)

A Couple of Kooks and Other Stories about Love, Cynthia Rylant (1990)

Crush, Ellen Conford (1998)

Dear Austin: Letters from the Underground Railroad, Elvira Woodruff (1998)

Destination Unexpected, Donald Gallo (ed.) (2003)

Dirty Laundry: Stories about Family Secrets, L. R. Fraustino (1998)

Doing Time: Notes from the Undergrad, Rob Thomas (1997)

Face Relations: 11 Stories about Seeing beyond Color, Marilyn Singer (ed.) (2004)

Face to Face, Thomas Pettepiece and Anatoly Aleksin (1990)

Firebirds: An Anthology of Original Fantasy and Science Fiction, S. November (2003)

First Crossing: Stories about Teen Immigrants, Don Gallo (ed.) (2004)

Front Porch Stories at the One-Room School, Eleanora Tate (1992)

Funny You Should Ask, David Gale (ed.) (1992)

A Gathering of Flowers: Stories about Being Young in America, Joyce Thomas (1990)

Girl Goddess: Nine Stores, F. L. Block (1996)

A Glory of Unicorns, Bruce Coville (1998)

Going Where I'm Coming From, Ann Mazer (1995)

Help Wanted: Short Stories about Young People Working, Anita Silvey (1997)

Here There Be Ghosts, Jane Yolen (1998)

I Love You, I Hate You, Get Lost, Ellen Conford (1994)

Into the Widening World: International Coming-of-Age Stories, John Loughery (ed.) (1995)

An Island Like You: Stories of the Barrio, Judith Ortiz Cofer (1995)

FIGURE 6.5

Short story collections for young adults.

Join In: Multiethnic Short Stories by Outstanding Writers for Young Adults, Don Gallo (ed.) (1993)

Kissing the Witch: Old Tales in New Skins, E. Donoghue (1993)

The Leaving, Budge Wilson (1992)

Leaving Home: Stories, H. Rochman and D. Z. McCampbell (eds.) (1997)

The Library Card, Jerry Spinelli (1997)

Local News, Gary Soto (1993)

Lord of the Fries, Tim Wynne-Jones (1999)

Losing Is Not an Option, Rick Wallace (2003)

Love and Sex: Ten Stories of Truth, Michael Cart (2001)

Mindtwisters: Stories to Shred Your Head, N. Shusterman (1997)

Necessary Noise: Stories about Our Families as They Really Are, Michael Cart (2003)

A Nightmare's Dozen: Stories from the Dark, M. Stearns (ed.) (1996)

Night Terrors: Stories of Shadow and Substance, Lois Duncan (1996)

No Easy Answers: Short Stories about Teenagers Making Tough Choices, Don Gallo (ed.) (1997)

Odder than Ever, Bruce Coville (1999)

On the Edge: Stories at the Brink, Lois Duncan (2000)

On the Fringe, Don Gallo (ed.) (2001)

Our Stories Remembered: American Indian History, Culture and Values through Storytelling, J. Bruchac (2003)

Out of Bounds: Seven Stories of Conflict and Hope, Beverly Naidoo (2001)

The People Could Fly: American Black Folktales, Virginia Hamilton (1987)

Please Do Not Touch: A Collection of Stories, Judith Gorog (1993)

Rearranging and Other Stories, D. Gifaldi (1998)

Rio Grande Stories, Carolyn Meyer (1994)

Second Sight: Stories for a New Millennium, Peck et al. (1999)

Shelf Life: Stories by the Book, Gary Paulsen (2003)

Short Circuits: Thirteen Shocking Stories by Outstanding Writers for Young Adults, Don Gallo (ed.) (1992)

Soul Searching: Thirteen Stories about Faith and Belief, L. R. Fraustino (2002)

Stay True: Short Stories for Strong Girls, M. Singer (ed.) (1998)

Things That Go Bump in the Night: A Collection of Original Stories, Jane Yolen and Martin Greenberg (1989)

Thirteen Stories That Capture the Agony and Ecstasy of Being Thirteen, James Howe (2003)

Thirteen Tales of Horror, T. Pines (1991)

Tomorrowland, Michael Cart (1999)

FIGURE 6.5

Continued.

Trapped! Cages of the Mind and Body, Lois Duncan (1998)

Twelve Impossible Things before Breakfast: Stories, Jane Yolen (1997)

Twelve Shots: Outstanding Short Stories about Guns, Harry Mazer (1998)

2041, Jane Yolen (1991)

Ultimate Sports, Don Gallo (ed.) (1995)

A Walk in My World: International Short Stories about Youth, Ann Mazer (ed.) (1998)

Welcome to Your Life: Writings for the Heart of Young America, David Haynes and Julie Landsman (eds.) (1998)

With All My Heart, With All My Mind, Sandy Asher (ed.) (1999)

Within Reach: Ten Stories, Don Gallo (ed.) (1993)

What Do Fish Have to Do with Anything and Other Stories, Avi (1997)

What's in a Name?, Ellen Wittlinger (2001)

When Nobody's Home: Fifteen Baby-Sitting Tales of Terror, Judith Gorog (1996)

A Whisper in the Night, Joan Aiken (1984)

Zebra and Other Stories, Chaim Potok (1998)

FIGURE 6.5
Continued.

Most of the plays found in anthologies and used in classrooms are the classics and have limited relevance to young adults. A listing of the best dramas now available, some written for young adults and others for adults, appears in Figure 6.6. We hope *Center Stage* has created enough of a stir that other editors and publishers will publish new and creative plays for young adult readers.

Nonfiction

Young adult literature means young adult novels to most people, and some realize that poetry and short stories can also fall under this heading. However, few think of non-fiction, although many young adults—and adults—choose to read nonfiction.

Nonfiction for Young Adults: From Delight to Wisdom (Carter & Abrahamson, 1991) starts with a detailed description of how literature is cataloged in libraries and thus gives the reader a sense of how the label "nonfiction" was born. Authors Carter and Abrahamson then offer the following definition of nonfiction: "Simply put, it's any book that's not a novel or a short story" (p. xii). They go on to group nonfiction as "factual books about topics such as the solar system, automobiles, curiosities and wonders, and cooking," as well as "informational works characterized by beautifully written prose, definable themes, unifying structure, and stimulating topics" (p. xii).

If only it were this easy to distinguish between fiction and nonfiction. Novelists often gather many facts about the topic before they begin writing, and many informational writers make their literature exciting and stimulating for the reader. Perhaps, at best, all of it is just literature, whether it's a fictitious story based on data or a factual account with fictitious embellishments.

FIGURE 6.6

Drama for young people.

Across the Plains, Sandra Fenichel Asher (1995)

Children of a Lesser God, Mark Medoff (1980)

Dancing with Strangers, Sandra Fenichel Asher (1994)

Emma, Sandra Fenichel Asher (1997)

Langston, Ossie Davis (1982)

Little Old Ladies in Tennis Shoes, Sandra Fenichel Asher (1989)

Meeting the Winter Bike Rider and Other Prize Winning Plays, Wendy Lamb (1986)

The Night Thoreau Spent in Jail, Jerome Lawrence and Robert Lee (1972)

The Outsiders, adapted by Christopher Sergel (n.d.)

Plays: The Drama Magazine for Young People

Plays of Black Americans, Sylvia E. Kamerman (1999)

Seven Ages of Anne, Jennifer Fell Hayes (n.d.)

Sunday, Sunday, Sandra Fenichel Asher (1994)

Theatre for Youth: Twelve Plays with Mature Themes, Coleman A. Jennings and Gretta Berghammer (eds.) (n.d.)

The Wise Men of Chelm, Sandra Fenichel Asher (1992)

Under Thirty: Plays for a New Generation, Nina Shengold and Eric Lane

Who Cares? Gillian M. Wadds (n.d.)

Markets for Plays for Young People

Plays, Inc., 120 Boylston Street, Boston, MA 02116

Anchorage Press, Box 8067, New Orleans, LA 70182

Dramatic Publishing Company, 311 Washington Street, Woodstock, IL 60098

New Plays, Inc., Box 5074, Charlottesville, VA 22905

Young people like to read nonfiction. Interest and circulating surveys strongly indicate that children and young adults are avid readers of nonfiction, regardless of ability level. Surveys of reading habits indicate that low-ability students are as interested in nonfiction as gifted students are. Most of the surveys indicate that nonfiction is read as casual reading; little is read in the classroom. Because nonfiction has made its mark on the reading habits of young adults, it should be a part of the curriculum (Carter & Abrahamson, 1990).

As noted earlier in this chapter, nonfiction can be easily incorporated into the curriculum as parts of thematic units, as choices when groups read literature, or as choices on students' individual reading lists. Whether the nonfiction is a book on career or college choices, a self-help or how-to book, or one that details the atrocities of the Holocaust, students can and will benefit from the author's craft and the book's content. Our nonfiction suggestions are listed in Figure 6.7.

The Abortion Controversy, Carol Emmens (1991)

Almost a Woman, E. Santiago (1999)

An American Plague: The True and Terrifying Story of the Yellow Fever Epidemic of 1793, J. Murphy (2003)

The American Revolution: War for Independence, A. Carter (1992)

At Her Majesty's Request: An African Princess in Victorian England, Walter Dean Myers (1999)

Battle of the Ironclads: The Monitor and Merrimack, A. Carter (1983)

Black Dance in America, James Haskins (1990)

Black Pioneers: An Untold Story, William Katz (1999)

Black Potatoes: The Story of the Great Irish Famine, Susan Bartoletti (2002)

Blood on the Forehead: What I Know about Writing, M. E. Kerr (1998)

Born to the Land: An American Portrait, Brent Ashabranner (1989)

Caught by the Sea, Gary Paulsen (2001)

Chapters: My Growth as a Writer, Lois Duncan (1982)

Charles A. Lindbergh: A Human Hero, J. C. Giblin (1997)

China Past—China Future, Carter (1994)

The Civil War: American Tragedy, Carter (1992)

The Colonial Wars: Clashes in the Wilderness, Carter (1992)

Columbus and the World around Him, Milton Meltzer (1990)

The Cookcamp, Gary Paulsen (1991)

Crews, Maria Hinojosa (1995)

Don't Be S.A.D.: A Teenage Guide to Handling Stress, Anxiety, and Depression, Susan Newman (1991)

Don't Sweat the Small Stuff for Teens, Richard Carlson (2002)

Edgar Allen Poe: A Biography, Milton Meltzer (2003)

Ethics, Susan Neiburg Terkel (1992)

Escape from Saigon, Andrea Warren (2004)

Fighting Back: What Some People Are Doing about AIDS, S. Kuklin (1989)

Food Fight: A Guide to Eating Disorders for Preteens and Their Parents, Janet Bode (1997)

Foxfire, 12, Angie Cheek, Kaye Carver Collins and Foxfire Students (eds.) (2004)

Gay and Lesbian Youth, G. B. Steward (1997)

Girls Speak Out: Finding Your True Self, A. Johnston and G. Steinem (1997)

The Greatest Stories Never Told: 100 Tales from History to Astonish, Bewilder and Stupefy, R. Beyer (2003)

Growing Up in Coal Country, S. C. Bartoletti (1996)

Growing Up: It's a Girl Thing, M. Jukes and D. Tilley (1998)

FIGURE 6.7

Representative nonfiction books for young adults.

Guts, Gary Paulsen (2001)

Heartbreak and Roses: Real Life Stories of Troubled Love, Janet Bode and Stan Mack (1994)

Hear These Voices: Youth at the Edge of the Millennium, Anthony Allison (1998)

The Heart Knows Something Different: Teenage Voices from the Foster Care System, A. Desetta and J. Kozol (eds.) (1996)

Hole in My Life, Jack Gantos (2002)

I Have Lived a Thousand Years, Livia Britton-Jackson (1997)

Inside the Alamo, J. Murphy (2003)

Invisible Enemies: Stories of Infectious Diseases, J. Farrell (1998)

Iqbal Masih and the Crusaders against Child Slavery, Susan Kuklin (1998)

Irrepressible Spirit: Conversations with Human Rights Activists, Susan Kuklin (1996)

Kids (Still) Having Kids, Janet Bode (1992)

Kids at Work, Russell Freedman (1994)

King of the Mild Frontier, Chris Crutcher (2003)

Knots in My Yo-Yo String: The Autobiography of a Kid, Jerry Spinelli (1998)

The Life and Death of Crazy Horse, Russell Freedman and A. Bull (1996)

Life Strategies for Teens, Jay McGraw (2000)

Lincoln and Slavery, Peter Burchard (1999)

Love Ya Like a Sister: A Story of Friendship, Julie Johnston (ed.) (1999)

Martha Graham: A Dancer's Life, Russell Freedman (1998)

Me, Me, Me, Me, Me: Not a Novel, M. E. Kerr (1983)

My Bridges of Hope, Livia Britton-Jackson (1999)

My Life in Dog Years, Gary Paulsen (1998)

The New Way Things Work, David Macaulay (1998)

Now Is Your Time, Walter Dean Myers (1991)

Oh, Freedom!, Casey King and Linda Barrett Osborne (1997)

One More River to Cross, Jim Haskins (1992)

Our Stories: A Fiction Workshop for Young Authors, M. D. Bauer (1996)

Outspoken: Role Models from the Lesbian and Gay Community, M. T. Ford (1996)

Presenting Chris Crutcher, Terry Davis (1997)

Presenting Cynthia Voigt, Suzanne E. Reid (1995)

Presenting Judy Blume, Maryann Weidt (1909)

Presenting Madeleine L'Engle, Donald R. Hettinga (1993)

Presenting M. E. Kerr, Alleen Nilsen (1986)

Presenting Norma Fox Mazer, Sally Holtze (1989)

Presenting Norma Klein, Allene Phy (1988)

Presenting Ouida Sebestyen, Virginia Monseau (1994)

FIGURE 6.7

Continued.

Presenting Paul Zindel, Jack Forman (1988)

Presenting Richard Peck, Donald Gallo (1989)

Presenting Robert Cormier, Patricia Campbell (1989)

Presenting Rosa Guy, Jerrie Norris (1988)

Presenting S. E. Hinton, Jay Daly (1989)

Presenting Sue Ellen Bridgers, Ted Hipple (1990)

Presenting Walter Dean Myers, Rudine Bishop (1990)

Presenting William Sleator, James Davis and Hazel Davis

Presenting Zibby Oneal, Susan Bloom and Cathryn Mercier (1991)

Princess Lesson, Meg Cabot (2003)

Puppies, Dogs, and Blue Northers: Reflections on Being Raised by a Pack of Sled Dogs, Gary Paulsen (Paintings by Ruth Wright Paulsen) (1996)

Real Girl/Real World: Tools for Finding Your True Self, H. M. Gray, S. Phillips, and E. Farney (1998)

Samuel Adams: The Father of American Independence, D. Fradin (1999)

The Shared Heart Portraits and Stories Celebrating Lesbian, Gay, and Bisexual Young People, Adam Mastoon (1997)

Sickened: The True Story of a Lost Childhood, Julie Gregory (2003)

Surviving Hitler, Andrea Warren (2001)

Tell Them We Remember, Susan Bachrach (1994)

Ten Queens: Portraits of Women of Power, Milton Meltzer (1996)

Thomas Jefferson: Architect of Democracy, John B. Severance (1998)

Violence in Our Schools: Halls of Hope, Halls of Fear, T. Orr (2003)

The War of 1812: Second Fight for Independence, A. Carter (1992)

We Rode the Orphan Trains, Andrea Warren (2001)

Whatever You Say I Am: The Life and Times of Eminem, Anthony Bozza (2003)

The Wild Colorado, Richard Maurer (1999)

Witch Hunt: Mysteries of the Salem Witch Trials, M. Aronson (2003)

With Their Eyes: September 11th, The View from a High School at Ground Zero, Anne Thoms (2002)

Words West: Voices of Young Pioneers, Ginger Wadsworth (2003)

Working Like a Dog: The Story of Working Dogs through History, G. K. Gorrell (2003)

FIGURE 6.7
Continued.

One Book, One Student

The one book, one student organizational structure perhaps best considers the needs and interests of students. Reading interests and difficulty, developmental stages, and intellectual ability are all considered before suggesting a book to a particular student. Traditionally, this arrangement has been used for the book report. In most classrooms, book reports are due every 6 or 9 weeks; students usually have the optimum choice of reading for this assignment. This organization can also be used from time to time with regular classroom reading.

Leighton (1991) describes a similar program of reading that she calls "saturation reading." When students read their own books, the classroom becomes a reading laboratory. Although teachers usually use one book for the entire class or three or four books with groups, they should not be limited to those arrangements. These three organizations make up a continuum that moves students from the most restrictive to the least restrictive, from dependence to independence in their reading. Therefore, teachers may wish to include all arrangements in the classroom, using the first at the beginning of the year and the third toward the end of the year. In this way, students will have more responsibility for their literature program. Atwell (1998) describes her use of the readers' workshop as she saturates her classes with books appropriate for young adults.

What books should students read? This question frequently gives teachers pause, because there are so many from which to choose. Some teachers provide a list from which students choose their reading for a particular assignment. Others question this approach because they see a list as being too restrictive as all books cannot be listed. The list cannot be all inclusive, but many teachers need lists for suggestions, and therefore perhaps students need a source from which to select "just the right book."

We have not provided a list of books in this section; we have placed it in Appendix C. Students could readily use many of the books in their individualized reading programs. Teachers will find a wide variety represented. The list includes works by Robert Cormier, Sue Ellen Bridgers, Chris Crutcher, Lois Duncan, S. E. Hinton, Judy Blume, Bette Greene, Paula Danziger, M. E. Kerr, and others—all authors of quality literature for young people.

After students have read their individual books, other students should benefit from this reading. Part of the beauty of reading a wonderful piece of literature is sharing it with others, much like moviegoers share after viewing a film. To have students read good literature but not have them in some way share their reactions to that reading seems unfair and unwise. This sharing can take many forms: formal book talks to the class, sharing in small groups, displays of projects related to the books read, and a variety of writing activities that can be read by other students. We do not suggest that students take a test, because then responses to the work are shared only with the teacher.

A current program that has found its way into the schools is Accelerated Reading, a computerized assessment program of many pieces of literature. In the program, students read books, many of which are not age appropriate, then take an objective test through the computer. Although many teachers believe that this approach motivates students, we wonder at what cost. It seems to us that teachers are turning over to the computer a strategy that should be handled by them. There are many problems with this system. First, little if any time is reserved for oral or written discussion of the book. Second, the test that the students take is completely objective, containing questions that demand only factual recall. This approach seems so contrary to what we want to happen in a reading or English classroom. Third, many of the books that are in the program are not appropriate for young adults. We think that perhaps the most important problem is that teachers who use this program are giving the students the wrong message. What we know about reader-response theory has been set aside. Students do not get the wonderful experience of reading and sharing that reading with someone else.

The following activities are a few ideas that students should be using when sharing what they have read with their peers. Some are written, some are oral, and some can be either; all, we think, are creative:

1. Two students who have read the same book develop a "meet the author" spot for a talk show. One student assumes the identity of the host or interviewer and the other that of the author. Students can also try another version of the same activity, replacing the author with the main character.

2. Students can give an effective book talk, providing other students with information about their books. These book talks can be videotaped and placed in the library for others to view.

3. Students who are musical can select background music to enhance an oral reading of specific passages of their book. Students will need to provide background information so the passages will be fully understood.

4. Students who have read the same book can put a character in the book on trial for a crime he or she committed. The students then present the prosecutor's case and the defendant's case.

5. After choosing a national or school issue, students compose a speech on that topic to be given by one of the major characters in the book. The speech should reflect the character's personality and beliefs. In groups of five to seven, students share their books with each other. The sharing should include a general overview of the plot, setting, and theme, plus a personal response that should include why the students liked or disliked the book and similar information.

6. Students complete a responding report (see Chapter 3) and then make these reports available in various parts of the room so that students can read about books that others have read.

7. Students can write one of the following letters about books they have read. The letters are then displayed so other students can read them.
   a. A letter to a friend explaining why the student thinks the book will make for enjoyable reading
   b. A letter from one of the book's characters to another and a responding letter from the second character

    c. A letter of advice to a character on how to handle his or her problem

    d. A letter to the school librarian giving reasons why he or she should or should not recommend this book to other students

8. Students take an interesting character, other than the main character, and write an original short story with this secondary character as the main character.

9. Students write book reviews of their books and publish them in a class collection. Teachers may exchange these collections with other classes and other teachers.

10. Teachers organize a book fair in which book projects and book responses are displayed around the room. Students work with other students who have read the same book or books with similar themes to create an original display that represents their books. This display may include written responses, collages showing the thematic thread that runs through the books, pictures of well-known actors and actresses who could play the book characters in a film of the book and an explanation of why they made those choices, journals that were kept by students as they read their books, and so forth.

11. Students present to the class a rationale for why their books should be considered "quality" books. Reasons could include character development, plot structure, universal themes, and specific examples of the writer's craft.

12. Students create a "found poem" from the text of the novel that they are reading and discussing. A found poem is created from the actual text of the novel. It can come from a particular section of the novel or it can be created from the novel as a whole. The important consideration is that the poem reflect the theme found in the novel. The following is an example of a found poem created by students after they read Sarah Dessen's *Dreamland* (2000):

Cover

Cover

Keep the defense going

What happened?

I looked up

Worn Out

Broken

Saw the bruises

Blue

Color enhances

He had taken everything

I should have known

See you in dreamland

Another group of students created this found poem after reading S. Creech's *Walk Two Moons* (1994):

Tumbling and sliding downward

Bus on its side

Like an old sick horse

Grotesquely twisted

Jumbled mess

Fuzzy, green mold

Looking for something, anything familiar

One survivor, cadaver

Tombstone

Engraving of a maple tree

Not coming back

Happy Birthday

She's singing in the trees

Backberry kisses

Huzza, Huzza

Other students created this found poem on *Speak* (Anderson, 1999):

I believed in Santa Claus

IT sees me

Choke out an answer

My report card

Making it out of 9th grade alive

Me:

Locks my jaw

Ignore IT

Blah, Blah, Blah

You have a reputation

Utter silence

Unlady like

Creepy, in a good way

Burns my scabby lips

Paralyzed

Picasso

Hiding in the open

Not quite sure

I don't do parties

Cutting off the damage

Grow again

Lies

You've been through a lot

The importance of these or similar activities is that students are sharing what they have read, which will encourage others to read.

Young Adult Literature in the Content Classes

"Reading in and about content disciplines is important for students for they need to learn and recognize that words have power" (*Literature across the Disciplines,* Hazlett, Richardson, & Richardson, 2002, p. 1).

The English or language arts teacher can play an important role in spreading the word about the use of young adult literature in the middle and high school curriculum. He or she could suggest to the social studies teacher that using Paulsen's *Soldier's Heart* (1998) may help students to better understand the evil of wars in general and the Civil War in particular. Students who learn about the Civil War through reading about it in a textbook get at best a cursory glance of this devastating war. For students to internalize the horror of that Heart, students read of a real boy, Charley Goddard, who at a young age left his family and farm life in Minnesota in search of adventure. What he found was more than an adventure: He found a relentless, brutal, violent experience. Students who read this work are with Charley through each moment of preparation and battle and learn how he felt as he fought each battle. There is no question in our minds that today's students would have a better understanding of that war and how it affected ordinary people if they read *Soldier's Heart* as part of the unit.

And so it is with other curriculum areas in middle and high schools. In health education, students learn from the textbook about the use of drugs and alcohol, sexual abuse, and a variety of illnesses. Although the information from these texts is helpful, it often doesn't tell the human story. Fictional and nonfictional young adult literature can bring to the classroom stories and accounts of authentic situations from which students can learn about the real word in which they live. Literature such as Jacqueline Woodson's *I Hadn't Meant to Tell you This* (1994) and its sequel, *Lena* (1999), Norma Fox Mazer's *Out of Control* (1993), Chris Crutcher's *Chinese Handcuffs* (1989), Janet Bode's *The Voices of Rape* (1990), Laurie Anderson's *Speak* (1999), Alex Flinn's *Breathing Underwater* (2001), and many other fine works speak directly to the issue of sexual abuse. Paula Fox's *The Eagle Kite* (1995), Marilyn Kaye's *Real Heroes* (1993), M. E. Kerr's *Night Kites* (1986), Fran Arrick's *What You Don't Know Can Kill You* (1992), and M. T. Ford's *The Voice of AIDS* (1995) deal with AIDS-related issues. Drug and alcohol abuse are topics in Linda Glovach's *Beauty Queen* (1998),

Jan Cheripko's *Imitate the Tiger* (1996), Cynthia Grant's *The White Horse* (1998), W. Moragne's *Depression* (2001), C. Mackler's *Love and Other Four Letter Words* (2002), and Janet Carey's *Wenny Has Wings* (2002). These are but a few of the quality works of literature that could be used in a health education course. Figure 6.8 lists other literature that could be used effectively in various disciplines.

Another important way that young adult literature can be used effectively in the content classes is when the literature is part of a thematic unit taught by a multidiscipline team. Middle schools and some high schools are often organized around teams that are usually composed of English, social studies, math, and science curriculum areas. Themes provide the connection between these diverse disciplines. Frequently, students read, write, and discuss thematically relevant material in English class. Students also center their attention around the theme as they emphasize their content in math, social studies, and science classes.

For example, in late winter through early spring, middle school students often study about the Iditarod Sled Dog Race to coincide with the actual race that is in progress in Alaska. Students are involved in many activities from all of the content areas. Cooperative learning teams decide on a particular musher to follow throughout the race. Teachers display a large map of Alaska, along with pictures, daily race information, weather reports, and other race news. Students use pins to move their musher along the trail daily as the race progresses. As noted in Chapter 9, there are wonderful sites on the World Wide Web for use in English classrooms. For this unit, daily information about the running of the race is posted for all to use. Among the many sites available, the following two seem to be most useful: www.iditarod.com/iditarod and www.starfishsoftware.com/idog/index/html.

In addition, teachers and students can use these sources for background information, including material on the mushers, history of the Iditarod, and many other interesting points that students would find helpful.

As part of the interdisciplinary unit, students may read George's *Julie of the Wolves* (1972), *Julie* (1994), or *Julie's Wolf Pack* (1997), or Paulsen's *Woodsong* (1990), *Dogsong* (1985), or *Winterdance: The Fine Madness of Running the Iditarod* (1995). Another important source is *Iditarod: The Last Great Race to Nome: Curriculum Guide* (1998), which is a part of the Last Wilderness Adventure series by Shelly Gill. Another major work that is not specifically related to the Iditarod but provides valuable information about Alaskan culture is Deb Vanasse's *A Distant Enemy* (1997). This book would give readers a substantial amount of information about Alaskan life. The other content areas could easily incorporate map skills, math practice (including reading charts and graphs), weather studies, cultural lessons, geography, and animal rights issues.

This interdisciplinary team construction can work just as well at the high school level. In a unit on the family, students can learn and use language arts, math, science, and social studies skills through the study of this theme. Students may do some or all of the following activities:

Language arts: Read novels such as *Cast Two Shadows* (Rinaldi, 1998), *Anne Frank: The Diary of a Young Girl* (Frank, 1956), or *Life in the Fat Lane* (C. Bennett, 1998). Students can discuss the relationships among the members

The Arts

Birdland, Tracy Mach (2003)

Broken Chords, B. S. Gilbert (2000)

Come Sing, Jimmy Jo, Katherine Paterson (1995)

Harley Like a Person, C. Bauer (2000)

Hate You, G. McNamee (1999)

Jason and the Bard, Kate Gilmore (1993)

No More Dead Dogs, Gordon Korman (2000)

Cultures

Baseball in April and Other Stories, Gary Soto (1990)

The Beast, W. D. Myers (2003)

Bronx Masquerade, Nikki Grimes (2002)

Buried Onions, Gary Soto (1997)

Rain Is Not My Indian Name, Cynthia Leitich Smith (2001)

The Shakespeare Scribe, Gary Blackwood (2000)

The Shakespeare Stealer, Gary Blackwood (1998)

The Year of the Hangman, Gary Blackwood (2002)

War

Anne Frank and Me, Jeff Gotesfeld and Cherie Bennett (2001)

Cast Two Shadows, Ann Rinaldi (1998)

Fallen Angels, W. D. Myers (1988)

Mary Mehan Awake, Jennifer Armstrong (1997)

Milkweed, Jerry Spinelli (2003)

No Man's Land: A Young Soldier's Story, S. Bartoletti (1999)

Operation Homefront, Caroline Cooney (1992)

The River between Us, Richard Peck (2003)

Sarney: A Life Remembered, Gary Paulsen (1997)

Soldier Boy, B. Burks (1997)

Soldier's Heart, Gary Paulsen (1998)

Sonny's War, Valerie Hobbs (2001)

Soon Be Free, Lois Ruby (2000)

Stones in Water, Donna Napoli (1997)

Summer of My German Soldier, Bette Greene (1973)

With Every Drop of Blood, James and Christopher Collier (1994)

Psychology and Sociology

Drowning Anna, Sue Mayfield (2001)

The Giver, Lois Lowry (1993)

Joey Pigza Loses Control, Jack Gantos (2000)

Missing the Piano, Adam Rapp (1994)

No Kidding, Bruce Brooks (1989)

Skin Deep, Lois Ruby (1994)

Speak, Laurie Halse Anderson (1999)

Science and Math

Hatchet, Gary Paulsen (1987)

The Music of Dolphins, Karen Hesse (1996)

The Number Devil: A Mathematical Adventure, H. M. Enzensberger (1997)

Phoenix Rising, Karen Hesse (1994)

Sports

Heat, Michael Cadnum (1998)

High Heat, Carl Deuker (2003)

High Hoops, Carl Deuker (2000)

Home of the Braves, D. Klass (2002)

Racing the Iditarod Trail, Ruth Crisman (1993)

Roughnecks, Thomas Cochran (1997)

Running Loose, Chris Crutcher (1983)

Shots on Goal, Rich Wallace (1997)

Slam, W. D. Myers (1996)

Warrior Angel, Robert Lipsyte (2003)

Whale Talk, Chris Crutcher (2001)

Health

Emily Good as Gold, S. G. Ribin (1993)

Perk! The Story of a Teenager with Bulimia, L. F. Hall (1997)

Petey, Gen Mikaelsen (1998)

Tangerine, E. Bloor (1997)

FIGURE 6.8

Representative literature for non-English classes.

of the family and how members affect each other. They can also write about or discuss the relationship of plot, setting, characterization, conflict, and point of view in literature about family life. Activities in writing, discussion, and creative drama can all bring to life the theme found in these novels.

Social studies: Using the literature they have chosen, students can investigate the family structure portrayed in the novels. They can compare and contrast family life in different cultures. Students can investigate the breakup of the family structure and what leads to that process. In addition to work with the novels, students can work within the theme to investigate various concerns related to family life. How do families cope under various social conditions? Under crisis conditions?

Science: Students can connect scientific study to each of the novels read. What was the scientific knowledge base during the Revolutionary War (*Cast Two Shadows*)? What science techniques were used to help the family survive (*Anne Frank: The Diary of a Young Girl*)? What is the scientific basis for weight control and what can science offer Lara in her quest to lose weight (*Life in the Fat Lane*)? In addition to work with the novels, students can investigate the area of genetics and discover how family characteristics are passed from one generation to another. They can chart the genetic characteristics of class members' families.

Math: Students can graph the size of families in the 1800s, 1850s, 1900s, and into the new millennium. They can also compare the average family size in different countries. How has mathematics helped the family unit to cope with members' daily lives? Students can interview their parents or other adults and find out about the ways in which they use math skills and concepts in their professional or personal lives.

Another approach connects just two disciplines. For example, an integrated approach to science and language arts instruction has several benefits over instruction in separate content areas. Students make meaningful connections between disciplines and find relevance to their own interests and the world around them. Understanding reaches a higher cognitive level in both science and language arts as each enhances the understanding of the other.

In addition, motivation is high for students to develop research skills as they investigate scientific topics within their favorite literature. These investigations are likely to rise to a level higher than course requirements because the motivation is intrinsic.

Integration can also have a positive impact on reading skills. A meaningful, multifaceted study of literary works encourages students to adopt reading as a lifetime recreation, and researching scientific threads within enjoyable literature increases students' use of the written word to access information.

An integrated unit can revolve around a theme or a literary work or group of works. For example, using a theme such as the sea, students might choose from *The Girl of the Sea of Cortez* (1982), *The Deep* (1976), or *Jaws* (1974) by Peter Benchley, *The Music of Dolphins* by Karen Hesse (1996), *Changes in Latitude* by Will Hobbs (1988), *20,000 Leagues under the Sea* by Jules Verne (1872), *Leaving Protection* by Will Hobbs (2004), and *The Old Man and the Sea* by Ernest Hemingway (1952). Students could read poetry selections such as "Whales Weep Not" by D. H. Lawrence

(1976) and "as is the sea marvelous" (1994) and "swim so now million many worlds in each" (1950) by e. e. cummings. Nonfictional videotapes such as the six-tape set *Best of Cousteau* (Turner Home Video, 1990) could be used to establish readiness and to pique student curiosity, as well as for individual research projects.

A broad range of language arts skills can be developed through activities within an integrated thematic unit. For example, in the sea unit, teachers might use a young adult novel such as *The Music of Dolphins* by Karen Hesse (1996) for the activities that follow:

Journal writing on topics such as the following: What do you think are some of the most mysterious aspects of the sea? What is unknown about it that you would most like to know? Which of these mysteries are included in *The Music of Dolphins*?

I-search projects on topics such as dolphins, whales, scuba diving and snorkeling, language development, and feral children. (This is the perfect way to learn to use Internet search engines.)

Panel discussion or debates on environmental issues such as clean air and water legislation, international fishing and whaling regulations, and ethical treatment of test subjects.

Creative writing such as poetry, short story, personal narrative, and character biopoems based on the novel.

Expository and persuasive writing on environmental issue such as clean air and water legislation, international fishing and whaling regulations, and ethical treatment of test subjects.

Cooperative learning with jigsaw activities to learn and report back to a small group on science issues such as oceanography, cetology, ichthyology, sociolinguistics, and anthropology.

Language arts and science can be successfully integrated in any number of ways depending on the creativity of the teacher and the flexibility of the school's curriculum.

It is obvious that young adult literature can play an important role in bringing together the study of various disciplines. In the scenarios just suggested, the content teachers do not have to teach the young adult literature. That can be left to the English teacher; however, the content teachers can use the literature that their students will have read because they are members of the team. This literature can be used to further their study of their own discipline.

 *Learning Log Responses*

How do you determine the quality of a book? In your learning log, explain what a book has to do or have to be a quality book for you.

What arrangement for teaching literature best suits you? Do you prefer having one book read by everyone, a few books related by theme read by groups of students, or one book chosen by each student? Explain what approach you will use and why.

Choose and read a collection of poetry, short stories, or drama. Write a brief entry about the content of each collection, its appropriateness for young adults, and the way you would use the collection in your classroom.

Create a thematic unit for a team of teachers in which the unit draws on all of the disciplines represented. What objectives will you have? What skills will students learn?

References

Atwell, N. (1998). *In the middle* (2nd ed.). Portsmouth, NH: Boynton Cook/Heinemann.

Carey, M. Poster, Ottawa, KS: The Writing Conference.

Carter, B., & Abrahamson, R. (1990). Nonfiction: The missing piece in the middle. *English Journal, 80*(1), 52–58.

Carter, B., & Abrahamson, R. (1991). *Nonfiction for young adults: From delight to wisdom.* Phoenix, AZ: Oryx.

Gallo, D. (Ed.). (1984). *Sixteen*. New York: Dell.

Hazlett, L., Richardson, M., & Richardson, J. A. (2002). *Literature across the disciplines.* Ottawa, KS: The Writing Conference.

Holbrook, S. Poster. Ottawa, KS: The Writing Conference.

Janeczko, P. Poster. Ottawa, KS: The Writing Conference.

Leighton, D. (1991). Saturating students with reading: A classroom lab approach. *English Journal, 80*(6), 81–85.

C H A P T E R

7

Young Adult Literature and the Classics

Literature is greater, broader, wider, more encompassing than the classics. Literature is an ocean. The classics are like an inland sea. We don't need "great" books to bring out kids to literature. We need readable books that enchant and inform and move kids to want more.

Harry Mazer

*T*eachers are torn between teaching the literature they feel will be most useful to their students and the literature that everyone else thinks they ought to teach. The struggle is not just with high school English teachers but with middle and upper elementary language arts teachers as well.

As we visit classrooms and talk to teachers, we find more and more emphasis being placed on "the classics." In fact, a survey that asked 322 public schools to list the books most frequently required in those schools (Applebee, 1989) showed the following 10 most frequently cited titles: (1) *Romeo and Juliet*, (2) *Macbeth*, (3) *Adventures of Huckleberry Finn*, (4) *To Kill a Mockingbird*, (5) *Julius Caesar*, (6) *The Pearl*, (7) *The Scarlet Letter*, (8) *Of Mice and Men*, (9) *Lord of the Flies*, and (10) *Anne Frank: The Diary of a Young Girl*. Interestingly, when compared with a similar study done in 1963, little has changed in more than 30 years.

Our concern—in addition to the lack of women and minority writers represented—is that in the 27 most frequently mentioned titles in the Applebee study, the emphasis is still on literature that has very little relationship to the adolescent. However, at least in the top 10 mentioned, *To Kill a Mockingbird*, *Lord of the Flies*, *Romeo and Juliet*, *Anne Frank: The Diary of a Young Girl*, and *Adventures of Huckleberry Finn* have some connection to young adults. When we talk further with teachers about the literature in the classroom, we find that students do not enjoy what they are reading; in fact, many are not reading at all but simply hearing about what they were supposed to read—in essence, hearing a translation of the literature.

Why do teachers feel that they have to teach the classics? What does the research say about the relationship between young adults and the literature they read? What are the alternatives to a curriculum composed of only the classics? We explore these questions and others in the following pages.

What Do the Students Say?

In a time of school restructuring, school reorganization, and curriculum evaluation, many "experts" surface to tell school officials what to do and how to go about doing it. Most of these experts, however, are outside of education. Those who work within the schools every day don't have much credibility. Boards of education commission experts to analyze the various components of schooling and to offer assistance in the effort to make changes. Often the two groups most affected—teachers and students—are not asked for input regarding the changes that ought to be made. Therefore, a study such as that by Sullivan (1991), who asked her students for information about their reading interests and habits, is refreshing. The results of her survey were not surprising.

> There were a few exceptions. Very few. The trend was clear, undeniable. I can't say that this took me completely by surprise. I have suspected the dark truth for a long time, had been working to develop strategies for counteracting the forces that work in school to separate students from the pleasure and the transforming power of reading. But I had never had to stare the fact in the face like this before. What I saw was painful. It raised difficult questions. It was, ultimately, instructive.
>
> In some cases, school had caused these bright students to abandon reading completely. More often—thank goodness!—enthusiastic readers remained enthusiastic about their own outside-of-school reading and hated (or, at best, remained indifferent to) only what they had to do for school. They clung to the pleasure of reading in spite of us. Sometimes we made them suffer for the choice. (p. 40)

This summary of the students' attitudes toward school literature reminded us of a statement made by a ninth grader we know. He said, "I love to read, but I hate literature." When prompted to continue this thought, he suggested that what he was reading in school had nothing, or at least very little, to do with him. He told us that his book report (one due every 9 weeks) offered some relief because he could usually choose something that he knew he would like, but what he read in the classroom was, as he called it, "dumb."

Sullivan (1991) asked students to share their thoughts about the literature taught in schools and their relationship to that literature. The details these students offer support the previous summary. Most have an exciting experience with literature during their elementary schooling, but the break in this happy experience comes as they enter junior high or middle school. Their loss of interest in reading generally comes in the seventh or eighth grade and, most of the time, continues through high school. Some students are creative and work things out for themselves. Louis is a case in point: "Finally in tenth grade I just started reading all the time. At first it was because I actually had spare time, but then I really began reading because I started using 'Mr. Cliff' and then I had tons of time for my own reading" (Sullivan, 1991, p. 41).

Another student, Amy, makes an interesting point:

> In high school came the assigned movies and textbook reading. They were OK, but I would have liked to go through them a bit faster so that we could have read some more modern things. I hate that we only read "old" things. In English I read one of the modern short stories that we skipped in class. It was the best story in the book. (Sullivan, 1991, p. 42)

And Melissa:

> In my tenth grade English class, we had to choose something to read off a list. There were all sorts of wonderful things I wanted to read like *Lord of the Flies* and *I Never Promised You a Rose Garden*, but I chose mine too late because I couldn't make a choice. All the best had been taken and I found myself stuck with *The Death of a Salesman*. I hated it with a purple passion! After that assignment was over I went back to the library and found *I Never Promised You a Rose Garden*. (Sullivan, 1991, p. 42)

Although there were a number of relevant options from which Melissa could choose something that she liked, the tragedy is that there were not enough books she wanted to read on the list. Consequently, Melissa could not read something of her choice but had to read something that she hated.

There is obviously a wide chasm between what the school offers for students to read and what the students want to read in the literature program. It is also obvious to us that many students will get along some way within this dichotomy, but the question arises: Why should they have to? It is also obvious that many students are not successful—they simply stop reading. Vogel and Zancanella (1991) make an interesting point:

> Some of us spend a great deal of energy trying to draw a clear line between the serious study of "literature" and the undisciplined consumption of "entertainment." Others try to erase such lines so that Stephen King can slide up against Shakespeare. What such maneuvering often fails to take into account, however, are the realities of ongoing literary experiences of adolescents in and out of school. For all the recent quarrels about the canon, about what seventeen-year-olds should know, about who's culturally literate and who ain't, little attention has been paid to the kinds of "literary lives" teenagers lead and to how those lives connect or fail to connect with the learning of literature in English class. (p. 54)

Vogel and Zancanella go on to share the literary lives of four adolescents, and their findings are not unlike Sullivan's. These four adolescents have very little interest in the literature found in the classroom but are interested in what they read outside of school. And that interest outside the classroom is varied. One student has a fondness for romances; another thinks mysteries are great reading. "For Donnovan, school remains a problem. Literature in school means absorbing the viewpoint of the teacher. From his viewpoint his interpretation will always be unaccountably different from those of his teachers" (1991, p. 57). However, Donnovan's love for music, art, and movies shows a different set of interests.

Small (1972) shares Donnovan's concern. He points out that the generally accepted goal of high school literature programs seems to place the student at a great disadvantage while the teacher is positioned as the source for the meaning of the literature read. Students have had fewer experiences—and for some, no experience at all—in such areas as marriage and divorce, ambition, greed, and hate, so it is more difficult for them to make honest responses about what meaning is there for them. In contrast, when the book has a teenager as the protagonist and other young adult characters, the balance of knowledge and the authority that is brought to that reading is changed. Young adults are more easily able to evaluate the characters, their problems, and the resolution of these problems.

What Vogel and Zancanella are saying is very similar to what Langer found in her 1984 study, "Literacy Instruction in American High Schools: Problems and Perspectives." In this study, Langer suggests that literacy instruction is differentially determined by who the students are and what worldviews and interests they bring to the classroom.

> While syntax, word length, and vocabulary have been shown to affect text difficulty, more recent views of reading comprehension suggest that ease of comprehension is also a function of the reader's knowledge and experiences . . . the contextual variables that affect and are affected by the purpose for reading and the environment surrounding the reading experience. (Langer, 1984, p. 122)

In *Voices of Readers* (1988), Carlsen and Sherrill present excerpts from the literature autobiographies of their students. It is interesting to note the authors' summary regarding attitudes toward the classics:

> It seems fairly clear that most of these people's taste had to reach a certain level of maturity before the classics were appreciated. Some mention their senior high school English classes as being responsible for their interest in the classics, but more often, it was not until their college English courses that they began to understand the reasons for labeling a literary work as "classic." Even then, some respondents had been so traumatized by their earlier exposure to a particular title that they could never overcome their distaste for it. (p. 135)

Students seem to be saying that what they are asked to read in school is far removed from their experiences out of school and far removed from what is of interest to them. When students have something to read that reflects their interests, most will read. When they do not, students either do enough to get by or simply give up and stop reading.

Developing Lifetime Readers

As noted, one of the most important goals for any school at any level is to foster reading so that students develop into lifelong readers. We would argue that schools are not succeeding. Lesesne (1991) surveyed middle school students and found that "almost seventy-five percent of the middle school students reported reading less than one hour daily on a regular basis; twenty percent had read only one book for their own enjoyment in the last six months" (p. 61).

O'Connor (1980) believes it isn't that students in schools can't read, but that they don't want to read because of the lack of connection between them and the literature. Angelotti (1981) concludes that the literature curriculum has contributed to the lack of reading by adults. He suggests that school curricula have produced very few adults who read serious literature. A study of more than 200,000 sixth graders in California revealed that 70 percent rarely read for pleasure (Trelease, 1982).

Results of a study titled "A Profile of the American Eighth Grader" completed by the U.S. Department of Education (1990) show that eighth-grade students in public, private independent, and Catholic schools have something in common: They don't read much for fun. Regardless of where these students went to school, they spent 2 hours or less each week reading on their own. Schools have made some attempt to increase the amount of reading that occurs after formal schooling. Programs such as sustained silent reading, directed individualized reading, elective courses that allow students a choice of what they read, and modeling by teachers to show the importance of reading have made some impact, but not much. We still have a society that is made up of many nonreaders.

A study in 1997 (Bushman, 1997) indicates that the middle and high school students surveyed are similar to the students previously mentioned in this chapter. They are not reading much either. In this survey, students indicated that they didn't have much time for outside reading because the reading assigned in class took most of their time. The in-class reading for 6th and 7th graders was more likely to be young adult literature. The assigned reading for 8th through 12th graders was much different. The most frequently named assigned books by 8th graders were *Julius Caesar* and *Anne Frank: The Diary of a Young Girl*. Next in frequency were *Call of the Wild, Romeo and Juliet, Ulysses, Great Expectations,* and *Count of Monte Cristo*. Of the 48 books mentioned, six were young adult. Ninth- through 12th-grade assigned reading was much the same—predominantly classics. Outside reading was similar, too. Students often had no choice in what they read. Clearly, the amount of reading from 8th to 12th grade diminished. Students indicated that the reading done in class (classics) was enough and they had no desire to read beyond what was assigned.

The research indicates what makes lifelong readers (Lesesne, 1991), and from what students offer about their reading habits in and out of school, an additional change must occur in the English classroom. These add-ons to the English curriculum may provide some help, but the curriculum itself should be modified to include literature that allows students to make some connection between themselves and the text they read, to find relationships between them and the developmental tasks they must accomplish, and to read at a level at which comprehension can come with little difficulty. Reading of literature in the classroom must be closely related to the independent reading of literature outside of the classroom. Atwell (1987) suggests:

> If we want our adolescent students to grow to appreciate literature, another first step is allowing them to exert ownership and choose the literature they will read. Preliminary to that, we might take a giant step as readers ourselves and acknowledge that the term "literature" embraces more than the risk-free, prescribed junior high canon or second-rate Dickens (*A Tale of Two Cities*), second-rate Steinbeck (*The Red Pony*), and second-rate Hemingway (*Old Man and the Sea*). The last twenty years have witnessed an explosion in the numbers of novels and short stories written expressly for young adults, adolescent literature of such breadth and depth that no teacher need ever apologize for building a curriculum around kids' responses to their own books. (p. 161)

Certainly, out-of-classroom reading does not have to be identical to in-classroom reading because the classroom should foster growth in literary experiences. But as Probst (1984) indicates, if students read with no other purpose in mind than to find and recall information, we may legitimately wonder if they have had a more significant literary experience than that of the student who reads only a summary (p. 30). If a work touches on matters in which students have a vital interest, and if the students can read it with enough ease to be able to grasp the fundamental issues, then they may respond strongly enough to the text (p. 32).

Therefore, the decisions that must be made by teachers and curriculum directors seem obvious: Literature that relates in meaningful ways to adolescents in middle and high schools should be a strong part of the English curriculum if we want to increase the numbers of lifelong readers. Carlsen and Sherrill (1988) conclude that to produce readers, students at almost every level should be exposed to a variety of reading fare, participate in reader-centered discussions of literature, generate nontraditional book reports, and be allowed freedom of choice in what they read.

Why Emphasize the Classics?

The Back-to-Basics Movements

Throughout modern schooling, there has always been some concern about the quality of education. This emphasis surfaces periodically with new concerns, frequently about different issues. Not long ago, the concern centered on our students being able to compete with students in other countries; in the 1950s, during the Sputnik era, the concern was with the quality of science and math instruction. The nation's schools and society went through a much more liberal time during the 1960s and early 1970s.

Following this emphasis on experimentation and self-discovery, educators, some reluctantly, accepted the back-to-basics movement; teachers and administrators removed most electives composed of thematic units that emphasized more contemporary literature and replaced this more creative curriculum design with one that emphasized the use of the anthology. This approach usually provided the student with a chronological presentation of American literature for juniors and British literature for seniors. The anthologies for lower high school and middle school contained literature often thematically related but very little literature that could be identified as specifically for the young adult.

Curricula of the 1980s and 1990s continued this tradition of including the literature of the past—the literature most commonly called the classics. Publications that call for school and curricula reform often contain suggestions about the English curriculum, such as including literature that will help students understand their literary heritage. They often call for a standardized list—sometimes a list of literary works that all students should have read by the time they leave high school and sometimes a list of educational areas, topics, or concepts that all should know about.

One list is from E. D. Hirsch, Jr. In *Cultural Literacy: What Every American Needs to Know* (1987), Hirsch sets forth a plan for making cultural literacy an educational priority. He defines core knowledge, wants textbook writers to put more of this information in the textbooks, and wants to develop tests of core learning that students can use to measure their progress. His list includes titles, areas, and issues. *A Nation at Risk* (Commission on Excellence in Education, 1984) also calls for more emphasis on the study of literature that will increase students' cultural literacy.

Two dangers seem apparent with lists (Mullican, 1991): (1) Whose culture and whose literacy are represented by the lists? It seems that the diverse population is not considered. (2) Lists will probably mean that the "culturally literate need know only titles, not entire literary works" (p. 244). Educators discuss these concerns in *Educational Leadership* (December 1991–January 1992), volume 49, issue 4.

Our concern is that many students are not cognitively or emotionally ready to read and understand many of the works that appear on these lists. Because American education tries to educate the total population of students with varying ability levels from kindergarten through grade 12, many of these students cannot handle some of the specific works that are recommended. Many are just too difficult. As we read these lists and the tables of contents in anthologies, it is clear that adult literature is being recommended. For example, Charles Dickens wrote for adults: He shared with adults the social problems of 19th-century England as he saw them, and his writing was delivered to these adults in installments in periodicals. That information should give teachers pause as they think of selecting literature for 21st-century young people. Most of the teachers we talk to acknowledge that many of their students are not ready for this adult literature.

The Importance of the Anthology

Another very important reason for the continued emphasis on classic literature is the prominent place the anthology has in the English classroom. There is a mystique about placing literature in a hardback collection. Accompanying this collection are strategies on how to use the material, including questions that can be asked before, during, and after the reading of any piece of literature. Also, this total package often includes a testing program. By purchasing the anthology package, teachers receive more than just the literature.

Certainly the anthology makes it easier for school districts to buy materials for groups of students spread over a number of grades. But therein lies one of the difficulties. When teachers use a particular anthology, they are assuming that all students in a particular class can and will read the literature found in the book. Evidence indicates the contrary. All 8th graders or 11th graders are not alike. The reading level, the emotional level, and the developmental level of adolescents vary significantly in each grade level. We find it difficult to recommend the use of anthologies when teaching a diverse set of students.

Sullivan (1991) mentioned Amy's concern about having to read so many "old" pieces of literature. Amy and many teachers do not realize that including old pieces keeps the cost of the anthology down. Authors of literature in the public domain do not receive royalty payments when that literature is used in an anthology. Even with this consideration, the anthology is quite expensive, which leaves little money for supplemental reading material. Therefore, the emphasis is given to the literature in the collection.

The Chicken-or-Egg Theory of Classics

The major factor used to determine classics is time. Charles Dickens's literature is considered classic primarily because it has stood the test of time. Of course, classic literature addresses the human condition and has a particular quality that we have come to equate with "great" literature. Time, however, is the deciding factor, because contemporary literature that also addresses the human condition rarely is considered classic.

A number of questions arise concerning this time element. Have the classics withstood the test of time because they are great literature? Or have they withstood the test of time because they are required reading in college English classes and because they are included in anthologies that are "read" by thousands and thousands of public school students? We pose this question only to suggest further discussion about an important issue that has a major impact on the reading program of young adults.

The University Wants Them Taught

The influence on high school literature programs of postsecondary institutions is perceived rather than direct. Colleges and universities do not tell high school teachers or administrators what to teach, although that was not always true. During the early and mid-1900s, colleges and universities distributed lists of books that students who graduated from high school ought to have read, and it was expected that students would read the books.

Although this is no longer formally done, the lists still exist, and teachers who want their students to do well in college often consult the lists so that they can include these books in their high school English classes. They apparently operate on the philosophy that if it is good for college students, it is good for high school students.

It is important to note, however, the type of literature that is often taught in freshman and sophomore courses at colleges and universities. If our analysis is correct, most programs emphasize writing at the freshman level, with some literature in the form of essays and other short pieces. Sophomore English often focuses on a variety of contemporary literature with, again, an emphasis on writing. It is not until the junior year that the British and American canonical literature is taught; of course, students who take these courses are English majors or at least have majors closely connected to the English field. It would seem to us that the colleges and universities have, through their reading lists and course offerings, forced the teaching of the classics to the high school level. We believe that this practice is inappropriate. In keeping with what we know about the classics, they are far more appropriate for college-level students.

English professors whom we have talked to prefer incoming students who have competent writing, literary analysis, and discussion skills (all of which can be developed with quality young adult literature) instead of having a knowledge base of literature that they may or may not have understood in high school.

We should also point out that most college and university teacher education programs for English teachers include a major in English, which usually includes approximately 20 hours in British, American, and world literature, with almost all of those coming from the traditional classical literature. Many colleges and universities require some study of adolescent literature but may not have a separate course that connects the adolescent literature with the methods course. English teachers have little to use as models: Their high school literature and their college literature programs are classics oriented.

Guilt

We suppose that some teachers have a sense of guilt if they do not stick with the canon. Certainly, no one can attack teachers for believing that educated people ought to know something of their literary heritage. Generally, the middle and high schools have become the place where that occurs, regardless of whether it is appropriate for these students. Teachers feel, and rightly so, that they are members of a team and want to be a team player, so if the department chair or the curriculum guide says to teach *Silas Marner,* teachers are hard-pressed not to do it even if they believe it is a waste of time. However, there are a few teachers who don't go along with the crowd just because everybody is doing it. We take our hats off to them for the stands that they are taking.

The Classics and Why Young Adults Have Problems Reading Them

In addition to the other problems facing young adults and teachers as they read and teach classics, there are two built-in problems that are difficult to overcome: The classics were written for adults, and they were written for an audience that doesn't exist today.

The classics were really not intended to be read by young people at all. Even though this literature may speak to the universal human condition, young people have trouble relating because they have not experienced many of those human conditions. In addition, the classics are written in a style and with syntax and vocabulary that are often quite foreign to young adult readers. Along with the survival of time, the classics are lovingly guarded by some for their stylistic prestige. It is this stylistic prominence that elevates the classic to the high level. Yet it is this elevation that makes appreciation and understanding unattainable for most young adults.

O'Donnell (1983) chronicles attitudes concerning the use of classical literature in the classroom. In her report, she shares the opinion of Robert Carlsen: "It is true that classic literature is one of the most difficult, most subtle and most mature expressions of human beings, so it is no surprise that an understanding and enjoyment of the classics comes, if at all, fairly late in a reader's growth" (O'Donnell, 1983, p. 48). Holbrook (1982) agrees: "Unfortunately, students are often introduced to these often difficult and irrelevant works just when their lives hold so much to distract them from reading . . . it takes a special kind of story to maintain their interest in reading" (p. 378).

To revisit Vygotskian theory, learning occurs only in one's zone of proximal development—"the level at which [learners] can do things with help that they cannot do alone" (Wilhelm, p. 10). Although students may produce impressive results through reading analysis and journaling, as well as after-reading essays and projects, if they are reading material that is in their "zone of actual development," with text that is easy for them to comprehend, we have taught them nothing, simply because they came to the reading already with the skills in their command. As a result, we are certainly not promoting that students be assigned readings that are too easy for them, not challenging their reading skills to mature. On the other hand, if we assign them reading material that is far too difficult and out of reach, these works many times being the works of Shakespeare, Dickens, Hawthorne, and Austen, we are asking students to work at a level beyond their proximal development, causing them to see reading and comprehension as a hopeless task that they cannot achieve and leaving them in, what Wilhelm calls, "the student's frustrational reading level" (p. 17). As a result, for many students, works by Robert Cormier, Chris Crutcher, M. T. Anderson, Mildred Taylor, Gary Soto, and so many other young adult authors fit the bill, taking students just where they are and, accompanied by effective instruction, moving them forward to higher levels of comprehension. Skipping over the students' zone of proximal development leaves students behind, regardless of the accompanying instruction and activities.

Because understanding and enjoyment of the classics rarely occur in many students at the middle and high school levels, teachers resort to picking apart and dissecting the literature so that the students can get something out of the classroom presentation. Shaw's (1935) comment may still be appropriate today: "Well meaning English teachers once dissected them [the classics] for us, poked around for the intangible in them, tried to unscrew the inscrutable for us and fixed us for the most part so we shall never open these books again" (p. 110). Robert Frost makes a similar point:

I don't want to analyze authors. I want to enjoy them. I want the boys in class to enjoy their books because of what's in them. . . . Youth, I believe, should not analyze its enjoyments. It should live. Criticism is the province of age, not youth. They'll get to that soon enough. Let them build up a friendship with the written word first. (Newdick, 1936, p. 632)

Carlsen and Sherrill (1988) summarize why some adults are not interested in reading:

> The most tragic of all the records, however, are those describing the traumatic experiences that children had with teachers and other adults. They were told they were poor readers, which made them feel inadequate as human beings and thereby fueled their determination to stay as far away as possible from this demeaning activity. Others became embarrassed in front of their classmates because of their teachers' comments about their poor oral reading skills. And still others were forced to read books that they found distasteful because these books were beyond either their comprehension or their interests. (p. 143)

The argument is not that students cannot make literary analyses in what they read or that they should never read a classic. The argument centers on what we know about the young adult, what we know about that body of literature we have come to call the classics, and how this knowledge can lead teachers to do what is appropriate for their students. If teachers want their students to hone their thinking skills and they want to use literature to aid in the process, then teachers should select literature that students can understand and respond to. When this happens, students have a common core of knowledge that is suitable for them to use in these thinking processes.

> *Classics: Books people praise but don't read.*
>
> Mark Twain

Of course, quality young adult literature can also be explored. It is folly to think that students can respond to universal themes, literary techniques, and the craft of specific authors only by reading and studying the classics. Literary analysis can and does occur with most young adult literature recommended for middle and high school students. In addition, some students may have progressed to the point where they are emotionally, experientially, cognitively, and developmentally ready to read this traditional adult literature. If they reach that point, teachers should encourage students to explore what interests them with the classics, but until then, teachers may find more success if they have students read the literature that is best suited for them. If students can have success with young adult literature, they may well continue the reading process as they move from the school setting. Daigon (1969) sums up this point of view in his response to a critic of young adult literature:

> Yes, you say, but what of the wisdom of ages, the great ideas and passions of the most sensitive and the most skilled, the great canon of the literary tradition, the great books, the noble concepts, the jewels of our intellectual and aesthetic heritage?
>
> Do we have the courage to confront the cruel reality that the literary heritage barely lives and does so in the minds of a handful of critics, intellectuals, and teachers? And it is losing ground fast as the media revolution and general antagonism to traditions and establishments gain momentum.

If we feel that literature does offer modes of experience and pleasures not otherwise available, and if we feel that these experiences and pleasures are worth passing on to new generations, the principles of relevance, variety, involvement, and developmental appropriateness will surely have to play major roles in literature instruction in the secondary school. If we feel that we cannot or should not do these things, let us honestly put literature away in a museum display case with other relics to be viewed, to be revered, and to be eulogized in hushed tones reserved for the dead. (p. 39)

Young Adult Literature as a Bridge to the Classics

Still, another struggle with students reading the classics deals with students' prior knowledge. "In general, the degree of prior knowledge (schemata) one has about a topic, event, or idea has a substantial impact on what will be learned" (Cooter & Flynt, 1996). According to brain researcher David Sousa, the criteria for whether or not students are able to store new information in "long-range storage" is dependent on the degree to which students can make sense out of it, as well as to the degree it has meaning for the student. "Brain scans have shown that when new learning is readily comprehensible (sense) and can be connected to past experiences (meaning) there is substantially more cerebral activity followed by dramatically improved retention" (Sousa, 2001). We would advocate that herein lies another roadblock with the classics, as students are frequently reading about situations that are foreign to them, situations for which they have no prior knowledge, situations that many times have little meaning or make little sense to them. What do our students know about the societal hierarchies addressed in such works as Shaw's *Pygmalian*, Austin's *Pride and Prejudice*, Fitzgerald's *The Great Gatsby*, or Dickens's *Great Expectations*? What knowledge do they have of the toils and struggles of such characters as Willie Lohman, Oedipus, and Hester Prynne? What experiences do they share with Raskolnikov in *Crime and Punishment* or Ishmael in *Moby Dick*? Does this mean that all the aforementioned books should never be used at all? No, we're not saying that. However, if they are used, they need to be addressed so that students can be successful with them. One of those ways is to create prior knowledge for the students to help them make the connections once the reading occurs, and one of the ways to do that is to, first, introduce students to parallel texts—young adult literature that can serve as a bridge or stepping-stone to the more challenging classic, throughout the reading of the classic, being sure to guide students to make connections all along the way.

We hesitate to discuss the use of young adult literature as a bridge to reading and studying the classics because we are generally troubled when teachers use the classics at the middle and high school levels. We firmly believe that 12- to 17-year-olds need to read literature that helps them grow in making literary responses and analyses and that relates to each individual in meaningful ways. To those few juniors and seniors in high school who have grown significantly in meeting their interests and their developmental needs so that they can respond effectively to what they read, we certainly recommend selected classics for the curriculum. However, we know that even though many students have not arrived at this level, the classics are what they will read in their English classrooms.

Therefore, our suggestion is that teachers precede study of the classics with selected young adult literature that is similar in theme or focus to the classics. In this way, students can succeed at discovering meaning and understanding the literary craft in literature at their developmental level before undertaking the analysis of literature at a higher level. Small (1977) argues: "If you were, for example, trying to teach a child how a jet or automobile engine works, it surely would be better not to use the engines of a 747 or the most advanced racing cars" (p. 56). Experience with making personal responses, analyzing literary techniques, and evaluating the writer's craft with the young adult novel may provide readers with the needed tools in literature study to help in reading adult literature. This approach assumes that, to use Small's analogy again, students will be able to work with the jet engine after working with the automobile engine. Teachers assume that because students can read N. F. Mazer's *When We First Met* (1982), they will be able to immediately move on to read *Romeo and Juliet*. Some, and maybe many, will not. In the spirit of using young adult literature as a bridge to the classics, we'll start by discussing the connecting elements of a few pairings. Additional pairings follow. For a more in-depth study of pairings of young adult literature with the classics, see Kaywell's (1993–1997) *Adolescent Literature as a Complement to the Classics*.

The Pairings: A Few in Detail

The Scarlet Letter.   *The Scarlet Letter* by Nathaniel Hawthorne (1850) is found in most high school curricula and is often read by juniors. The novel's complex sentence structure and vocabulary present many problems for high school students. The contemporary student has additional difficulty understanding Puritanism as well as some of the complex emotions that Hawthorne includes: despair, anger, grief, guilt, vengeance, and purification by suffering. Hawthorne's use of symbolism and his use of the setting as an emotional companion contribute to the difficulty in understanding the novel.

Samuels and Lowery-Moore (1987) suggest using a young adult novel that offers much the same Puritan atmosphere. *The Witch of Blackbird Pond* (Speare, 1958) is the story of a young girl from Barbados who moves to Connecticut, where she finds a very repressive atmosphere.

They also suggest *Sharelle* (Neufeld, 1983) because it also offers many similarities to the Hawthorne novel. Sharelle is a young adult who becomes pregnant at a time in her life when she is in need of love and affection. In addition, the reader knows early in the novel the identity of the child's father; however, Sharelle (like Hester) does not reveal his identity. Throughout the novel, readers see Sharelle's personal growth.

Although the Neufeld novel is not of the same quality as the Hawthorne work, it offers a similar theme for young adults to address before attempting the older work. A few questions may be used to discuss both novels: Did Hester (Sharelle) have justification for having the affair? Why does Hester (Sharelle) keep the identity of the father secret? Does she ever regret her decision? Does Hester (Sharelle) take responsibility for her actions? Is she a good mother? Does Hester (Sharelle) benefit from her circumstances?

Another young adult novel with this theme of unplanned pregnancy is Eyerly's *Someone to Love Me* (1987). Again, the novel is similar in theme to the Hawthorne novel. Students can respond to this work before moving on.

Guilt, a strong force in *The Scarlet Letter,* is also found in Zindel's *The Pigman* (1968). The theme and plot of the two novels are not similar, but the idea of guilt in both could be explored by students in the Zindel novel before they read the older work. Shortly after John and Lorraine discuss guilt with Mr. Pignati, he has a heart attack while roller-skating with the two young people. Discussing the guilt in the young adult novel may make the discussion in the classic more relevant to the readers. A discussion of the guilt that Louie feels after Becky's death in *Running Loose* (Crutcher, 1983) may also help. Students can also discuss the effects of guilt in *The One-Eyed Cat* (Fox, 1984).

Connections could also be made addressing how the community in which Hester lives ostracizes her. Similarly, Nick Andreas, in *Breathing Underwater* (Flinn, 2001), is ostracized for abusing his girlfriend. Even Nick's best friend turns against him and ignores him at school. Likewise, Melinda, in *Speak* (Anderson, 1999), is ostracized at the beginning of her freshman year in high school after she calls the police during a late-summer party—her peers having no idea that she had been raped and was in shock while making the call. Finally, there is Ailen, in *Ties That Bind, Ties That Break* (Namioka, 1999), who is disowned by her family for refusing to have her feet bound, a tradition in her Chinese society in the early 1900s. Students could make connections with Hester, comparing the circumstances and the aftereffects of what the characters go through.

One other area that may be explored in young adult literature first is the concept of emotionalized landscaping and the symbolism that goes with it. Setting is an integral part of the plot in Hawthorne's novel. Before reading *The Scarlet Letter*, students may benefit from reading *Z for Zachariah* (O'Brien, 1974), *Roll of Thunder, Hear My Cry* (M. Taylor, 1976), or *Deathwatch* (R. White, 1972). The emphasis on the setting in these young adult novels can help students understand this concept before moving on to *The Scarlet Letter.*

Romeo and Juliet.   The book and musical *West Side Story* (Laurents, 1956) is an updated, contemporary *Romeo and Juliet* that students can read, understand, and enjoy. The theme is basically the same; the major differences lie in the contemporary language and depth of quality found in the Shakespearean drama. Reading the script of *West Side Story* first may help students come to some understanding of the motivation of the two young people in love, of the interaction of the street gangs, and of the roles that parents play in the lives of young people and in their desire to be together.

A similar theme is found in N. F. Mazer's *When We First Met* (1982). Jenny and Rob can't be happier. They both believe their love will last forever. Jenny then finds out that Rob's mother is the drunken driver who killed Jenny's sister. She struggles with loyalty to her family but doesn't want to lose Rob. If this understanding comes through the more easily read literature, more time can be spent on the difficulties found in the Shakespearean drama. Certainly, having students compare and contrast the two will help in their understanding.

In a more recent novel, Sharon Draper presents a lively updated version of the Shakespearean tale in *Romiette and Julio* (1999). In this novel, the young lovers meet through the Internet, and Destiny is not the future but the name of Romiette's best friend. The major conflict is not with warring families, although early in the novel Julio's father is less than enthusiastic about Julio's relationship with Romiette, but with a school gang called the Devildogs that is opposed to Romiette, an African American, dating Julio, a Hispanic. Many of the themes that occur in Romiette and Julio also occur in Shakespeare's work. Interestingly, the major characters refer to the fact that their names are similar to Romeo and Juliet, and when tragedy strikes, all are concerned about the possibility of the tragic ending.

This suicide theme in *Romeo and Juliet* is quite troublesome. Young people often find this act difficult to understand. Even though they may have friends who have committed suicide, they still struggle with it. Reading R. Peck's *Remembering the Good Times* (1985) and Pfeffer's *About David* (1980) may help in that understanding. Both young adult authors treat the subject honestly, sincerely, and with great emotional care. Young people may then be able to understand Romeo and Juliet's actions when they realize their love cannot be.

If students read Hinton's *The Outsiders* (1967), they can get a sense of what societal gangs are all about and their effects on individuals. How alike are the Montagues and Capulets to the Greasers and Socs? The understanding that comes from reading Hinton's work may transfer when reading about similar actions in *Romeo and Juliet*.

To what extent will young people honor a commitment they have made? Some students reading *Romeo and Juliet* struggle with the idea that if they cannot be together, they will not live. Many novels have protagonists that make a commitment and have the strength to carry it out even when they are faced with great danger. One such novel is *Summer of My German Soldier* (Greene, 1973). Patty, a Jewish teenager, puts her life in danger by hiding Anton, her German soldier, after he escapes from a train taking him to a detention camp in Arkansas.

Walden. Two Paulsen novels, *The Island* (1988) and *Hatchet* (1987), work well to prepare readers for the more difficult *Walden* (Thoreau, 1854). The concept of learning from nature as well as learning through self-discovery runs through both of Paulsen's novels. In *The Island,* Wil finds his island and communes with nature, probing his understanding of what life is about and his relationship to the land and the water and to the life that is found there. In addition, both Wil and Thoreau turn to writing to help make their discoveries meaningful. Readers will relate well to Wil, a teenage boy, as he struggles with the world around him. Readers will also have a better chance of understanding limited isolation and self-study when it is done by one of their own. They can then take this concept to their reading of Thoreau's work.

Similarly, Brian Robeson, the protagonist in *Hatchet,* finds himself alone in the Canadian wilderness with nothing to draw on but a hatchet, the clothes that he wears, and his will to survive. Although landing the plane in the wilderness was not his choice, Brian learns about himself as he fights to stay alive in the rugged environment.

In *The Island,* the interaction with nature is by choice; in *Hatchet,* it is not. In both, the results are the same: Two young boys learn about themselves, their relationships to the world around them, and the meaning of life as they live it.

In the pairings in Figure 7.1, we have provided one or more young adult novels as companions to the older, traditional adult literature. In these listings, our organizing premise is to find a work with a similar theme—a theme that can more easily be rendered in the young adult novel than in the older work. Having the security of understanding and enjoying the young adult novel may make the job of reading and understanding the classic easier.

Other Pairings

There are other ways of making connections between the classics and young adult literature. For example, if the point of comparison is the general attitude of the region of the country, then it would be helpful to read *Johnny Tremain* (Forbes, 1944), *A Day No Pigs Would Die* (R. N. Peck, 1972), and *Homecoming* (Voigt, 1981) to get some understanding of the New England value system before reading *The Scarlet Letter* (Hawthorne, 1850). If the connecting theme is what it means to be southern, then students might read *Shuttered Windows* (Means, 1938), *Roll of Thunder, Hear My Cry* (M. Taylor, 1976), *M. C. Higgins, The Great* (Hamilton, 1974), *Home before Dark* (Bridgers, 1976), and *Sounder* (Armstrong, 1969) before reading the literature of Eudora Welty, Carson Mc-Cullers, William Faulkner, Tennessee Williams, and Flannery O'Connor.

The theme of social relationships and social status runs through *The Great Gatsby* (Fitzgerald, 1925). Perhaps students could read *Everything Is Not Enough* (Asher, 1987), *Permanent Connections* (Bridgers, 1987), or *Ordinary People* (Guest, 1977) before tackling the Fitzgerald novel.

The law, or at least a trial, plays an important part in *To Kill a Mockingbird* (H. Lee, 1960/1988), *The Stranger* (Camus, 1954), and *Billy Budd* (Melville, 1924). It may be helpful if students first read *Permanent Connections* (Bridgers, 1987) or *Summer of My German Soldier* (Greene, 1973). Discussion could center on the connections between the law of the time and how that law was integrated into the trials.

The decision theme may be used to make connections among young adult novels and the classics. Although there are many elements to explore in *The Crucible* (A. Miller, 1952), *Kidnapped* (Stevenson, 1886), *Of Mice and Men* (Steinbeck, 1937), *The Old Man and the Sea* (Hemingway, 1952), and *The Pearl* (Steinbeck, 1947), the decisions element may best be served by reading *Across Five Aprils* (Hunt, 1964), *The Catcher in the Rye* (Salinger, 1951), *Edgar Allan* (Neufeld, 1969), *A Separate Peace* (Knowles, 1960), *The Duplicate* (Sleator, 1989), or *The Accident* (Strasser, 1988).

We believe that if teachers are going to teach classics, then they must do everything possible to help their students have success when reading this adult literature. One way, perhaps the most meaningful way, offers students a bridge—something that connects their understanding of the world around them through their literature with the literature of the past, which may have little or no relevance to their world. In this way, young adult literature serves the teacher well.

Brave New World, **Aldous Huxley (1931)**
- *Feed,* M. T. Anderson (2002)
- *Gathering Blue,* Lois Lowry (2000)
- *The Giver,* Lois Lowry (1993)

Death of a Salesman, **Arthur Miller (1949)**
- *Dancing on Dark Water,* Alden Carter (1990)
- *Notes for Another Life,* Sue Ellen Bridgers (1981)
- *The Runner,* Cynthia Voigt (1985)

The Grapes of Wrath, **John Steinbeck (1939)**
- *All Together Now,* Sue Ellen Bridgers (1979)
- *Homecoming,* Cynthia Voigt (1981)
- *Make Lemonade,* Virginia Euwer Wolff (1993)
- *Out of the Dust,* Karen Hesse (1997)

Great Expectations, **Charles Dickens (1860–1861)**
- *Bud, Not Buddy,* Christopher Paul Curtis (1999)
- *Buried Onions,* Gary Soto (1997)
- *Catalyst,* Laurie Halse Anderson (2002)
- *Stargirl,* Jerry Spinelli (2000)

1984, **George Orwell (1950)**
- *The Chocolate War,* Robert Cormier (1974)
- *Forbidden City,* William Bell (1990)
- *The Kolokol Papers,* Larry Bograd (1981)

The Odyssey, **Homer (c. 850 B.C.E.)**
- *I Am the Cheese,* Robert Cormier (1977)
- *The Road to Memphis,* Mildred Taylor (1990)
- *Walk Two Moons,* Sharon Creech (1994)
- *The Watsons Go to Birmingham—1963,* Christopher Paul Curtis (1995)

Of Mice and Men, **John Steinbeck (1937)**
- *Big Mouth and Ugly Girl,* Joyce Carol Oates (2002)
- *Freak the Mighty,* Rodman Philbrick (1993)
- *Miriam's Well,* Lois Ruby (1993)
- *Staying Fat for Sarah Byrnes,* Chris Crutcher (1993)

Othello, The Moor of Venice, **William Shakespeare (1603–1604)**
- *Chernowitz,* Fran Arrick (1981)
- *Othello: A Novel,* Julius Lester (1995)
- *Monster,* Walter Dean Myers (1999)

The Red Badge of Courage, **Stephen Crane (1894)**
- *Fallen Angels,* Walter Dean Myers (1988)
- *My Brother Sam Is Dead,* James Collier and Christopher Collier (1974)
- *Soldier's Heart,* Gary Paulsen (1998)
- *Wolf by the Ears,* Ann Rinaldi (1991)

To Kill a Mockingbird, **Harper Lee (1960/1988)**
- *All Together Now,* Sue Ellen Bridgers (1979)
- *Roll of Thunder, Hear My Cry,* Mildred Taylor (1976)
- *Words by Heart,* Ouida Sebestyen (1981)

FIGURE 7.1

Pairings: A listing.

Learning Log Responses

Based on what you have read in this chapter about teaching the classics, present your views on why you will or will not teach them.

Identify a classic not discussed in this chapter. What young adult novel would you use to help your students connect to your chosen classic? Explain the connection. How will you promote in your classroom the concept of developing lifelong readers?

References

Angelotti, M. (1981). Uses of the young adult literature in the eighties. *English in Texas, 13,* 32–34.

Applebee, A. (1989). *The study of book-length works taught in high school English courses.* Albany, NY: Center for the Study of Teaching and Learning of Literature.

Atwell, N. (1987). *In the middle.* Portsmouth, NH: Boynton/Cook.

Bushman, J. H. (1997). Young adult literature in the classroom—or is it? *English Journal, 86*(3), 35–40.

Carlsen, G. R., & Sherrill, A. (1988). *Voices of readers: How we come to love books.* Urbana, IL: National Council of Teachers of English.

Commission on Excellence in Education. (1984). *A nation at risk: The full account.* Washington, DC: Author.

Cooter, R. B. & Flynt, E. S. (1996). *Teaching reading in the content areas.* Columbus, OH: Merrill.

Daigon, A. (1969). Literature and the schools. *English Journal, 58*(1), 30–39.

Hirsch, E. D., Jr. (1987). *Cultural literacy: What every American needs to know.* Boston: Houghton Mifflin.

Holbrook, H. T. (1982). Adolescent literature: More than meets the eye. *Journal of Reading, 25,* 378–381.

Kaywell, J. (Ed.). (1993–1997). *Adolescent literature as a complement to the classics* (Vols. 1–3). Norwood, MA: Christopher-Gordon.

Langer, J. (1984). Literacy instruction in American high schools: Problems and perspectives. *American Journal of Education, 93*(11), 107–132.

Lesesne, T. (1991). Developing lifetime readers: Suggestions from fifty years of research. *English Journal, 80*(6), 61–64.

Loeb, A. J. (Ed.). (1996). *The wit and wisdom of Mark Twain.* New York: Barnes & Noble Books.

Mayer, H. (1992). Big books, sex and the classics: Some thoughts on teaching literature. In D. Gallo, *Author's insights* (pp. 1–18). Portsmouth, NH: Heinemann.

Mazer, H. (1992). Quoted in D. Gallo, *Author's insights* (p. 8). Portsmouth, NH: Heinemann.

Mullican, J. (1991). Cultural literacy: Whose culture? Whose literacy? *English Education, 23*(4), 244–250.

Newdick, R. (1936). Robert Frost as teacher of literature and composition. *English Journal, 25*(6), 632.

O'Connor, M. E. (1980). *A study of the reading preferences of high school students.* (ERIC Document Reproduction Service No. ED 185 524)

O'Donnell, H. (1983). Death to the classics. *English Journal, 72*(3), 48–50.

Probst, R. (1984). *Response and analysis* (2nd ed.). Portsmouth, NH: Heinemann.

Samuels, B., & Lowery-Moore, H. (1987, Winter). Bridging the basics: The young adult novel in a back-to-basics society. *ALAN Review, 14*(38), 42–44.

Shaw, L. (1935). Touching the intangible. *Wilson Library Bulletin, 10,* 110–112.

Small, R. (1972). Teaching the junior novel. *English Journal, 61*(2), 222–229.

Small, R. (1977). The junior novel and the art of literature. *English Journal, 66*(6), 55–59.

Sousa, D. (2001). *How the brain learns* (2nd ed., pp. 46–48). Thousand Oaks, CA: Corwin Press.

Sullivan, A. M. (1991). The natural reading life: A high school anomaly. *English Journal, 80*(6), 40–46.

Trelease, J. (1982). *The read aloud handbook.* New York: Penguin.

U.S. Department of Education. (1990). *A profile of the American eighth grader.* Washington, DC: Author.

Vogel, M., & Zancanella, D. (1991). The story world of adolescents in and out of the classroom. *English Journal, 80*(6), 54–60.

Wilhelm, J. (2001). *Strategic reading: Guiding students to lifelong literacy 6–12.* Portsmouth, NH: Boynton/Cook.

8

Diversity in Young Adult Literature

With Lisa Hazlett, *University of South Dakota*
and Judith Hayn, *Loyola University*

Contemporary Classroom Changes

Today's classrooms are increasingly diverse and inclusive, much more so than in past years. Currently, the United States has a greater variety of cultures than at any other time in its history. These changes largely began after World War II due to immigrants from Latin and Central America, Asia, Europe, the Caribbean, South America, and other regions (U.S. Census Bureau, 2003).

This diversity is found within all schools: urban, suburban, and rural. Demographers state that 39% of all public school students are considered part of a minority or non-White racial/cultural/ethnic group, with this number growing (U.S. Census Bureau, 2003a), and the National Clearinghouse for English Language Acquisition reported in 2002 that approximately 9% (4.4 million) of U.S. public school students' native language is not English.

Moreover, America's ever-changing society now encompasses sex, age, national origin, physical and mental ability, disability, sexual orientation, religion, and socio-economic and experiential background into its contemporary view of diversity, creating an even more inclusive definition of the term.

Today's classrooms no longer house 30 students viewed as one. Now, a classroom consists of 30 *individuals,* each with a variety of diversities. Adolescents and their parents increasingly desire that *their* background, culture, situation, beliefs, and values be represented in the classroom and literature read, as well as learning of others'. One size no longer fits all—even among students within like groups.

Where Am I in the Traditional Canon?

Is there such a thing as a typical classroom anymore? Although students and their needs have changed, curricula vary in meeting those needs. Whereas some schools represent their students well by using a variety of works, in others the traditional classical canon continues to be solely and reverentially taught. Reflect on the following student scenarios regarding the traditional canon and diversity in secondary language arts classes:

- *Devon* has an African American heritage and refers to himself as Black. He is interested in African American history and has noticed that African Americans are represented well only during his school's Black History Month, with its featured literature from outside the canon.

- *Susan* views herself as a strong, confident female. Her mother teaches women's studies courses, and she and Lensey have visited some of these classes. Susan is interested in female authors and protagonists and learning about women throughout history. She is concerned about the paucity of women in her canonical reading.

- *Lensey* has a Japanese heritage and prefers being called a Japanese American. She enjoys books featuring intelligent, proactive females, especially Asians, but so far her reading on these topics has come from libraries or Susan, not the classroom.

- *Maria*'s family recently immigrated to America from Mexico via a church sponsorship, and her parents are employed by her city's large industrial plant. Maria finds America an abrupt change from her native Mexico. Although she is becoming adept with the English language, most of her classical reading assignments are too difficult for her and she does not find herself in the canon. She enjoys books featuring Hispanics (her family's term) or others facing adversity.

- *Trudi,* a Midwesterner, loves her small rural town. Through travel, the Internet, and the media, she is familiar with other geographic locations and various diversities. As she opens her text to yet another story set in Victorian England, she wonders if there is *anything* set in her part of the country—or even in her country.

- *Scott* dislikes many of the contemporary reading selections assigned, feeling they usurp traditional American stories, values, and views. Scott considers himself a White American and believes immigrants are taking American jobs—like those held by Maria's parents—and thinks needy Americans should be assisted before sponsoring immigrants. How can Scott's needs be met in tandem with the needs of his classmates?

- *Billy* is the only Native American (he prefers Indian) in his grade, and he has no Native American teachers. Like Devon, he wants to learn more about his heritage and read stories with indigenous characters. He's increasingly angered by the canon's few native peoples frequently portrayed as either noble helpmates or vicious savages, causing him to skip the reading and assignments he views as irrelevant or demeaning. His grades are slipping, and he is considering dropping out of school.

- *Illene,* a lesbian, refers to herself as Queer. She has never read a canonical piece prominently featuring homosexuality. Illene reads books with gay and lesbian characters, but is tired of works with homosexuality being a central, even terrible, problem and wonders if any books exist featuring characters whose sexuality is secondary and not always problematic.

- *Jim* is a cancer survivor and an aide for special education students. He wants to expand his teacher's library of books featuring special-needs students (his preferred term). Like the others, he sees little in the canon regarding disabilities or chronic illnesses. He's seeking titles for a variety of disabilities, but knows he must search outside the canon.

- *Wayne* is Baptist, *Kim* is Buddhist, and *Carrie* is Catholic who is questioning her faith due to disagreement over many church policies. All want to read more about religious issues and see faith embedded within the characters they are reading about. Of course, the contemporary religious issues that most interest these students do not exist in the canon. How can the classics possibly meet their needs?

These are similar concerns in classrooms all over the country. The traditional canon—although it contains wonderful literature—often fails in meeting contemporary students' immediate interests and concerns. All of the students described have one question in common: "*Where am I in the canon?*" Although our students have changed, our literature has largely remained the same—to all students' detriment.

Our Changing Society

Our classrooms directly reflect contemporary society. Many teachers' classrooms little resemble the ones in which they spent time as students. Consider these current societal, and thus classroom, realities:

- More than 400 languages are spoken in the public schools, with 76% claiming Spanish as their native language. Asians and Pacific Islanders form more than 34 ethnic groups and speak 300-plus languages and dialects; they compose approximately 4% of the U.S. population (U.S. Census Bureau, 2003d).

- African Americans constitute approximately 13% of the U.S. population, but Hispanic Americans are the fastest growing racial group, accounting for about 10% of the population. By 2010, the Hispanic population should reach 14%, surpassing African Americans as the country's largest minority group (U.S. Census Bureau, 2003b).

- Native Americans and Alaskan Natives represent less than 1% (2 million) of the total U.S. population (U.S. Census Bureau, 2003b).
- The *Kids Count Data Book, 2002* states that almost 20% of students' families live below the poverty line, and another 25% have parents who do not have stable employment. One percent of the U.S. population (2 million to 3 million) is homeless, with half of the homeless population having minor children (U.S. Department of Health and Human Services, 2002).
- Gender issues have become politicized, with various groups charging either boys or girls fare worse or better in classrooms and testing. Regardless, in a 1997 study Willingham and Cole found that boys and girls were fairly evenly matched in most test areas. Still, boys perform better in math/science, with girls' achievement highest in language arts areas.
- The academic achievement of all minority groups except Asian Americans is lower than that of Whites. Approximately 85% of students complete high school, but poor, minority, and urban students are most likely to drop out. Native Americans tend to leave school earliest, during or after eighth grade (U.S. Census Bureau, 2003d).
- Technology is increasingly sophisticated in schools, and while more Whites own home computers than any other group, computer use and knowledge among all students is almost equivalent in schools (U.S. Census Bureau, 2003d).
- The seminal Kinsey, Pomeroy, and Martin study (1948) stated that approximately 10% of the population is homosexual, with that number remaining in today's estimates (U.S. Census Bureau, 2003d).
- Students with disabilities constitute approximately 13% of the school population (National Center for Education Statistics, 2002). And, although states' criteria vary for defining gifted and talented, Parkay and Stanford (2004) estimated that 3% to 5% of students fall in this category.
- Teen pregnancy impacts more than 1 million U.S. teens (one in nine women between the ages of 15 and 19) (Alan Guttmacher Institute, 1999).
- Approximately 20% of high school students regularly use illicit drugs; 22% use alcohol. High school girls smoke tobacco more than boys, 24% to 16%, with females most likely to begin smoking for weight control. Regarding weight, in 1999, 14% of all adolescents were overweight. This number has tripled in the past two decades (U.S. Census Bureau, 2003d).
- Approximately 9% of all students have been threatened or injured with a weapon on school property, with ninth graders most victimized (U.S. Census Bureau, 2003d).
- Two thirds of public school educators are female, and the U.S. Census Bureau (2003c) stated that the age group with the most teachers is that of 40 to 49, with the second those over 50. Whites account for more than 2 million teachers, compared to some 200,000 Blacks, and 169,000 Hispanics. Other groups constitute less than 0.05% of teachers.

- The *American School Board Journal* (2001) stated that females constitute 38% of school boards, males 61%. Minority board membership is approximately 14%. Moreover, board members' incomes are higher than for the general population, with 67% showing incomes well over $50,000.

Interestingly, the average teacher is a middle-class White female in her mid-40s, with the typical school board member an upper-class White male. These educators and board members must teach and make responsible decisions regarding their contemporary students, who are unlike them in multiple ways.

Quality Literature and Instruction for All Students

Regardless of the diverse student body now commonplace in schools, the traditional canon remains the norm in secondary school classrooms. Applebee's 1994 study of the literature taught in secondary English classes found that young adult literature use was sparse at best. His findings suggested that students performed better in those classrooms using young adult literature. In tandem, Bushman (1996) found that young adult literature was primarily used in grades 6 and 7, with study of the traditional canon beginning in eighth grade, replacing young adult literature. Few eighth-grade teachers used young adult literature, and fewer still in subsequent grades.

Why is the canon predominantly taught? Consider explanations from these beginning and veteran practicing English teachers:

Classics are quality literature. Young adult literature is fine for middle schoolers' free reading, but not sophisticated enough for high school. We must prepare students for college. . . . Classics educate the students.

I was taught the classics in school, and the parents expect us to teach them.

Young adult literature brings the censors running. . . . The classics are safe from censorship.

The classics are in our curriculum guide. . . . I can't teach anything else.

Are these academically responsible reasons for teaching the canon? Classics were written for educated adults of their era and as such are not always the most suitable books for contemporary adolescents. They certainly do not reflect the current social issues faced by teens, nor the classroom's diverse population.

Unfortunately, canon companions are *Cliffs Notes,* extensive study aids, guided notes, paraphrasing, worksheets, and—boredom. Ultimately, students are learning *about* the canon rather than *from* it—an important distinction often unrecognized, masked and created by the previously mentioned practices.

Minority students receive even less benefit from the classics than their majority counterparts, because they tend to be underrepresented or stereotyped in the canon. Additionally, majority students are given few opportunities to read works about or by minorities if only the canon is utilized, with other diversities also bypassed.

A good book is one that meets the needs of any particular group of students or individual students. At times, this is a classic. Often, however, young adult literature is a more suitable choice. Written for contemporary adolescents and discussing the issues and events most important to them, quality young adult literature allows for textual engagement, relevance, learning, and enjoyment. All teachers want their students to become involved with literature, understand its message, view it as relevant, respond to it, and become lifelong readers. For students to do so, though, they must first be given appropriate literature to read.

It can be difficult for contemporary students to relate to adult classics, especially if they do not see themselves represented within them. However, engagement is important if we expect students to connect with literature and respond to it meaningfully. Rosenblatt (1976), in defining her theories of readers and their responses to literature, stated that the teacher's responsibility is to "foster fruitful transactions between individual readers and individual literary works" (pp. 26–27). She continued by declaring that it is not enough to simply provide students with reading materials; choices must instead reflect knowledge of the possible links between the materials and the students' background experiences, as well as their present level of maturity and cognitive ability. Quality young adult literature fits these requirements well, but classics may not.

Surely Rosenblatt was referring to rote teaching methodology when she declared, "When the images and ideas presented by the work have no relevance to the past experiences or emotional needs of the reader, only a vague, feeble, or negative response will occur" (pp. 58–59). Moreover, she argued that studying literary history, authors, eras, and genres is largely useless unless students can relate these works to their personal experiences.

Rather than imposing a set of preconceived notions about the "right" way to respond to a piece, teachers should assist students in developing their own understandings in the context of their personal emotions and experiences. When students reflect on why they have responded in certain ways, they are learning to read more effectively and are becoming proficient in discovering personal meanings in literature.

Perhaps the most valuable skill students acquire from analyzing their responses is the ability to listen to others, understand what is said, and respond in kind. Literature is not learned in a vacuum; students need their classmates and teacher for sharing, discussion, and feedback. How can students discuss and share when they are not engaged with their reading assignments? How can diversities be recognized and discussed if they are poorly represented in the literature assigned?

Selecting Young Adult Literature for Contemporary Students

Consider how young adult literature would be more beneficial than the traditional canon to the students previously introduced in this chapter.

Maria's background and current situation are insufficient to connect with most classics assigned. Because she has abruptly changed cultures, books featuring other displaced characters would be helpful. Shea's *Tangled Threads: A Hmong Girl's Story* (2003) features a female Hmong refugee who immigrates to Rhode Island; Brown's *Little Cricket* (2004) follows Laotian Kia and her family's immigration to Minnesota via church sponsorship, both similar to Maria's experience. Maria, Susan, and Lensey can compare Hesse's *Aleutian Sparrow* (2003), about a female native Aleut displaced during World War II, to Otsuka's *When the Emperor Was Divine* (2002), featuring a Japanese family also sent to an internment camp during this war.

Numerous titles profile confident female protagonists or female authors for Susan and Lensey. In Whelan's *Chu Ju's House* (2004), Chinese law allows families two children; boys are favored. After Chu Ju's sister is born, Chu Ju runs away to save the baby from an orphanage. China's treatment and view of women can be discussed with Susan's mother; likewise, Lowery's *The Fattening Hut* (2003) features Helen who refuses her island tribe's tradition of fattening girls before marriage and then performing female circumcision. Cameron's *Colibrí* (2003) portrays Guatemalan Colibri, living for 8 years with a man she calls Uncle—actually her kidnapper; Mikaelsen's *Tree Girl* (2004) features another Guatemalan girl who survives a military massacre and must evade pursuant soldiers, also exciting titles for Maria.

Rosenblatt (1976) and Whaley and Dodge (1999) believe that males, as much or more than females, benefit from reading about strong female protagonists. Both need respite from the canon's narrow view of the feminine role and benefit by reading more works by women. Miller's nonfiction *Good Women of a Well-Blessed Land: Women's Lives in Colonial America* (2003) would be an informative historical overview for all and of special interest to Susan.

Both Native and African American protagonists are poorly represented in the canon. Devon should enjoy Myers's *The Dream Bearer* (2003), which portrays an African American family living in Harlem. Paulsen's *Brian's Hunt* (2003) should appeal to Billy, with Brian intending to assist Canadian Cree friends but instead making a grisly discovery.

Nonfiction for Devon includes Morrison's *Remember: The Journey to School Integration* (2004) and McKissack and McKissack's *Days of Jubilee: The End of Slavery in the United States* (2003). Recommended for Billy are Bruchac's *Our Stories Remember: American Indian History, Culture, and Values through Storytelling* (2003) and Tingle's *Walking the Choctaw Road: Stories from Red People Memory* (2003). Kanter's *Ordinary Wolves* (2004) describes the White author's boyhood among Alaskan Inuits, with his acceptance struggles also appealing to Maria, Scott, and Devon.

Trudi would enjoy titles reflecting her particular region. Halvorson's *Bull Rider* (2003) features rodeos and bull riding, important components of midwestern culture. Moranville's *Over the River* (2003) portrays Willa Mae's life between relatives in 1940s rural Illinois and Oklahoma; Williams's *Escaping Tornado Season: A Story in Poems* (2004) features Allie, shuttled to Minnesota after her father's death and mother's desertion; both are suggested for Maria.

Scott dislikes the diversity aspects of his reading along with his community's changing population. Rosenblatt (1976) stated if students' beliefs and attitudes are formed by only narrow experiences, then literature is crucial in broadening and deepening their insights toward others. She further declared that literature increases social sensitivity, so students should be reading from the widest body of titles possible.

Scott, like the others, would benefit from the short stories in Frost's *Keesha's House* (2003); *Face Relations: 11 Stories about Seeing beyond Color* (2004), edited by Singer; *Necessary Noise: Stories about Our Families as They Really Are* (2003), edited by Cart; and Hoobler and Hoobler's nonfiction *We Are Americans: Voices of the Immigrant Experience* (2003), all of which move the reader beyond viewing a particular diversity or situation as indicative of human value. Scott should be encouraged to read about and communicate with those unlike him to broaden his views and experiences. Scott can easily resent immigrants, for example, but once meeting Maria and learning more of her family, this attitude becomes harder to retain. Cummings's *Red Kayak* (2004) illustrates the disastrous clash between a region's waterman and environmentalists, an excellent complement for Scott when revisiting his community. While Scott, like all students, should be encouraged to read titles he enjoys, he should also be introduced to works featuring diversity in a nonthreatening way.

Homosexuality garners various reactions in schools and communities but is virtually nonexistent in the canon. Regardless, homosexual students deserve quality titles reflective of their own situations, needs, and dreams. Illene should enjoy Huntington's *Demon Witch* (2003), which features teen sorcerer Devon who battles demons with his ordinary friends—including Marcus who is gay, accepted, and admired. Levithan's *Boy Meets Boy* (2003) portrays a town and high school as if its majority population were homosexual, with Benduhn's *Gravel Queen* (2003), Hartinger's *Geography Club* (2003), and Johnson's *The Bermudez Triangle* (2004) featuring homosexual high school students. Nonfiction includes Garner's *Families Like Mine: Children of Gay Parents Tell It Like It Is* (2004) and Hugle's *GLBTQ: The Survival Guide for Queer and Questioning Teens* (2003). Susan and Lensey should also enjoy these titles.

The canon tends to portray traditional Christianity, but Wayne, Kim, and Carrie are eager to learn more about their religions and that of others. Flinn's *Breaking Point* (2002) portrays Christian school corruption; Armstrong's *The Keepers of the Flame* (2002) explores repressive Christian fundamentalism; Bardi's *The Book of Fred* (2001) looks at communes; and Clinton's *The Calling* (2001) examines healing—all suitable for those seeking thoughtful discussion. Historical titles include Crew's *Brides of Eden: A True Story Imagined* (2001), which features a charismatic and sinister Oregon preacher during 1903; Fletcher's *Walk across the Sea* (2001), set in 1886, features Eliza, whose family believes its town's Chinese people are heathens; and Fama's *Overboard* (2002), set in Sumatra, explores Islam; these titles again are recommended for Susan and Lensey. Nonfiction includes editor Joselit's *Immigration and American Religion* (2001), Mann, Numrick, and Williams's *Buddhists, Hindus, and Sikhs in America* (2001), and Macaulay's *Mosque* (2003), also recommended for Devon, Maria, Billy, and Lensey. Fraustino's *Soul Searching: Thirteen Stories about Faith and Belief* (2002) and Cotner's *Words for the Heart and Soul* (2002) should appeal to all.

Jim is seeking titles regarding special needs, nearly nonexistent in the canon. Abeel's *My Thirteenth Winter: A Memoir* (2003) introduces dyscalculia, the inability to understand mathematics; Trueman's *Stuck in Neutral* (2000) features cerebral palsy, and his *Inside Out* (2003) examines schizophrenia. Johnson's *A Cool Moonlight* (2003) portrays a girl allergic to light; Hautman's *Sweetblood* (2003) features a female diabetic who theorizes vampires of yore were actually diabetics; all of these titles may prove intriguing for Susan, Lensey, and Maria. Haddon's *The Curious Incident of the Dog in Night-Time: A Novel* (2003) portrays autism; Harrar's *Not as Crazy as I Seem* (2003) looks at obsessive-compulsives; Minchin's *The Beat Goes On* (2004) explores HIV/AIDS; Hallowell's *The Annunciation of Francesca Dunn: A Novel* (2004) considers eating disorders; and Atkins's *Alt Ed* (2003) portrays being overweight. Of course, any of these titles would be appropriate for the profiled teens, depending on interest or situation, and they emphasize a variety of diversities.

The Meaning of Diversity

What does *diversity* mean? If we subscribe to the broadest definition of the term, then we are all diverse. Population changes, technology, and schools' commitment to global education and awareness have allowed our students, more than ever before, to interact with more people who are unlike them in some way. A preservice teacher at an urban university came to this conclusion; Melissa writes:

> Diversity is more than skin deep, such as race, ethnicity, gender or the way someone dresses. Sometimes, diversity can be seen in terms of sexuality, religion, an internal disease, or even morals. Be it outwardly noticeable or not, diversity encompasses every classroom in America, which is why it is crucial to introduce diverse literature in the classroom.

Rather than focusing on the differences associated with diversity, we should instead be emphasizing the similarities among various peoples. We are all really more alike than different, and once we move past surface features, as Melissa notes, everyone experiences the same universal feelings. In particular, all adolescents likely share such things as forging new relationships with their parents; experiencing the changes of puberty; developing relationships with the opposite sex, peers, siblings, teachers, and other adults; establishing a personal belief system; and preparing for the future. By taking these universal similarities into consideration, teachers can assist adolescents in their understanding and appreciation of others unlike them by first focusing on the common ground shared by all.

With these thoughts in mind, it is important to provide all of our students with literature that would be somehow diverse to its reader. We must not stereotype our students by the reading we recommend and assign. It is important to provide students with literature that features characters like them and familiar situations. But it is just as—and probably more—important to provide them with works that portray differences. We learn more about ourselves through exposure, comparison, and discussion with others.

In both cases, literature engagement and responses arrive from students asking, "Where am I in this work?" These experiences are the best possible ones we can give our students regarding diverse literature; they provide opportunities to learn more about and appreciate others while gaining insight into oneself. Lisa, a Chicago teen of Asian Indian heritage, writes:

> As a young Indian girl, I didn't really talk to my girlfriends about boys and crushes because I wasn't used to doing that. I never knew how to handle situations like that, and it seemed like everyone was dating or liking someone at that age except for me. I know it would have been great to read books where I could identify with a character about my feelings. I also wish I could have read more books that had to deal with Hispanic kids and Black kids because that's what my neighborhood and school consisted of. I also wish we read books about young Indian kids because no one really understood me or where I was from. I was always just a little different and it did get to me once in a while. I remember going to the school library once and finding a book of Indian folktales on the back shelf, and I checked that book out every week because I was so happy someone knew Indian people existed and found the time to write about them.

Numerous young adult titles feature diversity in some way. Consider the works of an ever-growing collection of global young adult literature by diverse authors discussed in the following sections and how they might be enjoyed by the previously mentioned students, as well as others like them.

Making Multiethnic Connections through Literature

Contemporary African American authors, some familiar and others new to the classroom, continue to write for students. Teachers familiar with M. Taylor's classic saga of the Logan family in *Let the Circle Be Unbroken* (1981) and *Roll of Thunder, Hear My Cry* (1976) will welcome the prequel to Cassie's story in *The Land* (2001). Curtis continues his exploration of young African Americans growing up in and around Flint, Michigan, established in *The Watsons Go to Birmingham—1963* (1995). *Bud, Not Buddy* (2000) searches for his identity by pursuing an absent father in the Depression, and in *Bucking the Sarge* (2004), Luther keeps his slumlord mother and her boyfiend Darnell from using lead paint for properties during the 1950s and escapes her tyranny.

Other perennial all-stars who focus on African American youth keep writing quality literature. Myers continues writing his powerful stories of the young African American male experience in *Monster* (1999), where accused killer Steve Harmon's story is written as a television movie script covering his trial with the utilization of Steve's journal. Myers continues his focus on Harlem with 16-year-old Anthony "Spoon" Witherspoon's contrasting life at an exclusive prep school with the hopelessness of his neighborhood in *The Beast* (2003). *Shooter* (2004) relays the story of Leonard Gray, a student who brings three guns to his high school, shoots and kills a football player, and then himself. The story is told through a series of interviews, newspaper clippings, and Leonard's diary.

Woodson continues to explore identity development in *Miracle's Boys* (2000), *Hush* (2002), *Locomotion* (2003), and *Behind You* (2004). In the first, Ty'Ree, Charlie, and Lafayette must survive after the death of both their parents. The second deals with Toswiah's family experiences as they enter a witness protection program, while the third tells Lonnie C. Motion's story as he uses his poetry assignments to deal with life as a foster child. All of Woodson's work is highly lyrical, and the powerful story of Ellie and Jeremiah's doomed romance in *If You Come Softly* (1998) continues in *Behind You* (2004). The sequel examines the grief process that takes place after Jeremiah is mistakenly murdered by police pursuing an African American thief—the novel views grief from Jeremiah's viewpoint and also the viewpoints of his family, friends, and Ellie, his White Jewish girlfriend.

The works of other familiar authors include a posthumous novel by Hamilton, *Time Pieces: The Book of Times* (2002), where Valena experiences her 11th year through a series of vignettes where the injustices of slavery match with modern ones. Grimes writes of Mr. Ward's 18 English students at a high school in the Bronx who write poetry as they study the Harlem Renaissance in *Bronx Masquerade* (2002). A. Johnson in *The First Part Last* (2003), a prequel to *Heaven* (1998), tells Bobby's story as he becomes a single father when the mother dies. Williams-Garcia's *No Laughter Here* (2003) is the story of Akilah and her best friend Victoria. After a summer at home in Nigeria, Victoria returns as a different person after a special coming-of-age ceremony.

Newer voices emerge as Frank tells the story of America, who is 18, biracial, and living in a residential treatment facility for teens; he dialogues with his therapist, Dr. B., unveiling his story as one of society's lost children in *America* (2002). A book embraced by adults, too, is Kidd's *The Secret Life of Bees* (2002), where Lily journeys with the Black woman who has been her substitute mother to South Carolina where they find sanctuary with Black beekeeping sisters who hold the key to the truth about Lily's mother. L. A. Williams tells Shayla's story as she grows up in *When Kambia Elaine Flew in from Neptune* (2000) and *Shayla's Double Brown Baby Blues* (2001). Shayla Dubois lives in a Houston neighborhood called the Bottom, where life is colorful but never easy. Her estranged father comes back to town, and Shayla doesn't know what to make of her strange new neighbor, Kambia Elaine. In the sequel, Shayla's father and his new wife have a baby girl named Gift who has Shayla's special eyes (the eyes of a writer), her father's last name, and the love that should have been Shayla's.

The Asian American or Pacific American adolescent experience in literature is chronicled in works by young adult authors who address the issue of identity for young female Asians settling in this country. Worth citing again is the highly acclaimed *When the Emperor Was Devine* by Otsuka (2002), the moving chronicle of five family members' reactions to life in an internment camp in Utah. Na lets Young Ju narrate her story of her family's immigration experience as they move from Korea to America in *A Step from Heaven* (2001). In Hidier's *Born Confused* (2002), Dimple Lala, the only child of East Indian parents, is confused about her identity and trying to please her parents. Yee introduces *Millicent Min, Girl Genius* (2003), who at age 11 has finished her junior year of high school, and now her family wants her to branch out from academics by joining a volleyball team. In *Naming Maya* (2004), Krishnaswami has 12-year-old Maya return to India with her mother to sell the ancestral home; she grows estranged from her mother and builds a friendship with a mysterious former housekeeper.

The experiences of Asian American males are told in Mochizuki's *Beacon Hill Boys* (2002) and Son's *Finding My Hat* (2003). The first features Dan Inagaki, who doesn't fit in at his south Seattle high school or at home; a course in comparative American culture helps bridge conflicts for him. The latter is the story of Jim-Han, who comes of age as a first-generation Korean American in Chicago, Memphis, and Houston.

Several contemporary authors address the complexity faced by students of Mexican, Latin American, and Caribbean heritage. Cisneros continues to utilize her own life as she did in *The House on Mango Street* (1994) with her more recent *Caramelo* (2004), where Celaya (Lala) Reyes grows up in Chicago, then moves with her family to San Antonio in a complex novel of the conflict between two cultures.

Soto keeps his reputation as the author who addresses the needs of male teens of Mexican heritage growing up in the San Fernando Valley of Fresno, California. Augmenting *Jesse* (1994) and *Buried Onions* (1997), Soto has written a prequel to the latter in *The Afterlife* (2003), where Chuy narrates his short life and his experiences as a ghost. Velasquez continues to do the same for young women in *Teen Angel* (2003), where Celia Chavez, 15, gets pregnant by a boy who deserts her and decides to keep the baby, much to her father's disapproval. Ryan writes of Mexican American family life in *Becoming Naomi León* (2004), as Naomi León Soledad Outlaw, a shy and extremely quiet young girl, comes of age living in the suburbs of San Diego with her great-grandmother and her younger brother. The novel is a diversion from her lyrical *Esperanza Rising* (2000), a novel based on the experiences of early migrant workers.

Other writers focus on other regions of Latin America. Alvarez in *How Tia Lola Came to (Visit) Stay* (2000) has an irrepressible aunt visit a Dominican American family in Vermont and bring excitement to young Miguel's life. Osa in *Cuba 15* (2003) tells of Violeta Paz's attempt to reconcile her Cuban grandmother's expectations of a *quinceañera* with her own self-doubts about her Cuban American father's and Polish American mother's expectations. Some authors focus on the unrest that dominates in so much of the region. Placide tells Mardi's story in *Fresh Girl* (2002); she was born in America but spent several years in Haiti, and her memories of that stay threaten to destroy her. Danticat continues to examine the chaos of Haitian life in *Behind the Mountains* (2002); the diary of 13-year-old Celiane Esperance describes village life in the mountains of Haiti and her adjustment to New York City. Veciania-Suarez tells Yara's story in *Flight to Freedom* (2004) as the young girl's family flees Cuba for life in Miami, Florida.

Literature that features Native American teens includes Rees, who explores the maturation of Agnes Hearne, a Mohawk, descended from medicine women. She suspects that the heroine of *Witch Child* (2001), Mary NewBury, might be her ancestor; Agnes returns to the reservation to tell Mary's story in *Sorceress* (2002). Lipsyte creates a series starting with *The Contender* (1967), where boxing is featured; the next three books—*The Brave* (1993), *The Chief* (1995), and *Warrior Angel* (2003)—focus on Sonny Bear, a Moscondaga Indian. Sonny Bear, the youngest heavyweight champion of the world, finds conflict with his tribal beliefs in New York City's fight world and later returns to the reservation. In the latest novel, he meets a self-proclaimed Warrior Angel who sees himself as Sonny's redeemer. Turlo and Turlo tell the story of

Crystal Manyfeathers in *The Spirit Line* (2004), the most talented weaver on the Navajo reservation, who fights her ancestry even as she learns her craft from the ancient teachings of her mother. Olsen tells Jane's story in *The Girl with a Baby* (2004); Jane gives birth at 14 to a daughter, which brings her closer to the support and nurturing of her First Nation grandmother after her own mother dies.

These books look at diversity from viewpoints that primarily focus on adolescent Americans striving to find identity in the dominant culture. Other writers examine the live of teens who are growing up in African cultures. For instance, Adichie in *Purple Hibiscus* (2003) writes of 15-year-old Kambili and her older brother, Jaja, who live in Enugu, Nigeria. Mankell's *Secrets in the Fire* (2003) supports the Adopt-a-Minefield program with the story of Sophia, a young refugee of war-torn Mozambique. *Zulu Dog* (2002), by Ferreira, tells of 11-year-old Vusi's adventures living in the South African bush—where he finds a three-legged dog he hides from his parents—along with his friendship with a White neighbor girl.

Writing of Asian cultures, Whelan introduces Koly in *Homeless Bird*, who at 13 enters an arranged marriage with an ill boy and then must support herself after his death. In *The Flame Tree* (2004), Lewis tells Isaac's story; his parents are missionary doctors in Java, Indonesia. His best friend is Ismail, a Muslim boy, and violence affects their lives. Ellis adds to a series of books that tell Parvana's story beginning in *The Breadwinner* (2000) and *Parvana's Journey* (2002); Parvana is a young girl in Afghanistan, which is still under control of the Taliban. *Mud City* (2004) tells of her friend Shauzia, who, like Parvana, masquerades as a boy to feed herself and her family. In *The Conch Bearer* (2004), Divakaruni combines Indian culture, spiritualism, and magic to tell the tale of 12-year old Anand.

Adolescent life is depicted in Latin America by several writers. In Joseph's *The Color of My Words* (2000), 12-year-old Ana Rosa grows up in the Dominican Republic where she keeps a notebook and discovers the power of her words. In Tall T's story in *The Jacob Ladder* (2001), Hausman and Hinds use the latter author's experiences growing up in Jamaica where learning to read facilitates identity. Consuelo Signe grows up in the 1950s when Operation Bootstrap occurs. In *The Meaning of Consuelo* (2003) by Ortiz Cofer, she assumes the role of guardian for her sister Mili who is schizophrenic.

Dealing with Additional Facets of Diversity

A growing cadre of young adult authors deal with a variety of disabilities and their influences on teens who are trying to find who they are, too. Some address unusual physical appearances. In *Face* (2002), Zephaniah's story of popular Martin Turner turns to tragedy when he is trapped in a burning car and severely burns his face, causing his friends to treat him as if he were truly disabled. An unlikely overweight hero, Mike "Moo" Nelson, uncovers a police frame-up in *Kissing the Rain* (2004) by K. Brooks. In *Fat Kid Rules the World* by Going (2003), Troy (Big T) weighs 300 pounds and is suicidal.

Teens also struggle with balancing adolescence development and illness. Regan wants to be a dancer in Striegel's *Homeroom Exercise* (2002), but she is diagnosed with juvenile rheumatoid arthritis. Lila has an unusual allergy to sunlight in A. Johnson's *A Cool Moonlight* (2003). Leyla's close cousin Emma tests positive for HIV in Minchin's *The Beat Goes On* (2004); Leyla struggles to support her cousin and deal with all the other challenges of adolescence. Trueman continues the story he began in *Stuck in Neutral* (2000). In *Cruise Control* (2004), Paul McDaniel's perspective narrates the story of his brother Shawn's battle with cerebral palsy. Shawn cannot communicate but has full brain function and knows his father is contemplating mercy killing.

There are books that tell the stories of teens who cope with mental illness, either their own or those of family or friends. *Memories of Summer* (2000) by R. White tells of Lyric's older sister Summer's descent into schizophrenia and its effect on Lyric's childhood. Suzie, who is 12, is traumatized by a horrific family situation and enters a near-catatonic state in Shaw's *Black-Eyed Suzie* (2002). Shapiro's *Family History* (2003) is the story of the change in perfect daughter Kate as she goes to a world of darkness that ends in institutionalization. In Trueman's *Inside Out* (2003), 16-year-old Zach suffers from schizophrenia and hears two voices in his head; whenever he needs to take his medicines, Dirtbag and Rat tell him to kill himself. Devon narrates his own story of obsessive-compulsive behavior in *Not as Crazy as I Seem* (2003) by Harrar. Marty is institutionalized in *More Than You Can Chew* (2003) as Tokio intertwines her semi-autobiographical dilemmas with her protagonist's experiences. *Tending to Grace* (2004) by Fusco features Cornelia, who chooses not to speak. In *17: A Novel in Prose Poems* (2002), Rosenberg tells Stephanie's story of finding first love and coping with her mother's bipolar disease. Her boyfriend Denny lives with and enables an alcoholic father.

Young adult authors are willing to tackle issues of sexuality in a variety of novels; Cart (2004) examines trends in gay, lesbian, bisexual, transgender, and questioning [GLBTQ] literature in *The ALAN Review:*

> increasing numbers and varieties of opportunities, now being given to teens of every sexual identity, to see their faces in the pages of good fiction, and in the process, to find the comfort and reassurance of knowing they are not alone suggests that the day may be coming when the words "what a wonderful world" will no longer carry any hint of irony. (p. 52)

A lesbian relationship frames Shimko's *Letters in the Attic* (2002); 12-year-old Lizzie McCann's father leaves her and her mother for a younger woman. Mother and daughter wind up in a small upstate New York town where Lizzie falls in love with a girl she befriends. Myracle in *Kissing Kate* (2003) details the changing nature of best friends Lissa and Kate as they both confront their sexual identities. Benduhn in *Gravel Queen* (2003) features Aurin and her friends and the upheaval a newcomer causes in their lives as Aurin befriends Neila, a lesbian. Nicola Lancaster, the heroine of Ryan's *Empress of the World* (2001), is spending 8 weeks at a summer program for gifted youth where she meets and falls for Battle Hall Davies, a beautiful blond dancer. Peters tells

Holland Jaeger's story in *Keeping You a Secret* (2003); her world turns upside down when she begins an affair with lesbian Cece Goddard.

Other authors focus on identity and homosexuality. Sanchez's debut novel, *Rainbow Boys* (2001), chronicles the senior year of three gay teens struggling with issues ranging from coming out to first love to an HIV scare. In the sequel, *Rainbow High* (2003), their problems mount, and one of the young men comes out at great cost to his future as an athlete. Sanchez also writes in *So Hard to Say* (2004) of eighth grader Frederick, the shy new boy, and Xio, the bubbly *chica* who befriends him. When Xio decides she wants to be more than friends, Frederick instead finds himself thinking more about Victor, the captain of the soccer team. *Geography Club* (2003) by Hartinger is the story of Russel who is gay in a small town and forms the "club" as a gay-lesbian-bisexual support group.

Not only are the homosexual/lesbian aspects of sexuality addressed, but those who write for teens look at the issue from additional viewpoints. In *How I Fell in Love and Learned to Shoot Free Throws* (2003), Ripslinger writes of Angel McPherson, a superb basketball player attracted to fellow athlete Danny; Angel's secret is that she is a test-tube baby, the daughter of a lesbian. In *My Heartbeat* (2002) by Freymann-Weyr, Ellen adores her older brother Link and his best friend James, the only company she ever wants. Then someone at school asks if Link and James might be in love with each other. Watts in *Heavenly Faith* (2001) introduces H.F. as a runaway from a small Kentucky town who finds refuge with three homeless teens and members of Atlanta's gay community. Sixth grader Matthew realizes his brother Bennett is gay in *The Rainbow Kite* (2002) by Shyer. Plum-Ucci, in *What Happened to Lani Garver* (2002), has popular cheerleader Claire McKenzie befriend newcomer Lani Garver, whose sexuality is a mystery.

More groundbreaking than these novels perhaps are those that address taboo subjects not often examined, like incestuous love. In *Wasteland* (2003), Block takes on the theme of love and its many variations. Though Marina and her brother, Lex, struggle against their powerful love, the force is too strong to be denied. Marina is inconsolable after Lex dies. In *Luna* (2004), Peters deals with transgender; Regan's brother Liam is really a girl named Luna, a female born in a male body, and he expects his sister's help with the complete transition, help she is not sure she can give.

As GLBTQ subjects are featured in adolescent fiction, so is religious conflict. In *The Book of Fred* (2001), Bardi features Mary Fred who has lived for 15 years in a religious commune where medical help is forbidden. In *The Life of Pi* (2002), Martel explores a variety of faiths and much about nature through an allegory involving animals at the zoo run by Pi's father. Pedersen in *Beginner's Luck* (2003) has 16-year-old Hallie Palmer turn her back on school and her large Catholic family. *Faith Wish* (2003) is Bennett's story of Anne-Marie Morgan, who has attention deficit disorder and is born again. Brother Jackson has sex with her, impregnates her, and takes her to a cult camp. Miklowitz, in *The Enemy Has a Face* (2003), introduces Netta, who fears that her brother has been harmed by Palestinian schoolmates as the family has come from Israel to settle in Los Angeles. In *When We Were Saints* (2003), Nolan has Archibald Caswell dedicate his life to God after his dying grandfather calls him a saint. Hallowell, in *The Annunciation of Francesca Dunn: A Novel* (2004), has 14-year-old Francesca accepted as the Blessed Virgin by the homeless community. In *Godless* (2004), Hautman has the agnostic Jason Bock become bored with Catholicism, so he founds a new religion, the Church of the Ten-Legged God, which quickly grows out of control.

A topic with less controversy perhaps but equally important deals with diversity from a regional standpoint, and, thus, urban or rural settings. Classroom teachers need to be informed about authors who write specifically about the area where they teach. For instance, Peck continues to focus on his own background in rural central Illinois with *A Long Way from Chicago* (1998), where Joey and sister Mary Alice visit Grandma Dowdel from 1929 through 1942. In the sequel, *A Year Down Yonder* (2000), Mary Alice spends a year with her grandmother. In addition, *Fair Weather* (2001) is the story of a rural Illinois family who visits the Chicago exposition. In *The River between Us* (2003), 15-year-old Howard travels by car in 1916 with his father and young twin brothers from St. Louis to the tiny town of Grand Tower in southern Illinois to visit Howard's paternal grandparents. Nolan continues to write about southern teens like Janie, who wants to be called Leshaya, who has survived a tumultuous childhood and wants to be a singer in *Born Blue* (2001).

As mentioned previously, Soto still uses Fresno, California, while Curtis continues to focus on Flint, Michigan, and Myers uses Harlem to make use of urban settings that are specific to their stories. James has Gretchen narrate *Tomorrow, Maybe* (2003), where she relates her experiences as part of the world of New York street kids. In Strasser's *Can't Get There from Here* (2004), runaway teens struggle to survive on the streets of New York. J. McDonald sets *Brotherhood* (2004) at a prestigious prep school in upstate New York, taking Nate Whitely away from his Harlem home but not so far as to sever the strong ties to his neighborhood. The author also writes of teens who grow up in Brooklyn; *Twists and Turns* (2003) follows the Washington sisters as they set up a business braiding hair.

In contrast, rural settings are found in Donnelly's *A Northern Light* (2003); Mattie Gokey promises her dying mother that she will stay and care for her farm family, only to find her self-survival means she must leave. R. N. Peck, the veteran author of the classroom staple *A Day No Pigs Would Die* (1972), writes another tale of a rural lad growing into manhood in *Bro* (2004), set in Depression-era Florida. *Country Girl, City Girl* (2004), by Jahn-Clough, tells Phoebe's story. She lives on a small farm in rural Maine, and the summer before eighth grade, olive-skinned Melita comes from New York City to stay. *The Legend of Buddy Bush* (2004) by Moses is the story of 12-year-old Pattie Mae who is growing up in rural North Carolina in 1947 but dreams of city life in Harlem.

Introducing Diverse Literature into the Classroom

Although it may make some uncomfortable, teachers cannot ignore the world inside and outside their classrooms, no matter the issue. Boyd, Brock, and Rozendal, the editors of *Multicultural and Multilingual Literacy and Language: Contexts and Practices* (2004), remind us of the urgency of working together "to improve the literacy learning opportunities of children from diverse, ethnic, cultural, and linguistic backgrounds in U.S. schools" (2004, p. 10).

The authors of this chapter encourage teachers to continue to broaden their definitions of diversity to include all aspects. The texts mentioned in this chapter show that fictional teens, like their adolescent counterparts, deal with being different in all ways. The classroom teacher sensitive to the needs of his or her students will continue to search for quality selections that can touch whole class groups or individuals searching for a sense of self. Tiedt (2002) provides practical suggestions and help for the classroom teacher to help implement diverse literature in her indispensable guide, *Multicultural Teaching: A Handbook of Activities, Information, and Resources.*

Students need to make connections, and this is what multicultural teaching is about. This mission is clear: Honoring all our students' lives is crucial. White students can learn to accept glimpses into other cultures, into the lives of their classmates, into the histories of men and women who lived on this continent before the White race claimed it, and into the struggles of those who live daily with differences—those that are obvious and those that are hidden.

Looking at how the culture of our educational system is socializing students and at the alienation experienced by those who do not see themselves as Anglo may be the biggest challenge teachers in this country are facing in the 21st century. In their review of research on "Multiculturalism, Literature, and Curriculum Issues" in *Handbook of Research on Teaching the English Language Arts* (2003), Harris and Willis support this assertion:

> We agree and add that multicultural literature is important for all students, not just for Whites who need to be decentered in the curriculum and to learn about others but also for students of color who need to be added to the curriculum and have their cultures affirmed. Multicultural literature, especially the works that move individuals outside of their comfort zones, raise critical consciousness, and challenge the status quo, is needed. (p. 829)

The statistics that began this chapter reiterate the vastness of the issue. Wherever you teach, whoever your students, however you facilitate learning, the provision for introducing diversity through young adult literature supplied by this chapter provides you with the texts; now, you must provide the strategies. Our changing population and our changing students deserve it.

 *Learning Log Responses*

Choose and read one young adult novel mentioned in this chapter and write how you would use it to achieve the goal of having students tolerate and appreciate diverse values.

How will you encourage and help your students to develop lifelong reading habits that will include reading diverse literature?

References

Abeel, S. (2003). *My thirteenth winter: A memoir.* New York: Orchard.

Alan Guttmacher Institute. (1999). *Teenage pregnancy: Overall trends and state-by-state information.* New York: Author.

American School Board Journal. (2001, December). Education vital signs, 31–37.

Applebee, A. (1994). *Shaping conversations: A study of continuity and coherence on high school literary curricula.* Albany, NY: National Research Center on Literature Teaching and Learning.

Armstrong, J. (2002). *The keepers of the flame.* New York: HarperCollins.

Atkins, C. (2003). *Alt ed.* New York: Putnam's.

Bardi, A. (2001). *The book of Fred.* New York: Washington Square.

Benduhn, T. (2003). *Gravel queen.* New York: Simon & Schuster.

Boyd, F., Brock, C., & Rozendal, M. (2004). *Multicultural and multilingual literacy and language.* New York: Guilford Press.

Brown, J. (2004). *Little cricket.* New York: Hyperion.

Bruchac, J. (2003). *Our stories remember: American Indian history, culture, and values through storytelling.* Golden, CO: Fulcrum.

Bushman, J. H. (1996). Young adult literature in the classroom—or is it? *English Journal, 86*(3), 35–40.

Cameron, A. (2003). *Colibri.* New York: Farrar, Straus & Giroux.

Cart, M. (Ed.). (2003). *Necessary noise: Stories about our families as they really are.* New York: Joanna Cotler Books/HarperCollins.

Cart, M. (Ed.). (2004). What a wonderful world: Notes on evolution of GLBTQ literature for young adults. *The ALAN Review. 31*(2), 46–52.

Clinton, C. (2001). *The calling.* Cambridge, MA: Candlewick.

Collins, P. L. (2003). *The fattening hut.* Boston: Houghton Mifflin.

Cotner, J. (Ed.). (2002). *Words for the heart and soul.* New York: HarperCollins.

Crew, L. (2001). *Brides of Eden: A true story imagined.* New York: HarperCollins.

Cummings, P. (2004). *Red kayak.* New York: Dutton.

Curtis, C. P. (2004). *Bucking the sarge.* New York: Wendy Lamb Books/Random House

Fama, E. (2002). *Breaking point.* New York: HarperCollins.

Fletcher, S. (2001). *Walk across the sea.* New York: Atheneum.

Fraustino, L. R. (Ed.). (2002). *Soul searching: Thirteen stories about faith and belief.* New York: Simon & Schuster.

Frost, H. (2003). *Keesha's house.* New York: Farrar, Straus, & Giroux.

Garner, A. (2004). *Families like mine: Children of gay parents tell it like it is.* New York: HarperCollins.

Hallowell, J. (2004). *The annunciation of Francesca Dunn: A novel.* New York: HarperCollins.

Halvorson, M. (2003). *Bull rider.* Custer, WA: Orca.

Harrar, G. (2003). *Not as crazy as I seem.* Boston: Houghton Mifflin.

Harris, V. J., & Willis, A. I. (2003). Multiculturalism, literature and the curriculum. In J. Flood, D. Lapp, & J. M. Jensen (Eds.), *Handbook of research on teaching the English language arts: Vol. 2.* Mahwah, NJ: Erlbaum.

Hartinger, B. (2003). *Geography club.* New York: Harper Tempest.

Hattlr, J. A. (1999). Technology for pre-service teachers: Driver education for the information superhighway. *Journal of Technology and Teacher Education, 7*(4), 323–32. Retrieved September 18, 2004, from http://vnweb.hwwilsonweb.com.

Hautman, P. (2003). *Sweetblood.* New York: Simon & Schuster.

Hesse, K. (2003). *Aleutian sparrow.* New York: Simon & Schuster.

Hoobler, D., & Hoobler, T. (2003). *We are Americans: Voices of the immigrant experience.* New York: Scholastic.

Hugle, K. (2003). *GLBTQ: The survival guide for queer and questioning teens.* Minneapolis, MN: Free Spirit.

Huntington, G. (2003). *Demon witch.* New York: HarperCollins.

Johnson, A. (2003). *A cool moonlight*. New York: Dial.

Johnson, M. (2004). *The Bermudez triangle*. New York: Razorbill/Penguin.

Joselit, J. W. (2001). *Immigration and American religion*. Oxford: Oxford University Press.

Kantner, S. (2004). *Ordinary wolves*. Minneapolis, MN: Milkweed Editions.

Kinsey, A. C., Pomeroy, M., & Martin, C. E. (1948). *Sexual behavior in the human male*. Philadelphia: Saunders.

Levithan, D. (2003). *Boy meets boy*. New York: Knopf.

Macaulay, D. (2003). *Mosque*. Boston: Walter Lorraine Books/Houghton Mifflin.

Mann, G. S., Numrick, D. P., & Williams, R. (2001). *Buddhists, Hindus, and Sikhs in America*. Oxford: Oxford University Press.

McKissack, P. C., & McKissack, F. L. (2003). *Days of jubilee: The end of slavery in the United States*. New York: Scholastic.

Mikaelsen, B. (2004). *Tree girl*. New York: HarperCollins.

Miller, B. M. (2003). *Good women of a well-blessed land: Women's lives in colonial America*. Minneapolis, MN: Lerner.

Morrison, T. (2004). *Remember: The journey to school integration*. Boston: Houghton Mifflin.

Myers, W. D. (2003). *The dream bearer*. New York: HarperCollins.

National Center for Education Statistics. (2002). *Projections of education statistics to 2008*. Washington, DC: Author.

National Clearinghouse for English Language Acquisition. (2002). *Survey of the states' limited English proficient students and available educational programs and services*. Washington, DC: George Washington University, National Clearinghouse for English Language Acquisition.

Otsuka, J. (2002). *When the emperor was divine*. New York: Random House.

Parkay, F. W., & Stanford, B. H. (2004). *Becoming a teacher*. Boston: Pearson.

Paulsen, G. (2003). *Brian's hunt*. New York: Wendy Lamb Books/Random House.

Peck, R. (2003). *The river between us*. New York: Dial.

Rosenblatt, L. M. (1976). *Literature as exploration*. New York: Modern Language Association.

Shea, P. D. (2003). *Tangled threads: A Hmong girl's story*. Boston: Clarion.

Singer, M. (Ed.). (2004). *Face relations: 11 stories about seeing beyond color*. New York: Simon & Schuster.

Tiedt, P. L. (2002). *Multicultural teaching: A handbook of activities, information, and resources* (6th ed.). Boston: Allyn & Bacon.

Tingle, T. (2003). *Walking the Choctaw road: Stories from Red People memory*. St. Paul, MN: Cinco Puntos Press.

Trueman, T. (2000). *Stuck in neutral*. New York: Harper Tempest.

Trueman, T. (2003). *Inside out*. New York: Harper Tempest.

U.S. Census Bureau. (2003a). *Languages spoken at home by age group and language: 2000*. Washington, DC: Author.

U.S. Census Bureau. (2003b). *Population by race and Hispanic origin 2003*. Washington, DC: Author.

U.S. Census Bureau. (2003c). *Public elementary and secondary school teachers—Selected characteristics: 1999–2000*. Washington, DC: Author.

U.S. Census Bureau. (2003d). *Statistical abstract of the United States 2003*. Washington, DC: Author.

U.S. Department of Health and Human Services. (2002). *HHS Fact Sheet, February 26, 2002*. Washington, DC: Author.

Whaley, L., & Dodge, L. (1999). *Weaving in the women*. Portsmouth, NH: Boynton/Cook Heinemann.

Whelan, G. (2004). *Chu Ju's house*. New York: HarperCollins.

Williams, J. (2004). *Escaping tornado season: A story in poems*. New York: Harper Tempest.

Willingham, W. W., & Cole, N. S. (1997). *Gender and fair assessment*. Mahwah, NJ: Lawrence Erlbaum.

CHAPTER

9

Media and Young Adult Literature

With Jill Adams, *University of Kansas*

Technology doesn't necessarily improve education. Take a simple innovation like the pencil: One can use it to write a superlative essay, to drum away the time, or to poke out someone's eye.
S. Veenema and H. Gardner

For many people, vivid memories of elementary school may include the smell of the mimeograph machine, the sight of the dusty chalkboard, or the vision of one of the first computers in the classroom. In the past 25 years, however, the look of American classrooms has drastically changed from this image. SmartBoards, data projectors, laptop computers, and palm pilots are replacing chalkboards, mimeograph machines, and computers that took nearly 5 minutes to boot.

The term *technology* is used frequently in classrooms across the country. But what specifically does that mean? What does it look like in today's English classroom? To find out, dictionary.com came to the assistance:

> *Technology:* The word comes from the Greek word *tekhnologiã*, meaning a *systematic treatment of an art or craft.* An organized treatment of a craft means using technology as a part of something that is already being done. The treatment is simply a way of doing it *differently.*

Simply defined, then, "technology in the English classroom includes all the tools available in your classroom that when applied with skill can lead you to enrich, extend, and empower student understanding" (Kajder, 2003, p. 5). This term is far beyond most people's vision of how it is utilized in the classroom (such as writing papers on the computer) and the term encompasses other areas such as media, audio theater, video projects, online discussion boards, Internet searches, interaction PowerPoints and Web sites, among other things.

The rise of technology in the classroom did not just come about. Numerous individuals, organizations, and school boards focused on keeping their students up to date on the current technological tools available. Even President Clinton got into the act in 1996 during a presidential debate, noting that "Every classroom in America should be hooked up to the Internet by 2000" (Hattler, 1999). As a result of this new-found emphasis, numerous innovations of technology in the classroom emerged. With all of these opportunities to incorporate media in the English classroom, however, one must wonder why it isn't always being done.

There are indeed some challenges in implementing technology effectively. An example could be the lack of technical support within a school district or building. High expectations for the available technology can soon lead to frustration if training does not accompany the new tools. Also, the lack of available technology can be frustrating to instructors who would love to utilize media in the classroom but don't have the hardware or technical support to do so.

There are unfortunately no simple solutions to these problems (even though many wish there were!). It seems imperative, then, to overcome these obstacles and also to recognize the reasons why utilizing technology would be beneficial for our students. First of all, adolescents are being presented with mass amounts of information like at no other time in our nation's history (Loertscher & Woolls, 2002). Helping them sort through all of this information and taking the next step to show them how to utilize it effectively seems as if it should be a logical aim of our schools. In addition, educators must recognize that our students' landscape is changing. Don Tapscott noted that "Today's kids are so bathed in bits that they think technology is part of the natural landscape. To them, digital technology is no more intimidating than a VCR or toaster" (as cited in Kajder, 2003, p. 23).

Statistics support this notion. According to the National School Board Association (2001), 49% of students utilize Internet access at home, and 75% had access either at home or school. Researchers on this study also discovered that the main reason parents buy computers is for educational purposes, and that families who did not have computers expected schools to provide the necessary resources. Both home and school computers are frequently utilized, for the UCLA Internet Report (2003) noted that 97% of both 12- to 15-year-olds and 16- to 18-year-olds are using the Internet.

However, along with the current research on technology in the classrooms came some unexpected findings. Research by Cuban (2001) found that "even when equipment is made available, students aren't using it to extend, enrich, and enhance understanding. . . . They use it in school to complete assignments, play games, explore CD-ROMs for information, and conduct Internet researches" (as cited in Kajder, 2003, p. 8). This idea is also supported by the UCLA Internet Report, which found that 73% of students believe that the Internet has not raised nor hurt their grades. As a result, it seems as if students are not properly utilizing the tool to adequately support their schoolwork.

Perhaps one reason this occurs is that many teachers use technology to "sustain existing patterns of teaching rather than to innovate" (Cuban, 2001, p. 134.) This idea affirms that technology won't simply make learning happen; that occurs only when students are thinking and are engaged with the content. Golub and Pope (2000) agree. Teachers using technology in their English language arts classrooms are not only improving their instruction for their students; they are changing the very nature of that instruction (p. 89).

It is also important to realize that we're talking about a different generation of learners. Tapscott (1998) noted this in his text *Growing Up Digital: The Rise of the Net Generation.* In the book, Tapscott named the group of individuals aged 2 to 22 in 1999 the Net Generation (N-GEN) and also noted that this group uses technology for everything from shopping, to entertainment, to communication, and more. He also claims that the N-Gen is beginning to process and learn differently. It seems as if the teacher-driven, direct instructional methods may not be the best way to teach this group of learners. Therefore, changes must occur.

First of all, teachers must recognize the change in our culture and how it affects instruction. This paradigm shift helps instructors realize that things are simply different. The computer isn't the archrival of the book; along with the chalkboard, overhead, and paper gradebook, there are now SmartBoards, data projectors, and electronic grade books. Instruction also can change. Kajder (2003) agrees. She sees the teacher's role as changing to that of instructional designers, researchers, resource managers, and communication specialists. Therefore, along with the traditional activities we use in our classrooms, we must also teach our students how to deal with digital literacies. After all, that's where the world is going, and we want them to be prepared. It's essentially about making choices that instructors have been making since the first teacher emerged. According to Kajder, "We choose the texts . . . the challenges and exercises. . . . Now we need to choose the most efficient tools for our students as learners. Our toolkit already consists of books, pencils . . . the computer is simply another tool" (p. 27). Therefore, for technology integration to affect students as learners and thinkers, it must bring together the right task, the right tool, and the right student (Kajder, 2003).

Media Opportunities for the Classroom

As each year progresses, the number of technologies that can be utilized in the classroom increases. Knowing which tools can be useful in the classroom and how to operate them can be overwhelming. The following opportunities have been scrutinized and evaluated for their effectiveness and overall quality. I suggest using any or all of them in the English classroom.

Critical Viewing Strategies

Movies and television can be used as stepping-stones to novels and short stories. Why use media literacy? Media engages students. According to John Pungente, educator and international consultant on issues related to children, youth, and media, by the time the average North American graduates from high school, he or she will have spent twice as much time in front of the television set as in the classroom. Although this is changing to include the computer screen, the fact remains that students are intrigued with media. I have sometimes used media to cover literary terms as a springboard to writing a literary analysis. It has been an effective way to encourage students to dig deeper and acts as a stepping-stone to analysis.

Audio Theater

People love hearing others speak. This concept is utilized in the audio theater project. In this activity, students are able to work in groups to collect, write, and produce short audio stories. Using tape recorders, they can conduct interviews with sound effects, voices, and music. Critical thinking is a must with this engaging activity! (See Figure 9.1.)

Video Project

As you probably already know, students love videos. They're intrigued not only with watching them but with creating them as well. This particular assignment can be utilized in the English classroom by having groups create two news reports and commercials that capture a scene and issue from the book. (See Figure 9.2.)

Storyboards

These are a way to have students use graphic organizers to detail the plot of a text that they have read or will create themselves. Storyboards could be created with Inspiration, PowerPoint, or Hyperstudio. Information on this activity can be found at www.youthlearn.org/learning/activities/language/storyboard.asp.

Innovative PowerPoint Presentations

Instead of having students respond to young adult literature in the traditional way, have them create a wordless PowerPoint presentation that serves as an interpretive background for their creation. For example, there may be no words on the screen, but the mood and tone of the slide changes as the student reads through a poem.

Overview

When students read S. E. Hinton's *The Outsiders,* it is not uncommon for them to compare and contrast their own lives with the lives of Ponyboy, Johnny, and the other members of the greaser gang. Initially, many students may think that they do not have much in common with a group of parentless, rough boys. However, as students progress through the book, they often begin to see some similarities with the greasers and how the greasers value friendship and the importance of time spent with friends.

One way to enhance the reading of *The Outsiders* is to have students participate in an audio theater production of the concept of friendship (e.g., the importance of friendship, what it means to be a friend, or what friends do together).

- Students can work in groups of four to collect, write, and produce short audio stories of their fellow students and the concept of friendship.
- Using tape recorders, students will conduct interviews and capture sound effects pertinent to their audio stories.
- The final audio piece will be a combination of voices, music, and sound effects.
- Students can present their audio theaters to the class for peer review and teacher evaluation.
- Students will also present a written transcript of their audio theater production.

Step 1: Introduction to Audio Theater

Introduce students to the world of audio theater. Many old-time radio shows can be downloaded for free at *www.radiolovers.com.* The National Public Radio Web site also has numerous audio artifacts at *www.npr.org/programs/lnfsound.*

Listening to these on a classroom computer requires either Windows Media Player or Real Player, both of which are free downloads. If a computer is not available, you can purchase CDs to play in the classroom from the Web sites.

While students are listening, have them keep track of their thoughts on a **Listening Guide** (a sample is provided).

After students have completed the Listening Guide, engage them with the following types of questions:

Was the story too long or too short?

What was the impact of the audio theater?

How did the voices contribute to the story?

What was your emotional response to the story?

FIGURE 9.1

Audio theater: Connecting with *The Outsiders.*

Developed by Casey Hudson, Columbus, Kansas.

Step 2: Planning the Audio Theater Project

1. Inform students they will be participating in their own audio theater project by conducting interviews, recording sound effects, and producing a cassette tape of their story.

2. Ask students to brainstorm the concept of friendship. Create a list of their ideas on the board or in an area of the classroom where the information can remain for the duration of the project.

   For example:
   Question: What does it mean to be a good friend?

   Potential Responses:

having fun	keeping secrets	loyalty
honesty	sticking up for each other	hanging out

   Question: What types of things do you do with friends?

   Potential Responses:

hang out	talk on phone	play football
go to movies	gossip	party

3. Divide students into audio theater teams (four students per team). As a group, they will decide on *three* people they will interview to learn about the concept of friendship. They will also decide what types of questions to ask.

   Give students guidelines for making these decisions:
   a. Interviewees cannot be members of this language arts class.
   b. If interviewees are students, they should be in a different grade.
   c. Interview at least one adult (e.g., a teacher, a parent, a family member).
   d. Interview questions should be relevant to learning about the concept of friendship.
   e. Each interviewee must answer at least three questions.
   f. Create more interview questions than needed, and then be selective in what is used for the story.

   A **graphic organizer** for brainstorming is provided.

4. Provide students with the remaining guidelines and requirements.

   A **project guidelines, requirements, and pointers page** for students is included.

5. Remind students that they will also need to record sound effects that are thematically tied to their interviewees or interview questions. As students begin collecting interviews, they can consider what types of sound effects will be appropriate.

6. Provide students with a transcript of a similar audio theater project.

   A **sample transcript** is provided.

FIGURE 9.1
Continued.

Step 3: Producing the Audio Theater

Class time can be devoted to working on the audio theater stories. *To ensure that students get the most out of the class time that they will be devoting to the project, it would be useful to acquire some "quiet spaces" in the school so students can work on the recording aspect of their project. Quiet spaces might include the library, conference rooms, or an empty classroom (e.g., during another teacher's planning period).*

Provide students with a checklist so they can manage their time.

A **checklist** is provided.

Step 4: Audio Theater Presentation

On the day that the audio theater stories are to be turned in and presented, students will submit the following:

1. One cassette tape of their audio story
2. Two cassette tapes used in the initial recording (these can be reused for other projects)
3. One typed transcript of their audio story
4. Peer review sheets

Groups can present their audio theater stories to the class by playing them on a tape player that is centrally located in the classroom. Remind students of appropriate audience behavior.

While students are listening, they can be conducting peer reviews.

Peer review sheets are provided.

A **rubric** for teacher assessment is provided

FIGURE 9.1

Continued.

Listening Guide		
Prelistening	Title of program	
	Purpose/Audience	
	Type of program (talk show, documentary, radio play, other)	
	What I'm expecting is . . .	
While listening	The first thing I notice is . . .	
	What I relate to is . . .	
	What I predict about it is . . .	
	What I question is . . .	
Postlistening	My overall impression is . . .	
	If I were going to produce a similar presentation, I would . . .	
	Other comments:	

FIGURE 9.1
Continued.

Audio Theater Project

Interviewing Guidelines

- ❑ Interviewees cannot be members of this language arts class.
- ❑ If interviewees are students, they should be in a different grade.
- ❑ Interview at least one adult (e.g., a teacher, a parent, a family member).
- ❑ Interview questions should be relevant to learning about the concept of friendship.
- ❑ Each interviewee must answer at least three questions.
- ❑ Create more interview questions than needed, and then be selective in what is used for the story.

Audio Theater Guidelines

- ❑ Groups will be provided three cassettes. It is best to use one cassette to capture voices and one to capture sound effects. The third cassette can be used to combine the voices and sound effects and to turn in as the final production piece.
- ❑ Students can use their own cassette recorder equipment or check out equipment from the teacher.
- ❑ Using a microphone will improve the quality of the recordings.
- ❑ Students can use more advanced equipment if they have technology skills. However, no instruction will be provided on the advanced equipment, and points will be deducted for any technology glitches that may occur. No extra points will be given for using more advanced equipment.
- ❑ The group is responsible for creating the "cleanest" (i.e., easy to hear and understand) audio theater possible. However, the teacher understands the limitations of the tape recorder and will not deduct points for limited background noise.

Audio Theater Requirements

- ❑ The audio theater production must begin and end with a piece of music.
- ❑ All group members must have their voice represented in the story at least once.
- ❑ The story must begin with a title and the names of the authors.
- ❑ The story must include a brief (one or two sentences) description at the beginning of the story and a detailed (four to six sentences) conclusion at the end of the story.
- ❑ The stories should be between 7 to 10 minutes. Points will be deducted for stories that do not fall within this time requirement.

Audio Theater pointers

- ❑ Interviews will go more smoothly if you provide a list of questions to the interviewee in advance of the taped interview.
- ❑ Provide transitions between different parts of the story.
- ❑ Sound effects are fun, but make sure they relate and add to the story. Don't get carried away with sound effects; the meat of the story is in the words.
- ❑ Get more information than you will need; be selective in what you use.

FIGURE 9.1

Continued.

Brainstorming Graphic Organizer

Potential Interviewees

1.
2.
3.
4.
5.
6.

Potential Interview Questions

1.
2.
3.
4.
5.
6.
7.
8.
9.
10.

Sample Transcript

- Music at introduction
- Title and authors of the story (e.g., "After-School Practice," by Aimee, Kyle, and Logan)
- Brief description of the story (e.g., "This is our glance into the after-school lives of students at Butler High School.")
- Sound effect
    Fans cheering in a stadium
- Background information of first interviewee
    "First, we meet Marianne, a tri-county volleyball player."

FIGURE 9.1

Continued.

- Interview #1

    "Marianne, what do you do after school?"

    "Well, in the fall, I come straight to volleyball practice after school."

    "How long do you typically practice?"

    "Practices last 2 hours unless we have a game the next day, then those practices are shorter because we are looking at plays and learning about the other team."

    "Do you like coming to practice after school?"

    "Um, well, yeah. I mean, that's the only way we can get better as a team. Also, a lot of my friends play so we get to hang out together, too."
- Transition

    "Now we leave the confines of the school gymnasium and go to the practice football field behind the school."
- Sound effect

    Whistle and football players colliding with each other
- Background information of second interviewee

    "Next, we meet Todd, a member of the football team."
- Interview #2

    "Todd, what do you do after school?"

    "I hit the locker room and dress for football practice."

    "What time do you get home after practice?"

    "I'm usually home by 5:30. I get home about the same time my mom gets home from work."

    "Does football practice interfere with other parts of your life, like studying or hanging out with friends?"

    "Not really. The coach tells us we have to manage our time so we don't fall behind in school. If we don't make good grades, we can't play. I get to see my friends on the weekends."
- Transition

    "From the football field, we go over to the marching band."
- Sound effect

    School fight song
- Background information of third interviewee

    "Finally, we meet LaShandra, a member of the Butler High marching band."
- Interview #3

    "LaShandra, what do you do when the last school bell of the day sounds?"

    "Well, I meet a group of my friends by my locker and we hang out in the commons, but then at 3:30 I have to go to the band room and get my saxophone and meet out in the street for marching band practice."

    "Do you like being a member of the marching band?"

    "Oh, I love it. I love being outside and practicing our steps for the parades."

    "Do you wish sometimes you could just go home after school instead of practicing?"

    "Sometimes, if it's been a long day at school. But once I get out here I have fun. Our director is funny. He makes it easy to come to practice."
- Detailed conclusion with music

    "Well, that concludes our tour of the after-school lives of Butler High students. As you heard, many of them are busy for several hours after the end of each school day. They all seem to enjoy their after-school activities. None of them complained about being tired at the end of the day or that they were missing out on other things. It seems that after-school sports practice just adds to the fun of school for some students."

FIGURE 9.1

Continued.

AUDIO THEATER CHECKLIST

Students: Place a check next to these items as you complete the different steps of the audio theater project. I will be checking for progress by looking at this sheet.

_____ Three cassettes   _____ Access to tape recorder/microphone

_____ Three interviewees

Name: _____   Student / Adult

Name: _____   Student / Adult

Name: _____   Student / Adult

_____ Interview questions

Question 1:
_____

Question 2:
_____

Question 3:
_____

Question 4:
_____

Question 5:
_____

Question 6:
_____

_____ Music

Selection: _____

Selection: _____

_____ Sound effects

1. _____

2. _____

3. _____

_____ Brief introduction
_____
_____

_____ Detailed conclusion
_____
_____
_____

Final Considerations

_____ Interviews conducted   _____ Transitions between each piece

_____ Music and sound effects   _____ All authors' voices represented

_____ All points on the assessment rubric have been considered

FIGURE 9.1
Continued.

Peer Review Sheet

Group members: _____ , _____ , _____ , _____

	Needs Work	Good	Great
1. I could hear the voices.	1	2	3
2. I could hear the sound effects.	1	2	3
3. I was interested while listening.	1	2	3
4. My overall impression of the story is . . .	1	2	3

Things I liked about the story:

Things that could be improved:

Peer Review Sheet

Group members: _____ , _____ , _____ , _____

	Needs Work	Good	Great
1. I could hear the voices.	1	2	3
2. I could hear the sound effects.	1	2	3
3. I was interested while listening.	1	2	3
4. My overall impression of the story is . . .	1	2	3

Things I liked about the story:

Things that could be improved:

Peer Review Sheet

Group members: _____ , _____ , _____ , _____

	Needs Work	Good	Great
1. I could hear the voices.	1	2	3
2. I could hear the sound effects.	1	2	3
3. I was interested while listening.	1	2	3
4. My overall impression of the story is . . .	1	2	3

Things I liked about the story:

Things that could be improved:

FIGURE 9.1
Continued.

Audio Theater Assessment Rubric

Content of the cassette was relevant to the assignment
Score: 1   2   3   4   5   6   7   8   9   10   _____/10
Comments:

Group made best possible use of audio equipment (clear, easy to hear)
Score: 1   2   3   4   5   6   7   8   9   10   _____/10
Comments:

All group members' voices occurred on the cassette
Score: 1   2   3   4   5   6   7   8   9   10   _____/10
Comments:

Group gave (about) equal amounts of coverage to each aspect
Score: 1   2   3   4   5   6   7   8   9   10   _____/10
Comments:

Sound effects were appropriate
Score: 1   2   3   4   5   6   7   8   9   10   _____/10
Comments:

Selected interview questions were appropriate in depicting after-school life
Score: 1   2   3   4   5   6   7   8   9   10   _____/10
Comments:

Music choice was thematic
Score: 1   2   3   4   5   6   7   8   9   10   _____/10
Comments:

Included title and authors' names
Score: 1   2   3   4   5   6   7   8   9   10   _____/10
Comments:

Included a brief description and detailed conclusion
Score: 1   2   3   4   5   6   7   8   9   10   _____/10
Comments:

Connection was made between the greasers and student peers
Score: 1   2   3   4   5   6   7   8   9   10   _____/10
Comments:

Cassette was appropriate in length
Score: 1   2   3   4   5   6   7   8   9   10   _____/10
Comments:

Typed transcript matched the cassette
Transcript was typed in appropriate form (e.g., correct use of quotation marks)
Score: 1   2   3   4   5   6   7   8   9   10   _____/10
Comments:

FIGURE 9.1
Continued.

Overview

When students read Nancy Farmer's *The House of the Scorpion,* they encounter many real-world issues depicted in a futuristic sci-fi novel. For some students, this book may be the first time they have considered the social, moral, and economical impacts of issues such as cloning, the drug trade, and immigration.

One way to enhance the reading of *The House of the Scorpion* is to have students participate in a video project that researches some of the main themes depicted in the novel.

- Students can work in groups of four to create a video presentation (two news reports and a commercial) that captures a scene and an issue from the book.
- Students will use a video camera to record their news production and commercial.
- The final news report will be a description of a recent event (a scene from the book), a research update (an update of an issue from the book, e.g., the drug trade), and a commercial for a product from the book.
- Students can present the news reports and commercial to the class for peer review and teacher evaluation.
- Students will also present written transcripts of their news reports.

Step 1: Introduction to News Reporting and Commercials

Introduce students to the world of news reporting and product commercials. Bring recorded samples for the class to view.

While students are watching, have them keep track of their thoughts on a **Watching Guide** (a sample is provided).

After students have completed the Watching Guide, engage them with the following types of questions:

> Was the news report/commercial too long or too short?
> What was the impact of the news report/commercial?
> How did the reporters contribute to the news report?
> How did the actors contribute to the commercial?
> What was your emotional response to the news report?
> What was your emotional response to the commercial?

FIGURE 9.2

Video project: News Reports on *The House of the Scorpion.*
Developed by Casey Hudson, Columbus, Kansas.

Step 2: Planning the Video Project

1. Inform students they will be participating in their own video production of two news reports and a commercial.

2. Ask students to brainstorm some of the "newsworthy" scenes from *The House of the Scorpion*.

   For example:
   Question: What were some of the more amazing things that happened in the book?

   Potential Responses:

   Mateo's a clone   Mateo never saw sunlight before age 6
   El Patron turned 140   Mateo was kept locked up
   The dead eejit   Rosa disappeared

3. Ask students to brainstorm some of the hefty issues from *The House of the Scorpion*.

   For example:
   Question: What social, economical, or moral issues were covered in the book?

   Potential Responses:

   DNA   Cloning
   Creating eejits   Immigration
   Drug trafficking   Addiction

4. Divide students into video project teams (four students per team). As a group, they will decide to report on one "newsworthy" scene from the book, one social, economical, or moral issue in the book, and they will choose one product from the book to advertise.

    A **graphic organizer** for brainstorming is provided.

5. Provide students with the guidelines and requirements.

    A **project guidelines, requirements, and pointers page** for students is included.

6. Students will need access to the Internet to research the current status of the issue they choose to report. The news reports need to be factual and serious.

7. Provide students with the transcript worksheet for their news reports. Students are responsible for documenting the sources of their reports.

    A **transcript worksheet** is provided.

FIGURE 9.2
Continued.

Step 3: Producing the Video Projects

Class time can be devoted to working on the video projects. *To ensure that students get the most out of the class time that they will be devoting to the project, it would be useful to acquire some "quiet spaces" in the school so students can work on the filming aspect of their project. Quiet spaces might include the library, conference rooms, or an empty classroom (e.g., during another teacher's planning period).*

Provide students with a checklist so they can manage their time.

 A **checklist** is provided.

Encourage students to use visuals in their news reporting and advertisement.

Step 4: Video Project Presentation

On the day that the video projects are to be turned in and presented, students will submit the following:

1. One video cassette of their news report and commercial
2. A written transcript worksheet for both news reports
3. Peer review sheets

Groups can present their video projects to the class by playing them on television and using a VCR. Remind students of appropriate audience behavior.

While students are watching, they can be conducting peer reviews.

 Peer review sheets are provided.

 A **rubric** for teacher assessment is provided.

FIGURE 9.2
Continued.

Watching Guide		
Prewatching	Title of program	
	Purpose	
	Predictions	
While watching	The first thing I notice is . . .	
	What I notice about the people is . . .	
	What I notice about their voices is . . .	
	What I notice about the music is . . .	
	What I notice about the "story" is . . .	
Postwatching	My overall impression is . . .	
	If I were to make a similar piece, I would . . .	
	Other comments:	

FIGURE 9.2
Continued.

Brainstorming Graphic Organizer

Potential Scenes

Potential Scenes	Positive	Negative

Potential Issues

Potential Issues	Positive	Negative

Potential Product Advertisements

Potential Products	Positive	Negative

FIGURE 9.2
Continued.

Video Project

Requirements and Guidelines

- ❑ You must have two components to your news report (a scene from the book and a social, economical, or moral issue from the book).
- ❑ You must have one product advertisement that is relevant to the book (you can be creative and invent your own product, but it must be relevant to the book).
- ❑ Three of your group members must appear in front of the camera during the production. Only one group member can be the cameraperson.
- ❑ News reports *must be factual* and serious. You can have fun with the commercial.
- ❑ You *must* document where you found your information (e.g., Web site addresses).
- ❑ If you are a news reporter, dress for the role.
- ❑ Each of the three components *cannot* be more than 4 minutes. There is a 12-minute time limit to your production. Points will be deducted for videos that are longer.
- ❑ Each group will get approximately 30 minutes to work with the camera. On the day you are to produce, you must be prepared.
- ❑ Students can use more advanced equipment if they have technology skills. However, no instruction will be provided on the advanced equipment, and points will be deducted for any technology glitches that may occur. No extra points will be given for using more advanced equipment.
- ❑ The group is responsible for creating the "cleanest" (i.e., easy to hear and understand) video project possible. However, the teacher understands the limitations of the recording and will not deduct points for limited background noise.

FIGURE 9.2
Continued.

Transcript Worksheet

SCENE	ISSUE
REPORTER	REPORTER
REPORT	REPORT
WEB SITES CONSULTED	WEB SITES CONSULTED

FIGURE 9.2
Continued.

Video Project Checklist

Students: Place a check next to these items as you complete the different steps of the video project. I will be checking for progress by looking at this sheet.

_____ A scene has been chosen

_____

_____ An issue has been chosen

_____

_____ A product has been chosen

_____

_____ Product approval from teacher

_____ Three people in front of camera   _____

                                                   _____

                                                   _____

_____ Cameraperson   _____

_____ Transcript 1

_____ Transcript 2

_____ Visuals have been created

_____ Filming day chosen   _____

_____ All points on the assessment rubric have been considered

FIGURE 9.2
Continued.

PEER REVIEW SHEET

Group members: _____ , _____ , _____ , _____

The first news report was . . .

The second news report was . . .

The commercial was . . .

Things I liked were . . .

PEER REVIEW SHEET

Group members: _____ , _____ , _____ , _____

The first news report was . . .

The second news report was . . .

The commercial was . . .

Things I liked were . . .

PEER REVIEW SHEET

Group members: _____ , _____ , _____ , _____

The first news report was . . .

The second news report was . . .

The commercial was . . .

Things I liked were . . .

FIGURE 9.2
Continued.

Video Project Assessment Rubric

Content of the video was relevant to the assignment
Score: 1   2   3   4   5   6   7   8   9   10   _____/10
Comments:

Group made best possible use of video equipment (clear, easy to hear)
Score: 1   2   3   4   5   6   7   8   9   10   _____/10
Comments:

All group members participated in the video production
Score: 1   2   3   4   5   6   7   8   9   10   _____/10
Comments:

Group gave (about) equal amounts of coverage to each aspect
Score: 1   2   3   4   5   6   7   8   9   10   _____/10
Comments:

First news report was relevant and clear
Score: 1   2   3   4   5   6   7   8   9   10   _____/10
Comments:

Second news report was clear
Score: 1   2   3   4   5   6   7   8   9   10   _____/10
Comments:

Commercial was informative
Score: 1   2   3   4   5   6   7   8   9   10   _____/10
Comments:

Visuals were appropriate
Score: 1   2   3   4   5   6   7   8   9   10   _____/10
Comments:

Connections were made between the book and the news reports
Score: 1   2   3   4   5   6   7   8   9   10   _____/10
Comments:

Connections were made between the book and the commercial
Score: 1   2   3   4   5   6   7   8   9   10   _____/10
Comments:

Transcripts matched the news reports
Score: 1   2   3   4   5   6   7   8   9   10   _____/10
Comments:

Transcripts included source information
Score: 1   2   3   4   5   6   7   8   9   10   _____/10
Comments:

FIGURE 9.2
Continued.

Interactive PowerPoint Lesson

Teachers can create a PowerPoint presentation that serves as a guide for students as they dig into a text. Chapter questions, journal response prompts, and assignments/activities are just a few of the features that could be added. An example can be found at www.people.ku.edu/~hudson. (See Figure 9.3.)

Electronic Portfolio

Today, there's an option of creating an electronic portfolio (e-folio) that could replace all the manila folders in your file cabinet. Students enjoy creating these on the computer, as they reflect on the progress made throughout the course. (See Figure 9.4.)

Discussion Board

Classroom discussions are not just face to face anymore. The opportunities for online talks can electrify the classroom. Consider these words of advice when thinking about incorporating the discussion board into your class: practice, practice, practice. Discussion boards can be an invaluable addition to a classroom; they can also be a mess. I've seen both. The key to success is to train students to write the kinds of responses that you are looking for and to get them to look critically at the posts they are reading and writing. Dan Rothermel, author of "Threaded Discussions: A First Step" (2001), recommends making the online entries a priority, assessing students' knowledge of technology before they begin, maintaining choices while still being directive, and finding a mentor to help you if the need arises. Many more tips are included on the project sheet. (See Figure 9.5.)

E-Literature Circles

Do you have a friend who teaches the same class/grade level as you do? Well, this idea may be for you. Students can participate in traditional literature circle activities in the classroom while also utilizing discussion boards to facilitate further conversation with students from another school in a different town, city, or state.

Web Log (Blog)

Put away those notebooks and try a blog instead of a journal in your classroom. A blog (short for *Web log*) is a space online that users can create to record personal thoughts, like an online diary. They can share these thoughts with other "bloggers" and get feedback from them. People can share their thoughts with people all around the world. Students may not be used to writing in this format, so it will be imperative that you let them know what you're looking for in their responses. Blogs are read with the latest information first, so you begin at the end as opposed to reading the oldest entry first with traditional journals. Consult www.blogger.com to see how Web logs work.

Overview

PowerPoint is a powerful and user-friendly program that is typically used to create multimedia presentations. PowerPoint can also be used to create an interactive reader's guide to assist students in making connections with their reading and to support a student's independent reading.

An interactive reader's guide slide show can contain background information about the author and book, and it can also provide prompts and instructions for lessons and assignments. Used properly, the PowerPoint interactive readers' guide allows students to read at their own pace while ensuring that students are making successful progress with the book. Also, by having an interactive reader's guide available to students, class time can be devoted to other types of activities.

- By using PowerPoint, teachers can create a slideshow that allows students to interact with a book.
- Students can move through the book at their own pace, using the interactive reader's guide at appropriate chapter breaks (designated by the teacher).
- The interactive reader's guide is meant to enhance the student's independent reading of a book. The guide can contain background information and prompts for activities.

Will the Interactive Reader's Guide Work in Your Classroom?

Using PowerPoint to create an interactive reader's guide is relatively easy, even if you are unfamiliar with the program. The tutorial and help options will likely provide answers to many of your questions. PowerPoint is such a commonly used program that you may be able to recruit help from colleagues as well.

There are at least two things to consider before creating an interactive reader's guide:

1. **How will students access the reader's guide?** Does your classroom have a single computer or several computers? Is the school's computer lab a place that students can use easily? Having access to a computer lab is probably not necessary, but depending on the number of students in your class, you will probably want to have several computer terminals available for students to use. As students come to designated chapter breaks, they will need access to a computer to work with the reader's guide.

   If there is a computer shortage in your classroom, one option may be to save the reader's guide to a floppy and let the students save the PowerPoint file to their home computer. If a student's home computer does not have the PowerPoint program, a PowerPoint viewer can be downloaded for free from the Microsoft Web site (www.microsoft.com).

2. **What types of text are suitable for PowerPoint interactive reader's guides?** The potential to use PowerPoint for an interactive reader's guide exists for any type of text. It may be worthwhile to create a reader's guide for a relatively short piece (e.g., short story) first, to determine how your students react to the interface. Because you want all students to participate, you would likely want to use a piece that you assign for all students to read.

FIGURE 9.3

PowerPoint: Using PowerPoint to create an interactive reader's guide for your students.
Developed by Casey Hudson, Columbus, Kansas.

What Should You Include in the Interactive Reader's Guide?

Creation of the reader's guide will go much smoother if you do some initial planning before the designing. First, decide the purpose of your reader's guide. Possible options include

a. providing additional information
b. guiding students in their reading
c. enhancing students' connections to their readings
d. a combination of all of these

Will your interactive reader's guide have images? An easy way to find images (e.g., a photo of the author, a copy of the book's cover) is by searching for images on the Internet. When an appropriate image is found, you can copy and paste the image from the Internet into your PowerPoint slideshow. *If you use images, it is important that you document from where these images were borrowed by recognizing the source of the image.*

The following pages provide templates for each slide of the PowerPoint slideshow for an interactive reader's guide for *When Zachary Beaver Came to Town* by Kimberly Willis Holt.

This PowerPoint slideshow is not chronological (i.e., continually clicking to progress through the slideshow is not necessary). Instead, by creating links in the slideshow, students can click through the slideshow in a way that is similar to navigating through the Internet. The PowerPoint help menu provides step-by-step instructions on how to link slides. Once the content of the reader's guide is established, it is helpful to create a flowchart of how the PowerPoint slideshow works. This will help ensure you have provided all of the links for students to navigate through the reader's guide.

 A sample flowchart is provided.

FIGURE 9.3
Continued.

Keypals

This is a new twist on an old idea. Instead of having traditional penpals, the concept of keypals utilizes safe and appropriate Web sites that pair up educators and their classes with other students around the world. Of course, modeling effective e-mail communication is a must before beginning this activity. Students could also respond to literature in this format. For example, if students were responding to each other while reading a book like *The Giver*, they could have various prompts that they needed to address in their e-mail. In addition, including such skills as having critical, insightful, fair, and complete responses could form the components of an effective rubric. The book *10 Easy Ways to Use Technology in the English Classroom* (Firek, 2003) recommends ePALS.com, which is one of the largest and safest spots, and Intercultural Email Classroom Connections at www.iecc.org is a smaller alternative.

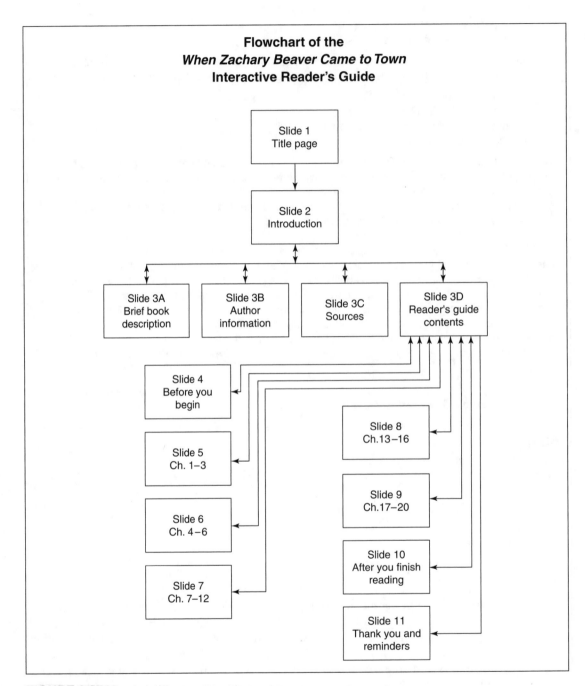

FIGURE 9.3
Continued.

Advantages:
- Ease of storage
- Can include other works besides simple documents
- The ability to scan items into the computer
- Students also gain computer skills
- Students can e-mail their work to their parents, guardians, grandparents, and others

Disadvantages:
- Where did it go?
- Missing the ability to read actual "papers"
- Frustration of technical issues (computer accessibility, down server, etc.)

1. Have students create a folder to hold all files and documents from your English class. Name it "Jenny Smith's Portfolio." *All* files—including documents, clip art, and so on—will have to be saved in this folder in order to be added to the e-folio.

2. There are three types of portfolios: working, showcase or display, and assessment. Decide which method will work best for your needs.

3. Some common characteristics include the following:
   - Many samples
   - Variety of genres
   - Student selection
   - Opportunities for revision
   - Reflection

4. What should be included? I have always included the following:
   - Introductory reflective letter
   - Table of contents
   - Pieces with hyperlinks to introductory reflections
   - Self-assessed rubric

5. Some helpful hints:
   - Involve students in the process.
   - Make sure to back up all files.
   - Show examples as models.
   - Provide checkpoints or deadlines.
   - Set high expectations.

Reading E-folio

"If you asked a teacher to show you high-quality work, he/she wouldn't show you a standardized test." Sally Loughlin

Purpose: To promote understanding of yourself as a reader and learner and to show growth over the semester in improvement in critical reading skills.

You will need to have the following selected items:

1. Portfolio table of contents with theme tie-ins. The order of the portfolio is up to you; think through the possibilities and find what organizational approach will work for you. The table of contents should provide links to all of the materials that follow. You may also choose to lead your audience through your piece by having the next link at the bottom of the piece.

FIGURE 9.4
Electronic portfolios.

2. One-page introductory reflective letter to introduce your audience to your theme. This should also describe your work this semester, progress you made, challenges that still exist, and so forth. Mention the various assignments or activities in the portfolio in your explanation. You are also inviting your audience into your portfolio.

3. Reading goals and reading list for this semester. Reading goals for the future (set five in the same format as the reading goals for the semester).

4. Revised and edited Portrait of Myself as a Reader (*update* the piece as well)

5. Reader-response journal. You should have one entry per week (either through the jump starts, dialogue journal, or vocab-a-toon). This should have a one-paragraph introductory reflection. The introduction could include your thoughts on the process, what you learned, why it's an important part of your portfolio, and so forth.

6. Three other activities or notes from class (your choice of which ones to include). Link *a* one-paragraph introductory reflection for *all* of them (why they would be important to include might be a good approach).

7. Self-assessed portfolio rubric.

> *Remember I like to be impressed! Concentrate on showing growth as a writer through having __personal__ and __insightful__ reflections/intros. In addition, make your portfolio easy and enjoyable for someone to peruse.*

Rubric for Reading Portfolio

	1	2	3	4	5
Presentation/Organization	Organization needs work; no creative effort put forth.		Some organization evident; a little creativity displayed.		Well organized! Creative effort is shown off!
Materials Included	Less than half of required materials included.		Majority of selected materials from choices are included.		All of chosen materials from choices are present
Personal Growth	Set some goals or no effort put forth on them; reflective letter missing.		Goals set but not actively worked on; reflective letter present but still in progress or not fully developed.		Goals set and reflective letter is insightful and well done.

Total Points: /15 × 10 = 150

Reflection on score:

FIGURE 9.4
Continued.

Okay, I know many of you may have already written on discussion board entries before. No, don't do it. Don't give me that yawn. Seriously. Through my years of incorporating discussion boards into my classes, I've realized the importance of establishing the Standards of Netiquette:

- Don't e-mail what you wouldn't say face to face.
- Respect others' time.
- Spelling, grammar, and punctuation still count in e-mail interactions and discussion board postings.
- Include a meaningful subject line in all e-mails.
- Always include contact information when e-mailing.

Sara Kajder, *The Tech-Savvy English Classroom*

Other Tips

➢ The discussion board could be viewed as an outside-of-class opportunity to respond to books and activities related to them.
➢ Inside of the classroom walls, the discussion could be "silent" in nature.
➢ Practice before you let them loose.
➢ Demonstrate effective threading.
➢ Give examples of excellent posts.
➢ Give examples of posts that aren't there quite yet.
➢ Have them evaluate several posts—ability to put forth a clear message, prompts additional commentary, adequately responds to initial post, and so on.
➢ Give them guidelines on how many minimum responses they should post (while also encouraging that they go beyond this) and also on how much the activity is worth grade-wise. (Is it worth 5% of their grade or 50 points?)
➢ Keep an eye on the activity.
➢ If something is inappropriate, delete it (you have the power to do so) and then follow up with the student.

Some sample rubrics for expectations follow.

Discussion Board Evaluation

Original posting:

Did you . . .

Mention at least two specific points from the text/class?	Yes	No
Relate new information to old?	Yes	No
Discuss at a deeper level (not just repeating facts)?	Yes	No
Provide an in-depth response that fully explores your point?	Yes	No

FIGURE 9.5

Discussion board guidelines.

Reply to others' postings:

Did you . . .

Discuss what you agreed with and piggyback on ideas?	Yes	No
Discuss what you may have disagreed with in a constructive way?	Yes	No

Discussion Board Self-Reflection

Did you . . .

Write at least 10 substantive posts this semester?	Yes	No
Post a balance of original postings and replies to others?	Yes	No

With your original postings, did you . . .

Relate old information to new?	Yes	No
Discuss at a deep level?	Yes	No
Go ih depth?	Yes	No

Considering your commentary toward others' postings, did you . . .

Discuss what you liked/agreed with and delve deeper into their ideas?	Yes	No
Discuss what you disagreed with in a positive way?	Yes	No

FIGURE 9.5

Continued.

Category	4	3	2	1
Discussion Board Rubric				
Delivery	The writer demonstrates a strong grasp of spelling and conventions	Only a few errors occur in postings	Errors occur often enough to be somewhat distracting	There are numerous errors that make the text difficult to read
Relevance	Always posts topics related to discussion topic; cites additional references related to topic	Mostly posts topics that are related to discussion content; prompts further discussion of topic	Occasionally posts are off topic; most posts are short in length and offer no further insight	Posts topics that do not relate to the discussion content; makes short or irrelevant remarks
Expression	Expresses opinions and ideas in a clear and concise manner with obvious connections made	Opinions and ideas are clear but may occasionally lack connection to topic	Unclear connection to topic and minimal expression of opinions or ideas	Does not express opinions or ideas clearly; no connection to topic
Contribution to discussion	Frequently attempts to motivate the group discussion	Mostly attempts to direct the discussion and to present relevant viewpoints	Occasionally makes meaningful reflection on group's efforts; marginal effort in involvement	Does not make effort to participate; seems indifferent
Timeliness	All required responses are posted early in the discussion as well as throughout the discussion	All the required responses are present, although some were not posted in time for others to read or respond to	All the required responses are present, although most were completed at the last minute without allowing for response time	Some or all of the required posts are missing

FIGURE 9.5
Continued.

Hyperlinked Essays

Hyperlinked simply means that the text is interactive; in other words, there are links within the text that lead to other spots. These other locations might be other writing pieces or perhaps even online resources. When writing reactions to young adult literature, students can create links that relate to what is being discussed in the text. For example, if a student is writing a piece titled "Athletic Shorts," he or she might include a link under Chris Crutcher's name that leads to his Web site, www.aboutcrutcher.com. Instead of a linear piece, the student ends up with text that conveys information in a different manner.

TrackStar

What's great about TrackStar? It's run by a nonprofit Web site that aims at making educational resources available. Many instructors use TrackStar to provide students with links to Web sites, thus limiting their search to "safe" areas. TrackStar can also be utilized to plan activities and other curriculum. The Web site to check out is www.scrtec.org, then hit TrackStar.

WebQuest

A WebQuest is simply a quest—or search—on the Web. Basically, a teacher designs the search for the student and therefore avoids a lot of the clutter that students can find online. The good news is that there are a lot of them out there. The bad news is that it may take some time to search through them to find one that you can adjust for your own needs. I typically find a site I like and use it as a springboard to develop a search for my own objectives. The best spot to start is the San Diego State University WebQuest site: http://webquest.sdsu.edu/. Other sites to investigate are www.bestwebquests.com and www.webquest.org. Also, sometimes completing a search for the name of a book and the word *WebQuest* is a great starting spot.

Gary Paulsen's Iditarod

With this Web site, students can follow along the Iditarod as it is being run. Kids love his adventures, and there are others detailed on this site: www.randomhouse.com/features/garypaulsen/index.html. Sometimes the Iditarod site is down when the race isn't being run.

Web Design

Each school district now seems to host sites where teachers can create and update their own Web sites. Although it takes time—both for design and upkeep—most parents and students appreciate the effort and are glad to have the outside communication that may detail such instructional aids as calendars, assignments, and so on. My advice is to keep your eye out for workshops on Web design in your district. I also recommend becoming friends with a technology guru in your school. Here are just a couple of typical English teacher Web sites: www.people.ku.edu/~hudson and http://teachers.usd497.org/prsalvat.

Young Adult Novel Research Activity

Students can also research young adult authors via an Internet project. Both guided and independent author searches would be held in addition to young adult teen book site searches, a novel recommendation activity, and a research project involving the exploration of a teen problem. This idea is based on an activity created by Annette Collins of Oskaloosa High School in Oskaloosa, Kansas.

Web Sites for Educators and Their Students

Disclaimer: The links provided here have been scrutinized for their appropriateness. However, because the Internet is constantly changing, it is advisable that you preview all of the links before introducing them to students.

About the Mountain Laurel

www.mtnlaurel.com/about/abouttml.htm

Through this site, you can journey to the "heart of the Blue Ridge Mountains." Links include mountain places, tales, memories, crafts, Mayberry, and more, many of which could directly relate to books or stories that students are reading.

African American Literature Book Club

www.aalbc.com

Although this site is mainly for adults, there are also links for young adult literature, including various African American young adult authors, writer's resources, awards (Coretta Scott King), and books/bestsellers.

American Libraries Association (www.ala.org)

- **Award Winning Books (www.ala.org/ala/alsc/awardsscholarships/awardsscholarships.htm)** This site is sponsored by the Association for Library Service for Children's Awards and Scholarships and is a great source for a listing of award-winning books, for all of the young adult books that won a major award are listed.
- **Book List (www.ala.org/ala/yalsa/booklistsawards/booklistsbook.htm)** The Book List includes links to the Alex Awards, Best Books for Young Adults, the Margaret A. Edwards Awards, the Michael L. Printz Awards, Outstanding Books for the College Bound, Popular Paperbacks for Young Adults, Quick Picks for Reluctant Young Adult Readers, Selected Audiobooks, Selected DVDs and Videos, and Teens' Top Ten.

- **Teen Read Week (www.ala.org/ala/yalsa/teenreading/teenreading.htm)**
  The ALA celebrates the annual teen read week.

America Writes for Kids!

http://usawrites4kids.drury.edu

Sponsored by the Drury University School of Education and Child Development, this site allows guests to search for information about authors and their books. According to the site, its goal is to "promote literacy and creativity by introducing young readers, parents, teachers, and librarians to the work of 'real, live' children's authors." Authors such as June Rae Wood and Vicki Grove are featured. Numerous other links to young adult Web sites are also provided.

The Assembly for Literature of Adolescents of NCTE

www.alan-ya.org

Sponsored by the Assembly on Literature for Adolescents (an NCTE special-interest group), this Web site features numerous articles about young adult literature and young adult authors. Also included are book reviews, weekly columns, the ALAN Award, *ALAN Review*, ALAN Speakers Bureau, ALAN Workshop, Authors' Bureau, Bill's Books, and the Ted Hipple Award.

The Author's Corner

http://ccpl.carr.org/authco

If you want to find a young adult author, you can go to this site. It also has a listing of the Newbery Award winners and quotes from them. Other links include mid-Atlantic authors, MAE Award Authors, other authors, and The Reading Corner.

Aztec Folk Tales

http://www.sdcoe.k12.ca.us/score/Aztec/aztectg.html

Developed by the Schools of California Online Resources for Educators Project, the site has several activities for middle school students to respond to literature. In one activity, students read "Aztec Snow White" and compare it to the Grimm version. Another example includes a volcano poem as a response to information on the landform.

Blogger

http://www.blogger.com

A blog (short for *Web log*) is a space online that users can create to record personal thoughts, like an online diary. They can share these thoughts with other "bloggers" and get feedback from them. Students can share their thoughts with people all around the world.

Bookspot

http://www.bookspot.com

The bookspot is your resource for everything that has to do with books, including young adult literature.

Carol Hurst's Children's Literature Web Site

www.carolhurst.com

Reviews of books for kids and ways to implement them in the classroom are a focus of this Web site. Also included are various collections of books that focus on certain subject areas, themes, and professional topics.

The Children's Literature Web Guide

www.ucalgary.ca/~dkbrown/index.html

This site, sponsored by the University of Calgary, features authors on the Web, stories on the Web, readers' theater, lists of recommended books, journals, and book reviews, research guides and indexes, Internet book discussion groups, and resources for teachers, parents, storytellers, writers, and illustrators. Tons of information is provided by each link.

Connections

www.nescbwi.org/connections.php

This site is a free directory of all New England authors and illustrators who make school visits. The New England Society of Children's Book Writers and Illustrators (New England SCBWI) compiled the directory.

CyberGuides

www.sdcoe.k12.ca.us/score/cy912.html

These CyberGuides, created by Schools of California Online Resources for Education, contain links to texts as well as virtual museums. In addition to classic literature, young adult links include such texts as *Night, The Pigman,* and *Farewell to Manzanar. Night's* link includes an introduction, overview, and five student activities.

Educational Paperback Association

www.edupaperback.org/showauth.cfm?authid=41

Designed for both educators and librarians, this site includes many links for children's book distributors and publishers (including young adult literature), Web resources (children's author and illustrator Web sites, education and library resources, journal/magazine/newsletter sites, literacy resources, and book awards), Top 100 Authors (divided up by K–4, 5–8, and 9–12), and author/illustrator bios.

Fairrosa Cyber Library of Children's Literature

www.fairrosa.info

Archived literature discussions, a reference shelf, a showcase, and information on authors are some of the links posted on this page. Students can also take the Newbery Honor Books Survey or see the results of the survey online.

Favorite Teenage Angst Books

www.grouchy.com/angst

What teen doesn't have angst? This site will help teenagers find a book to go along with their current struggles.

Global Access to Educational Sources: A Cybrary for Middle School and Beyond

www.geocities.com/Athens/Academy/6617/stures6.html

This Web site boasts numerous links for literature. Myths, Legends, Reader's Theater, Youth Web Sites, Judy Blume, *Snow White,* and Authors on the Web are just a few of the links listed.

Guys Read

www.guysread.com

Developed by Jon Scieszka, this site aims at helping boys find books that they'll enjoy reading. Visitors can find a book, read guys' picks (divided into elementary, middle, and high school levels), and learn about Scieszka and his books. Also included are reasons the site was created. Because Scieszka grew up with five brothers, taught elementary school for 10 years, and has been a young adult author for 15 years, he believes he has a good idea as to why boys aren't already crazy about reading.

The Horn Book, Inc.

www.hbook.com

The Horn Book, Inc., features publications about books for children and young adults. The online edition features recommended new paperbacks; lists of the Newbery, Caldecott, and other ALA Awards; the magazine's choices for best books; and previews of the upcoming publication. Other links of interest include a parents' page, future classics, and authors/illustrators.

Inspiration

www.inspiration.com

Inspiration is a program that allows teachers and students to organize their thoughts and ideas with diagrams, graphic organizers, and outlining. After the students organize their ideas, they can move them to a word processing program. This is great for prewriting.

International Reading Association

www.reading.org

This packed Web site contains multitudes of links for young adult literature. Article archives, book lists, discussion, headlines, news briefs, ReadWriteThink, and much more are available. Teachers and librarians probably are already familiar with this site.

Internet Public Library

www.ipl.org/div/kidspace/browse/rzn9000

KidSpace @ the Internet Public Library focuses on allowing students to learn more about their favorite books and authors. Numerous links to various Web sites allow students to discover these topics for themselves. Additional features include a culture quest, ask a question, story hour, the Reading Zone, and "fun stuff."

Jim Trelease's Read-Aloud Handbook

www.trelease-on-reading.com/rah_treasury.html

Great suggestions are given on effective read-aloud pieces for the classroom. The site also includes short texts as well as novels.

Kairos: A Journal of Rhetoric, Technology, and Pedagogy

English.ttu.edu/kairos

This refereed online journal publishes Web texts or pieces that are written to publish on the Web. These scholarly articles include reviews, news stories, announcements, interactive exchanges, and examinations of large-scale issues related to special topics.

Kathy Schrock's Guide for Educators: Literature and Language

artshttp://school.discovery.com/schrockguide/arts/artlit.html

More than 75 links provided here all share the same focus: the language arts classroom. Ask the Young Adult Author, book talks, YA author birthdays, cool quotes, literacy resources on the Net, Readers' Theater, and the Young Adult Librarian's Help/Homepage are just a few of the worthwhile links. A lot of information is presented.

KidsReads.com

www.kidsreads.com/index.asp

Aimed at students, this lively Web site fosters polls (e.g., "Do you go to events in local bookstores or libraries to meet authors?"), a newsletter, featured books, series books, new books, author information, reviews, a question of the week (e.g., "Besides J. K. Rowling, what author would you most like to meet?"), information on books being adapted into movies, book clubs, reading lists, trivia, word scrambles, and more. Middle-level students would especially like this one.

kidSPEAK!

www.kidspeakonline.org

Aimed at allowing an outlet for kids to speak out on free speech, this site contains links for information on censorship, up-to-date kidSPEAK news, what students are saying about such issues as the First Amendment, censorship, IQ, and what individuals can do to get involved with the group.

Lesson Plans and Resources for Adolescent and Young Adult Literature

www.cloudnet.com/~edrbsass/edadolescentit.htm

Numerous links to lesson plans and other resources for adolescent and young adult literature are present on this site. Short stories and mysteries are included. Although much of this site focuses on classic literature, young adult authors are also interspersed, such as Avi, Robert Cormier, Anne Frank, and S. E. Hinton, to name a few.

Linda's Links to Literature

www.richmond.k12.va.us/readamillion/LITERATURE/lindas_links_to_
literature.htm

This extensive Web site claims to have more than 16,500 links to lesson plans and activities for young adult and children's literature (I didn't try them all). Organized alphabetically, one can search for the book title of choice. *The Chocolate War* yielded the following links: a theme activity, two book talks, a master list of words, games for chapters, a lesson for journaling and discussion, a novel guide, an online quiz, questions for discussion, a reading guide, a study guide, and a WebQuest.

Marcopolo: Internet Content for the Classroom

www.marcopolo-education.org/index.aspx

The Marcopolo Web site combines various featured partners to produce numerous lesson plan ideas and professional development opportunities. Lessons are created by ARTSEDGE'S Art Quotes, EconEdLink's Data Links, EDSITEment's Calendar, Illumination's Interactive Math*lets, ReadWriteThink, Science NetLinks's Weekly Science Updates, and Xpeditions Atlas. Search using language arts and literature for one's respective grade level, and numerous hits will pop up. Although I initially thought that I would only find lessons from ReadWriteThink, I also discovered lessons through EDSITEment, ArtsEdge, Xpeditions, and Science NetLinks.

Mrs. Bradley's English Pages

www.members.accessus.net/~bradley

This Web site boasts units for the 7th-, 8th-, 9th-, and 10th-grade levels. The designed units are grouped by literature, grammar, writing, short stories, and poetry. Young adult literature includes *The Diary of Anne Frank* and *The Pigman*.

MysteryNet.com

www.mysterynet.com

"For everyone who loves a mystery." Both an adult and kid Web site, this page has links to kids' mysteries (solve-it mini-mystery, short scary stories, quick solve minimystery, and magic tricks) in addition to the mystery greats like Alfred Hitchcock, Edgar Allan Poe, Sherlock Holmes, Agatha Christie, and Nancy Drew. There are also links to TV and movies, including *CSI, Law & Order,* and *Monk*.

National Council of Teachers of English

www.ncte.org

An overview of NCTE, membership information, professional development opportunities, publications, programs, and related groups are just a few of the links on this extensive site. Current announcements in addition to an online teaching resource collection (adolescent literacy, literacy coaching, and more) make this site an invaluable reference to all who are working with our nation's readers.

Native American Authors

www.ipl.org/div/natam

Providing information on Native North American authors, this Web site also has links to online resources including interviews and tribal Web sites. Authors are listed with bibliographies of their work.

NCTE Inbox

www.ncte.org/about/over/inbox

Sponsored by the National Council of Teachers of English, this Web site sponsors a free weekly e-mail service that one can sign up to gain access to up-to-date teaching ideas, news, announcements, and viewpoints.

The Online Books Page

http://digital.library.upenn.edu/books/bannned-books.html

This site is just as it sounds—it's about banned books. This is a good resource if one wants to know the history and read some of the earliest banned books.

The Reading Corner

www.carr.org/read

Aimed at grades 2–8, this site contains numerous book reviews for readers and provides more information than a typical library catalog. Divisions include Caldecott, Fiction, Newbery, New Books, Nonfiction, Picture Books, State Awards, Young Adult, and Author Corner.

Reading Is Fundamental

www.rif.org

"Creating a Nation of Lifelong Readers" is still the motto of the nation's largest nonprofit children's literacy organization. Links for parents, educators, and co-ordinators will produce advice, articles, book lists, professional development programs, motivational activities, and more. Also available are monthly reading activities and writing contests. If you're interested in getting involved with RIF, there is a link for that, too.

Reading Online

www.readingonline.org

Published by the International Reading Association, this journal focuses on K–12 practice and research. Links include articles, international perspectives, the electronic classroom, a "from years past" page, new literacies, and online communities.

Reading Rants!

www.tln.lib.mi.us/~amutch/jen/info.htm

This Web site contains numerous "out of the ordinary teen booklists" that are aimed for teens, not teachers or librarians. Lists include the following: fiction about weight, best boy reads, gay fiction for teens, books about being in a band, teen vampire stories, sci-fi/fantasy, spiritual issues, historical fiction that isn't a snore, nail biters, teen tear jerkers, and much, much more.

Scholastic

www.scholastic.com

This extensive site has links for kids (games, contests, and books), families (activities, information, and advice), teachers (lessons, activities, and tools), administrators (news, trends, and solutions), and librarians (products, services, and resources). There are also free discussion guides available to help "kids get more out of reading in the classroom, library, or at home."

School Library Journal Homepage

www.schoollibraryjournal.com

A great resource for teachers and librarians, this site has a book of the week, SLJ's current issue, SLJ reviews, curriculum connections, professional resources, and SLJ archives.

Secondary English

www.secondaryenglish.com

This young adult site contains literature book reviews, articles, books on teaching English, PowerPoint presentations, and more. It is supported by a review board consisting of college instructors from across the country.

Seedwiki

www.seedwiki.com

According to CNN.com, "Wiki comes from the Hawaiian term for 'quick'." And, like a Web log, it's a fast and easy way to publish online. Unlike a Web log (which typically publishes a single voice), a Wiki is a collection work of numerous authors. Students cannot only publish online, but they can get their writing edited by people around the world.

TaskStream

www.taskstream.com

This is a handy Web site for all teacher practitioners as well as preservice students and student teachers/interns. The site can be used as a tool to create lesson plans. Also, it's able to connect the lesson to each state's standards. Definitely a must see!

TeacherVision

www.teachervision.fen.com/tv

A 7-day trial will allow you to explore this site before determining whether you will subscribe. Features include cross-curricular lessons and activities. A lesson-planning center with plans, rubrics, printables, graphic organizers, and more is a focus of this site. In addition, links on classroom management and teacher tools are available.

TeachingBooks.net

www.teachingbooks.net

A free trial will allow you to explore this site, which boasts of features such as authors up close, book guides, book reading, thematic book lists, book awards, and other valuable links.

TeachNet.com

www.teachnet.com

This Web site claims to offer "smart tools for busy teachers." Reading links include a literature list for grades 4–8, a paperback exchange, ideas for alternative book reports, reading in the real world, interviewing book characters, and promoting reading at home.

TeenLit.com

www.teenlit.com

Started in 1999, this site was created and is managed by two full-time English teachers. Teens can volunteer to help with the maintenance of the site. Links include teen writing, writers' workshop, book reviews, Web guides, discussion forums, cool teen links, contests, a bookshop, and a link for teachers.

Teenreads.com

www.teenreads.com

Boasting links to authors, reviews, and a newsletter, this teen reads Web site has numerous books that are read and discussed. Features include turning books into movies and polls taken through the site. Also available are book club and reading guides (some examples included *Stargirl* and *The Sisterhood of the Traveling Pants*).

TeenSpace

www.ipl.org/div/teen

Created for adolescents, this Web site features term paper help, ideas for what to read, help for girls' success, and career options. Other features include arts and entertainment, books and writing, clubs and organizations, college and career, computer and Internet, dating and "stuff," health, homework help, issues and conflicts, money matters, sports, and style. The University of Michigan sponsors it.

Visitingauthors.com

www.visitingauthors.com

Looking for an author to visit your school? This Web site will definitely come in handy as you plan the event. Links on how to plan a successful visit is a great starting place. Presentations, author bios, and author books give detailed information on the presentation style of the author, costs for the visit, and the books he or she has written. Also included are links to a request form, book ordering information (including an order form), and helpful articles.

Voice of Youth Advocates

www.voya.com

A library magazine for "those who serve young adults," this site spotlights articles that include ideas for librarians such as creating a YA book nook. The site also features links for top 10 book lists and a teen pop culture quiz.

Web English Teacher

www.webenglishteacher.com

Loaded with links, this Web site can connect you to the following: Advanced Placement and International Baccalaureate (AP and IB), book reports, children's literature, critical thinking, drama, English as a Second Language (ESL), grammar, interdisciplinary resources, journalism, just for fun, literature, media literacy, mythology/folklore/the hero, poetry, professional resources, reading, Shakespeare, speech/debate, study guides, vocabulary, writing, young adult literature, and more. The site aims at the following: "Beginning teachers can find guidance; experienced teachers can find inspiration."

Welcome to Blue Web'n

www.kn.pacbell.com/wired/bluewebn

Blue Web'n is a resource for teachers to find lessons on the Web. It is full of different sites that can be used to teach a variety of subjects.

What to Read: An Adolescent Literature Website

www.people.virginia.edu/~jkb3y/project/home.html

This site, designed for both teachers and students, provides reviews of literature (which were written by graduate students in the young adult literature class at the University of Virginia). Also present is the opportunity to share your ideas about books. The site divides books into topics (adventure, animals, biography, ethnic, historical, humor, problem novels, and science fiction), author (Chris Crutcher, S. E. Hinton, and Paul Zindel are listed), and genre (*The Chocolate War, The Giver,* and *Ironman*).

William Allen White Children's Book Award

www.emporia.edu/libsv/wawbookaward/index.htm

Sponsored by Emporia State University, this site showcases the winners of the William Allen White Book Award. Kansas students in grades 3–8 can vote on the books. Past winners include *Surviving Hitler: A Boy in the Nazi Death Camps; Dovey Coe; Bud, Not Buddy;* and *Holes.*

The Writing Conference, Inc.

www.writingconference.com

This Web site includes many opportunities for teacher and student activities. Links for students include the opportunity to enter in writing contests, voting opportunities for the Heartland Award for Excellence in Young Adult Literature, information on attending a writing camp and the Literature Festival at the University of Kansas. Also included is *The Writer's Slate,* which publishes original poetry and prose from K–12 students. Teachers may also be interested in attending the Conference for Writing and Literature, which is held at the University of Kansas in February.

Yahoo Young Adult Literature

http://dir.yahoo.com/arts/humanities/literature/genres/young_adult

Sponsored by the Yahoo Web site, this site includes the categories of authors, magazines, recommended reading lists, reviews, series, and Web-published literature. Some of the site listings include About.com: Young Adult Books (reviews, interviews, lists of awards and banned books) and papertigers.org (books from and about the Pacific Rim and South Asia), among others.

Author Pages

Laurie Halse Anderson, www.writerlady.com

Avi, www.avi-writer.com

Judy Blume, www.judyblume.com

Betsy Byars, www.betsybyars.com

Alden Carter, www.aldencarter.com

Sharon Creech, www.sharoncreech.com/index.html

Chris Crutcher, www.aboutcrutcher.com

Christopher Paul Curtis, http://christopherpaulcurtis.smartwriters.com

Roald Dahl, www.roalddahl.com

Carl Deuker, http://members2.authorsguild.net/carldeuker

Sharon Draper, http://sharondraper.com

Lois Duncan, http://loisduncan.arquettes.com

Madeleine L'Engle, www.madeleinelengle.com

Paul Fleischman, www.paulfleischman.net

Jack Gantos, www.jackgantos.com

Jean Craighead George, www.jeancraigheadgeorge.com

Nikki Giovanni, www.nikki-giovanni.com

Nikki Grimes, www.nikkigrimes.com

Virginia Hamilton, www.virginiahamilton.com

Daniel Hayes, www.danielhayes.com

S. E. Hinton, www.sehinton.com

Will Hobbs, www.willhobbsauthor.com

Sara Holbrook, www.saraholbrook.com

Kimberly Willis Holt, www.kimberlyholt.com

Gordon Korman, http://gordonkorman.com

Lois Lowry, www.loislowry.com

Anne McCaffrey, www.annemccaffrey.org

Ben Mikaelsen, www.benmikaelsen.com

Scott O'Dell, www.scottodell.com

Katherine Paterson, www.terabithia.com

Richard Peck, http://richardpeck.smartwriters.com

Rodman Philbrick, www.rodmanphilbrick.com

Tamora Pierce, www.tamora-pierce.com

Ann Rinaldi, www.annrinaldi.com

J. K. Rowling, www.jkrowling.com

Lois Ruby, www.loisruby.com

Cynthia Rylant, www.cynthiarylant.com

Louis Sachar, www.louissachar.com

Cynthia Leitich Smith, www.cynthialeitichsmith.com

Gary Soto, www.garysoto.com

Jerry Spinelli, www.jerryspinelli.com/newbery_001.htm

Joyce Carol Thomas, www.joycecarolthomas.com

Elie Wiesel, www.eliewieselfoundation.org/default.htm

There are also numerous links to the authors through the various publishers' Web sites.

 *Learning Log Responses*

Write a rationale (addressed to your administrator) for any technology named in this chapter that you could use in your classroom.

Plan a multimedia activity using three works of young adult literature.

Plan a young adult literature activity with students in another school using e-mail.

What do you think about current technology in the classroom?

Do you enjoy reading a novel or short story on your palm pilot?

What are the advantages and/or disadvantages of these technologies?

References

Cuban, L. (2001). *Oversold and underused: Computers in the classroom.* Cambridge, MA: Harvard University Press.

Firek, H. (2003). *10 easy ways to use technology in the English classroom.* Portsmouth, NH: Heinemann.

Golub, J. N., & Pope, C. A. (2000). Preparing tomorrow's English language arts teachers today: Principles and practices for infusing technology. *Contemporary Issues in Technology and Teacher Education 1*(1), 89–97.

Hattler, J. A. (1999). *Technology for pre-service teachers: Driver education for the information superhighway 7*(4). Retrieved September 18, 2004, from H. W. Wilson Company database.

Kajder, S. B. (2003). *The tech-savvy English classroom.* Portland, ME: Stenhouse.

Loertscher, D. V., & Woolls, B. (2002). Teenage users of libraries: A brief overview of the research. *Knowledge Quest.* Retrieved September 18, 2004, from H. W. Wilson Company database.

National School Boards Foundation. (2001). *Smart and safe: Research and guidelines for children's use of the Internet.* Retrieved April 29, 2002, from www.nsbf.org/safe-smart/full-report.htm.

Rothermel, D. (2001). Threaded discussions: A first step. *TechLearning.* Retrieved September 19, 2004, from www.techlearning.com.

Tapscott, D. (1998). *Growing up digital: The rise of the net generation.* New York: McGraw-Hill.

UCLA Center for Communication Policy. (2003). UCLA World Internet Project. Retrieved November 3, 2004, from http://ccp.ucla.edu/pdf/UCLA-Internet-Report-Year-Three.pdf.

Veenema, S., & Gardner, H. (1996). Multimedia and multiple intelligences. *The American Prospect Online.* Retrieved November 11, 2004, from www.prospect.org.

CHAPTER

10

The Censorship Issues

*T*he power to control what one reads, hears, and views is the essential component in the philosophical base of the censor. The censor takes many forms, some that are generally acceptable and others that are not: government (these materials are classified because they may threaten national security), courts (hearings are kept closed because they may infringe on the rights of individuals), public agencies, most notably school boards (books, films, and records or tapes have offensive material of some sort and are not appropriate for young people in general), and parents (this book, film, or record or tape has offensive material of some sort and is not appropriate for our children).

The general public has accepted the government's and courts' decisions, although many file suits and base arguments on the Freedom of Information Act, which makes some material open to the public. Those issues do not necessarily directly concern those who read or teach young adult literature, however. Most people would agree that parents have every right to determine the reading, listening, and viewing habits of their own children—even if many parents do not exercise that right. What is of concern to librarians, teachers, students, and some in the general public is the attempt by special-interest individuals and groups to keep specific works of literature, film, and recordings away from groups of students in an educational setting. In this chapter, we discuss these important issues as they relate to the English classroom.

A Historical View

Censorship is not a 20th-century American phenomenon. Ideas have been censored since the beginning of time, or so it seems. Some argue that Plato first used many of the same measures suggested by contemporary censors. He believed that many of the writers of his time were out of step with his thinking, and he made sure that they were banished from society because they were not working for the well-being of the young. This belief system may have laid the groundwork for the censors of the 1990s. Since Plato, numerous incidents over the centuries have added to censorship's long and notorious history.

History records that the works of Confucius were burned in China, Julius Caesar burned the Library of Alexandria, and the Bible was destroyed publicly in England. The Catholic Index of Forbidden Works, the first known literature "hit list," was published in 1555 in England. The Soviet Union was notorious for altering encyclopedias and journals before dissemination throughout the country. For example, *Science*, along with other foreign publications, was routinely censored. Whole articles, usually from the "News and Comment" section, were removed. Many people remember reading about the book burning that took place in Nazi Germany. There are many others—too many to mention here. Suffice it to say that censorship throughout the world has been alive and well for many, many years.

In America, censorship was rooted in the Blue Law controversy. These laws were enacted to close most businesses on Sundays; however, little was done to enforce the closing. Anthony Comstock, upset that most business and law enforcement people ignored the laws, founded the Society for the Suppression of Vice in New York in 1872. He went on to Washington to lobby for the passage of a federal statute against obscenity, abortion, and other evils as he saw them. With this new law in hand, Comstock began his journey, destroying what he considered bad literature and imprisoning the authors of these works. Comstock's most famous book, *Traps for the Young* (1883), listed the traps that young people could fall into: reading light literature, newspaper advertisements, and literature received through the mail. His list of taboos also included gambling, playing pool, using contraceptives, smoking, and drinking alcoholic beverages.

As more literature was written and became available to the general public, the censors had more targets. During the early history of American and British literature, the works censored were, of course, the traditional classics. Attacks on young adult literature did not start until the mid-1990s. In the early days, Swift's *Gulliver's Travels* (1726) was condemned as being "wicked and obscene," and Shakespeare's *The Merchant of Venice* (1596–1597) was removed from New York high schools because it was thought to be anti-Semitic. Voltaire's *Candide* was seized and labeled obscene in 1929; Mark Twain's *The Adventures of Huckleberry Finn* (1885) was banned by the Concord (Massachusetts) Public Library the year it was published because of its interracial friendships; the Texas State Board of Education banned Merriam-Webster's *New Collegiate Dictionary* because it included seven particular words thought to be obscene; Whitman's *Leaves of Grass* was banned in 1855 by the Boston Society for the Suppression of Vice;

and Joyce's *Ulysses*, considered one of the world's most significant pieces of literature, was seized by the Collector of Customs in 1930 before it could get to the publishers. It also was labeled obscene. Steinbeck's *The Grapes of Wrath* (1939) and *Of Mice and Men* (1937) are continually censored in one way or another. In fact, between 1982 and 1991, *Of Mice and Men* held the title as the most challenged book (People for the American Way, 1991, p. 123).

As young adult literature began to mature, it too became the target of censorship. Before the 1960s, young adult literature was considered "safe"—that is, the themes were harmless and were certainly not offensive to any segment of society. Most of the novels centered on the "all-American" family, with young people participating in a very sterile environment. The literature was phony, the language was pure and clean, the plots involved prom dates and similar activities, and the characters were WASPs. This unrealistic literature made no mention of pregnancy, drugs, sexual abuse, divorce, alcohol abuse, violence, prejudice, suicide, profanity, or other teenage problems.

Then two important phenomena changed everything: After World War II, the paperback book became popular, and in the late 1960s, realism invaded the literature. As a result, the censor has been knocking at the schoolroom door ever since. The paperback brought literature to the hands and pockets of almost every student. It was easy to read and to carry around, and the price was right. Paperbacks had not been popular in the classroom up to this point. Teachers did not use them primarily because of their lack of quality and low-grade appearance.

The publication of J. D. Salinger's *The Catcher in the Rye* (1951), Ann Head's *Mr. and Mrs. Bo Jo Jones* (1967), S. E. Hinton's *The Outsiders* (1967), and Paul Zindel's *The Pigman* (1968) changed the relationship between young adults and their reading. With the publication of these works and those that followed, young people were off and running with literature that spoke directly to them. Consequently, the censors were also off and running because they now had something more to denounce: the literature used in the schools.

Following on the heels of these first publications were others that also received harsh reviews: Robert Lipsyte's *The Contender* (1967), John Donovan's *I'll Get There. It Better Be Worth the Trip* (1969), and Paul Zindel's *My Darling, My Hamburger* (1969). The field of young adult literature continued to grow and change as it reflected a more sophisticated and complex society. The literature of the 1970s, 1980s, 1990s, and now into the 2000s became increasingly more mature in its treatment of the issues of the day. Consequently, books that dealt with controversial topics were open to criticism from those who disagreed with the issues or the placement of those issues in classrooms and libraries.

Who Are the Censors?

Censors have various motivations and agendas, and they make their attitudes and criticisms known to the classroom teacher in different ways. Some are individuals who simply do not want a particular piece of literature to be taught in the classroom; others are members of special-interest groups that have taken stands against having particular literature taught in schools. Most of the time, censors are at the extreme—either far to the left or far to the right of the political spectrum. Ellen Brinkley (1999) suggests that "would-be censors take a variety of positions that can be plotted on a continuum anchored by the most radical and most reactionary perspectives: Radical Censorship, Liberal Censorship, Conservative Censorship, Totalitarian Censorship" (p. 32). A few censors take the form of public agencies. Whatever the form, these censors often place an insurmountable burden on the classroom teacher. On some occasions, teachers are the censors themselves. We rarely think of teachers as censors; normally we think of them as those who feel the brunt of the censor. However, occasionally a teacher, perhaps acting as a parent, files a challenge to a work.

Some argue that teachers are censors when they select the materials to be used in the classroom; however, we do not consider them censors in this role. Teachers should make the decisions on what materials will be ordered by school districts and what books students will read. Because the classroom or the library cannot order all published books, some selections must be made. We hope that books will be chosen based on the quality of the literature and how the literature best meets the needs of young people. The major difference between people making decisions on the selection of the materials and those who wish to censor materials is that "selection seeks to promote the right of the reader to read; censorship seeks to protect not the right—but the reader himself from the fancied effects of his reading. The selector has faith in the intelligence of the reader; the censor has faith only in his own" (Asheim, 1953, p. 67).

School administrators, at both the building and district levels, often find themselves acting as censors. Whether as a result of input from another source or simply from their own objections, administrators have a tremendous amount of power in determining what is in the curriculum and what is not. Many administrators are very concerned about public relations and would rather not have to fight a battle about whether a piece of literature should be retained in the curriculum. Therefore, the literature may be banned before it even gets into the classroom.

Administrators may act after the works are in the classroom as well. A well-known incident in Drake, North Dakota (Massie, 1980), involved the burning of several books, including Vonnegut's *Slaughterhouse-Five* (1969). In 1990, a school official in Palm Springs, California, objected to having *Julie of the Wolves* (George, 1972) on the required reading list for seventh-grade English classes. The official thought that some sections of the work might be interpreted as describing an incestuous relationship. The book was removed from the core reading list for being too controversial. In Longview, Washington, *Stotan!* (Crutcher, 1986) was challenged by a school official for alleged profanity, sadism, violence, sexism, racism, and jokes about sex, and the official requested its removal from the eighth-grade optional reading. On appeal, the school board agreed to retain the book (People for the American Way, 1991).

In September 2003, in Baldwin City, Kansas, the superintendent of schools pulled the Cormier novel *We All Fall Down* (Cormier, 1991) from a freshman class in health education. He removed the book after a parent complained about the apparent sexually explicit language in the book. Because there was no policy for handling complaints for classroom curriculum materials, he simply removed the book. A review committee was formed to evaluate the book and made a recommendation to the board of education (Dymacer, 2003, p. 1). The policy for handling reviews of books has been rewritten; the book can be in the classroom but only as a "choice" book; the health curriculum does not contain *We All Fall Down* anymore, but the book is back in the library.

In some states, state education agencies approve lists of books to be used. These agencies may also act as censors. Acquiescing to pressure from national groups, in 1990 the Alabama State Textbook Committee removed 10 books from the state-approved list for fear of "Eastern religious practices" and discussion of homosexuality (People for the American Way, 1991). Although the 10 books were not novels and therefore not of direct concern to English teachers, the state agency's influence in determining curriculum is worth noting. State committees do not always follow the wishes of censors: the Texas State Textbook Committee withstood an effort to have some 100 items of literature removed from the list it recommends to school districts (Simmons, 1991).

Perhaps the largest group of censors is composed of parents. Sometimes parents act in accordance with their own beliefs; other times they are simply pawns for special-interest groups. As we have noted, parents who do not want their child to read a certain selection have every right to ask that a different book be assigned; it is only censorship if parents request that books be kept from all students. A few examples of censorship and attempts to censor are worthy of note.

One parent in Alabama brought action against *A Wrinkle in Time* (L'Engle, 1968) because "the book deals with New Age religion and describes women dressed as witches" (People for the American Way, 1991, p. 17). After evaluation by various school officials, the book remains in use. An interesting article by F. Todd Goodson (1998) addresses the censorship issue in relation to science fiction and fantasy. Goodson suggests that most of the time science fiction—but not fantasy—escapes the censors. He notes "the objections to fantasy raised by fundamentalist book protesters" is that "fantasy texts promote witchcraft, involvement in the occult, and so on" (p. 6).

In Barron, Wisconsin, a community member went to the Barron High School and asked the librarian to compile a list of books that depicted "alternative lifestyles." The librarian came up with 14 titles. Now four of those books have been removed from the shelves and another four are being challenged. The four that were removed were *Baby Be-Bop* by Francesca Lia Block (1995), *When Someone You Know Is Gay* by Susan and Daniel Cohen (1992), *Two Teenagers in Twenty: Writings by Gay and Lesbian Youth* by Ann Heron (1995), and *The Drowning of Stephan Jones* by Bette Greene (1991) (People for the American Way, 1996, p. 6).

A community member in Anaheim, California, complained that Toni Morrison's novel *Beloved* was too graphic for high school students. The Anaheim Union High School District removed the book from a proposed reading list for an advanced placement English class by a 4 to 1 vote of the school board. The book choice was recommended by an English teacher and approved by the district's Instructional Materials Review ("Book Banned," *Kansas City Star*, 1998, p. 9A).

A parent in Paola, Kansas, objected to Cormier's *The Chocolate War* (1974), although in his request to have the book reconsidered, he called the novel *Chocolate Wars*. He objected to "negative religious overtones," "sexual implications utilized by the author," and "inappropriate language" (Dilmore, 1990, p. 1A). A review committee was established to hold a formal hearing. The committee, composed of school and community leaders, voted 6 to 3 to recommend to the board of education that the book be retained. In its meeting of October 30, 1990, the board of education voted 4 to 3 to retain *The Chocolate War* (Dilmore, 1990). After the meeting, a teacher was overheard saying, "Well, it stays for now, but after the next [board of education] election, it could go the other way."

Annie on My Mind (Garden, 1992) was almost censored in the Kansas City area. The book was successfully defended in the Shawnee Mission School District (Kansas), but students and parents had to sue the Olathe (Kansas) board of education to keep Garden's book available in the library. A federal judge ruled that the school system had violated students' First Amendment rights when it ordered that all copies of the book be removed from high school libraries. It is interesting to note that *Annie on My Mind* had been available in the Olathe school libraries for more than 10 years without incident (National Coalition against Censorship, 1996).

An e-mail to an elementary school teacher from a university professor in Kansas offered this complaint about *Son of the Mob* (Korman, 2002):

> I read *Son of the Mob* and I strongly DO NOT recommend it for reading for the sixth graders (or even higher grades). [The elementary teacher was in no way going to have her sixth graders read that book; they were to read a different book.] It has explicit instances of prostitution, sex among high-school aged teenagers (with the girl eager to have it and asking the boy to hurry up and get the blanket ready), and an overall tone of conciliation for typical mob-type activities, like beating people up and leaving them in the trunk of a car, breaking fingers, and murder. Although the son's dilemmas about his father's occupation, and his attempts to stay out of it might in some far stretch of the imagination, might be a topic worth writing about. The book ends with the idea that (mob) business is business, and there is nothing we can do about it and so that's just life.

The professor goes on to say:

> Imagine, years from now, when these children are adults and sitting on a jury trying a mob ringleader. In their subconscious they will remember the permissive nature of this book they read as a child, and it could cause them to acquit someone of breaking the law, just because there was, in a fictional story, a son who wrestled with his conscience about his father's (and relatives') occupation, and ended up justifying it as legitimate.

(We hope the same logic doesn't affect those students who read *Romeo and Juliet.*)

The goal of many special-interest groups is to purge school systems of offensive materials. These materials may be young adult novels; reading anthologies; textbooks used in English, biology, or history classes; films; or records and tapes. The definition of offensive is, of course, determined by the special-interest group. Based on *Attacks on the Freedom to Learn* (People for the American Way, 1991), the names of some of the major special-interest groups that objected to certain school materials follow. Because representatives of these interest groups frequently invite themselves into a censorship problem in a local school, educators need to be aware that local issues often become national issues when these interest groups are present.

- American Family Association Law Center
- Central Council of Parent Teacher Associations
- Citizens for Excellence in Education (CEE)
- Committee to Restore Ethical and Traditional Education (CREATE)
- Concerned Women in America
- The Christian Coalition
- Eagle Forum (Phyllis Schlafly)
- Educational Research Analysts (Mel and Norma Gabler)
- Excellence in Children's Educational Literature (EXCELL)
- Family Research Council
- Focus on the Family
- National Association for the Advancement of Colored People (NAACP)
- Parents Exercising Action for Children and Education (PEACE)

Other groups with similar objectives include People of America Responding to Educational Needs of Today's Society (PARENTS), Citizens United for Responsible Education (CURE), Let's Improve Today's Education (LITE), and American Christians in Education (ACE).

We have often cited the People for the American Way Foundation in our list of examples of censorship. Readers of this text should know that the organization is now online (www.pfaw.org).

The Basis for Censorship

The major difference between the objectives of the private-interest groups and those of public education is the philosophical base from which the groups operate. Individuals involved in public education want change to occur—that is, educators believe that the truth is found through open but guided inquiry. The censors act from a position of absolute certainty. The conflict occurs between the inquiry process of learning and the absolutist doctrine of "I know what is right!" The former believe books are for finding out what is and making judgments about it; the censor is afraid of what is and thinks it will hurt the reader.

These philosophical differences are quite broad and need further clarification through detailed objections raised by the censors. Many of these objections have been cited in challenges to specific books earlier in this chapter. The objections seem to be of four different types: moral, political, religious, or social. Censorship has also been broken into the three S's: sex, Satanism, and swearing. Donelson (1974) places the objections into eight specific categories:

1. Sex

2. Politics

3. War and peace

4. Religion

5. Sociology and race

6. Language

7. Drugs

8. Inappropriate adolescent behavior (p. 48)

In "Dirty Dictionaries, Obscene Nursery Rhymes, and Burned Books," Jenkinson (1979b) increases the categories for objections to 14. In addition to those already mentioned, Jenkinson includes literature of homosexuals; ideas, methods, or books that seem to emulate "secular humanism"; role-playing; absence of grammar rules; materials that contain negative statements about parents; and phase-elective English programs. In later writings, Jenkinson adds to his list to make a grand total of 67 objections (1979a, 1979c, 1980). Brinkley (1999) suggests seven: offensive language, sexuality, violence, racial stereotypes, gender stereotypes, witchcraft and satanism, and New Age and the imagination (pp. 127–131).

Julian Thompson, a well-known author of young adult literature (*A Band of Angels*, 1986; *Simon Pure*, 1987; *Brothers*, 1998; and *Herb Seasoning*, 1990), has clear views on defending books against censorship. He states his reasons for why people censor books: "It seems to me three main reasons for burning, banning, and avoiding are that they're alleged to promulgate (or just contain) one or more of the following: (1) vulgar language, (2) sexual activity, and (3) anti-establishment attitudes" (Thompson, 1991, p. 2). In his defense of young adult literature, he argues that it is "normal and appropriate for kids to have a relationship of some sort with vulgarity . . . to be curious about sex—in terms of its mechanics and its context . . . to question and, at times, resist the edicts of those elements of the 'Establishment' they deal with day by day—the authority of parents, or of teachers, or of any other adult in their lives" (p. 4). He cautions readers not to be horrified by his suggestions without first realizing that by "normal and appropriate" he means behaviors that most adults engaged in when they were growing up. He continues:

> Don't misunderstand me here. I do believe that there are ways for kids to exercise their new-found and emerging sense of self. I'm not in favor of a world made up of bands of foul-mouthed, promiscuous kids running up to tell me, "I know what I can do." The Pharisees and censors paint the issues that we're raising here in blackest blacks and whitest whites, as either-or. My point is: there is a golden mean, a middle ground. What I'm speaking for is moderation, understanding—yes, appreciation of the way that normal people grow into a genuine adulthood. (p. 5)

Now, for the other side of the issue. Can anything be said in support of some of those who wish to question what is taught in the public schools? Small (1979) takes an interesting position when he points out that most educators are quite knowledgeable about the specific censorship cases (the specific dimension), arguments against censorship and defense of the freedom to read (the freedom dimension), and advice on what to do when the attack occurs (the professional dimension). He suggests that we must go beyond those dimensions. To be fair to all those who have some argument against what is taught in the schools, we must also be knowledgeable about the historical and social dimension, the educational dimension, and the human dimension.

To be knowledgeable about the historical and social dimension, educators must be aware of the basic premises that lead to schooling and the community school. Understanding the relationship between society and schools may help explain the sense of ownership some school patrons feel about what is taught in the classroom. The educational dimension that Small describes includes the basic questions of why literature is taught and whether there is some consistency between our thinking that "bad" literature will not harm the reader (that is our reaction to the censors) and that "good" literature will benefit young people. Small points out:

> We have led parents—out former students, after all—to believe that great works contain great truths and that masterpieces are such because of their power to influence. Why should it now be so surprising that parents, discovering curse words, scenes of sexual relations, arguments against the current American social order, questions about the existence of God, believe that we are now pushing those ideas as we formerly pushed the ideas in *Silas Marner* and *Julius Caesar?* (p. 59)

Those who argue against censorship often have few good things to say about the censors. We think of them as out of touch, ignorant, or even evil. We fail to understand the last dimension—the human dimension. Many parents, for whatever reason, are often frustrated about their relationships with the schools. "The schools are not responsive," they say. Regardless of the truth of the statement, parents sometimes feel the schools are ignoring their concerns. As a result, they strike out at something very specific—what is taught in the classroom, especially if they believe that it is incongruous with their values. The ever-changing society and thus the ever-changing school bring about the climate for censorship attacks. Consequently, we must know the community in which the school is set; we must know its culture, its historical roots, and, to some extent, the expectations that the community has for its schools. We would argue that if one or two parents object to a novel being in the library or being used in the classroom and the objections are based on "dirty words" or "sexual situations," for example, then the objection should be treated as an isolated incident by these parents. However, if these parents are supported by the vast majority of the community and the objections are based on differences in cultural heritage and basic philosophy that seem to be in conflict with materials presented in the classroom, then the school has a major concern to be worked out with this community at large.

Communitywide concerns fueled the struggle that occurred in Kanawha County, West Virginia, in 1974. This textbook controversy is by far the most unsettling and far-reaching conflict in the censorship history of America. At the center of the conflict was James Moffett's *Interaction*, a reading and language arts series composed of two film series, dozens of card and board games, 800 activity cards, hundreds of recorded selections, and other materials besides the 182 paperback books that completed the program. In describing the people of Kanawha County, Moffett (1988) says:

> The majority who opposed the books in Kanawha County were mountaineer funda-
> mentalists who have seldom received any attention but ridicule and who have been as
> grossly exploited as any group in our society. No region of the United States has been
> so plundered and taken over by outsiders. Miners die because companies cut corners
> on the expense of safety measures. But the mountaineer's proud code disdains welfare.
> . . . In fact, I have taken most seriously what was for them the heart of their outcry—
> their religious beliefs. (p. xi)

Although the controversy may have been started by the local school patrons because of a conflict between cultural and religious views and the materials selected for students, it quickly mushroomed into the large-scale conflict brought on, primarily, by the influx of outside support groups: the Hard Core Parental Group (Louisiana), the Heritage Foundation (Washington, D.C.), Mel and Norma Gabler (Texas), Citizens for Decency through Law (Los Angeles), and other groups.

Before his death, Jim Moffett had spent much of his time and energy reflecting on the Kanawha County controversy, and he had published *Storm in the Mountains: A Case Study of Censorship, Conflict, and Consciousness* (1988). Moffett explains why this book was so long in coming:

> I wanted very much to speak out about the issues but felt that my remarks might be
> taken as the vinegar of sour grapes. Actually, my reactions were very complex and in-
> cluded many other feelings and thoughts besides just hurt and anger. After ruminat-
> ing them for a good decade, I decided to set forth my views of what happened and
> explain how this case may illuminate phenomena bigger today than then. (p. x)

What Does the Teacher Do?

> *Failure to set down in writing precise regulations for processing*
> *challengers on library or curriculum materials is a prescription*
> *for disaster.*
>
> Beverly Becker, American Library Association, 2003

Before the Challenge

Teachers of English as well as teachers in other departments in schools must have a strong sense about the community in which they teach. Frequently, schools, perhaps at the district level, create task forces composed of school employees and school patrons to investigate, discuss, and explore a variety of social and educational issues. Although it may look as if the school district is pampering the positions of the community in this approach, it isn't; it is simply exploring, in a partnership arrangement, the issues facing both groups.

The schools and the community seem to be the beneficiaries of such a process. Teachers have an opportunity to learn about the community before they select materials for students. Whether these decisions are made in districtwide curriculum committees, school committees, or by individual teachers, information about the materials to be selected and the students who will use these materials will make the selection process more effective.

We are not suggesting that the community or its representatives need to be asked before materials are selected; on the contrary, professional educators ought to make those decisions. But they must those decisions with as much information as possible to prevent future confrontations. However, if the teacher or teachers believe that a particular work of literature is important and should be a part of the curriculum, then that work should indeed be used even if there is a possibility of challenge. If the selection meets the objectives set down by the decision makers and no alternatives are available, the material should be used.

How the selection will be used also affects the decision-making process. For example, will the young adult novel be read by every student, or will there be many novels from which each student will choose one novel to read? Another consideration involves the way the novel is used. Will students read the work as an in-class assignment or as an out-of-class assignment, such as for a book report? The more choices students have, the less potential there is for censorship. In Chapter 6 we discussed thematic units as an effective curriculum design. We reinforce that approach here because that design allows for diversity in the selection and treatment of literature.

We have also covered the importance of methodology in teaching young adult literature, in particular the use of reader-response practices in teaching the literature. We want to emphasize one component of that procedure because it may have some impact on the censorship issue. It is important for teachers, students, and parents to know that novels taught in the English classes will do more than just allow students to relate to a work from a humanistic view. Although students may respond to values and the portrayal of life, there is more to the study of literature. The quality of the work, which includes the author's craft, plays an important part in the consideration of the novel. Study that includes the use of literary strategies and elements as well as other more personal responses to the literature forces students to have a well-rounded understanding of the literature; understanding the stylistic value of a work may help quiet the would-be censor. Teachers, administrators, boards of education, and the general public should understand how the selection process works—who's involved and the basis on which decisions are made.

Teachers must know why they are teaching a particular piece of literature. Although it is not necessary to write rationales for each short story or each poem, it is important to be able to support the use of the anthologies that include these works of literature. We encourage teachers to prepare written rationales for longer pieces, such as novels and plays. These rationales should be on file and available for anyone to read. It takes some time to prepare the rationales; statements that reflect that teachers have given thought to why they are teaching a particular book may stop a challenge. Published collections of rationales may be helpful for teachers. Two collections seem appropriate: "Rationales for Challenged Materials," in *Statement: Journal of the*

Colorado Language Arts Society (1997), and *Rationales for Teaching Young Adult Literature* (Reid & Neufeld, 1999). In addition, the CD-ROM titled *Rationales for Challenged Books* (1998) by the National Council of Teachers of English (NCTE) and the International Reading Association (IRA) would be an invaluable resource.

In *Dealing with Censorship*, Shugert (1979) suggests eight elements that should be included in a rationale:

For what classes is this book especially appropriate?

To what particular objectives, literary or psychological or pedagogical, does this book lend itself?

In what ways will the book be used to meet those objectives?

What problems of style, tone, or theme or possible grounds for censorship exist in the book?

How does the teacher plan to meet those problems?

Assuming that the objectives are met, how would students be different because of their reading of this book?

What are some other appropriate books an individual student might read in place of this book?

What reputable sources have recommended this book? What have critics said of it? (This answer should cite reviews, if any are available.) (p. 188)

Rationales for two young adult novels follow. The rationale for *The Chocolate War* (Cormier, 1974) was written by the language arts teachers of Paola High School (Kansas) after a parent tried to have the text removed from the ninth-grade curriculum. The rationale for *Deliver Us from Evie* (Kerr, 1994) was written by Sara Pike and Amy Morgan, students at the University of Kansas, before any official challenge.

The Chocolate War: A Rationale.

The Chocolate War is taught in the ninth-grade curriculum at Paola High School.

Although it is a dark and sometimes disturbing book, *The Chocolate War* does increase students' awareness of the values, attitudes, and goals inherent in the human experience. It also allows them to examine some of the moral and social problems that face human beings in the modern world. The book provides the students with an image of good in the person of the protagonist, Jerry. He is an admirable character who tries in spite of overwhelming odds to do "the right thing." The book raises the issue of peer pressure and teaches that when you give in to peer pressure and do what you know you shouldn't, you feel worse. It focuses on the problem of the individual's responsibility for his own actions and teaches the student to be true to himself. It is only when Jerry tries to oppose his enemies with their own methods that he is ultimately defeated.

That defeat is realistic because it is a result of both his own actions and the world around him. Life doesn't always end happily, and institutions are not perfect. Jerry does not believe that he has any support system within his family, his church, or his school, and he doesn't reach out and try to gain any. This idea is extremely important for students, many of whom are dealing with problems in their own lives.

The language choices are appropriate to the characters. It is the antagonists who demonstrate their lack of morals, values, and ethical standards by the language they use. Jerry resorts to profanity only once and only under the most extreme pressure. The characters do not use profanity or vulgarity in the presence of authority figures or in the classroom, only when in their peer group. Although this is not desirable behavior for students, it is realistic.

This book is on the recommended reading lists of the American Library Association, the National Council of Teachers of English, Reading Circle, and, according to the State Department of Education, it is commonly taught in Kansas high schools and is available in virtually all of the middle and high school and public libraries in Kansas. It is included in college adolescent literature courses as a recommended text for middle and high school students. Area colleges and universities include the text in their adolescent literature courses. These are Kansas State University, Pittsburgh State University, Missouri Western State College, The University of Missouri at Kansas City, and The University of Kansas. It is included in the catalogs of the major educational publishing companies. *The Chocolate War* has been selected as an American Library Association Best Book for Young Adults, a *School Library Journal* Best Book of the Year, and a *New York Times* Outstanding Book of the Year.

As soon as we received the first objection to *The Chocolate War*, we offered an alternative novel, *The Old Man and the Sea* by Ernest Hemingway, and included assignments that would allow those students an opportunity to earn the same credit as students reading *The Chocolate War*. Perhaps we should have anticipated the controversy generated by *The Chocolate War*, but we feel we have dealt with it in a manner that was fair to everyone concerned. Because this is a newly adopted and somewhat controversial book, those students who have objections to the book have been provided with alternative literature. However, we are absolutely opposed to the removal of this book from the Paola High School curriculum, and we do not feel that the previously established curriculum would warrant other alternative assignments.

The issue has gone beyond the right of a parent to determine what his own child will read and study. We have seen to it that students whose parents object will not have to read *The Chocolate War*. What is at issue here is the removal of that same right from every other parent.

Deliver Us from Evie: A Rationale.   Most remember reading *Romeo and Juliet* in high school, and all are probably familiar with the plot of two star-crossed lovers who pursue true love despite the objections of their parents. Most, if not all, readers rooted for *Romeo and Juliet* as well as for Tony and Maria in *West Side Story* and countless other characters who pursued love for love's sake. The plot of *Deliver Us from Evie* also traces the story of two star-crossed lovers—only this time they are homosexual.

Deliver Us from Evie is the story of a young lesbian woman living on a farm in rural Missouri. Evie and her family must come to terms with her identity, which is not easy for any of them. They are also forced to deal with reactions from people outside the family, which proves to be challenging as lesbian farm girls are an oddity in Duffton, Missouri.

The American Library Association has named *Deliver Us from Evie* A Best Book for Young Adults and A Recommended Book for Reluctant Young Adult

Readers. The *School Library Journal* and the *New York Times Book Review* both praised the book.

The novel addresses themes of prejudice, betrayal, acceptance and tolerance, love and stereotyping. Evie is a good farmer who can fix anything mechanical. As such, she fits the stereotypes most people hold of lesbians, but her girlfriend Patsy is feminine and pretty in the traditional sense of the word. Kerr weaves stereotypes of farmers, religions, and class in with those of homosexuality, forcing the reader to examine the very nature of stereotypes, of how true they are (or aren't), and whom they affect.

The obvious censorship issue in this book is the lesbian relationship between Evie and Patsy. It is this very issue that would make this book a valuable addition to the curriculum, as well as the many important life lessons that are included.

In a mature and realistic way, *Deliver Us from Evie* promotes awareness and understanding of alternative lifestyles. Evie struggles to make her family and those around her realize that she isn't going through a phase and she won't outgrow it. She is what she is, and she is a lesbian. Her mother thinks clothes are the answer, her father thinks she just needs a boyfriend, and all she wants is for them to accept her as she is. The response from other community members is also a realistic example of prejudice. The entire family is treated differently as a result of Evie's lifestyle. Evie and her family are punished because she is different.

But why teach this particular book? Society is growing more and more diverse every day. There are people who have a different color skin, people who look different, people who walk differently, and people who talk differently, and people who don't talk at all. There are students in the classroom who are different. *Deliver Us from Evie* is a reminder that we shouldn't force those people to hide who they are. They shouldn't be treated differently because of who they are, and they shouldn't suffer because of who they are. Young adults need to know how to deal with people who are different. They cannot accept what they don't understand; they cannot understand what they are not allowed to see. It is precisely because homosexuality is a contemporary issue about which much of America is divided that gives us a reason why the novel should be taught. Students deserve the chance to confront their own ambiguities about this issue.

Deliver Us from Evie is a book about identity. It's about knowing who you are and what you want, and figuring out how to get there. That is something all of us must do. For people like Evie, it is harder than it is for most. It shouldn't be.

One additional decision should be made in advance of any challenge brought on by the censor. What policy will be in effect when the challenge comes? Will it be given to a committee for consideration? What is the makeup of that committee? Will there be a district review committee as well? Who will serve on that committee? All of these questions should be answered before any part of the process has to be initiated.

After the Challenge

The thought of having to face the censors and what they stand for is scary at best. As professional educators, teachers sense that what they do and the decisions they make, either

Hardcover ___

Author _____ Paperback ___

Title _____

Publisher (if known) _____

Request initiated by _____

Telephone _____ Address _____

City _____ Zip Code _____

Complaint represents

____ himself or herself

____ organization (please identify)_____

____ other group (please identify) _____

1. To what in the work do you object? Please be specific; cite pages _____

_____

2. What of value is there in this work? _____

_____

3. What do you feel might be the result of reading this work? _____

_____

FIGURE 10.1
Citizen's request for reconsideration of work.

individually or in concert with others, will be accepted by the community. Although this professionalism prevails throughout most communities, pockets of educational unrest surface from time to time, and teachers are faced with "Why are you teaching that filth to your students?" When that question arises, teachers are at the beginning of what can be a very long journey. At times within that journey, teachers will wonder why they ever thought they wanted to get involved with "kids." If the procedures have been thought through and are in place, the journey should be a little easier.

It would seem that the first step to take when a challenge has been made is for the challenger to meet with the teacher who is using the challenged material. This meeting is not an attempt to put off the formal, official objection but to bring the two people together so that some discussion can take place about the concerns of the would-be censor. Often after some clarification about why the novel was cho-

4. For what age group would you recommend this work? _____

_____

5. Did you read the entire work? _____ What pages or sections? _____

_____

6. Are you aware of the judgment of this work by critics?_____

_____

7. Are you aware of the teacher's purpose in using this work? _____

_____

8. What do you believe is the theme or purpose of this work? _____

_____

9. What would you prefer the school do about this work?

_____ Do not assign or recommend it to my child.

_____ Withdraw it from all students.

_____ Send it back to the English department for reevaluation.

10. In its place, what work of equal value would you recommend that would convey as valuable a picture and perspective of a society or a set of values?_____

_____

_____

Signature of Complainant

FIGURE 10.1
Continued.

sen, what objectives are being met by using such literature, or how the novel is being used in the classroom, the person making the challenge may understand and accept the decisions. There may be, too, a chance for the suggestion of alternative literature to be assigned instead of the challenged work. If the person or persons are not willing to make any change in their challenge, then the formal policy is implemented, and the censor is given a form to have the work or works formally reconsidered. That form may have been prepared by the local teachers or may be the one recommended by the National Council of Teachers of English (NCTE) or other similar groups. The Citizen's Request for Reconsideration of a Work prepared by NCTE is reprinted in Figure 10.1. This document is available along with other useful information in a booklet titled *The Students' Right to Read*. A single copy of this document is available from NCTE at no cost.

A Teacher's Library on Censorship

The following list of recommended sources does not and cannot include all of the books, articles, and helpful organizations concerning censorship; however, it is intended to help the classroom teacher get started in learning about censorship. Teachers will want to add to the list as they continue their reading in literary and professional journals. A well-informed teacher may well affect in a positive way the results of a literature challenge.

Resource Books

American Library Association. (1983). *Censorship litigation and the schools.* Chicago: Author.

American Library Association. (1983). *Intellectual freedom manual* (2nd ed.). Chicago: Author.

American Library Association. (1989). *Hit list: Frequently challenged young adult titles; References to defend them.* Chicago: Author.

Bosmajian, H. A. (Ed.). (1983). *Censorship: Libraries and the law.* New York: Neal-Schuman.

Bosmajian, H. A. (1987). *The first amendment in the classroom* (Vols. 1–5). New York: Neal-Schuman.

Boyer, P. (2002). *Purity in print: Book censorship in America from the Gilded Age to the Computer Age* (2nd ed.). Madison: University of Wisconsin Press.

Brinkley, E. H. (1999). *Caught off guard: Teachers re-thinking censorship and controversy.* New York: Allyn & Bacon.

Brown, J. E. (Ed.). (1994). *Preserving intellectual freedom: Fighting censorship in our schools.* Urbana, IL: National Council of Teachers of English.

Burress, L., & Jenkinson, E. B. (1982). *The students' right to know.* Urbana, IL: National Council of Teachers of English.

Committee on Bias and Censorship in the Elementary School. (1978). *Censorship: Don't let it become an issue in your schools.* Urbana, IL: National Council of Teachers of English.

Cox, B. C. (1977). *Censorship game and how to play it* (Bulletin No. 50). Washington, DC: National Council for the Social Studies.

Davis, J. E. (Ed.). (1979). *Dealing with censorship.* Urbana IL: National Council of Teachers of English.

DelFattore, J. (1992). *What Johnny shouldn't read: Textbook censorship in America.* New Haven, CT: Yale University Press.

Doyle, R. P. (1996). *Banned books, 1996 resource guide.* Chicago: American Library Association.

Foerstel, H. (2002). *Banned in the USA: A reference guide to book censorship in schools and public libraries.* Westport, CT: Greenwood Press.

Haight, A. L. (1978). *Banned books* (4th ed.). New York: R. R. Bowker.

Jenkinson, E. B. (1979). *Censors in the classroom: The mind benders.* Carbondale: Southern Illinois University Press.

Karolides, N. J. (2002). *Censored books II: Critical viewpoints, 1985–2000.* Lanham, MD: Scarecrow Press.

Karolides, N. J., Bald, M., and Sova, D. B. (1999). *100 banned books: Literature suppressed on political, religious, sexual, and social grounds.* New York: Facts on File.

Lehr, S. (Ed.). (1995). *Battling dragons: Issues and controversy in children's literature.* Portsmouth, NH: Heinemann.

Lewis, F. F. (1976). *Literature, obscenity, and law.* Carbondale: Southern Illinois University Press.

Lobbying for freedom: A citizen's guide to fighting censorship at the state level. (1975). New York: St. Martin's.

Moffett, J. (1988). *Storm in the mountains: A case study of censorship, conflict, and consciousness.* Carbondale: Southern Illinois University Press.

Monks, M. M., & Pistolis, D. R. (1996). *Hit list: Frequently challenged books for young adults.* Chicago: American Library Association.

National Council of Teachers of English. (1982). *The students' right to read*. Urbana, IL: Author.

National Council of Teachers of English and International Reading Association (1998). *Rationales for challenged books* [CD-ROM]: Urbana, IL: Authors.

People for the American Way. (1991). *Attacks on the freedom to learn, 1990–1991 report*. New York: Author. (All yearly reports are interesting.)

Power, B. M., Wilhelm, J. D., & Chandler, K. (1997). *Reading Stephen King: Issues of censorship, student choice, and popular literature*. Urbana, IL: National Council of Teachers of English.

Simmons, J. S. (Ed.). (1994). *Censorship: A threat to reading, learning, thinking*. Newark, DE: International Reading Association.

Simmons, J. S., & Desang, E. (2001). *School censorship in the twenty-first century: A guide for teachers and school library media specialists*. Newark, DE: IRA.

Stanek, L, W. (1976). *Censorship: A guide for teachers, librarians, and others*. New York: Dell.

West, M. I. (1997). *Trust your children: Voices against censorship in children's literature*. New York: Neal-Schuman.

Articles

Arons, S. (1979). Book burning in the heartland. *Saturday Review, 21*, 24–29.

Broz, W. (2001, July). Hope and irony: Annie on my mind. *English Journal, 90*, 47–53.

Burger, R. H. (1982). The Kanawha County textbook controversies: A study of communication and power. *Library Quarterly, 48*, 584–589.

Byorklun, E. C. (1988). Secular humanism: Implications of court decisions. *Educational Forum, 52*, 211–221.

Cormier, R. (1988). The authors speak. In M. I. West (Ed.), *Trust your children: Voices against censorship in children's literature* (pp. 29–39). New York: Neal-Schuman.

Donelson, K. L. (1981). Shoddy and pernicious books and youthful piety: Literary and moral censorship, then and now. *Library Quarterly, 51*, 4–19.

Edwards, J. (1986). The new right, humanism, and "dirty books." *Virginia English Bulletin, 36*, 94–99.

Greenbaum, V. (1997). Censorship and the myth of appropriateness: Reflections on teaching reading in high school. *English Journal, 86*(2), 16–20.

Hentoff, N. (1983). When nice people burn books. *Progressive, 47*, 42–44.

Janeczko, P. (1975). How students can help educate the censors. *Arizona English Bulletin, 17*, 78–80.

Larsen, T. J. (1980). The power of the board of education to censor. *Educational Leadership, 38*, 139–142.

Leo, J. (2002, June 17). Heck hath no fury. *U.S. News and World Report*, p. 53.

MacRae, C. D. (1998). The myth of the "bleak" young adult novel. *Voice of Youth Advocates, 21*(5), 325–327.

Mazer, N. F. (1997). Shhhh! *ALAN Review, 24*(2), 46–48.

Peck, R. (1986). The genteel unshelving of a book. *School Library Journal, 32*, 37–39.

Rationales for commonly challenged taught books. (1983). *Connecticut English Journal*, 15. (Entire collection of rationales will be helpful.)

Salvner, G. M. (1998). A war of words: Lessons from a censorship case. *ALAN Review, 25*(2), 45–49.

Simmons, J. (1991). Censorship in the schools— No end in sight. *ALAN Review, 18*(2), 6–8.

Small, R. C., Jr. (1976). Censorship and English: Some things we don't seem to think about very often (but should). In J. Davis (Ed.), *Dealing with censorship* (pp. 54–62). Urbana, IL: National Council of Teachers of English.

Small, R. C., Jr. (2002, Winter). Censorship as we enter 2000 or the millennium, or just next year. *Journal of Youth Services Libraries, 13*, 19–23.

Staples, S. F. (1996). What Johnny can't read: Censorship in American libraries. *ALAN Review, 23*(2), 49–50.

Suhor, C. (1997). Censorship—When things get hazy. *English Journal, 86*(2), 26–28.

Weiss, M. J. (2002, Spring/Summer). Rumbles! Bangs! Crashes! The road of censorship. *ALAN Review, 29*, 54–57.

Organizations

Only information regarding censorship is included here. See Appendix A for additional information about these and other organizations related to reading and teaching young adult literature.

American Civil Liberties Union, 132 W. 43rd Street, New York, NY 10036

American Library Association, 50 East Huron Street, Chicago, IL 60611 (Hit List)

National Coalition against Censorship, 2 West 64th Street, New York, NY 10023 (Censorship News)

National Council for the Social Studies, 3615 Wisconsin Avenue, NW, Washington, DC 20016 National Council of Teachers of English, 1111 Kenyon Road, Urbana, IL 61801 (Censorship and Professional Guidelines, Censorship: Don't Let It Become an Issue in Your Schools, The Students' Right to Know, The Students' Right to Read, SLATE: Support for the Learning and Teaching of English, Common Ground)

National Education Association Human and Civil Rights, 1201 16th Street, NW, Washington, DC 20036

Office of Intellectual Freedom, 50 East Huron Street, Chicago, IL 60611 (Newsletter on Intellectual Freedom, Freedom to Read Foundation News, Banned Books Resource Guide)

People for the American Way, 2000 M Street, NW, Suite 400, Washington, DC 20036 (Attacks on the Freedom to Learn [Yearly reports on censorship], and frequent reports on the Internet: [pfaw-aflo@lists.pfaw.org])

Literature with Censorship Themes

Avi. (1991). *Nothing but the Truth*. New York: Orchard.

Blume, J. (Ed.). (1999). *Places I Never Meant to Be*. New York: Simon & Schuster.

Clements, A. (1999). *The Landry News*. New York: Simon & Schuster.

Garden, N. (1999). *The Year They Burned the Books*. New York: Farrar, Straus & Giroux.

Hentoff, N. (1982). *The Day They Came to Arrest the Book*. New York: Dell.

Lasky, K. (1994). *Memoirs of a Bookbat*. San Diego: Harcourt Brace.

Malmgren, D. (1989). *The Ninth Issue*. New York: Bantam Doubleday Dell.

Miles, B. (1980). *Maudie and Me and the Dirty Book*. New York: Knopf.

Neufeld, J. (1982). *A Small Civil War*. New York: Ballantine.

Peck, R. (1995). *The Last Safe Place on Earth*. New York: Delacorte.

Philbrick, R. (2000). *The Last Book in the Universe*. New York: Blue Sky Press.

Thompson, J. F. (1995). *The Trials of Molly Sheldon*. New York: Holt.

Tolen, S. (1993). *Save Halloween*. New York: William Morrow.

 *Learning Log Responses*

Choose a young adult novel not discussed in this chapter and write a defense for its use in a middle or high school classroom.

What is your understanding of why censors try to remove books from classrooms and libraries?

What will you do in your classroom to make it less likely that censors will make a challenge?

Become familiar with at least one of the publications on censorship listed in this chapter. Write a brief summary of what that publication offers the classroom teacher.

References

Asheim, L. (1953). Not censorship but selection. *Wilson Library Bulletin, 28,* 67.

Becker, B. (2003, October 5). Quoted in Carpenter, T. Baldwin lacks policy for challenged books, *Lawrence Journal World,* p. 1b.

Book banned. (1998, May 17). *Kansas City Star,* p. 9-A.

Brinkley, E. (1999). *Caught off guard: Teachers rethinking censorship and controversy.* New York: Allyn & Bacon.

Comstock, A. (1883). *Traps for the young.* (n.p.).

Dilmore, K. (1990, October 31). *The Chocolate War* Trials. *Miami County Republican,* pp. 1A, 10A.

Donelson, K. (1974). Censorship in the 1970s: Some ways to handle it when it comes (and it will). *English Journal, 63*(2), 47–51.

Dymacer, K. (2003). Book's appropriateness in class questioned. *Baldwin City Signal,* 5(30), 1.

Goodson, F. T. (1998). Science fiction, fantasy, fundamentalist censors, and imaginative thinking: Motives of the censors, possible solutions for teachers. *SIGNAL Journal, 22*(1), 4–9.

Jenkinson, E. (1979a). *Censors in the classroom: The mind benders.* Carbondale: Southern Illinois University Press.

Jenkinson, E. (1979b). Dirty dictionaries, obscene nursery rhymes, and burned books. In J. Davis (Ed.), *Dealing with censorship* (pp. 2–13). Urbana, IL: National Council of Teachers of English.

Jenkinson, E. (1979c). Protest groups exert strong impact. *Publishers Weekly, 216,* 42–44.

Jenkinson, E. (1980). Sixty-seven targets of the textbook protesters. *Missouri English Bulletin, 38,* 27–32.

Massie, D. (1980). Censorship in the schools: Something old and something new. *Today's Education, 59*(4), 30–34.

Moffett, J. (1988). *Storm in the mountains: A case study of censorship, conflict, and consciousness.* Carbondale: Southern Illinois University Press.

National Coalition against Censorship. (1996, May). *Books in Trouble,* pp. 1–4.

National Council of Teachers of English. (1982). *The students' right to read.* Urbana, IL: Author.

National Council of Teachers of English and International Reading Association. (1998). *Rationales for challenged books* [CD-ROM]. Urbana, IL: Authors.

People for the American Way. (1991). *Attacks on the freedom to learn, 1990–1991 report.* Washington, DC: Author.

People for the American Way. (1996, February). *Attacks on the freedom to learn,* online (AFLO), Issue 3.1, www.pfaw.org.

Rationales for challenged materials. (1997). *Statement: Journal of the Colorado Language Arts Society, 33*(3), 3–63. Author.

Reid, L., & Neufeld, J. (1999). *Rationales for teaching young adult literature.* Portland, ME: Calendar Islands.

Shugert, D. (1979). How to write a rationale in defense of a book. In J. Davis (Ed.), *Dealing with censorship* (pp. 187–191). Urbana, IL: National Council of Teachers of English.

Simmons, J. (1991). Censorship in the schools— No end in sight. *ALAN Review, 18*(2), 6–8.

Small, R. C., Jr. (1979). Censorship and English: Some things we don't seem to think about very often (but should). In J. Davis (Ed.), *Dealing with censorship* (pp. 54–62). Urbana, IL: National Council of Teachers of English.

Thompson, J. (1991). Defending YA literature against the Pharisees and censors: Is it worth the trouble? *ALAN Review, 18*(2), 2–5.

CHAPTER

11

Young Adult Literature: A Brief History

Many think literature for young people developed in the 1950s and 1960s with the publication of Salinger's *The Catcher in the Rye* (1951) or Hinton's *The Outsiders* (1967); however, literature directed to and for young people began much earlier.

Although it seems impossible, we can trace the emphasis on modeling good behavior for children and young adults through literature back to the 15th and 16th centuries. This literature was written for adults, not young people. It was profoundly different from the literature young adults have today, but it did exist, and adults wanted young people to read it. This chapter traces the changes from the didactic literature of the early periods to the current body of literature for young adults.

Rules to Live By

The literature that adults wanted children and young adults to read reflected the mores of the time and was used to guide young people in their behavior. Literature closely tied to religion and mythology was set before young people as models. Wintle and Fisher (1974) discuss the characteristics of education in the Middle Ages:

> Education in the Middle Ages was grounded in Latin. Ideally, children were taught to read and write in a foreign language. . . . At a precociously early age, they could tackle the works of the masters. An understanding of literature in the vernacular was not re-

garded as the proper object of learning, even though popular romances had as much appeal to the young as to the old. (p. 11)

The books of the Middle Ages took stands that children were to emulate. *A Book of Courtesy* (1477) is said to be the first book published specifically for young readers in England. At approximately the same time, *Aesop's Fables* (1475–1480) appeared primarily as a book for adults, but its audience shifted to children and young adults. Malory's *Le Morte d'Arthur* (1485) enjoyed a considerable circulation among older children.

During this period adults felt strongly that young people should read the classics and not the more popular romances that were available (which sounds much like the current trend). The philosophy appears ever so strongly in Hugh Rhodes's *Book of Nurture* (c. 1545), which "fulminated against reading for pleasure and this reflected common opinion among the literate" (Wintle & Fisher, 1974, p. 12). The prevailing attitude was that children (especially the well born) were to read to learn how to act like adults and take on adult responsibilities if the need arose. Wintle and Fisher characterize this attitude toward children well: "Throughout the Tudor century childhood was merely an inconvenient period when one was not an adult" (p. 12).

The 17th century, while holding on to the traditions of the past, brought some changes, however slight. A somewhat different attitude toward children was found in the picture book *The Visible World in Pictures* by John Amos Comenius (1659). This was the first book to convey information to children through pictures of real children. It should be said, however, that the primary emphasis in the 17th century was on religious publication and faith in the Christian word. The King James Bible (1611) was standard reading for young and old; John Milton's *Paradise Lost* (1667), the 12-book epic based on the creation, the fall of Satan, and Adam and Eve, was written to put humans right with God; and John Bunyan's *The Pilgrim's Progress from This World to That Which Is to Come* (1678) taught God's way through religious allegory, with people and places representing vices and virtues.

As the 18th century dawned, children were still seen as deficient adults who needed all the help they could get. Books of the time reflected this didactic attitude: Benjamin Keach's *War with the Devil, or The Young Man's Conflict with the Powers of Darkness, in a Dialogue Discovering the Corruption and Vanity of Youth, the Horrible Nature of Sin, and the Deplorable Condition of Fallen Man* (1707) and James Janeway's *A Token for Children: Being an Exact Account of the Conversion, Holy and Exemplary Lives and Joyful Deaths of Several Young Children to Which Is Added: A Token for the Children of New England* (1700). Smith (1967) quotes Janeway's purpose for writing the book:

You may now hear (my dear Lambs) what other good Children have done, and remember how they wept and prayed by themselves; how earnestly they cried out for an interest in the Lord Jesus Christ. . . . Would you be in the same condition as naughty Children? O Hell is a terrible place, that is a thousand times worse than Whipping. God's Anger is worse than your Father's Anger. (p. 42)

In addition to this religious and didactic literature of the 17th and 18th centuries, two very important works that had a tremendous impact on children's literature were published. In 1719, Daniel Defoe published *The Life and Strange Surprising Adventures of Robinson Crusoe*, and shortly thereafter Jonathan Swift published *Gulliver's Travels* (1726). These two works were quickly adapted for younger readers and became early children's classics.

In the mid-1700s, John Newbery began publishing children's books as a business. Newbery wrote and published attractive small books for children. His attitude, contrary to the prevalent philosophy, was that children could read just for fun. However, Newbery's attitude was not the prevailing one. Most of the literature was still moralistic and didactic. Hannah More was the prolific writer of *Repository Tracts* (1795–1798), in which she preached moralistic lessons. These became standard reading for young people, as did the writing of Mary Sherwood (1778–1851). Sherwood's morally didactic fiction was widely read throughout the end of the 18th century and into the 19th century.

The 19th century was "the first age of great children's books" (Wintle & Fisher, 1974, p. 14). Literature for young women emphasized home and family values, conforming to societal expectations. Literature for boys largely emphasized that hard work would be rewarded by success, and traditional values were upheld even by their literary heroes. Wintle and Fisher comment on the literature of this period:

> It was the first age of great children's books: . . . *The Adventures of Tom Sawyer* (1876) and *The Adventures of Huckleberry Finn* (1885) by Mark Twain; *Black Beauty* (1877) by Anna Sewell; *The Wind in the Willows* (1908) by Kenneth Grahame, and so on and so on. There is no single explanation for such an assemblage. The accidents of genius, the dynamics of the market, cheaper printing methods, the swelling of the middle class, the increased sophistication of editors, the post-romantic sentimentalizing of the child, an abundance of literacy, the loosening of church morality, the awareness of class, the growth of advertising, and so on and so on again. (p. 14)

Also in the 1800s, Mason Locke Weems (also known as The Parson) wrote his adventurous, and reportedly inaccurate, books about Washington's exploits (*A History of the Life and Death, Virtues and Exploits, of General George Washington,* 1800; *The Life of George Washington,* 1808; and *The Life of Washington the Great,* 1806), which were widely read by young people in search of adventure. In 1825, the first of 170 Peter Parley books on moralistic standards was published.

In the mid-1800s, a new genre appeared: the domestic novel. This new literature had a tremendous impact on the American book-reading public. Leading the list of domestic novels was *The Wide, Wide World* by Susan Warner (1850). Domestic novels, including Warner's, successfully taught and preached traditional values and moral lessons—no tobacco, alcohol, adultery, or divorce was allowed in domestic novels. Warner wrote approximately 20 novels of this kind. *The Wide, Wide World* was one of the four most widely read books during the 1890s; the other three were the Bible, *The Pilgrim's Progress* (Bunyan, 1678), and *Uncle Tom's Cabin* (Stowe, 1852). Donelson and Nilson (1989) describe the domestic novel:

> Born out of a belief that humanity was redeemable, the domestic novel preached morality; woman's submission to man; the value of cultural, social, and political con-

servatism; a religion of the heart and the Bible; and the glories of suffering. . . . Heroines differed more in name than in characteristics. Uniformly submissive to—yet distrustful of—their betters and men, they were self-sacrificing and self-denying beyond belief, interested in the primacy of the family unit and a happy marriage as the goal of all decent women. They abhorred sin generally, but particularly tobacco, alcohol, divorce, and adultery. (p. 468)

One other domestic novel that must be mentioned is *St. Elmo*, by Augusta Jane Wilson (1867). It is said to be the most popular domestic novel written—only *Uncle Tom's Cabin* exceeded it in sales. Its popularity came from its strong domestic novel. components, especially the dominance of a good woman who triumphs over an evil man. Donelson and Nilson (1989) comment on the popularity of Wilson's novel: "No other novel so literally touched the American landscape—thirteen towns were named or renamed St. Elmo, as were hotels, railway coaches, steamboats, one kind of punch, and a brand of cigars" (p. 469).

At about the same time as the domestic novels, the dime novel made its entrance with the publication of Ann Stephens's *Malaeska: The Indian Wife of the White Hunter* (1860), a 128-page book that sold some 65,000 copies. These short 10-cent novels were first written for adults, but when publishers realized that young boys were reading them, they changed the audience and the price (they sold for 5 cents and the books were shorter, but people still called them dime novels). Some of the most popular characters included Revolutionary War scout Seth Jones, detectives "Old Sleuth" and Nick Carter, and western hero Deadwood Dick. The novels were quick, formulaic reading. They included standard characters, contrived plots, and values that reinforced family life.

The series books began with the publication of *The Boat Club* by Oliver Optic (1855). *The Boat Club* was the first of six volumes and 60 editions. Optic was a prolific writer—more than 123 novels are credited to him. Because this book was the first, it set the pattern that was to follow for later series. Harry Castlemon wrote *Frank, the Young Naturalist* (1864), the first of five adventurous Frank books. Martha Farquharson Finley wrote primarily for women. Her Elsie Dinsmore series (which included *Elsie Dinsmore*, 1867; *Christmas with Grandma Elsie*, 1888; and *Elsie in the South*, 1899) is said to have been the most popular series of its time for young women. The virtuous and Christian Elsie can be followed from childhood to grandmotherhood in 28 popular and profitable volumes.

These various novels—domestic, dime, and series—gave rise to a great deal of literature that was read by young people. It also gave rise to competition among publishing houses. As a result of the popularity of Optic's books, a competing publisher urged Louisa May Alcott to write a book especially for young girls. The novel *Little Women* was born. The story appeared in two volumes, *Little Women: Meg, Jo, Beth, and Amy. The Story of Their Lives: A Girl's Book* (1868) and *Little Women: Meg, Jo, Beth, and Amy, Part Second* (1869). Alcott and Horatio Alger, Jr., were the first writers for young people to gain national attention. Alger published the first of his estimated 119 novels in 1867. Alger's most successful books (they sold some 16 million copies) were the Ragged Dick books, such as *Ragged Dick and Mark, the Watch Boy* (1868), and the Richard Hunter books. Ragged Dick is a young and poor hero who is honest above everything else—he drinks, smokes, and gambles but refrains from lying or stealing, even in the worst of times and situations.

Literature went through a number of changes from the Middle Ages to the mid-1800s. There was one constant, however. Practically all of the literature still held values and morals high and came down on the side of what was considered "right." One difference between *A Book of Courtesy* in 1477 and Alcott's *Little Women* in 1868 was the intended audience. The major shift during this time was that the earlier literature was written for adults but read by children to model behavior. In *Little Women*, Alcott wrote specifically for young female readers.

A shift in the treatment of characters occurred in 1870 with the publication of Thomas Bailey Aldrich's *The Story of a Bad Boy*. With Aldrich's work—partly autobiographical—there soon appeared literature about "bad boys," literature that told about boys as they were, not as parents wished them to be. Other authors followed his lead, and bad-boy stories flourished. The realism about boys in literature mirrored the realism of Alcott's *Little Women*. Other bad-boy literature included Mark Twain's *Adventures of Tom Sawyer* (1876), soon to become the most loved mischievous bad boy of the 19th century. Peck's *Bad Boy and His Pa*, by George Wilbur Peck, followed in 1883. Two years later, Twain's *Adventures of Huckleberry Finn* became an immediate hit with young readers, despite being immediately banned by libraries in Concord, Massachusetts, and Brooklyn, New York, because it was seen as trashy, vicious, and unfit. Both *Tom Sawyer* and *Huck Finn* would be frequently banned ever after, yet remain reading favorites.

Other literature read by young people continued to flourish. *Twenty Thousand Leagues under the Sea* was written by Jules Verne in 1872 and provided young readers with one of the first examples of science fiction. A second novel by Verne, *Around the World in Eighty Days,* appeared in 1873. In 1877, Anna Sewell wrote the extremely popular *Black Beauty* as a protest against cruelty to horses.

Two adventure stories published in 1883 had an immediate impact on the reading of young people and continue to be popular reading today. Robert Louis Stevenson's *Treasure Island* and Howard Pyle's *The Merry Adventures of Robin Hood* are two of literature's all-time great adventure tales. In 1892, Arthur Conan Doyle contributed to the mystery and suspense genre with his *Adventures of Sherlock Holmes.*

Formula fiction dominated literature for young adults in the late 19th century and into the 20th century. Variations of stock plots and themes made the stories predictable, but young readers loved them. Edward Stratemeyer is credited with developing formula fiction to its fullest. Writing under numerous pen names, Stratemeyer first created the Old Glory series, which centered on two young boys and war themes. This series was followed by numerous other series of books—many of which are still read today. Among Stratemeyer's successes are contemporary battle books, *Soldiers of Fortune* (1900–1906); school-like and sports books, the Lakeport series (1904–1912); the adventurous Rover Boys books (1899–1926), of which 30 adventures were published; and mystery books centered on the Hardy Boys (1927–) and Nancy Drew (1927–). Remarkable young inventor Tom Swift also proved to be exciting and popular reading for young adults.

Although Stratemeyer is credited with producing more than 1,000 titles, it is well known that many of the novels were written by a writing syndicate headed by Stratemeyer. He provided other writers with chapter-by-chapter plot lines, and they completed the stories. Stratemeyer ensured the accuracy of events by comparing new books with others in the series, making changes as he wished, and then sending them off to be published.

The Stratemeyer books were widely popular. In a major survey of reading interests conducted by the American Library Association (1926), 98% of the young people surveyed listed a Stratemeyer title as a favorite. These stories displayed the elements that young readers most admired: mystery, excitement, and suspense, and a protagonist who would always triumph against terrible odds. Although far from good literature—with their stereotyped characters, poorly constructed plots, and lack of relationship to reality—these did keep young people reading and paved the way for the better young adult literature to follow. An interesting phenomenon surfaced again with the Stratemeyer books: Popularity and quality did not necessarily go hand in hand. This is true even today, and not only in young adult literature.

An early young adult novel that broke away from the unrealistic characteristics of the earlier literature was *Seventeen* by Booth Tarkington. Written in 1902, this novel is one of the first "reality" novels about the joys and problems of young people, with no sugarcoating. The literature of this period was a mixed bag. Tarkington's novel offered some sense of reality, but other literature seemed to stay with the tried and true. Laura Lee Hope's The Bobbsey Twins series, begun in 1904, was a great success. It offered pure entertainment for young readers. Also in 1904, Kate Douglas Wiggin's *Rebecca of Sunnybrook Farm* became one of the first of many popular novels in which young children significantly brighten the lives of people around them. Between 1906 and the 1920s, Zane Grey romanticized the Old West in more than 60 novels. Among the most successful were *The Spirit of the Border* (1906), *The Wanderers of the Wasteland* (1923), and *Riders of the Purple Sage* (1912).

In 1934, publishers first began to publish literature especially for young adults. The publishing company of Longmans, Green marketed Rose Wilder Lane's novel *Let the Hurricane Roar* (published earlier as an adult novel) as the first of its novels in a new marketing division termed "Junior Books." Other publishers would soon follow Longmans's lead and establish their own junior book divisions. The official junior or young adult novel was off and running. Although many of the young adult books were popular romances or series books, a few, such as Lane's novel, broke out of that tradition.

Let the Hurricane Roar was historical; it told about the pioneering days of Dakota and the struggle of a young couple fighting for survival in the hostile environment of the northern plains. *Shuttered Windows,* written by Florence Crannel Means in 1938, is considered the first novel for adolescents to portray Blacks realistically. The novel tells of the trials of a 16-year-old girl who leaves Minnesota and lives with her grandmother in South Carolina. The quality of writing leaves much to be desired, but the work does portray Blacks as worthwhile and dignified people. One other book of historical fiction published about this time was Esther Forbes's *Johnny Tremain* (1944), the story of a 14-year-old silversmith's apprentice and his life during the American Revolution.

Sports stories dominated the reading of young men. John Tunis was said to be the most widely read sports author, with such titles as *The Iron Duke* (1938), a novel about the football hero Jim Wellington, and *All-American* (1942), the story of Black athlete

Ronald Perry and the injustices he suffered because of racial prejudice. Many critics believe that Tunis's greatest story is *His Enemy, His Friend* (1967), which combines the aftermath of war memories with Tunis's favorite topic, sports.

A phenomenon that flourished in the 1930s and 1940s and peaked in the 1950s was the career novel. Publishers were eager to provide young readers with books for every vocation (except the least desirable). Unquestionably, books about nursing led the group in numbers and popularity. A representative writer in the genre was Helen Boylston, whose Sue Barton series (1936–1952) ran to seven volumes. Another widely read book was *Peggy Covers the News* (1936) by Emma Bugbee (Hauck, 1984).

Inaccurate Representation

Generally, young adult novels of the 1940s and 1950s focused on traditional social behavior: family, jobs, sports, dating, and so forth. The themes of most of these novels were moralistic and superficial. However, realism began to creep into the writing of a few popular young adult writers, and its use became a significant milestone in the direction of young adult literature. Hauck (1984) comments:

> Throughout the 40's and 50's lesser novelists also focused on genuine adolescent concerns, although the range of adolescent experience examined was still fairly narrow. Families, jobs, dating, and athletics were common themes, but such controversial subjects as drugs, alcohol, illegitimate pregnancy and the like were seldom introduced except to be decried. . . . All the protagonists in the novels are good, clean-hearted, clean-limbed, middle class Americans. In the antiseptic settings, sexual dilemmas are never allowed to intrude and difficulties rather readily are overcome. (p. 90)

Seventeenth Summer (1942), by Maureen Daly, is frequently credited with being the first contemporary young adult novel to meet these new criteria. It was the first classic love story for teenagers. The portrayal of teenagers as they really were set this story apart from others of its time. Daly recognizes drinking, smoking, homosexuality, and other taboo topics as realistic aspects of life. As one might expect, Daly's book was not well received by the adult population, but it did not go unnoticed by young adult readers.

Henry Gregor Felsen joined Daly in writing about young adults in an honest and serious fashion. He, too, ruffled the feathers of adults by writing about such taboo topics as adolescent failure and teenage pregnancy. One of his most popular books was *Two and the Town* (1952), about a young girl who becomes pregnant, which forces her boyfriend and her to marry. In the 1950s, Felsen's books about cars were immensely popular among young men. *Hot Rod* (1950), *Street Rod* (1953), and *Crash Club* (1958) were the hot titles.

In 1951, the novel that began the shift to what is called the new realism was J. D. Salinger's *The Catcher in the Rye*. The literature that followed this novel is cynical and reflects the economic, political, and social problems of the era. *Catcher* remains noteworthy in part because of its frankness in both language and the negative light in which it portrays adults. Ironically, the novel was written for the adult market, but it captured the young adult reader's attention like no other book has done.

Two other novels, although they did not have the impact of *Catcher*, contributed to the literary field. *Miracles on Maple Hill* (1957), by Virginia Sorenson, received the Newbery Medal, but it was heavily criticized for dealing with subject matter inappropriate for young adult readers: dissension in the home and the possibility of divorce. During this time, restrictions on subject matter were declining, but many adults still attempted to maintain unrealistic values of the past in current literature. The second book was *To Kill a Mockingbird* (1960) by Harper Lee. This novel depicts racial problems in the South and, to the horror of many adults of the time, it does not portray the White population favorably.

But for a few exceptions, "much of the literature written for young adults from 1940 through 1966 goes largely and legitimately ignored today" (Donelson & Nilson, 1989, p. 555).

Literature: Self-Discovery

Meanwhile, the influence of the media, especially television, and the more permissive climate of the sixties were also having their effect. . . . The middle sixties ushered in this "new realism" as it came to be called. These novels depicted young people in ordinary situations without censoring their language or glossing over their conduct. Premarital sex, unwed motherhood, abortion, illicit drugs, all these issues and many more found their way into the stories. . . . With few exceptions, these new problem novels, as they were also called, have several characteristics in common. They are told from the point of view of a rather precocious adolescent [and] . . . parents are unsympathetic or incompetent. . . . They generally end with the protagonist taking a small step forward in maturity or self-understanding. The language is conversational, with few descriptive passages or niceties of style, and the setting is a mere backdrop for the action. (Hauck, 1984, p. 91)

The early books in this new age of realism emphasized this "unsympathetic or incompetent" parent characteristic. Leading the pack is Paul Zindel. In his 1968 novel *The Pigman*, John and Lorraine, the two narrators, have little positive to say about their parents. John always refers to his father as "Bore," and Lorraine realizes that her mother is obsessed about the dangers that men may bring. In Zindel's next book, *My Darling, My Hamburger* (1969), the parents don't fare much better. Liz's father is extremely abusive, and her decision to have an abortion is due to her boyfriend's father, who believes it is better to spend a little to prevent the embarrassment.

Although this attitude toward parents may be the negative side of young adult literature at this time, Zindel and other authors offered a great deal more on the positive side for adolescents. *The Pigman* has been widely praised by critics and the young adults who read it. It offers young readers an understanding of and compassion for human nature. In addition, it shows an improvement in the quality of the writer's craft. An alternating point of view between John and Lorraine is one example of writing skill that is not common in previous young adult literature.

In *The Outsiders* (Hinton, 1967), parents are not effective or are not present, but this issue is not what Hinton emphasizes in this novel. Her motive for writing *The*

Outsiders was the realism that is found in street gangs, rigid social class structure, and violence in the community and the schools. She tells of the Greasers and the Socs from the point of view of Ponyboy, a Greaser. This new age of realism also was found with stories of the poor and minority groups. *Where the Lilies Bloom* (Cleaver & Cleaver, 1969) is set in the Appalachian Mountains, where 14-year-old Mary Call Luther struggles to keep her family together after the death of her father. The reader experiences the struggles of a poverty-stricken family. Readers also experience a well-written novel.

Also in 1969, William Armstrong wrote about a poverty-stricken Black family of tenant farmers in *Sounder*. In *The Contender* (1967), Robert Lipsyte writes about a Black young adult boxer who hopes his athletic ability will get him out of the slums. Hunter's *The Soul Brothers and Sister Lou* (1968) has a similar theme. It portrays the life of Blacks in a northern ghetto and shows the conditions that give rise to racial strife. The bleak and stark realities of racial prejudice are also presented effectively in Mildred Taylor's writings. Her novels follow the lives of the Logan family as they experience the struggle to hold on to their land and the persecution of White neighbors.

Books by Judy Blume also contributed to this new realism in young adult literature. *Are You There God? It's Me, Margaret* (1970) focuses on a preadolescent girl's fears and concerns about menstruation and other problems of growing up. In *Blubber* (1974), Blume writes about the issue of obesity as well as the lesser issue (perhaps) of teacher weakness and ineffectiveness. In the same year, Paula Danziger also wrote about school and the unhappy life of an overweight girl in *The Cat Ate My Gymsuit*. In this novel, however, the teacher has a more positive role and is portrayed as courageous and compassionate. In *Deenie* (1973), Blume writes of a pretty girl whose mother wants her to become a model, but this dream seems unachievable when Deenie develops scoliosis and must wear a back brace. A realistic view comes with Deenie's concern that the back problem may have developed because she masturbates. Perhaps the most controversial of Blume's novels is *Forever* (1976), which addresses teenage romance and includes graphic details of sexual intercourse.

Readers experience another type of realism in the works of Jean Craighead George. In *Julie of the Wolves* (1972), a young Eskimo woman struggles with two cultures: the past and the modern way of life. The agonizing conflicts that this woman faces in choosing the "right" direction for her are described vividly.

As the genre evolves, the literature reflects more conditions of society, and these conditions are told in straightforward stories that young people want to read. As we look at the evolution of young adult literature, we find that the literature from the mid-1970s to the present not only reflects the mountains and valleys of society but does so with high-quality writing. Some of the earlier novels were well written, of course, but quality was not generally the most important characteristic of young adult literature. There is more of a push in that direction as literature for young adults continues to evolve.

Most, if not all, of Robert Cormier's novels reflect this quality of writing. Cormier's literature offers complicated, sophisticated plot structure, fully developed characters, settings that complement the plot and characters, a variety of literary devices, and complex, universal themes. Although some criticize Cormier for the pessimistic view of life expressed in his early novels, he is perhaps only reflecting the reality that many of life's problems are difficult to overcome and sometimes cannot be overcome.

Chris Crutcher, a writer and former child abuse therapist, believes that if stories are to be told, they must be told in an honest, forthright way. His literature—*Running Loose* (1983), *Stotan!* (1986), *The Crazy Horse Electric Game* (1987), *Chinese Handcuffs* (1989), *Athletic Shorts* (1991), *Ironman* (1995), and *Whale Talk* (2001)—reflects this attitude. Crutcher believes that there are stories to be told about love, death, racism, bigotry, and sexual abuse, and these stories need to be told to young adults with honesty; if they are not told honestly, young people will see through them in a flash. Crutcher writes in an honest, straightforward style. He includes just the right amount of humor and other literary techniques to make young people want to read his works.

Literature: The Present and Beyond

Other writers of young adult literature who could be mentioned in this history of young adult literature have been included in other parts of this book, usually in discussions of their quality of writing and their positive contributions to the field of young adult literature. Certainly, the quality writers in the immediate past and present who will continue to write and contribute to the reading of young adults in the future include Norma Fox Mazer, Harry Mazer, Sue Ellen Bridgers, Richard Peck, Cynthia Voigt, Julian Thompson, Gary Paulsen, Mildred Taylor, Sandy Asher, Paul Zindel, S. E. Hinton, Judy Blume, Lois Duncan, Walter Dean Myers, Katherine Paterson, Robert Lipsyte, M. E. Kerr, Chris Crutcher, and others discussed in this text. Many others who are just publishing their first young adult novels will also be important authors of young adult literature.

What will the literature of the future be like? Certainly, like the literature of the past, it will reflect the concerns of an ever-changing society. The young adult literature of the present and the future will include stories about the problems young people face: child and sexual abuse, the family and its inability to stay together, political abuses in the United States and abroad, the stress of economic instability, sexually transmitted diseases and their effects on young people, and the general conflicts that go with growing up in a society that is sometimes unkind to its youth.

We also believe that the nonfiction genre will continue to grow and will meet the needs of young adults. A renewed interest will be apparent in the books on preparing for college and careers. There will be more how-to books and self-help books. Young adults will continue to read the books of Milton Meltzer, Brent Ashabranner, David Macaulay, and others who write nonfiction.

Young people themselves are developing new avenues in which they can write and read the writing of other young adults. Zines (pronounced *zeens*) are very popular. "A zine is any publication put together and distributed by the creator (or creators) for love and not profit. Most of the zines you'll read about these days are more like mini-magazines, but with a personal touch" (Dyer, p. 1). Zines are Web site publications written primarily by young people. They are about subjects that young people want to deal with and writers believe there is little written about these subjects in regular magazines. Whether one or more of these zines will turn into the new young adult novel remains to be seen.

Our guess is that soon in most schools, the teacher will simply say "take out your palm pilot and turn on *My Louisiana Sky* (Holt, 1998); scroll down to page 37 and let's talk about the setting there." So instead of students opening books, they simply will turn on technology. More and more schools are funding this technology for students to use in their reading and writing. One problem now is that much of the literature found on the palm pilot is classic literature. The inclusion of classics makes for less costs as very little or no royalty is paid on classic literature. The technology is available and it will not be long before the use of palm pilots or something similar will be used by students to read young adult literature as well as the classics.

Learning Log Responses

What realizations did you come to while reading this chapter? How has the genre evolved? How do recent series novels compare with earlier series novels?

References

American Library Association. (1926). *Children's reading interests*. Chicago: Author.

Donelson, K., & Nilson, A. (1989). *Literature for today's young adults*. Glenview, IL: Scott, Foresman.

Dyer, S. (n.d.). Action Girl Online: Questions and Answers about Zines. *Action Girl Newsletter*, www.houseoffun.com/action/index.html.

Hauck, P. (1984). Literature for adolescents: Gold or dross? *Journal of Educational Research, 18*(2), 88–102.

Smith, J. (1967). *A critical approach to children's literature*. New York: McGraw-Hill.

Wintle, J., & Fisher, E. (1974). *The pied pipers*. New York: Paddington.

Support for Teaching Young Adult Literature

Teachers are a busy group of professionals. Because both authors taught in the public schools, we know what it is like to teach 100 to 140 students each day. Simply trying to keep up with lesson plans, grading, and all of the administrative/clerical work that is asked of teachers is a full-time job. Little time is left for library research to find appropriate sources of support for teaching young adult literature. We attempt to provide an easy reference to these sources in this appendix.

Sources That Include Reviews of Young Adult Books

The ALAN Review
Assembly on Literature for Adolescents, NCTE
1111 Kenyon Road
Urbana, IL 61801

Booklinks
50 E. Huron Street
Chicago, IL 60611

Booklist
American Library Association
50 E. Huron Street
Chicago, IL 60611

Books for the Teen Ager
Office of Young Adult Services
New York Public Library
455 Fifth Avenue
New York, NY 10016

Bulletin for the Center for Children's Books
P.O. Box 1334
S. Oak Street
Chicago, IL 61820

Children's Literature in Education: An International Quarterly
Agathon Press
233 Spring Street
New York, NY 10013

English Journal
NCTE
1111 Kenyon Road
Urbana, IL 61801

Horn Book
14 Beacon Street
Boston, MA 02108

Horn Book Guide
14 Beacon Street
Boston, MA 02108

Interracial Books for Children Bulletin
1841 Broadway
New York, NY 10023

Journal of Adolescent and Adult Literacy
PO Box 8139
Newark, DE 19711

The Journal of Reading
International Reading Association
P.O. Box 8139
Newark, DE 19714

Journal of Youth Services in Libraries
American Library Association
50 East Huron Street
Chicago, IL 60611

Kirkus Reviews
200 Park Avenue South
Suite 1118
New York, NY 10003

Kliatt Young Adult Paperback Book Guide
425 Watertown Street
Newton, MA 02158

Language Arts
NCTE
1111 Kenyon Road
Urbana, IL 61801

McNaughton Young Adult Reviews
McNaughton Book Service
P.O. Box 926
Williamsport, PA 17705

The New Advocate
480 Washington Street
Norwood, MA 02062

The New York Times Book Review
New York Times Company
229 W. 43rd Street
New York, NY 10036

Publishers Weekly
P.O. Box 1979
Marion, OH 43302

The School Library Journal
P.O. Box 16388
North Hollywood, CA 91695

SIGNAL Newsletter
IRA
P.O. Box 8139
Newark, DE 19714

Voice of Youth Advocates (VOYA)
Scarecrow Press, Inc.
4720A Boston Way
Lanham, MD 20706

Voices from the Middle
NCTE
1111 Kenyon Road
Urbana, IL 61801

Wilson Library Review
950 University Avenue
Bronx, NY 10452

The Writers' Slate
The Writing Conference, Inc.
P.O. Box 664
Ottawa, KS 66067

Indexes of Reviews of Young Adult Literature

Book Review Digest
1905 to date
H. W. Wilson Company

Book Review Index
1965 to date
Gale Research Company

Children's Book Review
1975 to date
Gale Research Company
A. Block and C. Riley, Ed.

Children's Literature Review
1976 to date
Gale Research Company

High-Interest Books for Teens: A Guide to Book Review and Biographical Sources
Joyce Nakamura, Ed.
Gale Research Company
1988

Masterplots II, Juvenile and Young Adult Literature
Frank N. Magill, Ed.
Salem Press
1991

Olderr's Young Adult Fiction Index
Stevn Olderr, Ed.
St. James Press
1988

Writers for Young Adults, 4 vols.
Ted Hipple, Ed.
Simon & Schuster
Vols. 1–3, 1997; Vol. 4, 2000

Young Adult Book Review Index
Barbara Beach, Ed.
Gale Research Company
1988

Awards Presented to Young Adult Books

Best Books for Young Adults—The annual list of books is chosen by a committee of the American Library Association. The list is published in the March issue of *School Library Journal* or is available from the American Library Association.

Booklist Editors' Choices—The list of best books is published each January in *Booklist*.

Books for the Teenager—The best books list is published yearly by the New York Public Library.

Books for Young Adults—The list is generated from the evaluations sent in by young adult readers. It is published by the University of Iowa.

Boston Globe–Horn Book Award—Awards are given annually for the best in fiction and nonfiction. Acceptance speeches of those receiving the awards are published in the January/February issue of *Horn Book Magazine*.

The Heartland Award for Young Adult Literature (The Writing Conference, Inc., Ottawa, KS)—Teachers and librarians nominate books. A committee chooses the 10 finalists. Students nationwide read at least three of the nominated books and select the winner. The winner is invited to address the Literature Festival in October.

Horn Book Fanfare Books—This list of best books is selected by the editors of *Horn Book Magazine* and is published in the December issue of *Horn Book Magazine*.

Newbery Award—The annual award winner and the honor books are chosen by a committee of the American Library Association. The award is announced in January. The winning author's acceptance speech appears in the July/August issue of *Horn Book Magazine*.

Recommended Books for the Reluctant Young Adult Reader—The annual list of books is chosen by a committee of the American Library Association.

School Library Journal Best Books of the Year—The annual list of books is published in the December issue of *School Library Journal*.

Other Sources Important to the Classroom Teacher

Periodicals

The ALAN Review—In addition to the reviews of young adult literature, the journal includes articles written by professional writers of young adult literature as well as by professional educators who offer criticisms and practical applications of young adult literature.

Bulletin of the Center for Children's Books—In addition to the reviews, this source also includes articles about the way young adult literature may be used in the curriculum.

Children's Literature in Education: An International Quarterly—The international journal offers readers a more detailed analysis and scholarly criticism than many others.

English Journal—Although the journal tries to meet the needs and interests of the junior high/middle and high school English teacher with articles covering all aspects of teaching English, it does often have a focus, frequently on young adult literature.

Horn Book Magazine—Primary emphasis is given to scholarly reviews of children's and young adult literature; however, there are feature articles of interest to the classroom teacher.

Interracial Books for Children Bulletin—In addition to the reviews, this bulletin does include articles. The main emphasis is on social issues and their treatment in literature.

Journal of Reading—Aimed at the high school reading teacher, the journal emphasizes the teaching of reading; however, it does include articles on reading interests and literature.

Voice of Youth Advocates (VOYA)—Although primarily aimed at the librarian, this periodical offers interesting articles that would also be of interest to classroom teachers.

Wilson Library Bulletin—In addition to the reviews of books, the *Bulletin* includes interesting and relevant articles of interest to the young adult literature teacher.

Books

Bainhouse, R. (2000). *Recasting the part: The Middle Ages—young adult literature.* Westport, CT: Heinemann.

Bodart, J. (1992). *Booktalker.* Englewood, CO: Libraries Unlimited. *Explores booktalks and booktalking.*

Brown, J. E., & Stephens, E. C. (1995). *Teaching young adult literature: Sharing the connection.* Belmont, CA: Wadsworth.

Carlsen, G. R. (1980). *Books and the teen-age reader* (2nd ed.). New York: Harper & Row. *The first edition was one of the early books on young adult literature that connected with teachers. This book continues to connect.*

Carter, B., & Abrahamson, R., (1990). *Nonfiction for young adults: From delight to wisdom.* Phoenix, AZ: Oryx. *A thorough presentation of the nonfiction field, the book also includes interviews with prominent nonfiction writers.*

Criscoe, B. L. (Ed.). (1990). *Award-winning books for children and young adults: An annual guide, 1989.* New York: Scarecrow. *This directory of awards includes information on award sponsors, award background, and biographies of the winners.*

Day, F. A. (2000). *Lesbian and gay voices: An annotative bibliography and guide to literature for children and young adults.* Westport, CT: Greenwood Press. *Discusses literature connected to gay and lesbian voices.*

Donelson, K., & Nilsen, A. (2005). *Literature for today's young adults* (7th ed.). Boston: Pearson Education. *This book is often described as the complete text on young adult literature.*

Elliott, J., & Dupuis, M. (Eds.). (2002). *Young adult literature in the classroom: Reading it, teaching it, loving it.* Newark, DE: IRA. *Presents creative and interesting information about teaching young adult literature.*

Feehan, P., & Barron, P. (Eds.). (1991). *Writers on writing for young adults: Exploring the authors, the genre, the readers, the issues, and the critics of young-adult literature.* New York: Omnigraphs. *Essays in this work discuss the various aspects of young adult literature.*

Gallo, D. (Ed.). (1990). *Speaking for ourselves: Autobiographical sketches by notable authors of books for young adults.* Urbana, IL: National Council of Teachers of English.

Gallo, D. (Ed.). (1993). *Speaking for ourselves, too. More autobiographical sketches by notable authors of books for young adults.* Urbana, IL: National Council of Teachers of English.

Hipple, T. (Ed.). (1997–2000). *Writers for young adults,* 4 Vols. New York: Scribners. *These useful books contain sketches of well-known young adult authors, with information about each author's life and works.*

Kaywell, J. F. (Ed.). (1993–2000). *Adolescent literature as a complement to the classics* (Vols. I, II, III, IV). Norward, MA: Christopher Gordon. *These volumes contain many articles and suggestions on how to use young adult literature as a bridge to reading the classics.*

Kaywell, J. F. (Ed.). (1999–2004). *Using literature to help troubled teenagers series.* Westport CT: Greenwood Press. *Articles that speak to the issue of family matters and abuse.*

Kelly, P., & Small, R., Jr. (Eds.). (1999). *Two decades of the ALAN Review.* Urbana, IL: National Council of Teachers of English. *This book is a collection of articles, reviews, and interviews that have appeared in the ALAN Review over the past 20 years.*

Lynn, R. N. (1989). *Fantasy literature for children and young adults.* New York: R. R. Bowker. *The book contains annotated bibliographies of fantasy novels and short story collections.*

Matthews, D. (Ed.). (1988). *High interest–easy reading: For junior and senior high school students* (5th ed.). Urbana, IL: National Council of Teachers of English. *The emphasis is on books that meet the interests of reluctant adolescent readers.*

Monseau, V. R. (1996). Responding to young adult literature. Portsmouth, NH: Boynton/Cook. *This book emphasizes the reader-response strategy with young adult literature.*

Monseau, V. R., & Salvner, G. M. (Eds.). (1992). *Reading their world: The young adult novel in the classroom.* Portsmouth, NH: Boynton/Cook. *A variety of authors write about issues important to the teaching of young adult literature.*

Nathan, R. (Ed.). (1991). *Writers in the classroom.* Norwood, MA: Christopher Gordon. *In this book, writers share their writing, and writers and teachers share how they would teach writing. Chapters were written by young adult writers as well as professional educators.*

Probst, R. (1988). *Response and analysis: Teaching literature in junior and senior high school.* Portsmouth, NH: Boynton/Cook. *This book teaches about the teaching of literature in general and response-based teaching in particular.*

Reed, A. J. S. (1994). *Comics to classics.* New York: Penguin Books. *The material is an attempt to help teachers help students in choosing the right book for them to read given their abilities and interests.*

Responding: A reading/writing integrative approach to young adult literature (Vols. 1–4). (1994–2001). Ottawa, KS: Writing Conference. *This continuous series contains questions and statements about young adult literature to which students respond in writing.*

Spiegel, L. A. (1996). *Females in adolescent literature.* Ottawa, KS: The Writing Conference. *Each chapter of this book features a different genre of adolescent literature with strong female characters and protagonists. Discussion of books and characters is included as well as a lengthy bibliography.*

Spiegel, L. A. (1997–2001). *A thematic guide to adolescent literature: Annotations, critiques, and sources* (Vols. 2–4). Ottawa, KS: The Writing Conference.

Stover, L. T. (1996). *Young adult literature: The heart of the middle school curriculum.* Portsmouth, NH: Boynton/Cook. *A book that emphasizes young adult literature as it could be used in an interdisciplinary way in middle school.*

Stover, L. T., & Zenker, S. E. (Eds.). (1997). *Books for you: A booklist for senior high students.* Urbana, IL: National Council of Teachers of English. *Books are described by subject or theme. This publication is revised every 5 years.*

Twayne's United States author series: Young adult authors books. Boston: G. K. Hall. *This series presents the life and work of various young adult authors, including Judy Blume, Sue Ellen Bridgers, Robert Cormier, Rosa Guy, S. E. Hinton, M. E. Kerr, Norma Klein, Norma Fox Mazer, Richard Peck, Walter Dean Myers, and Paul Zindel. A list of specific titles in the Twayne series appears in Chapter 2; bibliographic information is included in Appendix B.*

Walder, E. (Ed.). (1988). *Book bait: Detailed notes on adult books, popular with young people* (4th ed.). Chicago, IL: American Library Association. *This bibliography provides detailed information about books that are of interest to young adults. It attempts to bridge the gap between young adult books and adult books.*

Ward, M., & Marquardt, D. (1990). *Authors of books for young people* (3rd ed.). New York: Scarecrow. *This book provides a snapshot reference of information about children's and young adult authors.*

Weiss, J. (Ed.). (1979). *From writers to students: The pleasures and pains of writing.* Newark, DE: International Reading Association. *The book contains interviews with selected young adult authors including Judy Blume, M. E. Kerr, and Norma and Harry Mazer.*

Zitlow, C. (2002). *Lost masterworks of young adult literature.* Lantham, MD: Scarecrow Press. *We recommend the thorough collection of sources presented in the Fall 1991 issue of* The ALAN Review. *"The Library Connection" column, by Donald J. Kenney, was titled "Familiarity with Reference." The column is extensive and demands the attention of any teacher of young adult literature.*

Conferences

Reading journals and books is just one of many ways to stay abreast of what is happening in the field of young adult literature. An effective way to come into contact with the literature, its writers, and its critics is to attend a conference that includes a young adult literature component. Most state English and reading organizations, perhaps affiliated with their national organizations, have annual conferences in which authors are invited to speak, and sessions on the writer's craft or the work itself are available for discussion. Teachers can learn a great deal from these conferences.

National conferences attract a wider audience and, thus, attract more and varied authors and sessions. In the national arena, prominent young adult authors participate in large group presentations as well as small group sessions. It is an excellent way for teachers of young adult literature to interact with the authors of the literature they are teaching in the classroom. Many groups across the nation meet and discuss young adult literature to some extent. Two in particular are the International Reading Association (IRA) and the Assembly on Literature for Adolescents—NCTE (ALAN). Both groups have extended workshops that include general presentations by authors, critics, and teachers of young adult literature as well as small-group sessions on related issues relevant to the classroom teacher.

Literature Festivals

Literature festivals also provide contact with popular young adult authors. These are particularly beneficial because they connect these authors with teachers, children, and young adults. These festivals usually last 2 to 3 days and involve hundreds of young people interacting with authors and specialists in young adult literature. Usually sessions are offered for the classroom teacher as well.

The field of young adult literature is growing rapidly. The quality of literature that is now available for young people demands that classroom teachers and librarians pay close attention to this genre. Resources are available so that teachers can keep up with this rapidly growing field. When teachers become knowledgeable about young adult literature, they and their students can only benefit.

 ## Learning Log Responses

Read the latest issue of *The ALAN Review.* Make an entry in your log about its content and its usefulness to you as a teacher of literature.

Peruse two other publications that may be helpful to the teacher of young adult literature. Make an entry showing how you might use these publications.

Works of Literature Cited

Books appropriate for middle school students are marked with an asterisk (*). Because many older titles are either no longer in print or are in the public domain and available from several sources, we do not list publishers for these works.

Abeel, S. (2003). *My Thirteenth Winter: A Memoir.* New York: Orchard.

Adichie, C. N. (2003). *Purple Hibiscus.* Chapel Hill, NC: Algonquin.

Adoff, A. (Ed.). (1970). *Black Out Loud: An Anthology of Modern Poems by Black Americans.* New York: Macmillan.

*Adoff, A. (1986). *Sports Pages.* New York: Lippincott.

Adoff, A. (1997). *I Am the Darker Brother: An Anthology of Modern Poems by African Americans.* New York: Simon & Schuster.

Aesop. (c. 6th century B.C.E.). *Fables.*

*Aguado, B. (2003). *Paint Me Like I Am: Teen Poems from Writers Corp.* New York: HarperCollins.

Aiken, J. (1978). *Street.* New York: Viking.

Aiken, J. (1984). *A Whisper in the Night.* New York: Delacorte.

Alcott, L. M. (1868). *Little Women: Meg, Jo, Beth, and Amy. The Story of Their Lives: A Girl's Book.*

Alcott, L. M. (1869). *Little Women: Meg, Jo, Beth, and Amy, Part Second.*

Aldrich, T. (1870). *The Story of a Bad Boy.*

Alger, H. (1868). *Ragged Dick and Mark, the Watch Boy.*

*Allison, A. (1998). *Hear These Voices: Youth at the Edge of the Millennium.* New York: Dutton.

Alvarez, J. (2000). *How Tia Lola Came to (Visit) Stay.* New York: Knopf.

Anaya, R. (1972). *Bless Me, Ultima.* Berkeley, CA: Tonatiuh, Quinto Sol International.

*Anaya, R. (1992). *Albuquerque.* Albuquerque, NM: University of New Mexico Press.

Anderson, L. H. (1999). *Speak.* New York: Farrar, Straus & Giroux.

Anderson, L. H. (2000). *Fever 1793.* New York: Simon & Schuster.

Anderson, L. H. (2002). *Catalyst.* New York: Viking.

Anderson, M. T. (2002). *Feed.* Cambridge, MA: Candlewick Press.

Angelou, M. (1970). *I Know Why the Caged Bird Sings.* New York: Random House.

Angelou, M. (1971). *Just Give Me a Cool Drink of Water 'fore I Die.* New York: Random House.

Angelou, M. (1975). *Oh, Pray My Wings Are Gonna Fit Me Well*. New York: Random House.

Angelou, M. (1978). *And Still I Rise*. New York: Random House.

Angelou, M. (1987). *Now Sheba Sings the Song*. New York: Dial.

Antle, N. (1993). *Tough Choices: A Story of the Vietnam War*. New York: Viking.

Appelt, K. (1996). *Just People and Paper/Pen/Poem: A Young Writer's Way to Begin*. New York: Absey.

Appelt, K. (2002). *Poems from Homeroom*. New York: Henry Holt.

Appleman-Jurman, A. (1988). *Alicia: My Story*. New York: Dell.

Armstrong, J. (2002). *The Keepers of the Flame*. New York: HarperCollins.

*Armstrong, W. (1969). *Sounder*. New York: Harper & Row.

*Armstrong, W. (1997). *Mary Mehan Awake*. New York: Knopf.

Arnoldi, K. (1998). *The Amazing "True" Story of a Teenage Single Mom*. New York: Hyperion.

Aronson, M. (2003). *Witch Hunt: Mysteries of the Salem Witch Trials*. New York: Atheneum.

Arrick, F. (1981). *Chernowitz*. New York: New American Library.

Arrick, F. (1992). *What You Don't Know Can Kill You*. New York: Bantam.

*Ashabranner, B. (1989). *Born to the Land: An American Portrait*. New York: G. P. Putnam's Sons.

*Ashabranner, B. (1989). *People Who Make a Difference*. New York: Cobblehill.

*Ashabranner, B., & Ashabranner, M. (1987). *Into a Strange Land: Unaccompanied Refugee Youth in America*. New York: G. P. Putnam's Sons.

Asher, S. (1980). *Summer Begins*. New York: Dutton.

*Asher, S. (1987). *Everything Is Not Enough*. New York: Dell.

Asher, S. (1987). Great Moves. In D. Gallo (Ed.), *Visions* (pp. 130–139). New York: Dell.

Asher, S. (1989). *Little Old Ladies in Tennis Shoes*. New York: Dramatic Publishing.

*Asher, S. (1989). *A Woman Called Truth*. Woodstock, IL: Dramatic Publishing.

*Asher, S. (1992). *The Wise Men of Chelm*. New York: Dramatic Publishing.

Asher, S. (1993). *Out of Here*. New York: Lodestar.

Asher, S. (1994). *Dancing with Strangers*. New York: Dramatic Publishing.

Asher, S. (1994). *Sunday, Sunday*. New York: Dramatic Publishing.

Asher, S. (1995). *Across the Plains*. New York: Dramatic Publishing.

Asher, S. (Ed.). (1996). *But That's Another Story*. New York: Walker.

Asher, S. (1997). *Emma*. New York: Dramatic Publishing.

Asher, S. (1999). *With All My Heart, with All My Mind: Thirteen Stories about Growing up Jewish*. New York: Simon & Schuster.

Asimov, I. (Ed.). (1985). *Young Monsters*. New York: Harper & Row.

Atkins, C. (2003). *Alt Ed*. New York: Putnam.

Austen, J. (1813). *Pride and Prejudice*.

Avi. (1989). *The Man Who Was Poe*. New York: Avon.

Avi. (1990). *The True Confession of Charlotte Doyle*. New York: Orchard.

*Avi. (1991). *Nothing but the Truth*. New York: Orchard.

*Avi. (1992). *The Blue Heron*. New York: Avon.

*Avi. (1997). *What Do Fish Have to Do with Anything? and Other Stories*. New York: Demco-Media.

*Avi. (1998). *Perloo the Bold*. New York: Scholastic.

Avi, L'Engle, M., Peck, R., Babbitt, N., Lisle, J. T., & Springer, H. (1999). *Second Sight: Stories for a New Millenium*. New York: Philomel Books.

*Ayres, K. (1998). *North by Night: A Story of the Underground Railroad*. New York: Delacorte.

*Bachrach, S. (1994). *Tell Them We Remember*. Boston: Little, Brown.

Baer, E. (1996). *Walk the Dark Streets*. New York: Random House.

Bailey-Williams, N. (2004). *Floating*. New York: Broadway Books.

Bardi, A. (2001). *The Book of Fred*. New York: Washington Square.

Barrett, P. (1986). *To Break the Silence: Thirteen Short Stories for Young Readers*. New York: Dell.

Bartoletti, S. C. (1996). *Growing Up in Coal Country*. Boston: Houghton Mifflin.

Bartoletti, S. C. (1999). *No Man's Land: A Young Soldier's Story*. New York: Hyperion.

Bartoletti, S. C. (2002). *Black Potatoes: The Story of the Great Irish Famine*. Boston: Houghton Mifflin.

*Bauer, C. (2000). *Harley Like a Person*. New York: Winslow Press.

*Bauer, J. (1992). *Squashed*. New York: Dell.

*Bauer, J. (1998). *Rules of the Road*. New York: Putnam.

*Bauer, J. (2000). *Hope Was Here*. New York: Putnam.

*Bauer, M. D. (Ed.). (1994). *Am I Blue? Coming Out from the Silence*. New York: HarperCollins.

*Bauer, M. D. (1996). *Our Stories: A Fiction Workshop for Young Authors*. New York: Clarion.

*Bauer, M.D. (2000). *What's Your Story?* New York: Clarion.

Bechard, M. (2002). *Hanging on to Max*. New York: Roaring Brook.

Beirhorst, J. (1987). *In the Trail of the Wind: American Indian Poems and Ritual Orations*. New York: Farrar, Straus & Giroux.

Bell, W. (1990). *Forbidden City*. New York: Bantam.

*Beltrán-Hernández, I. (1995). *Across the Great River*. Houston, TX: Pinata Books.

*Beltrán-Hernández, I. (1995). *The Secret of Two Brothers*. Houston, TX: Pinata Books.

Benard, R. (Ed.). (1989). *Do You Like It Here? and Other Stories—Twenty-One Views of the High School Years*. New York: Dell.

Benchley, P. (1974). *Jaws*. New York: Doubleday.

Benchley, P. (1976). *The Deep*. New York: Doubleday.

Benchley, P. (1982). *The Girl of the Sea of Cortez*. New York: Doubleday.

Benduhn, T. (2003). *Gravel Queen*. New York: Simon & Schuster.

Benjamin, C. (1991). *Nobody's Baby Now*. New York: Bantam.

Bennett, C. (1998). *Life in the Fat Lane*. New York: Delacorte.

Bennett, C., & Gottesfeld, J. (2004). *A Heart Divided*. New York: Delacorte Press.

*Bennett, J. (1980). *The Pigeon*. New York: Avon.

*Bennett, J. (1990). *Sing Me a Death Song*. New York: Fawcett.

*Bennett, J. (1994). *Dakota Dream*. New York: Scholastic.

Bennett, J. (1995). *The Squared Circle*. New York: Scholastic.

*Bennett, J. (2001). *Plunking Reggie Jackson*. New York: Simon & Schuster.

Bennett, J. (2003). *Faith Wish*. New York: Holiday House.

Beyer, R. (2003). *The Greatest Stories Never Told: 100 Tales from History to Astonish, Bewilder and Stupefy*. New York: HarperCollins.

Bishop, R. (1990). *Presenting Walter Dean Myers*. New York: Twayne.

Bitton-Jackson, L. (1997). *I Have Lived a Thousand Years*. New York: Simon & Schuster.

Bitton-Jackson, L. (1999). *My Bridges of Hope*. New York: Simon & Schuster.

Blackwood, G. (1998). *The Shakespeare Stealer*. New York: Dutton.

Blackwood, G. (2000). *The Shakespeare Scribe*. New York: Dutton.

Blackwood, G. (2002). *The Year of the Hangman*. New York: Dutton.

Block, F. L. (1989). *Weetzie Bat*. New York: HarperCollins.

Block, F. L. (1991). *Witch Baby*. New York: HarperCollins.

Block, F. L. (1995). *Baby Be-Bop*. New York: HarperCollins.

Block, F. L. (1996). *Girl Goddess: Nine Stories*. New York: HarperCollins.

Block, F. L. (2003). *Wasteland*. New York: HarperCollins.

Bloom, S., & Mercier, C. (1991). *Presenting Zibby Oneal*. New York: Twayne.

Bloor, E. (1997). *Tangerine*. New York: Scholastic.

Blos, J. (1979). *A Gathering of Days: A New England Girl's Journal*, 1830–32. New York: Aladdin.

*Blume, J. (1970). *Are You There God? It's Me, Margaret*. New York: Bradbury.

*Blume, J. (1973). *Deenie*. New York: Bradbury.

*Blume, J. (1974). *Blubber*. New York: Bradbury.

Blume, J. (1976). *Forever*. New York: Bradbury.

*Blume, J. (1981). *Tiger Eyes*. New York: Dell.

*Blume, J. (1986). *Starring Sally J. Freedman as Herself*. New York: Dell.

Blume, J. (1999). *Places I Never Meant to Be*. New York: Simon & Schuster.

*Bode, J. (1986). *New Kids in Town: Oral Histories of Immigrant Teens*. New York: Franklin Watts.

Bode, J. (1990). *The Voices of Rape*. New York: Franklin Watts.

Bode, J. (1992). *Kids (Still) Having Kids*. New York: Franklin Watts.

Bode, J. (1997). *Food Fight: A Guide to Eating Disorders for Preteens and Their Parents*. New York: Simon & Schuster.

*Bode, J., & Mack, S. (1994). *Heartbreak and Roses: Real Life Stories of Troubled Love*. New York: Delacorte.

Bograd, L. (1981). *The Kolokol Papers*. New York: Bantam.

Bograd, L. (1983). *Los Alamos Light*. New York: Farrar, Straus & Giroux.

Boissard, J. (1977). *A Matter of Feeling* (M. Feeley, Trans.). Toronto: Little, Brown.

*Bonham, F. (1965). *Durango Street*. New York: Dell. *A Book of Courtesy*. (1477).

Borland, H. (1963). *When the Legends Die*. New York: Lippincott.

Bosse, M. (1979). *The 79 Squares*. New York: Dell.

Boylston, H. (1936–1952). *Sue Barton* (series). Boston: Little, Brown.

Bozza, A. (2003). *Whatever You Say I Am: The Life and Times of Eminem*. New York: Crown.

Bradbury, R. (1973). *When Elephants Last in the Dooryard Bloomed*. New York: Knopf.

Brancato, R. (1977). *Winning*. New York: Dell.

Brancato, R. (1978). *Blinded by the Light*. New York: Knopf.

*Brancato, R. (1982). *Sweet Bells Jangled out of Tune*. New York: Knopf.

*Brancato, R. (1984). *Facing Up*. New York: Scholastic.

*Brancato, R. (1986). *Uneasy Money*. New York: Knopf.

Brashares, A. (2001). *The Sisterhood of the Traveling Pants*. New York: Random House.

Brashares, A. (2003). *The Second Summer of the Sisterhood*. New York: Random House.

Breslaw, E. G. (1996). *Tituba, Reluctant Witch of Salem*. New York: New York University Press.

Bridgers, S. E. (1976). *Home before Dark*. New York: Bantam.

*Bridgers, S. E. (1979). *All Together Now*. New York: Bantam.

*Bridgers, S. E. (1981). *Notes for Another Life*. New York: Bantam.

*Bridgers, S. E. (1987). The Beginning of Something. In D. Gallo (Ed.), *Visions* (pp. 213–228). New York: Dell.

Bridgers, S. E. (1987). *Permanent Connections*. New York: Harper & Row.

Bridgers, S. E. (1993). *Keeping Christina*. New York: HarperCollins.

Britton-Jackson, L. (1997). *I Have Lived a Thousand Years*. New York: Simon & Schuster.

Britton-Jackson, L. (1999). *My Bridges of Hope*. New York: Simon & Schuster.

Brontë, E. (1847). *Wuthering Heights*.

Brooks, B. (1984). *The Moves Make the Man*. New York: Harper & Row.

Brooks, B. (1986). *Midnight Hour Encores*. New York: Harper & Row.

Brooks, B. (1989). *No Kidding*. New York: Harper & Row.

Brooks, B. (1999). *Vanishing*. New York: HarperCollins.

Brooks, G. (1982). *Selected Poems*. New York: HarperCollins.

Brooks, K. (2002). *Martyn Pig*. New York: Scholastic.

Brooks, K. (2003). *Kissing the Rain*. New York: Scholastic.

Brooks, M. (2003). *True Confessions of a Heartless Girl*. New York: Farrar, Straus & Giroux.

Brown, J. (2003). *Tangled Threads*. Boston: Houghton Mifflin.

Brown, J. (2004). *Little Cricket*. New York: Hyperion.

Bruchac, J. (2003). *Our Stories Remembered: American Indian History, Culture and Values through Storytelling*. New York: Darly Creek.

Bugbee, E. (1936). *Peggy Covers the News*. New York: Dodd, Mead.

Bunting, E. (1982). *The Great White Shark*. New York: Julian Messner.

Bunyan, J. (1678). *The Pilgrim's Progress from This World to That Which Is to Come*.

Burchard, P. (1999). *Lincoln and Slavery*. New York: Simon & Schuster.

*Burks, B. (1997). *Soldier Boy*. San Diego: Harcourt Brace.

Burks, B. (1999). *Wrango*. San Diego: Harcourt Brace.

Burns, O. (1984). *Cold Sassy Tree*. New York: Dell.

Burt, G. (1994). *Sophie*. New York: Ballantine.

*Byars, B. (1985). *Cracker Jackson*. New York: Viking Penguin.

*Byars, B. (1991). *The Moon and I*. New York: Simon & Schuster.

*Cabot, M. (2003). *Princess Lesson*. New York: HarperCollins.

Cadnum, M. (1998). *Heat*. New York: Viking.

Cadnum, M. (1999). *Rundown*. New York: Viking.

Calhoun, D. (1999). *Firegold*. New York: Farrar, Straus & Giroux.

Cameron, A. (2003). *Colibri*. New York: Farrar, Straus & Giroux.

Campbell, P. (1989). *Presenting Robert Cormier*. New York: Twayne.

Camus, A. (1954). *The Stranger*. New York: Random House.

Carey, J. E. (2002). *Wenny Has Wings*. New York: Atheneum.

Carey, J. E. (2004). *The Double Life of Zoe Flynn*. New York: Atheneum.

Carlson, L. (1994). *Cool Salsa: Bilingual Poems on Growing Up Latino in the United States*. New York: Fawcett Juniper.

Carlson, R. (2002). *Don't Sweat the Small Stuff for Teens*. New York: Hyperion.

Carroll, J., & Wilson, E. (Ed.). (1997). *Poetry after Lunch: Poems to Read Aloud*. New York: Absey.

Cart, M. (1999). *Tomorrow Land*. New York: Scholastic.

Cart, M. (2001). *Love and Sex: Ten Stories of Truth*. New York: Simon & Schuster.

Cart, M. (2003). *Necessary Noise: Stories about Our Families as They Really Are*. New York: Harper Collins.

Carter, A. (1989). *Up Country*. New York: Scholastic.

Carter, A. (1990). *Dancing on Dark Water*. New York: Scholastic.

Carter, A. (1990). *Last Stand at the Alamo*. New York: Franklin Watts.

Carter, A. (1992). *The American Revolution: War for Independence*. New York: Franklin Watts.

Carter, A. (1992). *The Civil War: American Tragedy*. New York: Franklin Watts.

Carter, A. (1992). *The Colonial Wars: Clashes in the Wilderness*. New York: Franklin Watts.

Carter, A. (1992). *The War of 1812: Second Fight for Independence*. New York: Franklin Watts.

Carter, A. (1993). *Battle of the Ironclads: The Monitor and Merrimack*. New York: Franklin Watts.

Carter, A. (1994). *China Past–China Future*. New York: Franklin Watts.

Carter, A. (1994). *Dogwolf*. New York: Scholastic.

Carter, A. (1995). *Between a Rock and a Hard Place*. New York: Scholastic.

Carter, A. (1997). *Bull Catcher*. New York: Scholastic.

Castlemon, H. (1864). *Frank, the Young Naturalist*.

Cheek, A., Collins, K. C., & Foxfire Students (Eds.). (2004). *Foxfire, 12*. New York: Anchor Books.

Cheripko, J. (1996). *Imitate the Tiger*. Honesdale, PA: Boyds Mills Press.

*Childress, A. (1973). *A Hero Ain't Nothin' but a Sandwich*. New York: Avon.

*Childress, A. (1981). *Rainbow Jordan*. New York: G. P. Putnam's Sons.

*Childress, W. (1990). The Dreamer. In R. Peck (Ed.), *Sounds and Silences* (pp. 240–249). New York: Dell.

Cisneros, S. (1994). *The House on Mango Street*. New York: Knopf.

Cisneros, S. (2002). *Caramelo*. New York: Knopf.

Clark, M. H. (Ed.). (1995). *Bad Behavior*. Orlando, FL: Harcourt Brace.

*Cleaver, V., & Cleaver, B. (1969). *Where the Lilies Bloom*. New York: Lippincott.

Clinton, C. (2001). *The Calling*. Cambridge, MA: Candlewick.

Cochran, T. (1997). *Roughnecks*. San Diego: Harcourt Brace.

*Cofer, J. O. (1995). *An Island Like You: Stories of the Barrio*. New York: Orchard.

Cofer, J. O. (2003). *The Meaning of Consuelo*. New York: Farrar, Straus & Giroux.

Cohen, S., & Cohen, D. (1992). *When Someone You Know Is Gay*. New York: Bantam Doubleday Dell.

Cohn, R. (2003). *The Steps*. New York: Simon & Schuster.

Cole, B. (1997). *The Facts Speak for Themselves*. Arden, NC: Front Street.

Collier, J. (2004). *The Empty Mirror*. New York: Bloomsbury.

*Collier, J., & Collier, C. (1974). *My Brother Sam Is Dead*. New York: Macmillan.

*Collier, J., & Collier, C. (1976). *The Bloody Country*. New York: Macmillan.

*Collier, J., & Collier, C. (1994). *With Every Drop of Blood*. New York: Delacorte.

Collins, P. L. (2003). *The Fattening Hut*. Boston: Houghton Mifflin.

Comenious, J. (1659). *The Visible World in Pictures*.

Comer, J. (1988). *Maggie's American Dream*. New York: NAL-Dutton.

Comstock, A., & Bremner, R. (1967). *Traps for the Young*. Cambridge, MA: Harvard University Press.

*Conford, E. (1983). *If This Is Love, I'll Take Spaghetti*. New York: Scholastic.

*Conford, E. (1994). *I Love You, I Hate You, Get Lost*. New York: Scholastic.

*Conford, E. (1998). *Crush*. New York: HarperCollins.

*Conley, J. (1993). *Crazy Lady*. New York: HarperCollins.

Conrad, J. (1921). *Heart of Darkness*.

*Cooney, C. (1990). *Face on the Milk Carton*. New York: Bantam.

*Cooney, C. (1992). *Flight #116 Is Down*. New York: Scholastic.

*Cooney, C. (1992). *Operation Homefront*. New York: Bantam.

*Cooney, C. (1993). *Whatever Happened to Janie?* New York: Delacorte.

*Cooney, C. (1994). *Driver's Ed*. New York: Delacorte.

*Cooney, C. (1996). *The Voice on the Radio*. New York: Delacorte.

*Cooney, C. (1997). *The Terrorist*. New York: Scholastic.

*Cooney, C. (1999). *Burning Up*. New York: Delacorte.

*Cooney, C. (2000). *What Janie Found*. New York: Random House.

*Cooney, C. (2001). *Ransom of Mercy Carter*. New York: Random House.

*Cooper, S. (1975). *The Grey King*. New York: Collier.

Cormier, R. (1974). *The Chocolate War*. New York: Dell.

Cormier, R. (1977). *I Am the Cheese*. New York: Dell.

Cormier, R. (1979). *After the First Death*. New York: Dell.

Cormier, R. (1980). *8 Plus 1*. New York: Pantheon.

Cormier, R. (1983). *The Bumblebee Flies Anyway*. New York: Dell.

Cormier, R. (1985). *Beyond the Chocolate War*. New York: Dell.

Cormier, R. (1988). *Fade*. New York: Dell.

*Cormier, R. (1990). *Other Bells for Us to Ring*. New York: Delacorte.

Cormier, R. (1991). *We All Fall Down*. New York: Delacorte.

Cormier, R. (1992). *Tunes for Bears to Dance To*. New York: Delacorte.

*Cormier, R. (1995). *In the Middle of the Night*. New York: Delacorte.

Cormier, R. (1997). *Tenderness*. New York: Delacorte.

Cormier, R. (1998). *Heroes*. New York: Delacorte.

*Cormier, R. (1999). *Frenchtown Summer*. New York: Delacorte.

*Cormier, R. (2001). *Rag and the Bone Shop*. New York: Random House.

Corrigan, E. (2002). *You Remind Me of You: A Poetry Memoir*. New York: Push.

Cotner, J. (Ed.). (2002). *Words for the Heart and Soul*. New York: HarperCollins.

Coville, B. (1998). *A Glory of Unicorns*. New York: Scholastic.

Coville, B. (1999). *Odder than Ever*. Orlando, FL: Harcourt Brace.

Covington, D. (1991). *Lizard*. New York: Delacorte.

Crane, S. (1894). *The Red Badge of Courage*.

*Creech, S. (1994). *Walk Two Moons*. New York: HarperCollins.

*Creech, S. (1998). *Bloomability*. New York: HarperCollins.

*Crew, L. (1989). *Children of the River*. New York: Delacorte.

Crew, L. (2001). *Brides of Eden: A True Story Imagined*. New York: HarperCollins.

Crisman, R. (1993). *Racing the Iditarod Trail*. New York: Dillon Press.

Crossroads: Classic Themes in Young Adult Literature. (1995). Glenview, IL: Scott, Foresman.

Crow, C. (2002). *Mississippi Trial—1955*. New York: Putnam.

Crow, C. (2003). *Getting Away with Murder: The True Story of the Emmett Till Case*. New York: Dial.

Crutcher, C. (1983). *Running Loose*. New York: Dell.

Crutcher, C. (1986). *Stotan!* New York: Dell.

Crutcher, C. (1987). *The Crazy Horse Electric Game*. New York: Dell.

Crutcher, C. (1989). *Chinese Handcuffs*. New York: Greenwillow.

Crutcher, C. (1991). *Athletic Shorts*. New York: Greenwillow.

Crutcher, C. (1991). A Brief Moment in the Life of Angus Bethune. In *Athletic Shorts* (pp. 5–25). New York: Greenwillow.

Crutcher, C. (1993). *Staying Fat for Sarah Byrnes*. New York: Greenwillow.

Crutcher, C. (1995). *Ironman*. New York: Greenwillow.

Crutcher, C. (2001). *Whale Talk*. New York: HarperCollins.

Crutcher, C. (2003). *King of the Mild Frontier*. New York: HarperCollins.

cummings, e. e. (1950). Swim So Now Million Many Worlds in Each. In *Xaipe*. New York: Liveright.

cummings, e. e. (1994). As is the Sea Marvelous. In G. J. Firmage (Ed.), *E. E. Cummings: Complete Poems 1904–1962* (p. 45). New York: Liveright.

Cummings, P. (2004). *Red Kayak*. New York: Dutton.

*Curtis, C. P. (1995). *The Watsons Go to Birmingham—1963*. New York: Bantam Doubleday Dell.

*Curtis, C. P. (1999). *Bud, Not Buddy*. New York: Delacorte.

*Curtis, C. P. (2004). *Bucking the Sarge*. New York: Random House.

*Daly, J. (1989). *Presenting S. E. Hinton*. New York: Twayne.

*Daly, M. (1942). *Seventeenth Summer*. New York: Dodd, Mead.

*Daly, M. (1990). *First a Dream*. New York: Scholastic.

Danticat, E. (1995). *Breath, Eyes, Memory*. New York: Random House.

Danticat, E. (1996). *Krik? Krak! Stories*. New York: Random House.

Danticat, E. (2002). *Behind the Mountains.* London: Orchard.

*Danziger, P. (1974). *The Cat Ate My Gymsuit.* New York: Dell.

*Danziger, P. (1983). *The Divorce Express.* New York: Dell.

*Danziger, P. (1986). *This Place Has No Atmosphere.* New York: Dell.

*Danziger, P. (1992). *Not for a Billion Gazillion Dollars.* New York: Delacorte.

Davis, J. (1988). *Sex Education.* New York: Dell.

*Davis, J., & Davis, H. (1991). *Presenting William Sleator.* New York: Twayne.

Davis, O. (1982). *Langston.* New York: Delacorte.

Davis, R. F. (2003). *Jake Riley: Irreparably Damaged.* New York: HarperCollins.

Davis, T. (1993). *If Rock and Roll Were a Machine.* New York: Delacorte.

Davis, T. (1997). *Presenting Chris Crutcher.* New York: Twayne.

Deem, J. (1994). *3 NB's of Julian Drew.* Boston: Houghton Mifflin.

DeFelice, C. (2000). *Death at Devil's Bridge.* New York: Farrar, Straus & Giroux.

DeFelice, D. (2003). *Under the Same Sky.* New York: Farrar, Straus & Giroux.

Defoe, D. (1719). *The Life and Strange Surprising Adventures of Robinson Crusoe.*

DeGuzman, M. (2002). *Melonhead.* New York: Farrar, Straus & Giroux.

De Hoyos, A., Milligan, B., & Milligan, M. (1998). *Floricanto Si!: A Collection of Latina Poetry.* New York: Viking.

Desetta, A., & Kozol, J. (1996). *The Heart Knows Something Different.* New York: Persea.

Dessair, H. T. (2002). *Born Confused.* New York: Scholastic.

Dessen, S. (2000). *Dreamland.* New York: Puffin.

Dessen, S. (2004). *The Truth about Forever.* New York: Viking Press.

Deuker, C. (2000). *High Hoops.* Boston: Houghton Mifflin.

Deuker, C. (2003). *High Heat.* Boston: Houghton Mifflin.

*Dhondy, F. (1993). *Black Swan.* Boston: Houghton Mifflin.

Dickens, C. (1859). *A Tale of Two Cities.*

Dickens, C. (1960–1961). *Great Expectations.*

Dickinson, P. (1988). *Eva.* New York: Dell.

Donnelly, J. (2003). *A Northern Light.* Orlando, FL: Harcourt.

Donoghue, E. (1993). *Kissing the Witch: Old Tales in New Skins.* New York: State Mutual Book and Periodical Service.

Dowell, F. O. (2000). *Dovey Coe.* New York: Atheneum.

Doyle, A. C. (1892). *The Adventures of Sherlock Holmes (and Others).*

Draper, S. (1994). *Tears of a Tiger.* New York: Aladdin.

Draper, S. (1997). *Forged by Fire.* New York: Atheneum.

*Draper, S. (1999). *Romiette and Julio.* New York: Atheneum.

*Draper, S. (2002). *Double Dutch.* New York: Atheneum.

Draper, S. (2003). *Battle of Jericho.* New York: Atheneum.

*Dresbach, G. (1990). *The Cave.* In R. Peck (Ed.), *Sounds and Silences* (pp. 121–130). New York: Dell.

Drimmer, F. (1985). *The Elephant Man.* New York: G. P. Putnam's Sons.

*Duncan, L. (1978). *Killing Mr. Griffin.* New York: Dell.

*Duncan, L. (1982). *Chapters: My Growth as a Writer.* Boston: Little, Brown.

*Duncan, L. (1989). *Don't Look behind You.* New York: Dell.

Duncan, L. (1992). *Who Killed My Daughter?* New York: Dell.

Duncan, L. (1993). *On the Edge: Stories at the Brink.* New York: Simon Pulse.

*Duncan, L. (1996). *Night Terrors: Stories of Shadow and Substance.* New York: Simon & Schuster.

*Duncan, L. (1997). *Gallows Hill*. New York: Bantam Doubleday Dell.

Duncan, L. (1998). *Trapped! Cages of the Mind and Body*. New York: Simon & Schuster.

Dunning, S., Lueders, E., & Smith, H. (Eds.). (1969). *Some Haystacks Don't Even Have Any Needles and Other Complete Modern Poems*. New York: Lothrop, Lee & Shepard.

Dunning, S., Lueders, E., & Smith, H. (Eds.). (1995). *Reflections on a Gift of Watermelon Pickle* (2nd ed.). Glenview, IL: Scott, Foresman.

Edelman, B. (Ed.). (1985). *Dear America: Letters Home from Vietnam*. New York: Norton.

Ellis, D. (2000). *The Breadwinner*. Vancouver, BC: Groundwood/Douglas & McIntyre.

Ellis, D. (2002). *Parvana's Journey*. Vancouver, BC: Groundwood/Douglas & McIntyre.

Ellis, D. (2004). *Mud City*. Vancouver, BC: Groundwood/Douglas & McIntyre.

Ellis, S. (1998). *Back of Beyond: Stories of the Supernatural*. New York: McElderry.

Emmens, C. (1991). *The Abortion Controversy*. New York: Julian Messner.

English, K. (1999). *Francie*. New York: Farrar, Straus & Giroux.

Enzensberger, H. M. (1997). *The Number Devil: A Mathematical Adventure*. New York: Metropolitan Books.

*Esbensen, B., & Stadler, J. (1987). *Words with Wrinkled Knees*. New York: HarperCollins.

Fama, E. (2002). *Overboard*. Chicago: Cricket Books.

Farmer, N. (1994). *The Ear, the Eye, and the Arm*. New York: Orchard.

Farmer, N. (2002). *The House of the Scorpion*. New York: Atheneum.

Farmer, N. (2004). *The Sea Trolls*. New York: Atheneum.

Farrell, J. (1998). *Invisible Enemies: Stories of Infectious Diseases*. New York: Farrar, Straus & Giroux.

*Felsen, H. G. (1950). *Hot Rod*. New York: Dutton.

*Felsen, H. G. (1952). *Two and the Town*. New York: Scribner's.

*Felsen, H. G. (1953). *Street Rod*. New York: Random House.

*Felsen, H. G. (1958). *Crash Club*. New York: Random House.

Filipovac, A. (1994). *Zlata's Diary: A Child's Life in Sarajevo*. New York: Viking.

Finley, M. F. (1867). *Elsie Dinsmore* (series).

*Finley, M. P. (1998). *Soaring Eagle*. Austin, TX: Eakin Press.

*Finley, M. P. (2000). *White Grizzly*. Palmer Lake, CO: Filter Press.

*Finley, M. P. (2003). *Meadow Lark*. Palm Lake, CO: Filter Press.

Fitzgerald, F. S. (1925). *The Great Gatsby*.

Fletcher, S. (2001). *Walk across the Sea*. New York: Atheneum.

Flinn, A. (2001). *Breathing Underwater*. New York: HarperCollins.

Flinn, A. (2002). *Breaking Point*. New York: Harper Tempest.

*Forbes, E. (1944). *Johnny Tremain*. Boston: Houghton Mifflin.

Ford, M. T. (1993). *100 Questions and Answers about AIDS: What You Need to Know Now*. New York: Beech Tree.

Ford, M. T. (1995). *The Voice of AIDS*. New York: Beech Tree.

Ford, M. T. (1998). *Outspoken: Role Models from the Lesbian and Gay Community*. New York: Morrow.

*Forman, J. (1988). *Presenting Paul Zindel*. New York: Twayne.

*Fradin, D. (1999). *Biography of Samuel Adams*. New York: Lothrop, Lee & Shepard.

*Frank, A. (1956). *Anne Frank: The Diary of a Young Girl*. New York: Random House.

Frank, E. R. (2002). *America*. New York: Simon & Schuster.

Frank, E. R. (2003). *Friction*. New York: Simon & Schuster.

Fraustino, L. R. (1998). *Dirty Laundry: Stories about Family Secrets*. New York: Viking.

Fraustino, L. R. (2002). *Soul Searching: Thirteen Stories about Faith and Belief*. New York: Simon & Schuster.

Frederich, M. (2003). *True Meaning of Cleavage*. New York: Atheneum.

Frederich, M. (2004). *Head Games*. New York: Atheneum.

*Freedman, R. (1994). *Kids at Work*. New York: Clarion.

*Freedman, R. (1998). *Martha Graham: A Dancer's Life*. New York: Clarion.

*Freedman, R., & Bull, A. (1996). *The Life and Death of Crazy Horse*. New York: Holiday House.

Freymann-Weyr, G. (2002). *My Heartbeat*. Boston: Houghton Mifflin.

Friedman, C. (1991). *Nightfather*. New York: Persea.

Frost, H. (2003). *Keesha's House*. New York: Farrar, Straus & Giroux.

Frost, H. (2004). *Spinning through the Universe*. New York: Farrar, Straus & Giroux.

Fusco, K. N. (2004). *Tending to Grace*. New York: Knopf.

Gaiman, N. (2002). *Coraline*. New York: HarperCollins.

Gaines, E. (1983). *A Gathering of Old Men*. New York: Knopf.

Gale, D. (Ed.). (1992). *Funny You Should Ask*. New York: Delacorte.

*Gallo, D. (Ed.). (1984). *Sixteen*. New York: Dell.

*Gallo, D. (Ed.). (1987). *Visions*. New York: Dell.

*Gallo, D. (Ed.). (1989). *Connections: Short Stories by Outstanding Writers for Young Adults*. New York: Dell.

*Gallo, D. (1989). *Presenting Richard Peck*. New York: Twayne.

*Gallo, D. (Ed.). (1990). *Center Stage: One-Act Plays for Teenage Readers and Actors*. New York: Harper & Row.

*Gallo, D. (Ed.). (1992). *Short Circuits: Thirteen Shocking Stories by Outstanding Writers for Young Adults*. New York: Bantam Doubleday Dell.

*Gallo, D. (Ed.). (1993). *Join In: Multiethnic Short Stories by Outstanding Writers for Young Adults*. New York: Delacorte.

*Gallo, D. (Ed.). (1993). *Within Reach: Ten Stories*. New York: HarperCollins.

*Gallo, D. (Ed.). (1995). *Ultimate Sports*. New York: Delacorte.

*Gallo, D. (Ed.). (1997). *No Easy Answers: Short Stories about Teenagers Making Tough Choices*. New York: Delacorte.

*Gallo, D. (Ed.). (2001). *On the Fringe*. New York: Penguin USA.

*Gallo, D. (Ed.). (2003). *Destination Unexpected*. Boston: Candlewick.

*Gallo, D. (Ed.). (2004). *First Crossing: Stories about Teen Immigrants*. New York: Candlewick Press.

*Gantos, J. (1998). *Joey Pigza Swallowed the Key*. New York: Farrar, Straus & Giroux.

*Gantos, J. (2000). *Joey Pigza Loses Control*. New York: HarperCollins.

Gantos, J. (2002). *Hole in My Life*. New York: Farrar, Straus & Giroux.

*Gantos, J. (2002). *What Would Joey Do?* New York: Farrar, Straus & Giroux.

Garden, N. (1999). *The Year They Burned the Books*. New York: Farrar, Straus & Giroux.

Garland, S. (1992). *Song of the Buffalo Boy*. Orlando, FL: Harcourt Brace.

Garner, A. (2004). *Families Like Mine: Children of Gay Parents Tell It Like It Is*. New York: HarperCollins.

*George, J. (1972). *Julie of the Wolves*. New York: Harper & Row.

*George, J. (1994). *Julie*. New York: HarperCollins.

*George, J. (1997). *Julie's Wolf Pack*. New York: HarperCollins.

George, J. (1999). *Frightful's Mountain*. New York: Dutton.

George, J. (2001). *My Side of the Mountain*. New York: Puffin Books.

*Giblin, J. C. (1997). *Charles A. Lindbergh: A Human Hero*. New York: Clarion.

Gibson, W. (1959). *The Miracle Worker*. New York: French.

Gifaldi, D. (1998). *Rearranging and Other Stories*. New York: Simon & Schuster.

Gilbert, B. S. (2000). *Broken Chords*. New York: Random House.

Gill, S. (1998). *Iditarod: The Last Great Race to Nome: Curriculum Guide.* New York: Paws IV.

*Gilmore, K. (1993). *Jason and the Bard.* Boston: Houghton Mifflin.

Giovanni, N. (2002). *Quilting the Black-Eyed Pea.* New York: William Morrow.

*Glenn, M. (1982). *Class Dismissed! High School Poems.* New York: Clarion.

*Glenn, M. (1986). *Class Dismissed II: More High School Poems.* New York: Clarion.

*Glenn, M. (1987). *Back to Class.* New York: Clarion.

*Glenn, M. (1991). *My Friend's Got This Problem, Mr. Candler.* New York: Clarion.

*Glenn, M. (1996). *Who Killed Mr. Chippendale? A Mystery in Poems.* New York: Dutton.

*Glenn, M. (1997). *Jump Ball: A Basketball Season in Poems.* New York: Dutton.

*Glenn, M. (1997). *The Taking of Room 114: A Hostage Drama in Poems.* New York: Dutton/Lodestar.

*Glenn, M. (1999). *Foreign Exchange: A Mystery in Poems.* New York: Morrow Junior Books.

*Glenn, M. (2000). *Split Image.* New York: Dutton.

Glovach, L. (1998). *Beauty Queen.* New York: HarperCollins.

Going, E. L. (2003). *Fat Kid Rules the World.* New York: Putnam.

Gold, R. (Ed.). (1981). *Point of Departure: 19 Stories of Youth and Discovery.* New York: Dell.

Gold, R. (Ed.). (1981). *Stepping Stones: 17 Powerful Stories of Growing Up.* New York: Dell.

Golding, W. (1955). *Lord of the Flies.* New York: Coward, McCann.

*Gorog, J. (1993). *Please Do Not Touch: A Collection of Stories.* New York: Scholastic.

*Gorog, J. (1996). *When Nobody's Home: 15 Baby-Sitting Tales of Terror.* New York: Scholastic.

Gorrell, G. K. (2003). *Working Like a Dog: The Story of Working Dogs through History.* New York: Tundra Books.

Gotesfeld, J., & Bennett, C. (2001). *Anne Frank and Me.* New York: Putnam.

Graham, R. (1972). *Dove.* New York: Harper & Row.

Grant, C. (1998). *The White Horse.* New York: Atheneum.

Gray, H., Phillips, S., & Farney, E. (1998). *Real Girl/Real World: Tools for Finding Your True Self.* Seal Press.

Gregory, J. (2003). *Sickened: The True Story of a Lost Childhood.* New York: Random House.

Greene, B. (1973). *Summer of My German Soldier.* New York: Dial.

Greene, B. (1989). *Homecoming: When the Soldiers Returned from Vietnam.* New York: G. P. Putnam's Sons.

Greene, B. (1991). *The Drowning of Stephan Jones.* New York: Bantam.

Greene, B. (2004). *I've Already Forgotten Your Name, Philip Hall.* New York: HarperCollins.

Grey, Z. (1906). *The Spirit of the Border.*

Grey, Z. (1912). *Riders of the Purple Sage.*

Grey, Z. (1923). *The Wanderers of the Wasteland.*

Grimes, N. (1998). *A Dime a Dozen.* New York: Penguin Putnam.

Grimes, N. (2002). *Bronx Masquerade.* New York: Dial.

Grollman, E. (1993). *Straight Talk about Death for Teenagers: How to Cope with Losing Someone You Love.* Boston: Beacon.

*Grove, V. (1993). *Rimwalkers.* New York: G. P. Putnam's Sons.

*Grove, V. (1995). *The Crystal Garden.* New York: G. P. Putnam's Sons.

*Grove, V. (1998). *Reaching Dustin.* New York: G. P. Putnam's Sons.

Grove, V. (1999). *The Star Place.* New York: G. P. Putnam's Sons.

Grove, V. (2000). *Destiny.* New York: G. P. Putnam's Sons.

Guest, J. (1977). *Ordinary People.* New York: Ballantine.

* *The Guinness Book of World Records.* (1997). New York: Bantam.

Gunn, P., & Smith, P. C. (1996). *As Long as the Rivers Flow: The Stories of Nine Native Americans.* New York: Scholastic.

Haddix, M. P. (2004). *The House on the Gulf.* New York: Simon & Schuster.

Haddon, M. (2003). *The Curious Incident of the Dog in the Night-time.* New York: Doubleday.

*Hall, L. F. (1997). *Perk! The Story of a Teenager with Bulimia.* Carlsbad, CA: Gurze Books.

Halliday, J. (2003). *Shooting Monarchs.* New York: Simon & Schuster.

Hallowell, J. (2004). *The Annunciation of Francesca Dunn: A Novel.* New York: HarperCollins.

Halvorson, M. (2003). *Bull Rider.* Custer, WA: Orca.

*Hamilton, V. (1974). *M. C. Higgins, The Great.* New York: Macmillan.

Hamilton, V. (1984). *A Little Love.* New York: Berkley.

Hamilton, V. (1987). *The People Could Fly: American Black Folktales.* New York: Knopf.

Hamilton, V. (1987). *A White Romance.* New York: Philomel.

Hamilton, V. (1993). *Plain City.* New York: Blue Sky Press.

Hamilton, V. (2002). *Time Pieces: The Book of Times.* New York: Blue Sky/Scholastic.

Harrar, G. (2003). *Not as Crazy as I Seem.* Boston: Houghton Mifflin.

Hartinger, B. (2003). *Geography Club.* New York: HarperTempest.

Haskins, J. (1990). *Black Dance in America.* New York: HarperCollins.

Haskins, J. (1992). *One More River to Cross.* New York: Scholastic.

Hass, J. (2004). *Hoofprints: Horse Poems.* New York: Greenwillow.

Hausman, G., & Hinds, U. (2001). *The Jacob Ladder.* London: Orchard.

Hautman, P. (2003). *Sweetblood.* New York: Simon & Schuster.

Hawthorne, N. (1850). *The Scarlet Letter.*

Hayden, R. (1985). *Collected Poems.* New York: Liveright.

Hayes, J. (n.d.). *Seven Ages of Anne.* Charlottesville, VA: New Plays.

Haynes, D., & Landsman, J. (Eds.). (1998). *Welcome to Your Life: Writings for the Heart of Young America.* New York: Milweed.

*Head, A. (1967). *Mr. and Mrs. Bo Jo Jones.* New York: New American Library.

Hearne, B. (2003). *The Canine Connections: Stories about Dogs and People.* New York: Margaret K McElderry.

Hemingway, E. (1952). *The Old Man and the Sea.* New York: Prentice-Hall.

Heneghan, J. (1994). *Torn Away.* New York: Puffin.

*Henkes, K. (2003). *Olive's Ocean.* New York: Greenwillow.

Hentoff, N. (1981). *Does This School Have Capital Punishment?* New York: Dell.

*Hentoff, N. (1982). *The Day They Came to Arrest the Book.* New York: Dell.

Heron, A. (Ed.). (1995). *Two Teenagers in Twenty: Writings by Gay and Lesbian Youth.* Los Angeles: Alyson.

*Herriot, J. (1972). *All Creatures Great and Small.* New York: St. Martin's Press.

*Hesse, K. (1994). *Phoenix Rising.* New York: Holt.

*Hesse, K. (1996). *The Music of Dolphins.* New York: Scholastic.

*Hesse, K. (1997). *Out of the Dust.* New York: Scholastic.

*Hesse, K. (2001). *Witness.* New York: Scholastic.

*Hesse, K. (2003). *Aleutian Sparrow.* New York: Simon & Schuster.

*Hesser, T. S. (1998). *Kissing Doorknobs.* New York: Delacorte.

Hettinga, D. R. (1993). *Presenting Madeleine L'Engle.* New York: Twayne.

*Hewett, L. (1998). *Lives of Our Own.* New York: Dutton.

High, L. O. (2004). *Sister Slam and the Poetic Motormouth Roadtrip.* New York: Bloomsbury.

Hinojosa, M. (1995). *Crews.* Orlando, FL: Harcourt Brace.

*Hinton, S. E. (1967). *The Outsiders*. New York: Dell.

*Hinton, S. E. (1979). *Tex*. New York: Dell.

*Hinton, S. E. (1988). *Taming the Star Runner*. New York: Dell.

*Hinton, S. E. (1989). *That Was Then, This Is Now*. New York: Dell.

Hipple, T. (1990). *Presenting Sue Ellen Bridgers*. New York: Twayne.

Hobbs, V. (2001). *Sonny's War*. New York: Farrar, Straus & Giroux.

Hobbs, V. (2004). *Letting Go of Bobby James, or How I Found my Self of Steam*. New York: Farrar, Straus & Giroux.

*Hobbs, W. (1988). *Changes in Latitude*. New York: Horizons.

*Hobbs, W. (1989). *Bearstone*. New York: Avon.

*Hobbs, W. (1991). *Downriver*. New York: Atheneum.

*Hobbs, W. (1992). *The Big Wander*. New York: Atheneum.

*Hobbs, W. (1993). *Beardance*. New York: Atheneum.

*Hobbs, W. (1995). *Kokopelli's Flute*. New York: Atheneum.

*Hobbs, W. (1996). *Far North*. New York: Morrow Junior Books.

*Hobbs, W. (1997). *Ghost Canoe*. New York: Morrow Junior Books.

*Hobbs, W. (1997). *River Thunder*. New York: Bantam Doubleday Dell.

*Hobbs, W. (1998). *The Maze*. New York: Morrow Junior Books.

*Hobbs, W. (1999). *Jason's Gold*. New York: Morrow Junior Books.

*Hobbs, W. (2001). *Down the Yukon*. New York: HarperCollins.

*Hobbs, W. (2002). *Wild Man Island*. New York: HarperCollins.

*Hobbs, W. (2003). *Jackie's Wild Seattle*. New York: HarperCollins.

*Hobbs, W. (2004). *Leaving Protection*. New York: HarperCollins.

Hoffman, A. (2003). *Green Angel*. New York: Scholastic.

*Hohler, R. (1986). *I Touch the Future: The Story of Christa McAuliffe*. New York: Random House.

*Holbrook, S. (1990). *The Dog Ate My Homework*. Bay Village, OH: KID POEMS.

*Holbrook, S. (1990). *Feelings Make Me Real*. Bay Village, OH: KID POEMS.

*Holbrook, S. (1990). *Some Families*. Bay Village, OH: KID POEMS.

*Holbrook, S. (1992). *I Never Said I Wasn't Difficult*. Bay Village, OH: KID POEMS.

*Holbrook, S. (1995). *Nothing's the End of the World*. Honesdale, PA: Boyds Mills Press.

*Holbrook, S. (1996). *Chicks Up Front*. Honesdale, PA: Boyds Mills Press.

*Holbrook, S. (1997). *Which Way to the Dragon? Poems for the Coming on Strong*. Honesdale, PA: Boyds Mills Press.

*Holbrook, S. (1998). *Walking on the Boundaries of Change: Poems of Transition*. Honesdale, PA: Boyds Mills Press.

*Holbrook, S. (2002). *Wham! It's a Poetry Jam*. Honesdale, PA: Boyds Mills Press.

Holt, K. W. (2003). *Keeper of the Night*. New York: Henry Holt.

*Holtze, S. (1989). *Presenting Norma Fox Mazer*. New York: Twayne.

Homer. (c. 850 B.C.E.). *The Odyssey*.

Hoobler, D., & Hoobler, T. (2003) *We Are Americans: Voices of the Immigrant Experience*. New York: Scholastic.

*Hope, L. L. (1904). *The Bobbsey Twins* (series).

Hopkins, E. (2004). *Crank*. New York: Simon Pulse.

Houston, J. D., & Houston, J. W. (1973). *Farewell to Manzanar*. Boston: Houghton Mifflin.

Howe, J. (1997). *The Watcher*. New York: Atheneum.

Howe, J. (Ed.). (2001). *The Color of Absence: 12 Stories about Loss and Hope*. New York: Pulse Books.

Howe, J. (Ed.). (2003). *Thirteen Stories that Capture the Agony and Ecstasy of Being Thirteen*. New York: Pulse Books.

Howker, J. (Ed.). (1985). *Badger on the Barge and Other Stories*. New York: Greenwillow.

Hughes, D. (2004). *Soldier Boys*. New York: Atheneum.

Hughes, L. (1990). *Selected Poems*. New York: Random House.

Hugle, K. (2003). *GLBTQ. The Survival Guide for Queer and Questioning Teens*. Minneapolis, MN: Free Spirit.

*Hunt, I. (1964). *Across Five Aprils*. New York: Grosset & Dunlap.

*Hunt, I. (1966). *Up a Road Slowly*. New York: Berkley.

Hunt, I. (1987). *The Lottery Rose*. New York: Berkley.

*Hunter, K. (1968). *The Soul Brothers and Sister Lou*. New York: Szebineh's Sons.

Huntington, G. (2003). *Demon Witch*. New York: HarperCollins.

*Hurst, C. O., & Otis, R. (2003). *A Killing in Plymouth Colony*. Boston: Houghton Mifflin.

Hurston, Z. N. (1990). *Their Eyes Were Watching God*. New York: Perennial.

Huxley, A. (1998). *Brave New World*. New York: Perennial.

*Irwin, H. (1984). *I Be Somebody*. New York: NAL-Penguin.

*Irwin, H. (1992). *The Original Freddie Ackerman*. New York: McElderry.

Jackson, S. (1949). *The Lottery*.

James, B. (2003). *Tomorrow, Maybe*. New York: Scholastic.

*Janeczko, P. (Ed.). (1979). *Postcard Poems: A Collection of Poetry for Sharing*. New York: Bradbury.

*Janeczko, P. (Ed.). (1981). *Don't Forget to Fly*. New York: Bradbury.

*Janeczko, P. (Ed.). (1983). *Poetspeak: In Their Work, about Their Work*. New York: Bradbury.

*Janeczko, P. (Ed.). (1984). *Strings: A Gathering of Family Poems*. New York: Bradbury.

*Janeczko, P. (Ed.). (1985). *Pocket Poems: Selected for a Journey*. New York: Bradbury.

*Janeczko, P. (1986). *Bridges to Cross*. New York: Macmillan.

*Janeczko, P. (Ed.). (1987). *Going Over to Your Place: Poems for Each Other*. New York: Bradbury.

*Janeczko, P. (Ed.). (1990). *The Place My Words Are Looking For*. New York: Bradbury.

*Janeczko, P. (Ed.). (1991). *Preposterous: Poems of Youth*. New York: Orchard.

*Janeczko, P. (1993). *Stardust Hotel*. New York: Orchard.

*Janeczko, P. (1994). *Poetry from A to Z*. New York: Bradbury.

*Janeczko, P. (Ed.). (1999). *Very Best (Almost) Friends: Poems of Friendship*. New York: Candlewick Press.

*Janeczko, P. (2001). *Dirty Laundry Piles: Different Poems in Different Voices*. New York: Candlestick Press.

*Janeczko, P. (2001). *How to Write Poetry*. New York: Scholastic.

*Janeczko, P. (2002). *Seeing the Blue Petween: Advice and Inspirations for Young Poets*. New York: Candlestick Press.

*Janeczko, P. (2003). *Opening a Door: Reading Poetry in the Middle School Classroom*. New York: Candlestick Press.

*Janeczko, P. (2004). *Worlds Afire: The Hartford Circus Fire of 1944*. New York: Candlestick Press.

Janeway, J. (1700). *A Token for Children: Being an Exact Account of the Conversion, Holy and Exemplary Lives & Joyful Deaths of Several Young Children to Which Is Added: A Token for the Children of New England*.

Jenkins, A. M. (2001). *Damage*. New York: HarperCollins.

Jennings, C., & Berghammer, G. (n.d.). *Theatre for Youth: Twelve Plays with Mature Themes*. New Orleans, LA: Anchorage.

*Johnson, A. (1998). *Heaven*. New York: Simon & Schuster.

*Johnson, A. (1998). *The Other Side: Shorter Poems*. New York: Orchard.

Johnson, A. (2002). *Looking for Red*. New York: Simon & Schuster.

Johnson, A. (2003). *A Cool Moonlight.* New York: Dial.

*Johnson, A. (2003). *The First Park Last.* New York: Simon & Schuster.

Johnson, M. (2004). *The Bermudez Triangle.* New York: Penguin.

Johnston, A., & Steinem, G. (1997). *Girls Speak Out: Finding Your True Self.* New York: Scholastic.

Johnston, J. (Ed.). (1999). *Love Ya Like a Sister: A Story of Friendship.* New York: Tundra/ McClelland & Stewart.

Jones, D. (Ed.). (1985). *Warlock at the Wheel and Other Stories.* New York: Greenwillow.

Jones, R. (1993). *The Beginning of Unbelief.* New York: Atheneum.

Joseph, L. (2000). *The Color of my Words.* New York: Joanna Cotler Books.

Joyce, J. (1934). *Ulysses.*

Jukes, M., & Tilley, D. (1998). *Growing Up: It's a Girl Thing.* New York: Knopf.

Kadohata, C. (2004). *Kira-Rira.* New York: Simon & Schuster.

*Kamerman, S. E. (Ed.). (1999). *Plays of Black Americans.* Boston: Plays.

*Kassem, L. (1990). *A Haunting in Williamsburg.* New York: Avon.

*Katz, W. (1999). *Black Pioneers: An Untold Story.* New York: Simon & Schuster.

*Kaye, M. (1993). *Real Heroes.* Orlando, FL: Harcourt Brace.

Keach, B. (1707). *War with the Devil, or The Young Man's Conflict with the Powers of Darkness, in a Dialogue Discovering the Corruption and Vanity of Youth, the Horrible Nature of Sin, and the Deplorable Condition of Fallen Man.*

Kennemore, T. (1984). *Changing Times.* New York: Faber & Faber.

*Kerr, M. E. (1983). *Me, Me, Me, Me, Me, Not a Novel.* New York: Harper & Row.

Kerr, M. E. (1986). *Night Kites.* New York: Harper & Row.

Kerr, M. E. (1994). *Deliver Us from Evie.* New York: HarperCollins.

Kerr, M. E. (1997). *"Hello," I Lied.* New York: HarperCollins.

Kerr, M. E. (1998). *Blood on the Forehead: What I Know about Writing.* New York: HarperCollins.

Kidd, S. M. (2002). *The Secret Life of Bees.* New York: Penguin.

King, S. (2002). *On Writing: A Memoir of the Craft.* New York: Scribner.

King, C., & Osborne, L. (1997). *Oh, Freedom!* New York: Knopf.

Kittredge, M. (1991). *Teens with AIDS Speak Out.* New York: Julian Messner.

Klass, D. (1994). *California Blue.* New York: Scholastic.

Klass, D. (1996). *Danger Zone.* New York: Scholastic.

Klass, D. (2002). *You Don't Know Me.* New York: HarperCollins.

Klass, D. (2003). *Home of the Braves.* New York: Farrar, Straus & Giroux.

Klause, A. (1997). *Blood and Chocolate.* New York: Delacorte.

Knowles, J. (1960). *A Separate Peace.* New York: Macmillan.

Koertge, R. (2003). *Shakespeare Bats Cleanup.* New York: Candlestick Press.

Konigsburg, E. L. (2004). *The Outcasts of 19 Schuyler Place.* New York: Atheneum.

Korman, G. (1985). *Don't Care High.* New York: Scholastic.

*Korman, G. (1987). *A Semester in the Life of a Garbage Bag.* New York: Scholastic.

*Korman, G. (2001). *No More Dead Dogs.* New York: Hyperion.

Korman, G. (2002). *Son of the Mob.* New York: Hyperion.

Korman, G. (2004). *Son of the Mob: Hollywood Hustle.* New York: Hyperion.

Krishnaswami, U. (2004). *Naming Maya.* New York: Farrar, Straus & Giroux.

Kuklin, S. (1989). *Fighting Back: What Some People Are Doing about AIDS.* New York: G. P. Putnam's Sons.

Kuklin, S. (1993). *Speaking Out: Teenagers Talk on Sex, Race, and Identity.* New York: G. P. Putnam's Sons.

Kuklin, S. (1996). *Irrepressible Spirit: Conversations with Human Rights Activists.* New York: G. P. Putnam's.

Kuklin, S. (1998). *Iqbal Masih and the Crusaders against Child Slavery.* New York: Holt.

Lamb, W. (Ed.). (1986). *Meeting the Winter Bike Rider and Other Prize Winning Plays.* New York: Dell.

Lane, R. W. (1934). *Let the Hurricane Roar.* New York: Longmans, Green.

Lapine, W., & Pagel, S. (Eds.). (1997). *Absolute Magnitude.* New York: St. Martin's Press.

*Laurents, A. (1956). *West Side Story in Romeo and Juliet/West Side Story.* New York: Dell.

Lawrence, D. H. (1971). Whales Weep Not. In W. Roberts & V. de Sola Pinto (Eds.), *The Complete Poems of D. H. Lawrence* (pp. 694–695). New York: Viking Penguin.

Lawrence, J., & Lee, R. (1972). *The Night Thoreau Spent in Jail.* New York: Bantam.

Layne, S. (2001) *This Side of Paradise.* New York: North Star Books.

Lederer, R. (1987). *Anguished English.* Charleston, SC: Wyrick.

Lee, H. (1960). *To Kill a Mockingbird.* New York: Fawcett.

Lee, M. G. (1994). *Saying Goodbye.* Boston: Houghton Mifflin.

Lee, M. G. (1996). *Necessary Roughness.* New York: HarperCollins.

*Le Guin, U. K. (1976). *Very Far Away from Anywhere Else.* New York: Atheneum.

*L'Engle, M. (1968). *A Wrinkle in Time.* New York: Dell.

Les Becquets, D. (2001). *The Stones of Mourning Creek.* New York: Winslow Press.

Lester, J. (1984). *Do Lord, Remember Me.* New York: Holt.

Lester, J. (1995). *Othello: A Novel.* New York: Scholastic.

Leuders, E., & St. John, P. (Eds.). (1976). *Zero Makes Me Hungry: A Collection of Poems for Today.* New York: Scott, Foresman.

*Levertov, D. (1990). Gone Away. In R. Peck (Ed.), *Sounds and Silences* (pp. 47–59). New York: Dell.

Levithan, D. (2003). *Boy Meets Boy.* New York: Knopf.

Lewis, R. (2004). *The Flame Tree.* New York: Simon & Schuster.

Life through Poetry: Original Poems by Young Adults. (2000). Ottawa, KS: The Writing Conference.

*Lipsyte, R. (1967). *The Contender.* New York: Bantam.

*Lipsyte, R. (1977). *One Fat Summer.* New York: Harper & Row.

*Lipsyte, R. (1991). *The Brave.* New York: HarperCollins.

*Lipsyte, R. (1992). *The Chemo Kid.* New York: HarperCollins.

*Lipsyte, R. (1993). *The Chief.* New York: HarperCollins.

*Lipsyte, R. (2003). *Warrior Angel.* New York: HarperCollins.

Loughery, J. (Ed.). (1995). *Into the Widening World: International Coming-of-Age Stories.* New York: Persea.

Lowery, C. P. (2003). *The Fattening Hut.* Boston: Houghton Mifflin.

*Lowry, L. (1989). *Number the Stars.* New York: Dell.

*Lowry, L. (1993). *The Giver.* Boston: Houghton Mifflin.

*Lowry, L. (2000). *Gathering Blue.* Boston Houghton Mifflin.

*Lowry, L. (2003). *The Silent Boy.* Boston: Houghton Mifflin.

*Macaulay, D. (1988). *The Way Things Work.* Boston: Houghton Mifflin.

*Macaulay, D. (1998). *The New Way Things Work.* Boston: Houghton Mifflin.

*Macaulay, D. (2003). *Mosque.* Boston: Houghton Mifflin.

Mach, T. (2003). *Birdland.* New York: Scholastic.

Mackler, C. (2002). *Love and Other Four Letter Words*. New York: Candlewick Press.

Mackler, C. (2003). *The Earth, My Butt, and Other Big Round Things*. New York: Candlewick Press.

MacPhail, C. (2003). *Dark Waters*. New York: Bloomsbury.

Mahy, M. (2004). *Alchemy*. New York: Simon Pulse.

Major, K. (1978). *Hold Fast*. New York: Delacorte.

Malmgren, D. (1989). *The Ninth Issue*. New York: Dell.

Malmgren, D. (1990). Large Fears, Little Dreams. In D. Gallo (Ed.), *Center Stage: One Act Plays for Teenage Readers and Actors* (pp. 184–214). New York: Harper & Row.

Mankell, H. (2003). *Secrets in the Fire*. Toronto: Annick Press.

Malory, T. (1485). *Le Morte d' Arthur*.

Marchetta, M. (1999). *Looking for Alibrandi*. New York: Orchard.

Martel, Y. (2001). *Life of Pi*. Orlando, FL: Harcourt.

Martin, A. (1998). *Sunny: Diary Two*. New York: Scholastic.

Martinez, V. (1996). *Parrot in the Oven: Mi Vida*. New York: HarperCollins.

Mason, S. (1986). *Johnny's Song: Poetry of a Vietnam Veteran*. New York: Bantam.

Mastoon, A. (1997). *The Shared Heart: Portraits and Stories Celebrating Lesbian, Gay, and Bisexual Young People*. New York: Morrow.

*Matas, C. (1993). *Daniel's Story*. New York: Dell.

*Matas, C. (1999). *In My Enemy's House*. New York: Simon & Schuster.

*Mathis, S. (1972). *Teacup Full of Roses*. New York: Avon.

*Matthews, L. S. (2004). *Fish*. New York: Random House.

*Maurer, R. (1999). *The Wild Colorado*. New York: Crown.

Mayfield, S. (2004). *Drowning Anna*. New York: Hyperion.

Mazer, A. (Ed.). (1993). *American Street: A Multicultural Anthology of Stories*. New York: Persea.

Mazer, A. (Ed.). (1995). *Going Where I'm Coming From*. New York: Persea.

*Mazer, A. (Ed.). (1998). *A Walk in My World: International Short Stories about Youth*. New York: Persea.

*Mazer, H. (1985). *When the Phone Rang*. New York: Scholastic.

*Mazer, H. (1998). *Twelve Shots: And Other Stories about Guns*. New York: Bantam Doubleday Dell.

*Mazer, H. (2004). *A Boy No More*. New York: Simon & Schuster.

*Mazer, N. F. (1976). *Dear Bill, Remember Me? and Other Stories*. New York: Delacorte.

*Mazer, N. F. (1981). *Taking Terri Mueller*. New York: Avon.

*Mazer, N. F. (1982). *Summer Girls, Love Boys*. New York: Delacorte.

*Mazer, N. F. (1982). *When We First Met*. New York: Scholastic.

Mazer, N. F. (1987). *After the Rain*. New York: Avon.

Mazer, N. F. (1993). *Out of Control*. New York: Morrow.

Mazer, N. F. (1999). *Good Night Maman*. New York: HarperCollins.

McDaniel, W. (1985). Who Said We All Have to Talk Alike? In F. Conlon, R. da Silva, & B. Wilson (Eds.), *The Things That Divide Us* (pp. 1–6). Seattle, WA: Seal.

McGraw, J. (2000). *Life Strategies for Teens*. New York: Fireside Books.

McKay, H. (2004). *Indigos Star*. New York: McElderry.

McKissack, P. C., & McKissack, F. L. (2003). *Days of Jubilee: The End of Slavery in the United States*. New York: Scholastic.

McNamee, G. (1999). *Hate You*. New York: Random House.

McNamee, G. (2003). *Acceleration*. New York: Random House.

*Mead, A. (1998). *Junebug and the Reverend*. New York: Farrar, Straus & Giroux.

*Mead, A. (1999). *Soldier Mom*. New York: Farrar, Straus & Giroux.

Medoff, M. (1980). *Children of a Lesser God*. New York: Dramatists.

Meltzer, M. (1982). *The Truth about the Ku Klux Klan*. New York: Franklin Watts.

Meltzer, M. (1985). *Ain't Gonna Study War No More: The Story of America's Peace Seekers*. New York: Harper & Row.

Meltzer, M. (1988). *Rescue: The Story of How Gentiles Saved Jews in the Holocaust*. New York: HarperCollins.

*Meltzer, M. (1990). *Columbus and the World around Him*. New York: Franklin Watts.

*Meltzer, M. (1998). *Ten Queens: Portraits of Women of Power*. New York: Dutton.

*Meltzer, M. (2003). *Edgar Allen Poe: A Biography*. New York: 21st Century.

Melville, H. (1924). *Billy Budd*.

Merriam, E. (1983). *If Only I Could Tell You: Poems for Young Lovers and Dreamers*. New York: Knopf.

Meyer, C. (1994). *Rio Grande Stories*. Orlando, FL: Harcourt Brace.

Meyer, C. (1995). *Drummers of Jericho*. Orlando, FL: Gulliver/Harcourt Brace.

Meyer, C. (1996). *Gideon's People*. Orlando, FL: Gulliver/Harcourt Brace.

Meyer, C. (1997). *Jubilee Journey*. Orlando, FL: Gulliver/Harcourt Brace.

Meyer, C. (1999). *Mary, Bloody Mary*. Orlando, FL: Harcourt Brace.

Mikaelsen, B. (1998). *Petey*. New York: Hyperion.

Mikaelsen, B. (2001). *Touching Spirit Bear*. New York: HarperCollins.

Mikaelsen, B. (2002). *Red Midnight*. New York: HarperCollins.

Mikaelsen, B. (2004). *Tree Girl*. New York: HarperCollins.

*Miklowitz, G. (1985). *The War between the Classes*. New York: Dell.

Miklowitz, G. (1987). The Fuller Brush Man. In D. Gallo (Ed.), *Visions* (pp. 100–105). New York: Dell.

*Miklowitz, G. (1990). *Anything to Win*. New York: Dell.

Miklowitz, G. (2001). *Secrets in the House of Delgado*. Grand Rapids, MI: Eerdmans.

Miklowitz, G. (2003). *The Enemy Has a Face*. Grand Rapids, MI: Eerdmans.

Miles, B. (1989). *Maudie and Me and the Dirty Book*. New York: Random House.

Miller, A. (1949). *Death of a Salesman*. New York: Viking.

Miller, A. (1952). *The Crucible*. New York: Dramatists.

Miller, B. M. (2003). *Good Women of a Well-Blessed Land: Women's Lives in Colonial America*. Minneapolis, MN: Lerner.

*Miller, R. (1986). *Robyn's Book: A True Diary*. New York: Scholastic.

Milton, J. (1667). *Paradise Lost*.

Min, A. (2002). *Wild Ginger*. Boston: Houghton Mifflin.

Minchin, A. (2004). *The Beat Goes On*. New York: Simon & Schuster.

Minter, J. (2004). *The Insiders*. New York: Bloomsbury.

Minter, J. (2004). *Pass It On: An Insider's Novel*. New York: Bloomsbury.

Mochizuki, K. (2002). *Beacon Hill Boys*. New York: Scholastic.

Monseau, V. (1994). *Presenting Ouida Sebestyn*. New York: Twayne.

Moore, L. (1994). *Lifelines*. New York: Dutton's Children's Books.

Moragne, W. (2001). *Depression*. New York: Millbrook Press.

Moranville, S. B. (2002). *Over the River*. New York: Henry Holt.

More, H. (1795–1798). *Repository Tracts*.

Mori, K. (1993). *Shizuko's Daughter*. New York: Fawcett Juniper.

Moriarty, L. M. (2003). *The Center of Everything*. New York: Hyperion.

Morrison, T. (1987). *Beloved*. New York: Knopf.

Morrison, T. (2004). *Remember: The Journey to School Integration*. Boston: Houghton Mifflin.

Murphy, J. (2003). *An American Plaque: The True and Terrifying Story of the Yellow Fever Epidemic of 1793*. New York: Clarion Books.

Murphy, J. (2003). *Inside the Alamo*. New York: Delacorte Press.

*Myers, W. D. (1981). *Hoops*. New York: Dell.

Myers, W. D. (1987). Jeremiah's Song. In D. Gallo (Ed.), *Visions* (pp. 194–202). New York: Dell.

*Myers, W. D. (1987). *Motown and Didi*. New York: NAL-Dutton.

*Myers, W. D. (1987). *The Outside Shot*. New York: Dell.

Myers, W. D. (1988). *Fallen Angels*. New York: Scholastic.

*Myers, W. D. (1988). *Scorpions*. New York: Harper.

*Myers, W. D. (1988). *Won't Know Till I Get There*. New York: Puffin.

Myers, W. D. (1991). *Now Is Your Time!* New York: HarperCollins.

*Myers, W. D. (1992). *Somewhere in the Darkness*. New York: Scholastic.

*Myers, W. D. (1993). *Malcolm X: By Any Means Necessary*. New York: Scholastic.

*Myers, W. D. (1994). *Darnell Rock Reporting*. New York: Delacorte.

Myers, W. D. (1994). *The Glory Field*. New York: Scholastic.

Myers, W. D. (1996). *Slam*. New York: Scholastic.

Myers, W. D. (1997). *Harlem: A Poem*. New York: Scholastic.

*Myers, W. D. (1999). *At Her Majesty's Request: An African Princess in Victorian England*. New York: Scholastic.

Myers, W. D. (1999). *Monster*. New York: HarperCollins.

Myers, W. D. (2003). *The Beast*. New York: Scholastic.

Myers, W. D. (2003). *The Dream Bearer*. New York: Amistad Books.

Myers, W. D. (2004). *Shooter*. New York: Scholastic.

Myracle, L. (2003). *Kissing Kate*. New York: Dutton.

Na, A. (2001). *A Step from Heaven*. Asheville, NC: Front Street.

Naidoo, B. (2001). *Out of Bounds: Seven Stories of Conflict and Hope*. New York: HarperCollins.

Namioka, L. (1994). *April and the Dragon Lady*. Orlando, FL: Harcourt Brace.

Namioka, L. (1999). *Ties That Bind, Ties That Break*. New York: Delacorte.

Napoli, D. J. (1997). *Stones in Water*. New York: Dutton.

Napoli, D. J. (2003). *Breath*. New York: Atheneum.

*Naylor, P. (1987). *How I Came to Be a Writer*. New York: Aladdin.

*Naylor, P. (1989). *Alice in Rapture, Sort Of*. New York: Macmillan.

*Naylor, P. (1998). *Outrageously Alice*. New York: Aladdin.

*Naylor, P. (1998). *Sang Spell*. New York: Atheneum.

Naylor, P. (2002). *Blizzard's Wake*. New York: Atheneum.

Neufeld, J. (1983). *Sharelle*. New York: New American Library.

Newman, S. (1991). *Don't Be S.A.D.: A Teenage Guide to Handling Stress, Anxiety, and Depression*. New York: Julian Messner.

*Nilsen, A. (1986). *Presenting M. E. Kerr*. New York: Twayne.

*Nix, G. (1997). *Shade's Children*. New York: HarperCollins.

*Nixon, J. L. (1987). *A Family Apart*. New York: Bantam.

Nolan, H. (2001). *Born Blue*. San Diego: Harcourt Brace.

Norris, J. (1988). *Presenting Rosa Guy*. New York: Twayne.

November, S. (2003). *Firebirds: An Anthology of Original Fantasy and Science Fiction*. New York: Firebirds Books.

Oates, J. C. (2002). *Big Mouth and Ugly Girl*. New York: HarperCollins.

Oates, J. C. (2003). *Freaky Green Eyes*. New York: HarperCollins.

O'Brien, R. (1974). *Z for Zacharia*. New York: Macmillan.

Olsen, S. (2004). *The Girl with a Baby*. Winslaw, BC: Sono Nis Press.

Optic, O. (1855). *The Boat Club*.

Orr, T. (2003). *Violence in Our Schools: Halls of Hope, Halls of Fear*. New York: Franklin Watts.

Orwell, G. (1950). *1984*. New York: Dutton.

Orwell, G. (1954). *Animal Farm*. New York: Harcourt Brace Jovanovich.

Osa, N. (2003). *Cuba 15*. New York: Delacorte Press.

Oswald, D. (n.d.). *Dags*. Woodstock, IL: Dramatic Publishing.

Otsuka, J. (2002). *When the Emperor Was Divine*. New York: Random House.

Park, L. S. (2001). *The Single Shard*. New York: Clarion Books.

*Paterson, K. (1977). *Bridge to Terabithia*. New York: Avon.

*Paterson, K. (1979). *The Great Gilly Hopkins*. New York: Avon.

Paterson, K. (1980). *Jacob Have I Loved*. New York: Avon.

*Paterson, K. (1988). *Park's Quest*. New York: Penguin.

*Paterson, K. (1995). *Come Sing, Jimmy Jo*. New York: Puffin.

*Paulsen, G. (1978). *The Night the White Deer Died*. New York: Dell.

*Paulsen, G. (1985). *Dogsong*. New York: Bradbury.

*Paulsen, G. (1987). *Hatchet*. New York: Puffin.

*Paulsen, G. (1988). *The Island*. New York: Dell.

*Paulsen, G. (1989). *The Voyage of the FROG*. New York: Dell.

*Paulsen, G. (1990). *Woodsong*. New York: Bradbury.

*Paulsen, G. (1991). *The Cookcamp*. New York: Orchard.

*Paulsen, G. (1993). *Harris and Me*. New York: Harcourt Brace.

*Paulsen, G. (1993). *Nightjohn*. New York: Bantam Doubleday Dell.

Paulsen, G. (1993). *Sisters*. Orlando, FL: Harcourt Brace.

*Paulsen, G. (1995). *Winterdance: Fine Madness of Running the Iditarod*. Orlando, FL: Harcourt Brace.

*Paulsen, G. (1996). *Puppies, Dogs, and Blue Northers: Reflections on Being Raised by a Pack of Sled Dogs*. San Diego: Harcourt Brace.

Paulsen, G. (1997). *Sarney: A Life Remembered*. New York: Delacorte.

*Paulsen, G. (1998). *My Life in Dog Years*. New York: Delacorte.

Paulsen, G. (1998). *Soldier's Heart*. New York: Delacorte.

*Paulsen, G. (1999). *Alida's Song*. New York: Delacorte.

*Paulsen, G. (2000). *The Beetfields*. New York: Random House.

*Paulsen, G. (2001). *Caught by the Sea*. New York: Random House.

*Paulsen, G. (2002). *Guts*. New York: Random House.

*Paulsen, G. (2003). *Brian's Hunt*. New York: Random House.

*Paulsen, G. (2003). *Shelf Life: Stories by the Book*. New York: Simon & Schuster.

Peck, G. W. (1883). *Peck's Bad Boy and His Pa*.

Peck, R. (1973). *Dreamland Lake*. New York: Dell.

*Peck, R. (1985). *Remembering the Good Times*. New York: Dell.

Peck, R. (1991). *Unfinished Portrait of Jessica*. New York: Delacorte.

*Peck, R. (1993). *Bel-Air Bambi and the Mall Rats*. New York: Bantam Doubleday Dell.

*Peck, R. (1995). *The Last Safe Place on Earth*. New York: Delacorte.

*Peck, R. (1998). *A Long Way from Chicago*. New York: Penguin Putnam.

Peck, R. (2000). *A Year Down Yonder*. New York: Penguin Putnam.

Peck, R. (2001). *Fair Weather*. New York: Dial.

Peck, R. (2003). *The River Between Us*. New York: Dial.

Peck, R. N. (1972). *A Day No Pigs Would Die*. New York: Dell.

*Peck, R. N. (1998). *Nine Man Tree*. New York: Random House.

*Peck, R. N. (1999). *Cowboy Ghost*. New York: HarperCollins.

Pedersen, L. (2003). *Beginner's Luck*. New York: Ballantine.

Peters, J. A. (2003). *Keeping You a Secret*. New York: Little, Brown.

Peters, J. A. (2004). *Luna*. New York: Little, Brown.

*Petersen, P. J. (1984). *Nobody Else Can Walk It for You*. New York: Dell.

Pettepiece, T., & Aleksin, A. (1990). *Face to Face*. New York: Philomel.

Peyton, J. (Ed.). (1989). *The Stone Canoe and Other Stories*. New York: McDonald.

Pfeffer, S. (1980). *About David*. New York: Dell.

Pfeffer, S. (1987). *The Year without Michael*. New York: Dell.

*Philbrick, R. (1993). *Freak the Mighty*. New York: Scholastic.

Phy, A. (1988). *Presenting Norma Klein*. New York: Twayne.

Pines, T. (Ed.). (1991). *Thirteen Tales of Horror*. New York: Scholastic.

Pirsig, R. (1974). *Zen and the Art of Motorcycle Maintenance: An Inquiry into Values*. New York: Morrow.

Placide, J. (2002). *Fresh Girl*. New York: Random House.

Plays: The Drama Magazine for Young People. Boston: Plays.

Plum-Ucci, C. (2000). *The body of Christopher Creed*. New York: Hyperion.

Plum-Ucci, C. (2002). *What Happened to Lani Garver*. San Diego: Harcourt.

*Porter, T. (1997). *Treasures in the Dust*. New York: HarperCollins.

Potok, C. (1998). *Zebra and Other Stories*. New York: Knopf.

Powell, R. (1999). *Tribute to Another Dead Rock Star*. New York: Farrar, Straus & Giroux.

Prose, F. (2003). *After*. New York: HarperCollins.

Pyle, H. (1883). *The Merry Adventures of Robin Hood*.

Rapp, A. (1994). *Missing the Piano*. New York: Viking.

Reaver, C. (1990). *Mote*. New York: Delacorte.

Reed, D. (1989). *The Dolphins and Me*. Boston: Sierra Club/Little, Brown.

Rees, C. (2001). *Witch Child*. Cambridge, MA: Candlewick.

Rees, C. (2002). *Sorceress*. Cambridge, MA: Candlewick.

Reid, S. (1995). *Presenting Cynthia Voigt*. New York: Twayne.

Rhodes, H. (c. 1545). *Book of Nurture*.

Ribin, S. G. (1993). *Emily Good as Gold*. New York: Browndeer Press.

Rinaldi, A. (1991). *Wolf by the Ears*. New York: Scholastic.

Rinaldi, A. (1992). *A Break with Charity*. Orlando, FL: Harcourt Brace.

Rinaldi, A. (1993). *In My Father's House*. New York: Scholastic.

Rinaldi, A. (1994). *Finishing Becca*. Orlando, FL: Harcourt Brace.

Rinaldi, A. (1997). *An Acquaintance with Darkness*. Orlando, FL: Harcourt Brace.

Rinaldi, A. (1998). *Cast Two Shadows*. San Diego: Harcourt Brace.

Rinaldi, A. (1999). *The Coffin Quilt: The Feud between the Hatfields and the McCoys*. San Diego: Harcourt Brace.

Rinaldi, A. (2001). *Girl in Blue*. New York: Scholastic.

Rinaldi, A. (2002). *Taking Liberty*. New York: Simon & Schuster.

Rinaldi, A. (2004). *Mutiny's Daughter*. New York: HarperCollins.

Ripslinger, J. (1994). *Triangle*. Orlando, FL: Harcourt Brace.

Ripslinger, J. (2003). *How I Fell in Love and Learned to Shoot Freethrows*. New York: Roaring Books.

Roberts, W. D. (2004). *Blood on his Hands*. New York: Simon & Schuster.

Robinson, M. (1990). *A Woman of Her Tribe*. New York: Fawcett Juniper.

Rochman, H., & McCampbell, D. (Eds.). (1997). *Leaving Home: Stories*. New York: HarperCollins.

*Rofes, E. (Ed.). (1985). *The Kid's Book about Death and Dying: By and for Kids*. Boston: Little, Brown.

Rose, R. (1969). Twelve Angry Men. In W. Kaufman (Ed.), *Great Television Plays* (pp. 78–91). New York: Dell.

Ruby, L. (1993). *Miriam's Well*. New York: Scholastic.

Ruby, L. (1994). *Skin Deep*. New York: Scholastic.

*Ruby, L. (1994). *Steal Away Home*. New York: Macmillan.

*Ruby, L. (2000). *Soon Be Free*. New York: Aladdin.

Ryan, S. (2001). *Empress of the World*. New York: Viking.

Rylant, C. (1990). *A Couple of Kooks and Other Stories about Love*. New York: Franklin Watts.

*Sachar, L. (1998). *Holes*. New York: Farrar, Straus & Giroux.

Salinger, J. D. (1951). *The Catcher in the Rye*. Boston: Little, Brown.

Salisbury, G. (1992). *Blue Skin of the Sea*. New York: Delacorte.

Sanchez, A. (2001). *Rainbow Boys*. New York: Simon & Schuster.

Sanchez, A. (2003). *Rainbow High*. New York: Simon & Schuster.

Santiago, E. (1999). *Almost a Woman*. New York: Vintage Books.

*Savage, D. (1997). *Under a Different Sky*. Boston: Houghton Mifflin.

*Savage, D. (1999). *Summer Hawk*. Boston: Houghton Mifflin.

Sebestyen, O. (1981). *Words by Heart*. New York: Bantam.

Sebestyen, O. (1987). *Girl in the Box*. New York: Dell.

Sebestyen, O. (1994). *Out of Nowhere*. New York: Orchard.

Sender, R. M. (1988). *Caged*. New York: Bantam Doubleday Dell.

*Sergel, C. (n.d.). *The Outsiders*. Woodstock, IL: Dramatic Publishing.

*Severance, J. B. (1998). *Thomas Jefferson: Architect of Democracy*. New York: Clarion.

Sewell, A. (1877). *Black Beauty*.

Shakespeare, W. (1595). *Romeo and Juliet*.

Shakespeare, W. (1596–1597). *The Merchant of Venice*.

Shakespeare, W. (1599). *Julius Caesar*.

Shakespeare, W. (1603–1604). *Othello*.

Shakespeare, W. (1606). *Macbeth*.

Shapiro, D. (2003). *Family History*. New York: Knopf.

Shaw, S. (2002). *Black-eyed Suzie*. Honesdale, PA: Boyds Mills.

Shea, P. D. (2003). *Tangled Threads: A Hmong Girl's Story*. Boston: Clarion.

Shengold, N., & Lane, E. (2004). *Under Thirty: Plays for a New Generation*. New York: Vintage Books.

Shimko, B. (2002). *Letters in the Attic*. Chicago: Academy Chicago.

Shiras, F. (n.d.). *Go Ask Alice*. Woodstock, IL: Dramatic Publishing.

Shusterman, N. (1997). *Mindtwisters: Stories to Shred Your Head*. New York: Tor Books.

Shyer, M. (2002). *The Rainbow Kite*. New York: Marshall Cavendish.

*Silvey, A. (Ed.). (1997). *Help Wanted: Short Stories about Young People Working*. New York: Little, Brown.

Singer, M. (1998). *Stay True: Short Stories for Strong Girls*. New York: Scholastic.

Singer, M. (Ed.). (2000). *I Believe in Water: Twelve Brushes with Religion*. New York: HarperCollins.

Singer, M. (Ed.). (2004). *Face Relations: 11 Stories about Seeing beyond Color*. New York: Simon & Schuster.

*Sleator, W. (1984). *Interstellar Pig*. New York: Dutton.

*Sleator, W. (1989). *The Duplicate*. New York: Dell.

*Sleator, W. (1999). *Rewind*. New York: Dutton.

Smith, S. L. (2001). *Rain Is Not My Indian Name*. New York: HarperCollins.

Son, J. (2003). *Finding My Hat*. London: Orchard Books.

*Sones, S. (1999). *Stop Pretending: What Happened When My Big Sister Went Crazy*. New York: Simon & Schuster.

*Sones, S. (2001). *What My Mother Doesn't Know*. New York: Simon & Schuster.

*Sones, S. (2004). *One of Those Hideous Books Where the Mother Dies*. New York: Simon & Schuster.

Sorenson, V. (1957). *Miracles on Maple Hill*. New York: Harcourt Brace.

*Soto, G. (1990). *Baseball in April and Other Stories*. New York: Harcourt.

*Soto, G. (1990). *A Fire in My Hands*. New York: Scholastic.

*Soto, G. (1993). *Local News*. Orlando, FL: Harcourt Brace.

Soto, G. (1994). *Jesse*. Orlando, FL: Harcourt Brace.

Soto, G. (1997). *Buried Onions*. Orlando, FL: Harcourt Brace.

Soto, G. (2003). *The Afterlife*. Orlando, FL: Harcourt Brace.

*Speare, E. (1958). *The Witch of Blackbird Pond*. Boston: Houghton Mifflin.

*Speare, E. (1983). *The Sign of the Beaver*. New York: Dell.

Spiegelman, A. (1986, 1991). *Maus* (Vols. 1–2). New York: Pantheon.

*Spinelli, J. (1988). *Who Put That Hair in My Toothbrush?* New York: Little, Brown.

*Spinelli, J. (1990). *Maniac Magee*. Boston: Little, Brown.

*Spinelli, J. (1997). *The Library Card*. New York: Scholastic.

*Spinelli, J. (1998). *Knots in My Yo-Yo String: The Autobiography of a Kid*. New York: Knopf.

*Spinelli, J. (2000). *Stargirl*. New York: Knopf.

*Spinelli, J. (2003). *Milkweed*. New York: Knopf.

Staples, S. (1996). *Dangerous Skies*. New York: HarperCollins.

Stearns, M. (Ed.). (1996). *A Nightmare's Dozen: Stories from the Dark*. San Diego: Harcourt Brace.

Steinbeck, J. (1937). *Of Mice and Men*. New York: Viking.

Steinbeck, J. (1939). *The Grapes of Wrath*. New York: Viking.

Steinbeck, J. (1947). *The Pearl*. New York: Viking.

Stephens, A. (1860). *Malaeska: The Indian Wife of the White Hunter*.

Stevenson, R. L. (1883). *Treasure Island*.

Stevenson, R. L. (1886). *Kidnapped*.

Stewart, G. B. (1995). *Life in the Warsaw Ghetto*. San Diego: Lucent Books.

Stewart, G. B. (1997). *Gay and Lesbian Youth*. San Diego: Lucent Books.

Stowe, H. B. (1852). *Uncle Tom's Cabin*.

Strasser, T. (1985). *A Very Touchy Subject*. New York: Dell.

Strasser, T. (2000). *Give a Boy a Gun*. New York: Simon Pulse.

*Stratemeyer, E. (1899–1926). *The Rover Boys* (series).

*Stratemeyer, E. (1900–1906). *Soldiers of Fortune* (series).

*Stratemeyer, E. (1904–1912). *Lakeport* (series).

*Stratemeyer, E. (1927–). *The Hardy Boys* (series).

*Stratemeyer, E. (1927–). *Nancy Drew* (series).

Striegel, J. (2002). *Homeroom Exercise*. New York: Holiday House.

*Sullivan, C. (Ed.). (1996). *Imaginary Animals: Poetry and Art for Young People*. New York: Harry N. Abrams.

Swanson, J. (1978). *142 Ways to Make a Poem*. St. Paul, MN: EMC Corporation.

Swift, J. (1726). *Gulliver's Travels*.

Tarkington, B. (1902). *Seventeen*.

*Tate, E. (1987). *The Secret of Gumbo Grove*. New York: Bantam.

Tate, E. (1992). *Front Porch Stories at the One-Room School*. New York: Bantam.

*Taylor, M. (1975). *Song of the Trees*. New York: Bantam.

*Taylor, M. (1976). *Roll of Thunder, Hear My Cry*. New York: Bantam.

*Taylor, M. (1981). *Let the Circle Be Unbroken*. New York: Bantam.

*Taylor, M. (1990). *Mississippi Bridge*. New York: Dial.

*Taylor, M. (1990). *The Road to Memphis*. New York: Dial.

*Taylor, M. (2001). *The Land*. New York: Phyllis Fogelman Books.

*Taylor, T. (1976). *The Cay*. New York: Avon.

Taylor, T. (1989). *Sniper*. New York: Avon.

Terkel, S. (1992). *Ethics*. New York: Lodestar.

Terris, S. (1990). *Author! Author!* New York: Farrar.

Thackeray, W. (1847). *Vanity Fair*.

Thomas, J. (1982). *Marked by Fire*. New York: Avon.

Thomas, J. (Ed.). (1990). *A Gathering of Flowers: Stories about Being Young in America*. New York: Harper & Row.

Thomas, R. (1997). *Doing Time: Notes from the Undergrad*. New York: Simon & Schuster.

Thoms, A. (2002). *With Their Eyes: September 11, The View from a High School at Ground Zero*. New York: HarperCollins.

Thoreau, H. D. (1854). *Walden*.

Tingle, T. (2003). *Walking the Choctaw Road: Stories from Red People Memory*. St. Paul, MN: Cinco Puntos Press.

Tokio, M. (2003). *More Than You Can Chew*. Plattsburgh, NY: Tundra.

Townsend, S. (1982). *The Secret Diary of Adrian Mole, Aged 13¾*. New York: Avon.

Trelease, J. (1989). *The New Read-Aloud Handbook*. New York: Penguin.

Trueman, T. (2000). *Stuck in Neutral*. New York: HarperCollins.

Trueman, T. (2003). *Inside Out*. New York: Harper Collins.

Trueman, T. (2004). *Cruise Control*. New York: HarperCollins.

*Tunis, J. (1938). *The Iron Duke*. New York: Harcourt Brace.

*Tunis, J. (1942). *All-American*. New York: Harcourt Brace.

*Tunis, J. (1967). *His Enemy, His Friend*. New York: Morrow.

Turlo, D., & Turlo, A. (2004). *The Spirit Line*. New York: Viking.

Twain, M. (1876). *Adventures of Tom Sawyer*.

Twain, M. (1885/1999). *Adventures of Huckleberry Finn*. (1999). (Original work published 1885). New York: Simon & Schuster.

*Vanasse, D. (1997). *A Distant Enemy*. New York: Lodestar.

Velasquez, G. (2003). *Teen Angel*. Houston: Arte Pablico.

*Velde, V. V. (1999). *Never Trust a Dead Man*. San Diego: Harcourt Brace.

Velde, V. V. (1999). *There's a Dead Person Following My Sister Around*. San Diego: Harcourt Brace.

Verne, J. (1872). *Twenty Thousand Leagues under the Sea*.

Verne, J. (1873). *Around the World in Eighty Days*.

Vivelo, J. (1997). *Chills in the Night: Tales That Will Haunt You*. New York: DK Publishing.

*Voigt, C. (1981). *Homecoming*. New York: Atheneum.

*Voigt, C. (1982). *Dicey's Song*. New York: Ballantine.

*Voigt, C. (1985). *The Runner*. New York: Atheneum.

Voltaire, F. (1901). *Candide*.

Vonnegut, K. (1969). *Slaughterhouse-Five, or The Children's Crusade*. New York: Dell.

Wadds, G. (n.d.). *Who Cares?* Woodstock, IL: Dramatic Publishing.

Wadsworth, G. (2003). *Words West: Voices of Young Pioneers*. Boston: Houghton Mifflin.

Wait, Lea. (2004). *Wintering Well*. New York: McElderry.

Walker, A. (1979). *Good Night Willie Lee, I'll See You in the Morning*. New York: Dial.

Walker, K. (1993). *Peter*. San Diego: Harcourt Brace.

*Wallace, R. (1996). *Wrestling Sturbridge*. New York: Knopf.

*Wallace, R. (1997). *Shots on Goal*. New York: Knopf.

*Wallace, R. (2003). *Losing Is Not an Option*. New York: Knopf.

Warner, S. (1850). *The Wide, Wide World*.

Warren, A. (2001). *Surviving Hitler*. New York: Harper Collins.

Warren, A. (2001). *We Rode the Orphan Trains*. Boston: Houghton Mifflin.

Warren A. (2004). *Escape from Saigon*. New York: Farrar, Straus & Giroux.

Weaver, W. (2001). *Memory Boy*. New York: HarperCollins.

Weems, M. L. (1800). *A History of the Life and Death, Virtues and Exploits, of General George Washington*.

Weems, M. L. (1806). *The Life of Washington the Great*.

Weems, M. L. (1808). *The Life of George Washington*.

*Weidt, M. (1989). *Presenting Judy Blume*. New York: Twayne.

Weiss, J., & Weiss, H. (2002). *Big City Cool: Short Stories about Urban Youth*. New York: Persea Books.

Wersba, B. (1997). *Whistle Me Home*. New York: Holt.

Whelan, G. (2000). *Homeless Bird*. New York: HarperCollins.

Whelan, G. (2004). *Chu Ju's House*. New York: HarperCollins.

White, E. (1987). *Life without Friends*. New York: Avon.

White, R. (1972). *Deathwatch*. New York: Dell.

White, R. (1996). *Belle Prater's Boy*. New York: Farrar, Straus & Giroux.

White, R. (2000). *Memories of Summer*. New York: Farrar, Straus & Giroux.

Whitman, W. (1855). *Leaves of Grass*.

Wiesel, E. (1960). *Night*. New York: Bantam.

Wiggin, K. D. (1904). *Rebecca of Sunnybrook Farm*.

Wigginton, E. (Ed.). (1972–). *The Foxfire Books* (series). New York: Doubleday.

Wilder, T. (1938). *Our Town*. New York: Samuel French.

Williams, J. (2004). *Escaping Tornado Season: A Story in Poems*. New York: Harper Tempest.

Williams, L. A. (2000) *When Kambia Elaine Flew in from Neptune*. New York: Simon & Schuster.

Williams-Garcia, R. (1995). *Like Sisters on the Homefront*. New York: Dutton.

Williams-Garcia, R. (2004). *No Laughter Here*. New York: HarperCollins.

Wilson, A. J. (1867). *St. Elmo*.

Wilson, B. (1992). *The Leaving*. New York: Philomel.

Wilson, N. (1998). *Flapjack Waltzes*. New York: Farrar, Straus & Giroux.

Wittlinger, E. (2001). *Razzel*. New York: Simon & Schuster.

Wittlinger, E. (2001). *What's in a Name?* New York: Simon Pulse.

Wittlinger, E. (2002). *The Long Night of Leo and Bree*. New York: Simon & Schuster.

Wittlinger, E. (2003). *Zig Zag*. New York: Simon & Schuster.

Wittlinger, E. (2004). *Heart on My Sleeve*. New York: Simon & Schuster.

Wolff, V. E. (1993). *Make Lemonade*. New York: Holt.

Wolff, V. E. (2001). *True Believer*. New York: Atheneum.

Wood, J. R. (1992). *The Man Who Loved Clowns*. New York: Putnam.

Wood, J. R. (1997). *Turtle on a Fence Post*. New York: Philomel.

Woodruff, E. (1998). *Dear Austin: Letters from the Underground Railroad*. New York: Knopf.

Woodson, J. (1991). *The Dear One*. New York: Delacorte.

Woodson, J. (1994). *I Hadn't Meant to Tell You This*. New York: Delacorte.

Woodson, J. (1998). *If You Come Softly*. New York: Putnam & Sons.

Woodson, J. (1999). *Lena*. New York: Delacorte.

Woodson, J. (2002). *Hush*. New York: G. P. Putnam & Sons.

Woodson, J. (2003). *Locomotion*. New York: G. P. Putnam & Sons.

Woodson, J. (2004). *Behind You*. New York: G. P. Putnam & Sons.

Wynne-Jones, T. (1995). *The Book of Changes*. New York: Orchard.

Wynne-Jones, T. (1999). *Lord of the Fries*. New York: D-K Publishing.

Yee, L. (2003). *Millicent Min, Girl Genius*. New York: Scholastic.

Yep, L. (Ed.). (1993). *American Dragons: Twenty-Five Asian American Voices*. New York: HarperCollins.

*Yolen, J. (1990). *The Devil's Arithmetic*. New York: Puffin.

Yolen, J. (Ed.). (1991). *2041*. New York: Delacorte.

Yolen, J. (1992). *Briar Rose*. New York: Tom Doherty & Associates.

Yolen, J. (1997). *Twelve Impossible Things before Breakfast: Stories*. San Diego: Harcourt Brace.

Yolen, J. (1998). *Here There Be Ghosts*. San Diego: Harcourt Brace.

Yolen, J., & Coville, B. (1998). *Armageddon Summer*. San Diego: Harcourt Brace.

Yolen, J., & Greenburg, M. (Eds.). (1989). *Things That Go Bump in the Night: A Collection of Original Stories*. New York: Harper & Row.

*Yumoto, K. (1999). *The Spring Tone*. New York: Farrar, Straus & Giroux.

Zephaniah, B. (2002). *Face*. London: Bloomsbury Publishing PLC.

*Zindel, P. (1968). *The Pigman*. New York: Bantam.

*Zindel, P. (1969). *My Darling, My Hamburger*. New York: Harper & Row.

Zindel, P. (1970). *The Effect of Gamma Rays on Man-in-the-Moon Marigolds*. New York: Dramatists.

*Zindel, P. (1974). *Let Me Hear You Whisper*. New York: Harper & Row.

*Zindel, P. (1987). *The Amazing and Death-Defying Diary of Eugene Dingman*. New York: Harper & Row.

*Zindel, P. (1989). *A Begonia for Miss Applebaum*. New York: Bantam.

Zindel, P. (1993). *David and Della*. New York: HarperCollins.

*Zindel, P. (1994). *Loch*. Orlando, FL: Harcourt Brace.

*Zindel, P. (1998). *Reef of Death*. New York: HarperCollins.

*Zindel, P., & Zindel, B. (1980). *A Star for the Latecomer*. New York: Harper & Row.

Zolotow, C. (1986). *Early Sorrow: Ten Stories of Youth*. New York: Harper & Row.

Book Lists

One Book, One Class

The following books are particularly appropriate when teachers are considering a book selection for all students in a class.

After the First Death, Robert Cormier (1979)

After the Rain, Norma Fox Mazer (1987)

Alt Ed., C. Atkins (2003)

America, E. R. Frank (2002)

The Battle of Jericho, Sharon Draper (2003)

Beyond the Chocolate War, Robert Cormier (1985)

Bless Me, Ultima, Rudolfo Anaya (1972)

Blizzard's Wake, Phyllis Reynolds Naylor (2002)

Bloomability, Sharon Creech (1998)

The Body of Christopher Creed, Carol Plum-Ucci (2000)

Bridge to Terabithia, Katherine Paterson (1977)

Bucking the Sarge, Christopher Paul Curtis (2004)

Bud, Not Buddy, Christopher Paul Curtis (1999)

Bull Catcher, Alden R. Carter (1997)

The Bumblebee Flies Anyway, Robert Cormier (1983)

Buried Onions, Gary Soto (1997)

Burning Up, Caroline Cooney (1999)

But That's Another Story, Sandy Asher (1996)

Catalyst, Laurie Halse Anderson (2002)

The Catcher in the Rye, J. D. Salinger (1951)

Chapters: My Growth as a Writer, Lois Duncan (1982)

Chernowitz, Fran Arrick (1981)

Children of the River, Linda Crew (1989)

Chinese Handcuffs, Chris Crutcher (1989)

The Chocolate War, Robert Cormier (1974)

The Coffin Quilt: The Feud between the Hatfields and the McCoys, Ann Rinaldi (1999)

Cold Sassy Tree, Olive Burns (1984)

The Contender, Robert Lipsyte (1967)

The Crazy Horse Electric Game, Chris Crutcher (1987)

Crazy Lady, Jane Conley (1993)

The Crystal Garden, Vicki Grove (1995)

Dark Waters, Catherine MacPhail (2003)

Daniel's Story, Carol Matas (1993)

Darnell Rock Reporting, Walter Dean Myers (1994)

A Day No Pigs Would Die, Robert Newton Peck (1972)

The Day They Came to Arrest the Book, Nat Hentoff (1982)

Death at Devil's Bridge, Cynthia DeFelice (2000)

Destiny, Vicki Grove (2000)

Dicey's Song, Cynthia Voigt (1982)

Dogwolf, Alden Carter (1994)

Don't Look behind You, Lois Duncan (1989)

Dove, Robin Graham (1972)

Dovey Coe, Frances O'Roark Dowell (2000)

Downriver, Will Hobbs (1991)

Down the Yukon, Will Hobbs (2001)

Driver's Ed, Caroline Cooney (1994)

Eva, Peter Dickinson (1988)

The Face on the Milk Carton, Caroline Cooney (1990)

Fallen Angels, Walter Dean Myers (1988)

The First Part Last, Angela Johnson (2003)

Fish, L. S. Matthews (2004)

Flight #116 Is Down, Caroline Cooney (1992)

Forbidden City, William Bell (1990)

Forged by Fire, Sharon Draper (1998)

Freak the Mighty, Rodnum Philbrick (1993)

The Giver, Lois Lowry (1993)

The Glory Field, Walter Dean Myers (1994)

Heat, Michael Cadnum (1998)

Heroes, Robert Cormier (1998)

High Heat, Carl Deuker (2003)

Holes, Louis Sachar (1998)

Home before Dark, Sue Ellen Bridgers (1976)

Home of the Braves, David Klass (2002)

Hope Was Here, Joan Bauer (2000)

I Am the Cheese, Robert Cormier (1977)

Interstellar Pig, William Sleator (1984)

In the Middle of the Night, Robert Cormier (1995)

Into a Strange Land: Unaccompanied Refugee Youth in America, Brent Ashabranner and M. Ashabranner (1987)

The Island, Gary Paulsen (1988)

I Touch the Future: The Story of Christa McAuliffe, Robert Hohler (1986)

Jackie's Wild Seattle, Will Hobbs (2003)

Jacob Have I Loved, Katherine Paterson (1980)

Jason's Gold, Will Hobbs (1999)

Keeper of the Night, Kimberly Willis Holt (2003)

Killing Mr. Griffin, Lois Duncan (1978)

The Last Safe Place on Earth, Richard Peck (1995)

Leaving Protection, Will Hobbs (2004)

Let the Circle Be Unbroken, Mildred Taylor (1981)

Loch, Paul Zindel (1994)

Locomotion, Jacqueline Woodson (2003)

A Long Way from Chicago, Richard Peck (1998)

Looking for Red, Angela Johnson (2002)

Make Lemonade, Virginia Euwer Wolff (1993)

The Maze, Will Hobbs (1998)

Meadow Lark, Mary Peace Finley (2003)

Memory Boy, Will Weaver (2001)

Milkweed, Jerry Spinelli (2003)

Mississippi Bridge, Mildred Taylor (1990)

Mississippi Trial, 1955, Chris Crow (2002)

Monster, Walter Dean Myers (1999)

The Moves Make the Man, Bruce Brooks (1984)

New Kids in Town: Oral Histories of Immigrant Teens, Janet Bode (1986)

Night Hoops, Carl Deuker (2000)

Night Kites, M. E. Kerr (1986)

No Easy Answers, Don Gallo (1997)

No Kidding, Bruce Brooks (1989)

Nothing but the Truth, Avi (1991)

Number the Stars, Lois Lowry (1989)

Olive's Ocean, Kenin Henkes (2003)

One Fat Summer, Robert Lipsyte (1977)

The Outcasts of 19 Schulyer Place, E. L. Konigsburg (2004)

Out of Control, Norma Fox Mazer (1993)

Out of Here, Sandy Asher (1993)

Out of the Dust, Karen Hesse (1997)

The Outsiders, S. E. Hinton (1967)

Park's Quest, Katherine Paterson (1988)

Permanent Connections, Sue Ellen Bridgers (1987)

Phoenix Rising, Karen Hesse (1994)

The Pigman, Paul Zindel (1968)

The Rag and Bone Shop, Robert Cormier (2001)

Reaching Dustin, Vicki Grove (1998)

Red Midnight, Ben Mikaelsen (2003)

Rescue: The Story of How Gentiles Saved Jews in the Holocaust, Milton Meltzer (1988)

Rimwalkers, Vicki Grove (1993)

The River between Us, Richard Peck (2003)

The Road to Memphis, Mildred Taylor (1990)

Roll of Thunder, Hear My Cry, Mildred Taylor (1976)

Romiette and Julio, Sharon Draper (1999)

Running Loose, Chris Crutcher (1983)

Sang Spell, Phyllis Reynolds Naylor (1998)

The Shakespeare Scribe, Gary Blackwood (2000)

The Shakespeare Stealer, Gary Blackwood (1998)

The Silent Boy, Lois Lowry (2003)

Skin Deep, Lois Ruby (1994)

Slam, Walter Dean Myers (1996)

Soaring Eagle, Mary Peace Finley (1998)

Soldier's Heart, Gary Paulsen (1998)

Star Girl, Jerry Spinelli (2000)

Steal Away Home, Lois Ruby (1994)

Stones in Water, D. J. Napoli (1997)

Stotan!, Chris Crutcher (1986)

Summer of My German Soldier, Bette Greene (1973)

Surviving Hitler, Andrea Warren (2001)

Taming the Star Runner, S. E. Hinton (1988)

Tunes for Bears to Dance To, Robert Cormier (1992)

Walk Two Moons, Sharon Creech (1994)

The War between the Classes, Gloria Miklowitz (1985)

Warrior Angel, Robert Lipsyte (2003)

The Watsons Go to Birmingham—1963, Christopher Paul Curtis (1995)

We All Fall Down, Robert Cormier (1991)

Wenny Has Wings, Janet Lee Carey (2002)

Whatever Happened to Janie?, Caroline Cooney (1993)

White Grizzly, Mary Peace Finley (2001)

Wild Man Island, Will Hobbs (2002)

Winning, Robin Brancato (1977)

Words by Heart, Ouida Sebestyn (1981)

A Wrinkle in Time, Madeleine L'Engle (1968)

A Year Down Yonder, Richard Peck (2000)

You Don't Know Me, David Klass (2001)

Z for Zacharia, Robert O'Brien (1974)

One Book, One Student

Teachers may include the following books on an individual reading list, along with any of the books from the previous list. Again, as in any literature program, it is important to realize that a book appropriate for one student may not be appropriate for another.

An Acquaintance with Darkness, Ann Rinaldi (1997)

After, Francine Prose (2003)

The Afterlife, Gary Soto (2003)

Alchemy, Margaret Mahy (2004)

Alicia: My Story, Alicia Appleman-Jurman (1988)

The Amazing "True" Story of a Teenage Single Mom, Katherine Arnoldi (1998)

Anything to Win, Gloria Miklowitz (1990)

April and the Dragon Lady, Lensey Namioka (1994)

Armageddon Summer, Jane Yolen and Bruce Covelle (1998)

The Beast, Walter Dean Myers (2003)

Beauty Queen, Linda Glovach (1998)

Bel-Air Bambi and the Mall Rats, Richard Peck (1993)

Between a Rock and a Hard Place, Alden Carter (1995)

Big Mouth and Ugly Girl, Joyce Carol Oates (2002)

Blood and Chocolate, Annette Klause (1997)

Blood on His Hands, Willo Davis Roberts (2004)

Blue Skin of the Sea, Graham Salisbury (1992)

Born Blue, Han Nolan (2001)

A Boy No More, Harry Mazer (2004)

The Brave, Robert Lipsyte (1991)

A Break with Charity, Ann Rinaldi (1992)

Breath, Donna Jo Napoli (2003)

Breathing Underwater, Alex Flinn (2001)

Brian's Hunt, Gary Paulsen, (2003)

The Center of Everything, Laura Moriarty (2003)

The Chemo Kid, Robert Lipsyte (1992)

The Chief, Robert Lipsyte (1993)

Coraline, Neil Gaiman (2002)

Crank, Ellen Hopkins (2004)

Crews, Maria Hinojosa (1995)

Cruise Control, Terry Trueman (2004)

The Curious Incident of the Dog in the Night-time, Mark Haddon (2003)

Dakota Dream, James Bennett (1994)

Damage, A. M. Jenkins (2002)

Danger Zone, David Klass (1996)

David and Della, Paul Zindel (1993)

Deliver Us from Evie, M. E. Kerr (1994)

The Devil's Arithmetic, Jane Yolen (1990)

Does This School Have Capital Punishment?, Nat Hentoff (1981)

Dogsong, Gary Paulsen (1985)

Don't Care High, Gordan Korman (1985)

The Double Life of Zoe Flynn, Janet Lee Carey (2004)

The Dream Bearer, Walter Dean Myers (2003)

The Drowning of Stephan Jones, Bette Greene (1991)

The Duplicate, William Sleator (1989)

The Ear, the Eye, and the Arm, Nancy Farmer (1994)

The Earth, My Butt, and Other Big, Round Things, C. Mackler (2003)

The Empty Mirror, James Lincoln Collier (2004)

Escape from Saigon, Andrea Warren (2004)

Facing Up, Robin Brancato (1984)

The Facts Speak for Themselves, Brock Cole (1997)

A Family Apart, Joan Lowery Nixon (1987)

Feed, M. T. Anderson (2001)

Fever 1793, Laurie Halse Anderson (2000)

Finishing Becca, Ann Rinaldi (1994)

Firegold, Dia Calhoun (1999)

Floating, Nicole Bailey-Williams (2004)

Food Fight: A Guide to Eating Disorders for Preteens and Their Parents, Jane Bode (1997)

Freaky Green Eyes, Joyce Carol Oates (2003)

Frightful's Mountain, Jean Craighead George (1999)

Gathering Blue, Lois Lowry (2000)

Getting Away with Murder: The True Story of the Emmett Till Case, Chris Crow (2003)

Girl in Blue, Ann Rinaldi (2001)

Good Night Maman, Norma Fox Mazer (1999)

Gravel Queen, T. Benduhn (2003)

Green Angel, A. Hoffman (2003)

The Grey King, Susan Cooper (1975)

Hanging on to Max, Margaret Bechard (2002)

Harris and Me, Gary Paulsen (1993)

Hatchet, Gary Paulsen (1987)

Head Games, Mariah Fredericks (2004)

Heart on my Sleeve, Ellen Wittlinger (2004)

Heaven, Angela Johnson (1998)

"Hello," I Lied, M. E. Kerr (1997)

Hole in My Life, Jack Gantos (2002)

The House of the Scorpion, Nancy Farmer (2004)

The House on the Gulf, Margaret Peterson Haddix (2004)

If Rock and Roll Were a Machine, Terry Davis (1993)

I Hadn't Meant to Tell You This, Jacqueline Woodson (1994)

Imitate the Tiger, Jan Cheripko (1996)

Indigo's Star, Hilary McKay (2004)

In My Enemy's House, Carol Matas (1999)

In My Father's House, Ann Rinaldi (1993)

Inside Out, Terry Trueman (2003)

The Insiders, J. Minter (2004)

Ironman, Chris Crutcher (1995)

I've Already Forgotten Your Name, Philip Hall and Bette Greene (2004)

Jake Riley: Irreparably Damaged, R. F. Davis (2003)

Jesse, Gary Soto (1994)

Julie's Wolf Pack, Jean George (1997)

Keeping Christina, Sue Ellen Bridgers (1993)

Keeping You a Secret, Julie Anne Peters (2003)

A Killing in Plymouth Colony, Carol Otis Hurst and Rebecca Otis (2003)

King of the Mild Frontier: An Ill-Advised Autobiography, Chris Crutcher (2003)

Kissing Doorknobs, Terry Spencer Hesser (1998)

Lena, Jacqueline Woodson (1999)

Letting go of Bobby James or How I Found Myself of Steam, Valerie Hobbs (2004)

Life of Pi, Yann Martel (2001)

Life without Friends, Ellen White (1987)

Lives of Our Own, Lorri Hewett (1998)

Lizard, Dennis Covington (1991)

Looking for Alibrandi, Melina Marchetta (1999)

Lord of the Flies, William Golding (1955)

Los Alamos Light, Larry Bograd (1983)

Malcolm X: By Any Means Necessary, Walter Dean Myers (1993)

Maniac Magee, Jerry Spinelli (1990)

The Man Who Was Poe, Avi (1989)

Marked by Fire, Julian Thomas (1982)

Martyn Pig, Kevin Brooks (2002)

Mary, Bloody Mary, Carolyn Meyer (1999)

Midnight Hour Encores, Bruce Brooks (1986)

Missing the Piano, Adam Rapp (1994)

Motown and Didi, Walter Dean Myers (1987)

Mutiny's Daughter, Ann Rinaldi (2004)

Nightjohn, Gary Paulsen (1993)

Nine Man Tree, Robert Newton Peck (1998)

Nobody Else Can Walk It for You, P. J. Petersen (1984)

Nobody's Baby Now, C. Benjamin (1991)

No Laughter Here, Rita Williams-Garcia (2004)

No More Dead Dogs, Gordon Korman (2000)

Other Bells for Us to Ring, Robert Cormier (1990)

Out of Nowhere, Ouida Sebestyn (1994)

Outside Shot, Walter Dean Myers (1987)

Pass It On: An Insiders Novel, J. Minter (2004)

The Perks of Being a Wallflower, Stephen Chbosky (1999)

Perloo the Bold, Avi (1998)

Razzle, Ellen Wittlinger (2001)

Real Heroes, Marilyn Kaye (1993)

Reef of Death, Paul Zindel (1998)

Rewind, William Sleator (1999)

Robyn's Book: A True Diary, Robyn Miller (1986)

Rules of the Road, Joan Bauer (1998)

Rundown, Michael Cadnum (1999)

Sarney: A Life Remembered, Gary Paulsen (1997)

Scorpions, Walter Dean Myers (1988)

The Sea Trolls, Nancy Farmer (2004)

The Second Summer of the Sisterhood, Ann Brashares (2003)

The Secret Life of Bees, Sue Monk Kidd (2002)

The Secret of Gumbo Grove, Eleanora Tate (1987)

Sex Education, Jenny Davis (1988)

Shooter, Walter Dean Myers (2004)

Shooting Monarchs, John Halliday (2003)

Sickened: The True Story of a Lost Childhood, Julie Gregory (2003)

The Single Shard, Linda Sue Park (2001)

Sing Me a Death Song, Jay Bennett (1990)

The Sisterhood of the Traveling Pants, Ann Brashares (2001)

Sisters, Gary Paulsen (1993)

Soldier Mom, Alice Mead (1999)

Somewhere in the Darkness, Walter Dean Myers (1992)

Son of the Mob, Gordon Korman (2002)

Son of the Mob Hollywood Hustle, Gordon Korman (2004)

The Spring Tone, Kazumi Yumoto (1999)

Squashed, Joan Bauer (1992)

The Star Place, Vicki Grove (1999)

Staying Fat for Sarah Byrnes, Chris Crutcher (1993)

The Steps, R. Cohn (2003)

Summer Hawk, Deborah Savage (1999)

Sweet Bells Jangled out of Tune, Robin Brancato (1982)

Taking Liberty: The Story of Oney Judge, George Washington's Runaway Slave, Ann Rinaldi (2003)

Taking Terri Mueller, Norma Fox Mazer (1981)

Tears of a Tiger, Sharon Draper (1994)

Tenderness, Robert Cormier (1997)

Tex, S. E. Hinton (1979)

There's a Dead Person Following My Sister Around, Vivian Vande Velde (1999)

3 NB's of Julian Drew, James M. Deem (1994)

Ties That Bind, Ties That Break, Lindsey Namioka (1999)

Tomorrow Land, Michael Cart (1999)

Torn Away, James Heneghan (1994)

Touching Spirit Bear, Ben Mikaelsen (2001)

Tribute to Another Dead Rock Star, Randy Powell (1999)

The True Confession of Charlotte Doyle, Avi (1990)

True Confessions of a Heartless Girl, M. Brooks (2003)

The Truth about Forever, Sarah Dessen (2004)

Under the Same Sky, Cynthia DeFelice (2003)

Uneasy Money, Robin Brancato (1986)

Unfinished Portrait of Jessica, Richard Peck (1991)

Vanishing, Bruce Brooks (1999)

The Voyage of the FROG, Gary Paulsen (1989)

Walk Two Moons, Sharon Creech (1994)

Wasteland, Francesca Lia Block (2003)

The Watcher, James Howe (1997)

The Weekend Was Murder, Joan Lowery Nixon (1992)

Whale Talk, Chris Crutcher (2001)

Whatever You Say I Am, Anthony Bozza (2003)

What Happened to Lani Garver, Carol Plum-Ucci (2002)

What You Don't Know Can Kill You, Fran Arrick (1992)

When the Phone Rang, Harry Mazer (1985)

When We First Met, Norma Fox Mazer (1982)

Who Killed My Daughter?, Lois Duncan (1992)

Wintering Well, Lea Wait (2004)

With All My Heart, with All My Mind: Thirteen Stories about Growing Up Jewish, Sandy Asher (1999)

Wolf by the Ears, Ann Rinaldi (1991)

A Woman of Her Tribe, Margaret Robinson (1990)

Words West: Voices of Young Pioneers, Ginger Wadsworth (2003)

Wrango, Brian Burks (1999)

The Year They Burned the Books, Nancy Garden (1999)

The Year without Michael, Susan Beth Pfeffer (1987)

Zig Zag, Ellen Wittlinger (2003)